CW00956438

41

41

Inside the Presidency
of George H. W. Bush

Edited by Michael Nelson
and Barbara A. Perry

CORNELL UNIVERSITY PRESS   ITHACA AND LONDON

PUBLISHED IN ASSOCIATION WITH THE UNIVERSITY OF VIRGINIA'S
MILLER CENTER

Frontispiece: President Bush in the Oval Office of the White House, Washington, DC. Courtesy of the George Bush Presidential Library and Museum.

Chapter 3 is reprinted with permission from *The Strategist* by Bartholomew Sparrow. Available from PublicAffairs, an imprint of The Perseus Books Group. Copyright © 2014.

First published 2014 by Cornell University Press
First printing, Cornell Paperbacks, 2014
Printed in the United States of America

Library of Congress Cataloging-in-Publication Data

41 (Nelson and Perry)
  41 : inside the presidency of George H.W. Bush / edited by Michael Nelson and Barbara A. Perry.
      pages cm
  "Published in association with the University of Virginia's Miller Center."
  Papers originally presented at a conference held in fall 2011 at the University of Virginia, White Burkett Miller Center.
  Includes bibliographical references and index.
  ISBN 978-0-8014-5263-5 (cloth : alk. paper)
  ISBN 978-0-8014-7927-4 (pbk. : alk. paper)
  1. Bush, George, 1924– —Congresses. 2. United States—Politics and government—1989–1993—Congresses. I. Nelson, Michael, 1949– editor of compilation. II. Perry, Barbara A. (Barbara Ann), 1956– editor of compilation. III. Nelson, Michael, 1949– George Bush. Contains (work): IV. White Burkett Miller Center, sponsoring body. V. Title. VI. Title: Forty-one.
  E881.A13   2014
  973.928092—dc23   2013033237

Cloth printing   10 9 8 7 6 5 4 3 2 1
Paperback printing   10 9 8 7 6 5 4 3 2 1

Contents

Foreword

Philip Zelikow

The popular image of George H. W. Bush, which has recently been reinforced by an HBO documentary produced by Jerry Weintraub and other Bush friends, is the portrait of an accomplished, good-natured, self-deprecating gentleman and sportsman. All this is true enough. Indeed, Bush seems highly qualified to be the president of any community's Rotary Club.

This does leave us, however, with a few puzzles.

First, why was this amiable fellow both so successful and so unsuccessful as a politician? It is interesting that Bush's abilities in winning people over at the personal level, which was abundantly in evidence in foreign capitals and on Capitol Hill, translated so poorly into abilities at the level of mass retail politics.

Perhaps he was not really all that outstandingly successful, except in the qualities that recommended him to Ronald Reagan in 1980 as an appropriate vice president. And then that pairing led to other things. The oral histories compiled by the University of Virginia's Miller Center and the perceptive essays in this volume that use them provide insightful conjectures. They portray Bush as a politician who was really, in some sense, outside of his time, an anachronism within his party and perhaps even in the world of American politics.

Second, although Bush practically had the word "prudent" tattooed to his forehead—in purple letters, not scarlet—there is little evidence that he was an especially analytical person in any formal sense of the term. He did read and listen. But his temperament was restless, constantly looking for something to do. He was a deeply emotional person—instinctive, intuitive in his reactions to people and situations. I believe one source of his characteristic inability to express himself very well in public settings is that a long-ingrained filter was in place habitually blocking the facile expression of these impulses. My hypothesis is of a person who forced himself, had seemingly always had to force himself, to pause and reflect. He would then make some big calls, yet do so in a way that seemed so diffident and unhistrionic that their importance might pass without notice.

So, third, we have the public image of Bush the cautious, Bush the prudent, Bush the risk averse. Against that we have the reality of some of the most radical moves any president has overseen in modern times. Part of this is just the empowerment of skillful subordinates in a true administration team—Scowcroft, Baker, Zoellick, the Nick Brady of the important "Brady plan," Cheney, Sununu, Darman, and others. But some of the biggest calls were very much Bush's own.

Contrary to much of the historiography, the end of the Cold War featured some breathtaking gambles. Bush and most (not all) of his advisors threw aside initial hesitations about how to make sense of the changes about two months into the new administration, toward the end of March 1989. I was a direct witness to this. Bush and his team (notably Baker and Scowcroft) called for a rollback of Soviet power—eventually to extend to a rollback to borders the Russian empire had not known since the eighteenth century. Throughout human history changes on this scale have happened only as the corollary of bloodily catastrophic war.

Bush unequivocally gambled on an all-out push for German unification and did so publicly—much noticed among world leaders—weeks before the Berlin Wall came down. He presided over the largest change in the U.S. force posture in Europe since the 1950s and the most ambitious nuclear and conventional arms control agreements ever signed before or since. If his agenda is compared to what foreign leaders privately wanted or expected or what public pundits such as Henry Kissinger and George Kennan were advocating in leading newspapers at the time, Bush's agenda was indeed extreme.

In the immediate aftermath of Iraq's August 1990 invasion of Kuwait, who in America envisioned or called for the dispatch of 500,000 American soldiers to the sands of Saudi Arabia who were prepared to reverse it? And then seek to do so with full UN support, seizing on the end of the Cold War as its embers were still glowing to revive for the first time since 1945 the long-latent dream of Franklin Roosevelt to make the UN Security Council a body of high-minded "policemen" (FDR's term)?

All this was afire with political controversy (the resolution authorizing the use of force passed the Senate by only five votes; his son's 2002 Iraq vote would pass by fifty). That was the context in which, barely a week before the 1990 midterm elections, Bush decided to double the U.S. troop commitment, including reserve call-ups that could touch every American community. The war plan of the theater commander was junked, and Joint Staff stepped in to help craft a far bolder plan, backed by a blank check of presidential commitment. Bob Gates's recollection of the October 30, 1990, meeting, preserved in his oral history interview, still echoes astonishment even twenty years later. Bush knew what he was doing. A week earlier, Baker and Colin Powell had privately conferred about where all this was going. Both men were uneasy, with Powell clearly wondering whether Bush was really "all in" and then being assured that he was. I believe from that day—October 30—forward, Colin Powell was George H. W. Bush's man, proud to count himself among a band of brothers.

However one characterizes all this, "prudent" does not do the job. The pictures of the frenetic golfer or fisherman, the self-deprecating, genial but rather hapless toastmaster, do not do the job. And future scholars will want to keep in mind that almost all of the American academic commentators who wrote about George H. W. Bush in the twentieth century can be presumed to have voted against him, based on what they thought they knew at the time.

Nor do such depictions do the job for the 1990 budget agreement, which turned out to be the first and most important of three budget deals struck between 1990 and 1996 that produced a balanced budget by the end of the decade for the first time since the Nixon administration. This book amply describes what this cost Bush. That this came as the country was quietly staggering from an enormous, dimly understood American financial crisis (the so-called savings and loan crisis that began toward the end of the Reagan administration) makes the issue more interesting still. That the budget deficit became the signature issue for the strange and ultimately quite significant third-party candidacy of that eccentric, vengeful snake-oil salesman Ross Perot, only redoubles the historical irony.

If puzzles like these pique your curiosity, make you want to take another look at this rather peculiar one-term president, read on. And then read the oral histories, which are available at http://millercenter.org/president/bush/oralhistory.

In weighing the value of these oral histories, consider that there are only two kinds of primary sources about the past. There are the material remnants of what happened—documents, coins, statues. Then there are the preserved recollections of the human observers. Some of these recollections take the form of formal memoirs.

From the time it was founded in the mid-1970s, the University of Virginia's Miller Center placed the study of the American presidency close to the center of its work. From the point of view of basic research into primary evidence, the most obvious way to supplement the work of the National Archives and Records Administration was to organize good oral history projects to set down the recollections of participants before they passed on. A modest effort of this kind was undertaken for the Ford presidency; a better one (helped by James Sterling Young's involvement) was conducted for the Carter administration. Then Young went on to other work at Virginia and, though director Kenneth Thompson did his best, these efforts went back to a relatively modest scale. This was a pity, because the quality of oral history work being conducted by the presidential libraries had always been up and down, mostly down, and candor was constrained by the fact that the libraries, with their institutional bias toward the presidents whose legacies they embodied, directly ran the projects.

One of my first tasks when taking over the directorship of the Miller Center in 1998 was to revive the oral history work and raise its standards. The goal was to provide as strong a complement to the documentary and memoir record as funds would allow, institutionalizing these practices for every presidency possible. Jim Young came back on board to help; he and I later recruited the current director, Russell Riley, whom we both knew to have been one of Dick Neustadt's finest students. The oral history work was complemented by another primary research effort, the careful annotated transcription of the presidential meeting and telephone recordings secretly compiled in several presidencies, above all between 1962 and 1973. These two research projects seemed to be the most important primary research projects possible, beyond the compilation of papers and other artifacts long being carried out by the National Archives.

The launching pad for the renewed oral history effort was the presidency of George H. W. Bush. His immediate successor, Clinton, was then still in office. I had served in Bush's administration in a rather junior position, as a career diplomat detailed to his National Security Council staff, and knew some of the principal figures. The Bush oral history project became a template for those to follow. The Miller Center has now forged partnerships to conduct such projects for the administrations of Reagan, Clinton, and George W. Bush as well. One of our alumni, Tim Naftali, was also able to use some of this experience to conduct a too-long-delayed and quite good oral history project for the Nixon administration when Naftali became the National Archives' director of the Nixon Library.

The Bush precedent involved financial support from Bush's presidential library foundation. They agreed to be fenced off from the research process itself. The Miller Center chose the interviewers, shaped the agenda, conducted the interviews, and then kept the results as private (including from the Bush library foundation) as the respondents wished. That kind of partnership would not have been easy for every presidential library foundation to swallow. And this one had some second thoughts about it, even third thoughts.

From a research point of view, the partnership with the Bush library foundation was fortunate. It set the right kind of precedent for scholarly integrity. That is a credit to Bush himself and the tone he set for some of his former aides who shared these instincts.

It was not as hard for them to set such a standard as it might have been for some other presidents and their aides. They had been involved in a presidency that, though it failed of reelection, had been practically unblemished by scandal and had produced notable policy successes—some of which were known and some of which (they thought) were not adequately known. So these men and women were not as insecure about what scholars would find as some other sets of "formers" might have been. Hence the good precedent.

This volume reflects an initial reappraisal by a superb group of scholars armed with this material along with additional material generated at a fall 2011 symposium that brought them together with Bush administration alumni at the Miller Center. I believe other scholars who take their time with this volume and the underlying material will find both to be quite important in revising our understanding of this very important, misunderstood, and, as discussed above, somewhat peculiar president.

Preface

Describing the University of Virginia Miller Center's oral history of his presidency, George H. W. Bush has written that although "the documentary record is vital," interviews with members of the administration "add the human side that those papers can never capture."

41: Inside the Presidency of George H. W. Bush offers another dimension—objective scholarly analysis of the Bush presidency, using the oral history interviews and other sources to expand our understanding of the forty-first president and of the Cold War era and its immediate aftermath. The book's chapters, all contributed by systematic observers of American politics, foreign policy, political ideology, and government institutions, analyze how President Bush organized and staffed his administration, approached the "new world order" and its challenges, applied his brand of Republican conservatism, handled legislative affairs, and made judicial appointments. Forming bookends for *41*'s core are Russell Riley's introduction and Sidney Milkis's conclusion. Riley's chapter combines an overview of the Bush oral history project, which he directed, with analysis of how it refines our knowledge of presidential power, especially in wartime. Milkis's conclusion synthesizes the theories and evidence presented in each chapter into a portrait of presidential politics, policy-making, and leadership in the twentieth century's last decade.

The volume is based on papers initially presented at the 2011 conference that accompanied the release of the Bush oral histories, jointly sponsored by the Miller Center and the George Bush Presidential Library Foundation. The conference included panels covering the Bush administration's foreign affairs, defense policy, political ideology, and domestic issues. Each panel convened Bush alumni, historians, and political scientists, who commented on the contributions that the oral history interviews make to our knowledge of the president and his administration. Panel chairs Philip Zelikow, Melvyn Leffler, Sidney Milkis, and Charles Jones provided expert guidance for the conversations among Bush officials and scholars. Offering first-hand observations of the Bush presidency were administration members Brent Scowcroft, David Jeremiah, John Sununu, Roman Popadiuk, Robert Kimmitt, Boyden Gray, Fred McClure, and Bobbie Kilberg. They were joined by Professors Bartholomew Sparrow, Jeffrey Engel, and Robert Strong, who spoke on war and statecraft; Michael Nelson and Hugh Heclo on Bush's conservatism; and Barbara Sinclair, Barbara Perry, and Henry Abraham on relations with Congress and the Supreme Court. C-SPAN's recordings of the conference and related material have been archived in the network's video library as the "President George H. W. Bush Oral History Project," at www.c-spanvideo.org/.

As a cooperative effort of the Miller Center and the George Bush Presidential Library Foundation, the Bush oral history project consists of fifty interviews with senior White House and Cabinet officials that were conducted from 1999 to 2011. Normally, interviews ran from seven to ten hours over a two-day period. A team that usually consisted of two to four scholars most often interviewed one official, but occasionally several Bush administration alumni would participate together. Typically, interviews explored officials' memories of their service with President Bush and their careers prior to joining the administration. Interviewees also offered political and leadership lessons they had gleaned as eyewitnesses to and shapers of history. (See Appendix 1 for a chronological list of interviews. Appendix 2 lists all of the scholars who participated.) The Bush Foundation imposed no influence over or constraints on the interviews or on the chapters drawing from them by scholars contributing to this volume.

The Miller Center has conducted oral histories of every president since Jimmy Carter. No questions are off limits; officials are encouraged to speak candidly to history. Each interview's audio recording is transcribed, then edited by the subject, and eventually becomes the authoritative record of the interview. In October 2011, the Miller Center released all Bush oral history transcripts that had been cleared by the interviewees. Cleared transcripts can be accessed at www.millercenter.org/president/bush/oralhistory; the headnotes of these transcripts provide a list of all participants in each interview. The site will post additional transcripts as their subjects agree to allow their release. Although presidential oral histories do not take the place of original presidential documents, they can be especially useful if members of an administration refuse to release their papers, despite Presidential Records Act mandates to do so.

Our profound gratitude goes to Philip Zelikow, not only for writing this book's foreword but also for establishing the George Bush Oral History Project during his directorship of the Miller Center. He persuaded James Sterling Young, the Center's founding father of its presidential oral history program, to eschew emeritus status and return to the Miller Center in order to launch the Bush project. Professors Stephen Knott, Tarek Masoud, and Darby Morrisroe ably assisted him.

We could not have enjoyed a more proficient administrator of the Miller Center's Presidential Oral History Program than Katrina Kuhn, who effectively arranged the interviews and organized the conference based on them. Equally dedicated were editor Jane Rafal Wilson and her team of transcribers, who painstakingly produced the written record of each interview. Information director Mike Greco and librarian Sheila Blackford led the Miller Center's talented technology team in digitally preparing and posting the transcripts online. And no interviews could have been conducted without the detailed briefing books prepared by our skilled researchers, Bryan Craig and Rob Martin, aided by a coterie of expert assistants.

Obviously, the Bush oral history could never have reached completion without the administration officials who generously gave their time to participate in interviews. We also thank the Miller Center, led by Governor Gerald L. Baliles, and its former managing director, W. Taylor Reveley IV, as well as the George Bush Presidential Library Foundation, guided by Roman Popadiuk. We appreciate the freedom afforded the authors of this book to follow the scholarship to its logical conclusions, based on careful readings of primary documents, oral history, and previous literature.

Michael Nelson and Barbara A. Perry

Of the forty-six men who have served as vice president of the United States, fourteen have become president, but only six of them have done so without first ascending to the office when the president died or resigned. George H. W. Bush had vast political experience before becoming Ronald Reagan's vice president in 1981. A transplanted New Englander who moved to Texas, succeeded in the oil business, and was elected to the U.S. House of Representatives from Texas's 7th District in 1966, Bush ran for the U.S. Senate in 1970. He lost, but as a reward for supporting President Richard Nixon's Vietnam policy, Nixon nominated him to be ambassador to the United Nations. When the Watergate scandal broke, however, Nixon needed a reliable ally as chair of the Republican National Committee and asked Bush to accept the position in 1973. After Nixon resigned in 1974, his successor, Gerald Ford, asked Bush to serve as the chief of the U.S. Liaison Office in China. His next post, from 1976 to 1977, was director of central intelligence, heading the Central Intelligence Agency until President Jimmy Carter, a Democrat, replaced him. Bush sought the Republican nomination for president in 1980 and finished second to Ronald Reagan, who chose him as his vice presidential running mate.

Bush loyally logged two terms as vice president. As is typical of modern vice presidents, he met weekly with the president over Oval Office lunches and led task forces, one involving deregulation and the other international drug smuggling. Bush also attended to the traditional duties of the vice president such as presiding over ceremonial events and representing the nation at funerals for foreign heads of state. Bush famously quipped, "You die; I fly!" Yet his wife, Barbara

Bush, correctly noted that such journeys gave her husband the opportunity to meet with dignitaries around the world, some of whom would soon become the leaders of their countries. Bush accumulated so much experience in this role that he decided to model his run for the GOP's presidential nomination on Vice President Richard Nixon's 1960 race to become his party's nominee, offering himself to Republican voters as a quasi-incumbent president.

In October 1987, Bush announced his candidacy for president in his adopted home town of Houston. Although he thought that he had positioned himself as the clear front-runner, the Reagan Administration's Iran-Contra scandal in 1985–1986 presented a potential stumbling block. In addition, he had to fight the stereotype that all vice presidents face of being viewed as a weak yes-man to the chief executive. Suddenly, the loyal party warrior and World War II naval pilot faced the media's insinuation that he was a "wimp."

Despite the scandal-induced dips in Reagan's approval ratings, he remained an iconic figure in the Republican Party. Placing too much distance between the president and himself clearly would jeopardize Bush's nomination. After a third-place finish in the Iowa caucuses, behind Senator Robert Dole of Kansas and televangelist Pat Robertson, the vice president decided to hew especially closely to Reagan's economic policies. Although he had once dismissed Reagan's proposal for massive tax cuts as "voodoo economics" during the 1980 nomination campaign, Bush now announced his opposition to any and all tax increases. That strategy, along with his campaign strategist Lee Atwater's ability to garner southern votes, secured the 1988 presidential nomination for Bush.

The vice president faced Democratic Massachusetts governor Michael Dukakis in the general election. In public opinion polls taken just after the Democratic convention in June, Bush trailed Dukakis by as many as 17 percentage points. Atwater urged an aggressive attack on Dukakis's liberalism, which Vice President Bush mounted that summer. He also repeated the no-tax pledge in his convention acceptance speech, prefacing it with a Clint Eastwood twist: "Read my lips: no new taxes." His choice of Indiana senator Dan Quayle for a running mate—a surprising selection to his staff, whom he did not consult fully—failed to energize the ticket. But the no-tax pledge energized the GOP, and the Bush campaign's assault on the Massachusetts governor's supposed lack of patriotism hit their mark. The ultimate weapon against Dukakis was campaign ads that portrayed the governor as soft on criminals because he supported his state's prison furlough program. An independent pro-Bush group added a racial theme to its ads, which focused on a black convict, Willie Horton, who had committed additional violent crimes while on furlough.

In the second presidential debate with the vice president, Dukakis inflicted a wound on himself from which his campaign never recovered. His unemotional answer to a hypothetical question about whether he would change his anti-capital punishment stance if his wife were raped and murdered sealed his fate. Bush swept to victory on November 8, 1988, winning forty states with 426 electoral votes and 53 percent of the national popular vote. In doing so he became the first incumbent vice president to win the presidency since Martin Van Buren in 1836.

41

HISTORY AND GEORGE BUSH

Russell L. Riley

We are told by those close to the man who was the forty-first president of the United States that he does not like discussions of the "L word," preferring to leave assessments of his presidential legacy to others. In this, George H. W. Bush's approach to his place in history is, to say the least, atypical, in a business where brazen self-promotion is expected and oblique boasting high art. Efforts to spin history usually continue long after a president leaves office. The White House memoir is an evergreen genre, and "reputational entrepreneurs" routinely seek to memorialize their leader's accomplishments—witness the ongoing effort to erect venerations to Ronald Reagan in every county in the country.[1] Indeed the urge to shape how history will recall a presidency is as old as the nation itself. George Washington and his family sanctioned an unusual public release of his last will and testament, almost surely to help fortify the first president's historical reputation for benevolence by highlighting his major gifts to education and the liberation of his slaves.[2]

Bush's evident reticence to engage in similar efforts to shape how history will remember him is rooted in a bred-in-the-bone aversion to self-referential behavior, learned at his mother's knee. His White House speechwriters knew, for example, to cull the first-person singular from his prepared remarks, because Bush otherwise would refuse to speak it. This practice produced a unique form of subjectless presidential rhetoric: "Worked in the oil business, started my own.... Moved from the shotgun [shack] to a duplex apartment to a house. Lived the dream—high school football on Friday night, Little League, neighborhood barbecue."[3] (By contrast, Harry Truman once used "I" eleven times on a single page of his draft memoir, an excess that Dean Acheson felt duty-bound to point out.)[4] The boy known fondly as "Have Half" for his disposition to share what he had with others grew into political manhood as someone who was more comfortable sharing the spotlight than elevating the importance of his own accomplishments in the public sphere.[5] This trait probably helps explain why as Vice President Bush was such an effective second to Reagan and why there were such unusual delays in setting up a campaign operation to highlight his own presidential achievements heading into the 1992 election. As his White House personnel chief Chase Untermeyer has remarked, Bush believed "his record was his record and he didn't need to campaign to create a ballyhoo about" it.[6]

Bush alone among recent presidents refused to compose a true autobiography, choosing instead to co-author, with National Security Advisor Brent Scowcroft, a shared, policy-based account of the end of the Cold War.[7] And when historical analysts approached him with requests for extended interviews, he persistently resisted their entreaties, expressing discomfort with the idea of being "stretched out on the couch" to reflect on his past.[8] As a political type, then, Bush has shown himself to be the polar opposite of Theodore Roosevelt, of whom it was observed that he wished to be the bride at every wedding and the corpse at every funeral.

Of course, it is possible that Bush also has made a rational calculation about his own limits in steering how future generations will view his public life. But whether his calculus is based on the optimistic assumption that ultimately history will get it right or the pessimistic one that his own judgments will be disregarded, we cannot know. It may be that in this instance the president takes the same fatalistic approach as his son. "George Washington, you know, they're still writing books about number one," George W. Bush once observed to Bob Woodward. Accordingly, "I'm not going to worry about what they're saying [now] about 43."[9] If the work of historians is perpetual and inconclusive, today's verdicts will probably be discarded tomorrow anyway.

Measured by the esteem of his fellow citizens, however, Bush 41 has already experienced a remarkable redemption for a man so thoroughly rejected when he last stood for public judgment. In November 1992, Bush suffered a rebuke of monumental proportions, securing only 37.5 percent of the popular vote. In the final opinion poll taken by Gallup prior to the election, Bush's job performance approval rating was only 34 percent, with 56 percent disapproving.[10] By roughly twenty years later, those public opinion figures were more than reversed. In Gallup's November 2010 retrospective poll on presidents who had served during the past fifty years, Bush registered 64 percent job approval and 34 percent disapproval, placing him in the upper half of those evaluated, in the company of John F. Kennedy, Ronald Reagan, and Bill Clinton. Clearly in the court of public opinion, George H. W. Bush was, to borrow a phrase from the 1992 campaign, "the Comeback Kid."

Although it is normal for a former president to enjoy an enhanced image as the patina of history accumulates, the speed of Bush's initial recovery in popular standing is so fast as to be almost inexplicable. It happened practically overnight, even before his presidency had ended. Gallup's January 1993 survey showed the president with a 56 percent approval rating less than ten weeks after his historic defeat. This was a leap in approval of 22 percentage points, placing Bush almost even with the incoming Clinton's rating as measured later that same month. Nothing remotely approaching this end-of-term boost has happened to any other president in the era of polling. (See Table 1.) In addition, Bush's recovery occurred during an interval when he was suffering extensive press criticism of his preemptive pardon of former secretary of defense Caspar Weinberger for offenses related to the Iran-Contra affair, to which over half of the American people objected.[11] How, then, can we account for this remarkable change? There are four probable answers.

The first is that the 1992 election itself may have drained much of the venom from the body politic. Having decisively dispatched the incumbent at the ballot box (a relatively rare punishment in the United States over the last century), American voters could reflect in this brief interval on the good Bush had accomplished without fear that any favorable evaluation would be misread by pollsters as an endorsement for him to continue in office.

Second, the nation's economic news began to reflect positive developments shortly after the election, giving strong indications that the recession that had so hobbled Bush's reelection effort was nearing an end. The timing of this recovery

TABLE 1 Post–World War II presidential approval ratings, end of presidential terms

	APPROVAL RATING, LAST SURVEY TAKEN BEFORE FINAL ELECTION IN OFFICE	APPROVAL RATING, LAST SURVEY STILL IN OFFICE	CHANGE IN RATING POINTS DURING THE TRANSITION OUT
George H. W. Bush	34 (10/12–14/92)	56 (1/8–11/93)	+22
Harry Truman	32 (10/9–14/52)	32 (12/11–16/52)	No change
Dwight Eisenhower	58 (10/18–23/52)	60 (12/8–13/60)	+2
Lyndon Johnson	42 (9/26–10/1/68)	49 (1/1–6/69)	+7
Gerald Ford	45 (6/11–14/76)	53 (12/10–13/76)	+8
Jimmy Carter	37 (9/12–15/80)	34 (12/5–8/80)	–3
Ronald Reagan	51 (10/21–24/88)	63 (12/27–29/88)	+12
Bill Clinton	58 (10/6–9/00)	66 (12/15–17/00)	+8
George W. Bush	25 (10/31–11/2/08)	29 (12/12–14/08)	+4

was a source of immense frustration to Bush's political team, who believed that a quicker turnaround might have salvaged their political fortunes. In the end, that good economic news—which included a jump in consumer confidence and (premature) reports of an improving unemployment rate—may also have put Americans in a forgiving state of mind for the lame-duck Bush.[12]

Third, there may have been some buyer's remorse. During the transition period immediately after the election, public attention shifted dramatically to Bill Clinton and his team, who found themselves increasingly owning the nation's problems. Moreover, immediately on taking office Clinton suffered a major political misstep on a pledge to reverse the military ban on gay and lesbian personnel, perhaps fueling suspicions that he was not the "New" Democrat he had purported to be during the campaign.[13]

Finally, to the surprise of many analysts at the time, Bush did not use defeat in November as an excuse for early retirement. Instead, he pursued until the end an aggressive agenda of foreign policy initiatives to round out his term. The most prominent of these was the decision to provide humanitarian military support to Somalia. "This is the most remarkable action ever taken by a lame-duck president," observed historian Leo Ribuffo at the time. "I think he is moved by a sense that he wants to be remembered as a humanitarian and not as a loser."[14] Subsequently, an early December 1992 Gallup poll, which already showed a leap in Bush's approval rating to 49 percent, also indicated that nearly three of four Americans agreed with this humanitarian effort.[15]

Bush left office, then, enjoying a substantial reversal in his public prestige. Since the time of his departure from the White House those early gains have been consolidated, but the main storyline of his evolving public reputation after leaving office has been its extraordinary dependency on popular evaluations of his two immediate successors in the Oval Office. It is true that every president is judged to some extent in comparison to others who serve in the lifetime of the observer. But Bush's has been an extreme case: his popular standing since leaving office has been notably hostage to the fortunes of others.

In Gallup's occasional retrospective polling about former presidents, two major swings have occurred in Bush's popular standing. In a January-February poll in 1998, his approval rating jumped sixteen points from its last measurement in late 1993, with 74 percent approving and only 24 percent disapproving of how Bush "handled [his] job as president." Some of this difference is probably the result of a gradual accretion in retrospective approval over time, but the magnitude of the leap surely owes much to the timing of the poll and the political realities it was reflecting. Just weeks before the survey was taken, Monica Lewinsky had become a household name in the United States, along with lurid details about Bill Clinton's behavior in the West Wing. It was in this environment that

1,013 randomly selected American adults were asked whether they approved of how Bush—a fabled family man—had conducted himself in office. The results were unsurprising.[16]

A reverse swing happened to Bush in June 2006. Although the public's judgment about most other former presidents was stable from Gallup's 2002 survey, Bush's numbers plummeted by thirteen points, leaving him almost twenty points below his high standing registered in February 2000. The reason is not hard to detect. This was, after all, as Gallup's revised questionnaire identified him, "The elder George Bush, father of the current president." Clearly the weight of public disapproval of George W. Bush, as it grew in the aftermath of the Iraq invasion and Hurricane Katrina, had the effect of pulling down his father's ratings. Indeed, George H. W. Bush's decline in popular approval in this interval is the most precipitous recorded in the multiple Gallup retrospectives of eight former presidents taken since 1990 and is all the more remarkable because it occurred during the same interval when he was famously engaged with Bill Clinton in a popular bipartisan effort to raise money for tsunami relief in the Indian Ocean.

To be sure, Bush's vulnerability to being measured by the yardstick of others' behavior is itself partly a sign of the ineffable quality of his presidency. There is in the popular memory no prominent and durable achievement that serves to anchor Bush in the public mind. The success of the first Gulf War faded in retrospect because it was a fast-won venture in a country few Americans knew and because Saddam Hussein's survival to fight another day became a persistent reminder of unfinished business. Bush's success in bringing the Cold War to a peaceful and satisfactory conclusion did not permanently elevate his public stature because his diplomacy was quiet, modest, and often indirect and because Ronald Reagan already occupied that particular pedestal. And Bush's major domestic victories were either in areas more closely associated with the life's work of others (such as Senators Edward Kennedy and Tom Harkin and the Americans with Disabilities Act) or created such polarizing political effects (such as the 1990 budget accord and Clarence Thomas's Supreme Court appointment, which is described in chapter 7 by Barbara A. Perry and Henry J. Abraham) that even today they constitute an indefinite public legacy.[17] Moreover, as both Michael Nelson (chapter 1) and Hugh Heclo (chapter 2) explain, Bush's uneven relationship with an evolving Republican Party left him at the end of his career without the kind of cohesive core constituency—"Bush Republicans"—to which a firm historical identity might be secured.

If the popular judgment about George H. W. Bush has been subject to wide swings, the overall scholarly assessments of his presidency to date have been practically inert. The best place to see this is in Bush's positioning in the historical rankings of presidents, those surveys of scholars occasionally compiled to arrange administrations from best to worst. The flaws in these rankings are often noted, but they do provide a rough picture of how historians and political scientists evaluate each president at a given moment. In one compilation of eleven of these surveys taken since Bush left office in January 1993, he has ranked almost exactly in the middle of the pack—between 20 and 22—eight times.[18]

This consistency in Bush's rankings is conspicuous during a period when other presidents continued to move over a considerable range: JFK has bobbed from 18 to 6 and back to 15, Nixon from 38 to 23 within a span of three years, and Carter from 19 to 34 then to 18. This movement suggests ongoing churning in the scholarly community among those trying to establish a consensus.[19] By comparison, the verdict on Bush has looked almost fixed: a median president.

It is of course possible that these assessments will change. Yet access to new evidence is a problem for anyone who would seriously reconsider the place in history of the forty-first president—or, for that matter, any recent president. An immense documentary record of original source materials is held in the presidential library system, but its release is governed by a set of legal and administrative constraints that slows the process to a virtual crawl. This starves historians of their basic sustenance. As of June 2012, for example, less than 20 percent of the holdings of the George H. W. Bush Presidential Library were ready for public inspection.[20] Moreover, decisions of the National Archives and Records Administration about opening presidential documents are often driven more by curiosity seekers and conspiracy theorists exploiting the Freedom of Information Act (FOIA) than by any systematic logic about which materials might add to our overall understanding of the president's tenure. One published account from 2007, for example, indicates that fully one-quarter of the FOIA filings at the Clinton Library were from a single UFO researcher.[21] Since the law gives such requests privileged status, this means, perversely, that we probably have relatively more information about Roswell, New Mexico, than about White House relations with the Kremlin.[22]

The absence of these original sources creates serious obstacles for students of the contemporary presidency. But there are at least two ways to circumvent them fruitfully, both of which are used in this book. The first is to seek out other data about the inner workings of the White House that can serve as a surrogate until the official records become available. The most prominent of these alternative sources is presidential oral history. Indeed, much that we would like to know about every presidency rests not in the documentary archive but in the memories of those who served with the president. A systematic debriefing of these officials provides extremely valuable evidence about the internal affairs of a presidency, providing a bridge to the time when the presidential records can be opened and also filling important gaps in what the written records will ultimately reveal.[23]

This book draws directly on thirty-one lengthy interviews with senior Bush officials, in the process casting new and important light on the inner workings of this White House.

A second alternative is to focus on the historic context of a presidency: the broad currents of American politics, the power situation, and the fundamental challenges the White House was required to confront. Such political trends and patterns drawn from already available evidence probably look different from the distance of time, in part because we have more complete knowledge about the full range of consequences. New perspectives can help resituate a presidency in American political history.

For example, it has been widely observed of George H. W. Bush that he was the first sitting vice president to be elected directly to the presidency since Martin Van Buren in 1836. Too, he also served as the first post–Cold War president, responding in 1989 and thereafter to the collapse of the Berlin Wall and its aftermath. These two facts are not, however, merely nuggets of trivia. Instead, they are important contextual features that make Bush genuinely distinctive historically and they merit deeper attention because of their great explanatory value. Together they created an extraordinarily difficult environment for the exercise of presidential leadership during the Bush presidency. Indeed, as will be explained below, because of these paired contextual factors Bush arguably served in one of the most challenging environments for national leadership ever experienced by an American president. Any fair assessment of his presidency ought to take into account the fullness of the barriers to presidential leadership he had to surmount. They were formidable.

Three Terms in the White House

We will begin here by examining the problems Bush confronted in proceeding from the vice presidency to a third consecutive term at the White House.

Reagan's Shoes

The most recognizable encumbrance George Bush bore as the direct successor to Ronald Reagan was one that Van Buren himself well understood: the travails of following a two-term political icon in the White House—in his case, Andrew Jackson. Both Van Buren and Bush were confronted with the unenviable task of serving in a role that had come to be personified in their immediate predecessors, who defined the party politics of their era. As a *Washington Post* headline warned on the day of Bush's 1989 inauguration, he had "Hard Shoes to Fill."

To understand the scale of Bush's burden, consider this casual observation about Reagan's footwear in Colin Powell's memoir. During his first meeting with the president after moving to the White House staff, Powell found himself seated on a couch in the Oval Office. "My eyes went to [Reagan's] feet, where I spotted something odd. How could his shoes, besides being mirrorlike," observed this spit-and-polish soldier, "have none of those creases across the instep caused by normal wear? On this and every other occasion, his shoes always looked as if they were being worn for the first time."[24] Reagan's appearance in the Oval Office was flawless; the image of him as president was strikingly perfect.

That apparently trivial detail is actually freighted with political significance. Reagan's awareness of the power of presentation was at once thorough and highly disciplined, making him a commanding public figure. And his ways were not so easily matched as one might imagine. Speechwriter Clark Judge remarks that

> I didn't appreciate this until . . . I had watched some tapes of [Reagan doing] ceremonial events, where I knew that there was tape marking his spot on the floor . . . and it all looked very natural. Then I'd look at other people . . . and there was no such discipline in it. There [is] nothing harder, that requires more discipline, than to appear spontaneous in front of a mass audience.[25]

By this point in Reagan's career he hit his mark effortlessly or, in the Hollywood tradition, by masking whatever effort it took to produce the special effect. Hard shoes to fill indeed.

Moreover, none of the creases of normal wear showed on Reagan, who left office after eight years with hardly a wrinkle added or a bronze hair out of place. That he had survived an assassin's bullets—with good humor and undiminished partisan scrappiness—added to the aura of invincibility. The political vernacular of the Reagan era reflected this reality. His opponents, bewildered by their inability to make their political charges stick, declared Reagan the "Teflon president." And his standing among his own partisans was protected by the so-called "Eleventh Commandment": "Thou shalt not speak ill of a fellow Republican." This injunction is usually credited to Reagan himself, but his sometime political advisor Stuart Spencer has divulged that the commandment was devised by Reagan's associates back in California precisely to shield him from in-party attacks. "We created that for his protection. . . . We didn't want anybody dumping on us."[26]

The image-promoting side of the Reagan presidency that served him so well involved habits that were foreign to his successor. Bush's communications director, David Demarest, recalls in his oral history that in 1992 Bill Clinton made an advance visit to their debate site to check on camera angles. Bush, he said, "no more would have done that than fly to the moon." He "hated that [sort of stuff]."

Thus, although Bush had great admiration for Reagan, he had little patience for the art or artifices that had helped sustain him. This included a focus on presidential rhetoric. Peter Robinson, once a Bush speechwriter, has observed that for Bush, "speeches were something that he had to do in addition to the real work," in "vivid . . . contrast" to Reagan.[27] Dan Quayle concurs: Bush "wasn't crazy about giving speeches. . . . If you gave him the choice between sitting in his office and solving problems all day or going out and making speeches, he'd solve the problems, because that's what he thought he was hired to do."

To be sure, by the time Bush assumed the office, there was some public weariness with the Reagan image and the White House spin operation. Thus, Bush's lack of polish was actually something of an advantage. In his own way, he, too, was a great communicator, but Bush's métier was the small room or the telephone or the handwritten note, methods better suited to a bygone day. Reagan's success in the use of mass communications meant that Bush was compelled to work more in that new world than he felt comfortable with, to his detriment. The expectations of high gloss remained, notwithstanding suspicions about the kinds of mechanisms and skilled manipulators needed to produce it. Demarest confirms that "the press didn't like it when Reagan 'manipulated' them, but [then] . . . we got castigated because we didn't [feed them] a line of the day. The collision of those two things I always thought was very amusing."

Reagan's substantive record added to Bush's burden. His policy successes in moving the country in a more conservative direction both set a high standard for meaningful presidential activism and created momentum on policy that largely set the terms for Bush's presidency. In this, Bush acutely felt what Stephen Skowronek has called the dilemmas of the "faithful son," the president who comes into office to continue the work of a successful predecessor.[28] As with all presidents, Bush desired to leave his own imprint on the nation. But his freedom of movement was checked, partly by his own political need to carry on with Reagan's legacy and partly by the simple policy momentum of the "Reagan Revolution."

The best example of these constraints arose in relation to budget politics. Bush's ill-fated declaration in his 1988 Republican nomination acceptance address—"Read my lips: no new taxes!"—arose precisely from the uncomfortable balancing act required of a faithful son emerging on his own under the watchful eye of a nervous party compelled to contemplate a future without its icon. That pledge was offered as reassurance of fundamental continuity (a point Hugh Heclo furthers in chapter 2).

Because of the realities of his situation—in effect, the momentum of a third term—Bush came to the presidency with much less freedom of action politically than a president who arrives at the White House under most other conditions.

And so when he decided, on the basis of his own considered judgment of the public good and his own reading of the opposition's leverage, to raise taxes—something Reagan had done more than once during his presidency without great political harm to himself—the president's party rebelled against what it felt was a singular betrayal.

The "Friendly" Transition

Scholars of the American presidency have built something of a cottage industry on the topic of transitions. Transition problems are especially consequential because of their opportunity costs: the political system is seldom as primed for presidential leadership as it is when a president comes to office fresh from an electoral victory. In addition, early failings reverberate throughout a presidency.

One might assume that Bush and his team had a major advantage on this count because they began their presidency with a running start. To some extent this was so. But it is an error to dismiss the transition as a nonexistent problem for President-elect Bush. On the contrary, some of those who experienced it first-hand have observed that a so-called friendly transition may be the most difficult of all. Indeed, Jeffrey A. Engel (chapter 4) quotes Bush's 1992 campaign manager, James A. Baker III, as asserting soon after that election that theirs was "*not* a friendly take-over" after all. Thus, in-party succession can mask the real problems inherent in this kind of transition.

Engel describes the problems Bush and his foreign policy team confronted in trying not to be captive to what they saw as the Reagan administration's excessive optimism about the Soviet Union. Bush's so-called pause was a formal mechanism for breaking from the existing policy trajectory, initiated to allow the administration to set a fresh course apart from the one it inherited. This experience in trying to reset foreign policy reveals both the aspiration for presidential independence and the difficulties of changing a course of action set into motion by a previous administration, especially when the successor is not free to repudiate openly the inherited policy.

Another major transitional issue for Bush was leftover personnel.[29] Van Buren dealt with this problem by bowing to it; he retained almost the entire Jackson cabinet. This was not an acceptable option for Bush, although many of the Reagan insiders wanted (even expected) to stay. So Bush had to make scores of decisions about senior executive branch jobs in a situation where any newly placed loyalist put an incumbent Reaganite out of work. Predictably, this generated resentments. Dan Quayle observes that conservatives soon came to him complaining that "the Reagan people are really getting shafted down in the bureaucracy." Reagan's close friend, Senator Paul Laxalt (R-Nev.), argues that Bush's subsequent political problems with Republican conservatives partly originated with these personnel changes: "[The] Bush people did not treat the Reagan people well. . . . They just literally put them into the street. And there was a lot of hard feeling in the Reagan camp across the country, which was a huge problem for George."[30] Bush's personnel director, Chase Untermeyer, objects to this "conservative shibboleth," asserting that the new administration took great care in dealing with the old team. Nonetheless, Bush experienced more than most presidents the frustration Thomas Jefferson voiced about patronage appointments: Every time I fill a vacant office I make one ingrate and a hundred enemies.[31] Bush's malcontents were in some ways more disgruntled than usual because he uprooted fellow Republicans from jobs already in their possession. Grumblings of betrayal in this environment were inevitable.

Fatigue and the Short Bench

The physical wear and tear of life in the White House is one of the most vivid images to emerge from oral histories. Presidents usually seem to age before our eyes. Yet in some ways they have it easier than the people who work for them, who do not have a small army assigned to their care and feeding and who have to keep up with household and family obligations away from the White House. (One senior presidential aide has confided in her oral history that she learned to alternate flossing uppers and lowers each night in order to save precious moments for sleep.) Such pressures afflict people who are at the White House even for short tenures. They become vastly more problematic the longer the team is in place. Accordingly, one of the underappreciated burdens of staying at the White House into a third term is fatigue, both physical and mental.[32]

Burnout thus becomes a problem. The conventional remedy is turnover, especially since most of those in senior White House positions can greatly improve their income by moving from the public to the private sector. However, turnover has to be managed. Too little and the accumulated fatigue of the staff that remains makes for poor staff work, poor decision-making, and stasis. Too much and there is a detrimental loss of continuity.

Turnover is also complicated by the fact that there is a limited universe of people with the talents and political credentials necessary to staff senior positions at the complex center of the federal government. This means that as a presidency endures, the talent pool dwindles. "[Over] time," observes David Demarest, "an administration kind of loses its ability to attract and retain." Therefore, the core problem for Bush, coming immediately on the heels of a two-term predecessor, was that the Republican bench was demonstrably shorter than the one Reagan began drawing on in 1980.

In addition, some senior Bush officials had worked for Reagan without a break for the entire two terms. Importantly, this included Bush himself. And although we do not hear much about fatigue early in his term, this changes as the years pass. In January 1992, Bush famously got sick on the prime minister of Japan, surely a sign that he was being pressed to perform beyond his physical limits. And his weariness probably affected his enthusiasm for reentering the grueling business of a reelection campaign. Timothy McBride, who as Bush's personal aide saw him up close as much as any staffer, concedes that Bush "seemed to be more tired and clearly not displaying the same zeal that he had during '87, '88, leading up to the campaign. It's hard to dispute that."

Finally, there is idea fatigue. Although Bush was in some ways a different kind of Republican than Reagan, their shared affiliation meant that they would frequently draw on the same partisan sources for new policy initiatives. After eight years, many of those new ideas had already been introduced. As policy advisor James Pinkerton says: "[If] you're in power, you play your best cards, you play your kings and your aces, first. And then you play your eights and nines and then you play your twos and threes. [By 1989] we were down to twos and threes. . . . [And we] lacked the capacity to identify . . . fresh ideas that would put juice back."

A Historically Unwieldy Congress

Contemplating midterm elections, Walter Dean Burnham has written that "by the sixth year [of a presidency,] grievances have had ample time to accumulate, and the regime often takes on a shopworn look."[33] The Congress that George H. W. Bush inherited on the first day of his term looked almost exactly like the one that had come to Washington during Reagan's sixth year, and its accumulated grievances were intact. Thus, Bush was forced from the very outset to confront a harsh partisan reality: Capitol Hill was dominated by an opposition that had bristled under Reagan's successes and its inability to penetrate his armor. Although Bush sought in his inaugural address to disarm congressional Democrats—"The American people await action. They didn't send us here to bicker. They ask us to rise above the merely partisan"—he could not wholly disassociate himself from the bitterness of the preceding eight years. His was far from a clean slate.

Reagan began his presidency with Republicans in control of the Senate (by a margin of 53–47) and Democrats in the majority in the House of Representatives (by a margin of 243–192). Southern Boll Weevil Democrats, however, often tilted the House in Reagan's direction. A Democratic surge at Reagan's six-year mark reversed control of the Senate (55 Democrats and 45 Republicans) and left Democrats with an enhanced 258–177 majority in the House. Those numbers were modestly worse when Bush took office. Since Zachary Taylor in 1848, only Bush and Richard Nixon had been elected to the White House with both chambers of Congress controlled by the political opposition. And both Taylor and Nixon became president after eight years of opposition party presidencies.[34] Accordingly, Bush found himself in an unprecedented political situation: No president in American history had ever continued his party's reign at the White House while confronting two congressional chambers arrayed against him. (Bush still remains alone on this count.) Further, as Barbara Sinclair emphasizes in chapter 6, Bush actually faced "a more formidable Congress" than his Republican predecessors because these Democrats were, as a result of long-term institutional developments on Capitol Hill, "better equipped and more experienced [than before] at building majorities in opposition to the president."

Bush's situation was unique in yet another way, again to his detriment. At the time of his inauguration, the House was entering its thirty-fourth year of continuous majority control by the Democratic Party. The corollary to this was more than three consecutive decades of minority status for House Republicans. No other congressional party has come close to this record of futility. The average amount of time any congressional party spent in minority status before this long run of Democratic rule was just over six years, and the previous record of twenty-four years was held by the gradually dying Federalist Party (1801 to 1825).[35] The Federalists ultimately dealt with their frustration by disbanding. The House Republicans of the 1980s, under the leadership of Georgia's Newt Gingrich, settled on a decidedly different course: guerrilla warfare.

Here, then, was Bush's governing predicament: to achieve legislative successes, he had to work from the very outset with invigorated opposition majorities in both chambers, and he had to do this at the same time that his own party was riven by "Young Turks" aggressively challenging the mainstream party leadership in the House, people who were of Bush's generation. That Bush had won the presidency in 1988 while the Republican ranks in the House actually dropped by two seats revealed a glaring disconnect between the condition of the presidential party and the condition of the congressional party. Some activists took that disjunction as confirmation that they could be rescued from their status as a "permanent minority" only by their own devices, steamrolling whatever partisan or institutional barriers stood before them. It is no wonder that energy for rebellion grew within the GOP. This was the backdrop for one of Bush's most embarrassing setbacks: the open rejection by House Republicans of his initial 1990 budget agreement with congressional Democrats. Whatever scruples Gingrich may have held against undermining the public standing of a Republican president were overwhelmed by his conclusion that the Republican minority in the House was otherwise destined to remain voiceless.

Roosting Chickens

An additional reason that an administration begins to take on a "shopworn" appearance over time is that the consequences of its actions accumulate. Anything negative that can be tied to administration behavior creates a rich and lasting target for partisan opponents and journalists. This was a special problem for Bush, who came into the Oval Office carrying eight years of incumbent's baggage. The consequences of Reagan-era budget deficits had left a set of disagreeable choices for Bush, which were made that much more difficult by the fact that he himself was complicit in decisions that had aggravated the deficit in the first place. (In an earlier parallel, Van Buren's own political fortunes fell victim to the economic collapse of his day, probably exacerbated by Andrew Jackson's war on the banks.) There was no way politically that Bush could have made this somebody else's problem, even if he had never uttered the words "Read my lips . . ." His bargaining power with Congress was at an ebb because the consequences of inaction, or failure of action, merely highlighted a problem with his fingerprints all over it. Politically, he needed a deal more than the Democrats did, and they knew it. After years of being beaten up by Reagan on the twin issues of spending and taxes, the Democrats took out their accumulated frustration on the president who was left to clean up the resulting deficit. This score-settling left chief of staff John Sununu fuming that Senate majority leader George Mitchell and Speaker Thomas Foley "were the most partisan congressional leaders the country has ever seen."

The experience of the Reagan years came back to haunt Bush in another way: the Iran-Contra scandal. Bush's role in that episode remained under investigation during the course of his presidency without a great deal of popular attention. But independent counsel Lawrence Walsh's decision to bring an indictment against former defense secretary Caspar Weinberger less than a week before the 1992 election and the public statements he made suggesting that Bush had been more deeply involved than was previously described shook the political world at a critical moment and, by some accounts, cut off a late-surging tide of popular momentum in Bush's favor. His cabinet secretary, David Bates, asserts in his oral history that Bush "was going to win but for Lawrence Walsh. Little known fact nowadays, but the Thursday night/Friday morning before the election, CNN likely voters polling track had him down minus one. . . . He was gaining ground, winning back the base. . . . Then that Walsh indictment came out, and by Saturday night/Sunday morning we dropped to about seven down."

Bush's continued service in the White House for a third consecutive term gave the Iran-Contra scandal political legs. Although Walsh's investigation was at bottom a legal proceeding, it was energized by—perhaps even, as the critics hold, motivated by—the fact that it involved behavior by the man then sitting in the

Oval Office. Had Bush not been elected in 1988, that investigation might have withered on the vine or at a minimum taken the modest course of finding facts and presenting a narrative of wrongdoing to the American people. What is clear, however, is that Bush's political fortunes took a direct hit late in his presidency, once again as a result of his time as vice president. The gestation period of that political scandal was not complete until his term as president was nearly at end. Even second terms have been notably burdened by scandals originating in first-term behavior.[36] Third terms merely extend the problem.

The Burdens of a Postwar Presidency

Whatever difficulties Bush confronted by rising to the presidency after eight years as Reagan's vice president were greatly exceeded by another simple fact of his time: He presided over the end of the Cold War. Mikhail Gorbachev's reform efforts were well under way by Bush's inauguration, and the Berlin Wall fell during his first year in office. Accordingly, much of his presidency was devoted to understanding and responding to a "new world order." The combination of the complexities of this global revolution and an altered dynamic for institutional power relations in Washington created an exceptionally thorny governing environment for the Bush presidency.

Late in 1991, Bush's pollster Fred Steeper passed along to the president a brief memo contemplating Bush's political vulnerabilities at a moment when his approval ratings were sparkling, scaring off the most prominent of his likely Democratic challengers for reelection. In scanning the political landscape, Steeper had grown increasingly worried about what he termed "the Churchill Factor or the Churchill Parallel."[37] Steeper detected a possibility that Bush's great foreign policy successes—including the end of the Cold War but more directly victory in the Gulf War—might be insufficient reason for the American people to give him a second term. He relied on the example most educated Americans understood without explanation. In perhaps the most stirring manifestation of democratic leadership ever, Winston Churchill had demonstrated extraordinary skill and courage in moving the English people through the hardships of World War II to ultimate victory. But once the enemy was vanquished, the electorate began to turn its attention inward, and, notwithstanding his wartime successes, Churchill was judged to be the wrong man for the peace. Only weeks after VE Day, he was unceremoniously dumped by the voters in favor of a Labor government led by Clement Attlee. Steeper, without elaboration, wanted to sound an alarm that the principal justifications for Bush's reelection might similarly be politically hollow.

Steeper's detection of this emergent force in the electoral environment was striking. But so too was his decision to rely on a foreign example. What Steeper did not know was that there is a rich, if largely unrecognized, tradition in U.S. history of the same kind of dynamic in which the voters are hostile to postwar executives. In this, George H. W. Bush shared a similar place in political time with a troubled cohort of postwar predecessors, most prominently Andrew Johnson, Woodrow Wilson, and Harry Truman. Johnson was impeached for defying a resurgent postwar Congress. Wilson was subjected to political repudiation about the structures of postwar global politics that was so humiliating as to hasten him to an early grave. And Truman found himself a few months after the end of World War II declaring to a Gridiron Dinner that "Sherman was *wrong*. . . . Peace is hell." "For President Truman, the postwar period did not simply arrive," wrote biographer Robert J. Donovan. "It broke about his head with thunder, lightning, hail, rain, sleet, dead cats, howls, tantrums, and palpitations of panic."[38]

There is a logic to this political behavior, although it has not been thoroughly explored.[39] What is widely understood is that war empowers and enlarges the presidency. As Clinton Rossiter explained in his 1948 classic *Constitutional Dictatorship: Crisis Government in the Modern Democracies*, since ancient times republican governments have found it necessary to confer vast powers on one leader in periods of crisis in order to survive. During the Civil War and World Wars I and II, as Rossiter recounts (and later with the Cold War presidency and George W. Bush's presidency after 9/11), the powers of Presidents Lincoln, Wilson, and Franklin Roosevelt grew to extraordinary proportions. The American people looked to the presidency for leadership, relaxing the usual constraints of constitutional limits and shared powers to permit the president the latitude necessary to defeat the enemy. It is widely recognized that this departure from constitutional norms is essential to achieve victory in a system that otherwise is not well suited for quick and decisive action.

But the rest of the sequence is typically misunderstood. "In war," Cambridge political scientist David Runciman has written, "democratic governments have often had to resort to emergency powers, but when the war is over, those powers get given back."[40] *Get given back*. That characterization is commonly assumed—and deeply flawed. Runciman implies that once the crisis has been met, the wartime leader engages in a collegial and accommodating restoration of the status quo antebellum, agreeably returning to the constitutional armory those powers borrowed and deployed for the duration of the crisis. The evidence—at least in the United States (and in Churchill's Great Britain)—indicates something quite different.[41]

The political contractions of immediate postwar periods have produced some of the most contentious episodes in American history. A rare kind of consensus has been the basis for establishing a wartime leadership regime in the first place. But when that consensus about threat evaporates, so, too, does deference to presidential direction, sometimes in a spectacularly messy fashion. In these instances, profound disagreements have erupted, especially between Congress and the White House, over the extent to which the wartime powers of the president ought to be left intact to deal with the problems of restoring peace. In every case, postwar periods have been characterized by a jealous reassertion of congressional prerogative, fueled in part by genuine concerns about the health of the Constitution and in part by pent-up resentment in Congress over being obligated by crisis to follow. Simply put, Congress has sought at the earliest opportunity after each crisis has ended to restore its equal position in the governing process. The same can be said, of others who during wartime have attenuated their constitutionally protected rights to challenge the president, including opposition party members, the press, and even the judiciary. In sum, presidents normally have not quickly or freely "given back" the wartime powers conferred to them. Rather, as war has ended, the other major constitutional actors have typically insisted on a precipitous and politically painful reclamation of their prerogatives and, in the bargain, have moved vigorously to cut the presidency back down to its proper constitutional dimensions. The speed and scope of these contractions have been politically traumatic.

To be sure, this pattern was not perfectly replicated following the wars in Korea, Vietnam, and Iraq, because in these instances the nation still found itself confronted by the perils of a protracted low-intensity conflict. The dangers of the Cold War and later the "Long War" created an enduring tolerance for heightened presidential power in order to secure the nation against global communism and Islamic terrorism, respectively. But it is striking that even in these cases of wars within wars the impulse to right-size the presidency appeared once these conflicts turned from hot to cold. The post-Vietnam period, for example, includes some of the most striking confirmatory evidence of the general pattern, including the War Powers Resolution of 1973 and the decision by Congress in 1976 to dismantle a long succession of emergency powers delegated to the president that began in 1933.[42]

Contributing to the usual institutional impulses for what Warren Harding called the return to "normalcy" is the increasing importance on the public agenda of issues more clearly in the orbit of congressional authority than is emergency management. Swords are normally a presidential business, plowshares the business of Congress, and turning the former into the latter, as one Bush-era member of Congress said, "is not painless."[43] Popular enthusiasm for exchanging guns for butter always runs ahead of the pace deemed prudent by the commander-in-chief. Accordingly, the very nature of postwar demobilization fosters the congressional urge to reassert its authority.

The end of the Cold War meant distinctive trouble for the Bush White House across a broad range of fronts—beginning, perhaps, as early as the Senate's unusual decision, described in Robert A. Strong's account of the John Tower nomination (chapter 5), to deny the president his first choice for leading "the [defense] department in austere times."

Abroad, Bush and his foreign policy team were immediately confronted after the collapse of the Berlin Wall with a first-order problem in international relations: how, in the aftermath of a sudden, unexpected, and profound change in the global environment, to ensure the security of American interests, especially when other government actors in Washington were increasingly focused on what the peace would mean at home.

Before November 1989, almost nobody, inside the government or out, had spent serious time thinking about how the Cold War might end and what the implications would be for American policy. By contrast, as John Lewis Gaddis has noted, "in both world wars elaborate postwar planning exercises were under way in Washington just weeks after the fighting had begun." Gaddis asserts that notwithstanding a long and durable commitment by Washington policymakers of both parties to a strategy of containment, few had bothered to consider seriously what the ultimate goal of containment was and thus what to do if it prevailed.[44] As a result, President Bush found himself, quite unexpectedly, compelled to help improvise a once- or twice-in-a-century remaking of the global order. That he navigated through this perilous environment as well as he did is in part attributable the team of experts he recruited to join him and to the policy-making process they created, both detailed by Bartholomew Sparrow in chapter 3.

Two major geopolitical problems dominated the attention of the White House: the fate of Germany (and more broadly of Europe) and the future of the Soviet Union. In both cases, there was a deficiency of reliable intelligence about rapidly changing developments and a persistent inability to predict whether U.S. intervention, modest or robust, would produce an intended effect or instead create a backlash against a meddling outsider. A misplayed hand at any of a dozen—perhaps any of a hundred—inflection points might well have poisoned the peace or even created a world in which new dangers were as threatening as the old. Such dangers preoccupied the Bush White House, and yet they were little appreciated by Americans happily liberated by the collapse of a longtime enemy.

In addition, one of the ascribed benefits of the Cold War had been its relative stability, keeping in check regional, ethnic, and religious conflicts that were safely embedded in the broader contest between the two dominant world powers. Consequently, two of Bush's most vexing foreign policy problems emerged from the destabilization of that bipolar world. One was the first Gulf War, which was provoked by Saddam Hussein's August 1990 invasion of Kuwait. According to Musallam Ali Musallam, "If a Cold War situation had existed, in which U.S.-Soviet tensions were acute, it is difficult to imagine Saddam Hussein's Iraq, a client of the Soviet Union, invading a major oil-producing state friendly to the United States." Joseph Nye has even called Kuwait "the first victim of the end of the Cold War world order."[45] Although the Gulf War produced arguably the greatest success of the Bush presidency, it required an enormous investment of presidential energy, which was surely drawn away from other initiatives.

The second regional conflict sparked by the end of the Cold War was the disintegration of Yugoslavia. For the most part, the Bush administration succeeded in keeping itself disengaged from this thicket of ethnic tensions, following Secretary of State Baker's colloquial guidance that "we don't have a dog in this fight." But this perhaps prudent absenting was not without major costs. How to stay out and how to justify a hands-off approach when Americans were presented with horrifying images of suffering was no simple matter, and the situation required attention and occasional recalibration. Although it is doubtful that nonintervention damaged Bush directly with the American electorate, there surely was an indirect cost to him: a growing perception of incapacity, which in itself poses a danger to a president, especially in an election year.[46]

But postwar problems for the Bush White House only began abroad. At least as challenging was the domestic side of the return to normalcy. One of the easiest places to see the impulse for Congress to reestablish its equal role with the presidency was, paradoxically, in its decision to authorize the use of military force to drive Saddam out of Kuwait. The conventional accounts of this episode tend to focus on Bush's shrewdness in asking for formal congressional approval. By deciding to "coopt" Congress and succeeding, Bush strengthened his hand at home and projected a more unified and powerful presence overseas.[47] That image of strength was enhanced by the fact that the president let it be known that he was prepared to go it alone, defiantly, if Congress voted not to support him.[48]

An alternative reading of this decision, however, leads to a starkly different interpretation of its meaning. Bush felt himself impelled by the realities of his political situation, including the increasing assertiveness of an independent-minded Congress, to seek its endorsement of his actions, notwithstanding the assurances of counsel Boyden Gray, defense secretary Dick Cheney, and the leadership of his own justice department that legal precedent was plainly on his side: the president, by Constitution and law, did not need Congress to approve.[49] That Bush nonetheless still sought legislative sanction was a sign of his political need for cover in an environment of congressional resurgence. *Congressional Quarterly*'s annual report for 1991 records the historic nature of that vote, which "reinstated a congressional role in going to war, missing in action since December 8, 1941."[50] Moreover, even with the president's prestige on the line and troops in theatre, the Senate vote was a bare 52–47, the "most narrow margin backing military action since the War of 1812."[51] Cheney observes that if Bush had decided to act unilaterally, as he had privately said he would if the vote had gone the other way, "there certainly would have been some impeachment resolutions introduced."

During the congressional debate over the authorization of force, Senator Daniel Patrick Moynihan (D-N.Y.) argued explicitly, both on the Senate floor and on the op-ed page of the *New York Times*, that Congress needed to use this occasion, after a long hiatus, to reestablish its primacy in the business of commencing war. "The Constitution took something of a beating during the cold war," Moynihan observed. "How could it not have in the course of 30 to 40 years in which Presidents knew they would have 10 minutes at most to decide whether to launch a thermonuclear second strike? All right; that was then. Now a certain normality reappears." With that return to normality, the long habits of the Cold War had to be broken—which was not easy. Moynihan's training as a sociologist led him to observe that "the manner and mode of the cold war . . . has been with us so long, we do not know how to act differently. We have not acquired the instincts, the institutions, the institutional memories, to do other than what we have been doing during the cold war. We know nothing else." These habits meant that when the first post–Cold War conflict arose, the White House would naturally deny the "primacy of Congress under the Constitution . . . just at that moment when it would seem possible to return to what was once the normal conduct of foreign affairs by the President and the Congress of the United States."[52] The inference was that Congress would be inclined, reflexively, to follow the president's lead.

Moynihan opposed the Persian Gulf War and hoped that Congress would deny the president authorization to intervene. He failed on the policy but succeeded on the basic principle: the president did come to Congress to get its imprimatur for military intervention. And as *Congressional Quarterly* asserted, the fact of that vote (to authorize) is as important as its immediate outcome, especially because it suggested that the restoration of "normal conduct" between the institutions was more advanced than Moynihan had understood.

Postwar demobilization also profoundly shaped the contentious politics of the federal budget in the Bush years, which led directly, many believe, to the president's political demise. The basic frame of Bush's challenge was how to manage pressures for a rapid post–Cold War build-down in the defense sector while simultaneously accounting for what was widely termed the "peace dividend."[53] "'Peace dividend, peace dividend,' we heard it over and over and over again," Cheney recollects in his oral history. Bush's core problem was not so much the dividend itself but rather what might be termed the dividend gap—that is, the difference between his own perception, as commander-in-chief, and those of his critics about how much money could responsibly be redeployed from national security to other purposes. For the remainder of his presidency after the fall of the Berlin Wall on November 9, 1989, Bush was enmeshed in political battles over both the supply and demand sides of the peace dividend: fending off calls to cut defense spending more precipitously than he thought wise and deflecting commitments to a host of other domestic priorities that others thought should be funded from the dividend as it was still taking shape. "A quip is going around Washington," one contemporaneous report had it, "that half the U.S. peace dividend . . . will be spent on education, half on the drug war, half on reconstructing Eastern Europe and half on the budget deficit."[54]

In a purely economic sense, Bush did not confront the same degree of transitional difficulty Truman experienced after World War II. The percentage of the nation's economy invested in defense was much lower in 1990 than in 1945, and Bush did not have to grapple with the systemic shock Truman confronted as the nation abandoned wartime price controls. But Bush's economic (and thus his political) problems were still acute.

First, Bush was commander-in-chief of an all-volunteer military force. This significantly changed the dynamic of demobilization. In the past, draftees had been delighted to be discharged. But with military careers at stake, the post–Cold War drawdown generated "an anxiety akin to layoffs at General Motors."[55] It was during this interval that the Pentagon began to fret about what was newly called "involuntary separation."[56] Second, the very length of the Cold War had created what had been understood by many Americans to be a permanent defense establishment—meaning that over the decades, communities across the country had become dependent on defense spending, through the presence of military installations or major contractors such as shipbuilders and munitions plants. The downsizing of the defense sector thus generated a frightened backlash from adversely affected communities, especially among members of Congress who sought to protect their constituencies. Bush's political difficulties were aggravated by the fact that defense expenditures were not evenly distributed across the national landscape, which meant that the economic pain was more pronounced in some places than others. Unfortunately for him, half of the nation's defense expenditures went to only eight states, and those eight would cast 203 electoral votes in the 1992 presidential election.[57]

It is also impossible to understand properly the politics of the momentous 1990 budget agreement without situating it in the post–Cold War context. In chapter 2, for example, Hugh Heclo describes the extent to which Bush's negotiating room was cramped during those critical negotiations by the approach of the Gulf War later that same year: "If he failed to get the agreement, the nation would be fighting a war with a divided government and no budget." And although that agreement is completely dominated in the popular memory by the president's abandonment of his "No new taxes" pledge, what is usually overlooked is what the commander-in-chief extracted from Democratic negotiators in exchange for this humiliation: the establishment of "fire-walls" between three major spending categories—defense, foreign aid, and domestic discretionary programs—such that money saved in one category could not be redistributed into another. Inasmuch as the savings in the fiscal year 1991 budget came disproportionately out of the defense sector, which experienced a $9.8 billion reduction from the previous year, the intent of the walls was clear: the defense budget was not to be treated as an ATM for funding domestic programs.[58] Any defense funds freed up by a still-inchoate peace dividend would have to remain in the defense silo or be used for deficit reduction.

The 1990 budget agreement's effect on Bush was politically devastating. But the existence of these legal firewalls gave the White House tremendous leverage in the budget process throughout the rest of his presidency. "What isn't appreciated," remarks Michael Boskin, "is how much of the budget agreement was Bush protecting defense . . . for another couple of years while he did what he had to do diplomatically and geopolitically." Indeed, the full effect of Bush's "success" did not become apparent until after late 1991. His initial concession on taxes occurred in June 1990, barely six months after the Berlin Wall fell, when there was great uncertainty about the future abroad because it was not known how serious the Soviet reformers were. By late 1991, the Soviet Union had ceased to exist. That profound development, which took place as the nation was about to enter a presidential election year, might well have caused a run on defense accounts to feed pent-up demand for other programs but for the walls constructed in the agreement forged in negotiations at Andrews Air Force Base.

Senate Budget Committee chair James Sasser (D-Tenn.), among others, tried vigorously to find a way to crack open the defense budget, claiming that "it would be foolish not to seize this opportunity . . . to go back to a policy of investing in America." Yet these efforts were frustrated by the terms of the 1990 agreement, which were reenforced, Sasser lamented, by "unreconstructed old Cold Warriors [who] strap on their rusty armor and come over here on the floor and tell us, 'Oh, no, you can't reduce this military spending.'"[59] Similar efforts failed in the House, beaten back by a coalition of budget-conscious conservatives and defense hawks who were joined by moderates and liberals seeking to protect defense jobs in their districts.[60] All operated with the knowledge that the president could and would veto any efforts to break down the Andrews walls for the purpose of raiding the Pentagon.

Bush succeeded, then, as a budget-conserving commander-in-chief, working with Cheney and joint chiefs chair Colin Powell to rationalize the contraction in the nation's defense sector.[61] But in consequence he failed as a political candidate.

The glow of twin victories over communism and Saddam Hussein left Americans unimpressed with their commander-in-chief's esoteric priorities.

Ultimately, the best place to see the full force of the changing postwar environment was, as Fred Steeper had feared, in the election season for the 1992 campaign. After more than four decades of obsession with foreign threats, American voters turned their sights inward that year with stunning force. In a June Associated Press survey, only 1 percent of respondents identified foreign policy as important in selecting their presidential candidate.[62] Bush's media advisor Sig Rogich explains that "On the Gulf War and foreign visits . . . we arranged for film crews to film every aspect of our trips without any fanfare. . . . And we didn't use any of [that footage in our campaign ads]. . . . Why? Because the polls didn't reflect that [as a winning issue]. . . . So we set aside the hallmark of his administration."

The winner of that 1992 contest, conversely, was the governor of a small state in the American heartland whose strongest foreign policy credential was two years abroad as a student in England. His campaign's informal slogan was, emphatically, "The economy, stupid," ridiculing any suggestion that other issues, such as foreign policy, might be meaningful that year. And only 6 percent of the text of Clinton's nomination acceptance address was devoted to foreign affairs, a nearly unparalleled low figure in contemporary American politics.[63] In the end, Bush's record of foreign policy successes appeared to benefit him not at all—he won the support of barely one in three voters.

Whether Bush might have pivoted more deftly to secure his reelection in 1992 is an intriguing question for alternative history.[64] His close advisors still believe that some fine-tuning here or a reversal of fortune there might have shifted the electoral calculus in their favor. Had Lawrence Walsh not dropped his bombshell in the campaign's closing days, had they not lost political operative Lee Atwater to brain cancer, had the president's doctors been able to diagnose and treat more quickly his enervating Graves' disease, had the national unemployment numbers shifted downward just two or three months earlier, had the president developed and vigorously promoted an "economic Desert Storm" agenda, or had Patrick Buchanan or Ross Perot decided not to challenge an incumbent Republican president, George H. W. Bush may well, by these accounts, have remained in the White House, meeting history's first test of presidential success: winning four more years. But in the end the stars did not align.

The harsh fundamentals of the White House's governing context, however, did not dissolve in January 1993, notwithstanding the change in presidents. Indeed, in some ways the postwar currents engulfed Bill Clinton more fully than they had George Bush. The centerpiece of Clinton's first-term agenda—establishing a national health care system—suffered from being introduced during a postwar period when, as economist Robert Higgs has shown, the prevailing public impulses are to retrench rather than to grow big government programs.[65] Clinton then endured a devastating loss of both houses of Congress in the 1994 elections, a rare but signature midterm repudiation limited in American history almost exclusively to postwar elections. (In the entire run of U.S. constitutional history, there have been only seven cases when a president has lost partisan control of both houses of Congress at a midterm, five of which were postwar elections.)[66] And Clinton became only the second president to be impeached, both cases inextricably enmeshed in the painful process of recalibrating the proper postwar relationships of the nation's governing institutions.[67] Reflecting on the idiosyncratic problems of his time compared to what had gone before, Clinton once wryly observed: "Gosh, I miss the Cold War."[68]

These epoch-driven forces surely would not have subsided had Bush managed to beat the odds and won in 1992. It does not require an active imagination, for example, to see an impeachment growing from Walsh's indictments, regardless of whether Bush had decided under the circumstances to make use of his pardoning power. As painful as that loss to Bill Clinton was, then, it inevitably spared George H. W. Bush four more years of enduring, even escalating, adversity as the political order continued its historic return to normalcy following the protracted departures of the Cold War. If so, Bush's ultimate standing in history may, ironically, benefit from the voters' decision not to reward him with a second term.

Part I
AMERICAN CONSERVATISM

GEORGE BUSH: TEXAN, CONSERVATIVE

Michael Nelson

George H. W. Bush's three-decade-long political career was shadowed, more than that of any other recent and prominent national leader, by public doubts about what he believed. From 1962, when he entered politics as the Harris County (Houston) party chair to 1993, when he exited the political scene after a single term as president, Bush worked within a Republican Party that became ever more adamantly and aggressively conservative on a wider range of issues. Along the way he was branded as everything from "the darling of the John Birch Society" to "somewhat center of center" to a "big government, 'me-too-Republican." By 1980, when Bush first sought his party's presidential nomination, the wrong answer for a Republican candidate who was asked about his political philosophy was scorn for "the vision thing." The right answer was "conservative."

Was Bush a conservative? Oral history interviews of longtime Bush associates by the University of Virginia's Miller Center, conducted for the George H. W. Bush Oral History Project, both illuminate and complicate this question.[1] According to Chase Untermeyer, who began working for Bush in Congress and later served as White House personnel director, "He's never been an ideological man in the sense of having a fixed core of principles that he would constantly mention or bring up in a debate a lot like Ronald Reagan." Bush "was sort of dismissive" of ideas, says James Pinkerton, who served him as research director in the 1988 campaign and as deputy domestic policy advisor in the White House. "He said, 'It's what's in my heart that matters, and if you know me, you'll like me,' and things like that. That's a great argument if you're Henry V, but it's not such a great argument if you're trying to get demotic people to vote for you." Unlike Bush, Vice President Dan Quayle "was really more of an ideologue than I realized, the President was not," according to 1988 Bush campaign advertising director Sig Rogich.

Quayle himself says that in the Bush presidency, "there wasn't any real ideological, conservative, domestic agenda, other than markets and free enterprise and things of that sort." But, Quayle adds, "when it came to the market," Bush's conservatism was "pure. . . . He really believed in it. He didn't feel that there was a huge role for government and that was a big part of it. He just felt that the less the government did, the better." The observations of White House chief of staff John Sununu extend Quayle's assessment. Bush's "broad philosophy," says Sununu, comprised a set of "fundamental conservative principles of minimizing government involvement, of free market, capitalism-oriented economy, of an unleashing of the growth potential of the country, of not overconstraining it, of fixing problems, and of a kinder, gentler (remember that phrase?) set of policies that deal with individual needs and recognizing that different people have different needs."

The account of Bush's brand of conservatism that emerges from these observations is complex but accurate, not just for the eight years Bush was vice president and the four years he was president but for the entirety of his political career. Bush-style conservatism was nonrhetorical. It was rooted in matters of character, temperament, and experience rather than in philosophy. It was centered, with firm conviction, on economic issues, and it valued spending and regulatory restraint over slashing income taxes. It was to some extent inconsistent and occasionally expedient. (The positive form of those words is "flexible" and "prudent.") And, as we will see, most elements of Bush's version of conservatism can be traced to his life and political activity in his adopted home state of Texas.

Growing Up

None of this is to say that Bush arrived in Texas unaffected by his upbringing and experiences as a child and young man. Far from it. From his mother, Dorothy Walker Bush, Bush derived an ethical code that, in personal relations, placed others above self. The lessons she taught were to share with, show interest in, and include those who might otherwise feel neglected. "She had these kind of truisms that served me in good stead even when I got to be president of the United States," Bush recalls. "She said, 'Nobody likes a braggadocio, don't be bragging about yourself all the time. Listen; don't talk all the time. Give the other guy credit.'"

Competition was another of his mother's canonical virtues, but always tempered by good sportsmanship and the primacy of the team's success over one's own performance. "She was the fastest mother in the mothers' races," Bush recalls, invoking a bygone sport. "She was the best pitcher on the mothers' softball team."[2]

Bush's father, Prescott Bush, broadened his son's amplitude of concern to encompass public service—indeed, full-time service once the financial security of one's family was established. "Through him we got the idea that you ought to do something, you ought to put something back, you ought to give something back," says Bush. Both parents were strong supporters of the United Negro College Fund (UNCF) and the Birth Control League of Connecticut, among other causes. Support for the latter organization's activities, which focused on providing contraceptive services to poor women, came at the risk of unpopularity in heavily Catholic Connecticut, where birth control devices were illegal even for married couples until 1965. In 1950, Prescott Bush lost his first bid as the Republican nominee for a seat in the U.S. Senate by a margin of one-tenth of one percentage point. Not coincidentally, two days before the election, radio personality Walter Winchell revealed Bush's support for the birth control organization. Prescott Bush was subsequently elected to the Senate and served until 1963.[3]

George Bush's most important experiences outside the family confirmed his parents' teaching: the service ethic instilled in students by his prep school, Phillips Academy; enlistment in the navy at the outbreak of World War II, in which he served as the service's youngest aviator and flew missions well beyond the number required after he was shot down in the Pacific; and even his postwar captainship of the soccer and baseball teams at Yale University, where he also headed the fund-raising campaign for the campus's UNCF chapter.[4]

As political scientist Hugh Heclo observes in chapter 2, Bush had already absorbed much of the prevailing midcentury version of American conservatism by 1948, the year he left New England for Texas at age twenty-four. As Heclo rightly describes it, the conservatism of Bush's formative years was "a disposition more than an ideological package of doctrines." This "disposition" was toward prudence, incrementalism, opposition to statism, and above all to duty—that is, to "public service in the form of community and political leadership." Although for the Bushes the commitment to public service was rooted more in social class than political ideology (hence the term noblesse oblige), the strong overlap between wealth and Republicanism that marked the era in this region of the country made the association between service and conservatism seem entirely natural to them. "Politics is a noble calling," Bush said near the end of his ninth decade, affirming a creed he first embraced during his youth. "It's worth serving something other than your own self, your own pocketbook."[5]

The Move to Texas

Sociologically, Bush's post–World War II move from Connecticut to Texas was part of a great migration of young northeastern veterans who were drawn by the burgeoning opportunities the state's booming oil economy offered. Personally, for Bush it was a way to strike out on his own without cutting ties to his family: Bush's access to loans and investments from family members in the East enabled him to fund his new business enterprises in Texas. His energies when he arrived in Texas were concentrated on raising his young family and establishing their financial security. Like his parents, Bush believed that once these goals had been achieved, he should turn to a life of public service. While living in Odessa and later in Midland, he was lightly and locally involved on behalf of the Republican ticket in the 1952 and 1956 presidential campaigns. The small Texas GOP was torn during the 1952 nominating contest between the state party's old guard, which existed mainly to reap federal patronage when the Republicans were in power and which supported Robert A. Taft, the conservative senator from Ohio, and younger Republicans and Republican-leaning independents, many of them newcomers to Midland, Houston, and other booming cities in the state, who preferred former general Dwight D. Eisenhower. In the test of strength at the national convention that decided the nomination, Ike's delegates from Texas, as well as those from Georgia and Louisiana, were seated instead of Taft's.[6]

Bush stayed out of this fight. He was busy with his business and his father had ties to both contenders. But during the general election campaign, Bush organized an airport visit by Eisenhower's vice presidential running mate, Richard Nixon. Bush also helped raise funds for the ticket's reelection campaign in 1956. "I am working locally on the Ike thing," Bush wrote to his uncle, George Herbert Walker, "being head of the publicity committee for newspaper work and for the finance comm." He found that many people were for Eisenhower (who carried the state both times with support from conservative state Democratic leaders such as Governor Allan Shivers), but "it is surprising how strong the prejudice against the Republicans is."[7]

With Bush's move to Houston in 1959, the circumstances were ripe for a serious entry into Republican politics. Financially he was set, having sold a large stake in Zapata, the oil company he co-founded with partners a few years after moving to Texas. Politically, he was at the epicenter of Republican politics in the state. "Houston was the largest city in the country to carry for Nixon" in 1960, Bush crowed in a March 18, 1963, letter to his Yale friend Thomas Ludlow (Lud) Ashley, a Democratic congressman from Ohio.[8] Although Nixon lost the state narrowly to a Democratic ticket that included Senate majority leader Lyndon B. Johnson of Texas as its vice presidential nominee, in 1961 John Tower, a history and political science instructor at Midwestern University in Wichita Falls, bush-whacked through an ideologically divided Democratic political landscape and won a 71-candidate special election to fill Johnson's vacated Senate seat, thereby becoming the only Republican senator from the South.

Harris County Republican Chair

The downside of the growing Republican success in Houston was that control of the party became something worth fighting for. As in Midland, most of the people joining the local GOP were young businessmen and professionals from the North who, like Bush, had moved to Texas because of the career opportunities they saw there, not just in oil but also in defense, electronics, finance, construction, insurance, real estate, law, medicine, and other enterprises. Their main political concern, like Bush's, was with the sort of traditional economic issues—balanced budgets, low inflation, and business-friendly government regulations and subsidies—that bonded Republicans nationally as a party. Because the Republican Party was ripe for rapid growth in traditionally (and monolithically) Democratic Texas, politically ambitious women, both northern migrants and native Texans, also found opportunities in the GOP that had previously been closed to them. Anne Armstrong, for example, a Vassar-educated native of New Orleans, moved to Texas with her husband two years after Bush and by 1966 was vice chair of the state party—en route to becoming President Richard Nixon's choice for vice chair of the Republican National Committee and, eventually, President Gerald Ford's ambassador to the Court of St. James.

Other new recruits to the Harris County party, however, were John Birch Society members and kindred extremists who were mainly interested in unmasking and uprooting communist influence in American life wherever they perceived it. The founder of the Birch society, Massachusetts candy manufacturer Robert Welch, perceived it nearly everywhere, even the Oval Office. Harry S. Truman, Welch argued in his 1962 book *The Politician*, was "passively *used* by the Communists with his knowledge and acquiescence." As for Eisenhower, whom Welch had previously described as "a dedicated, conscious agent of the Communist conspiracy," he now wrote that "it is difficult to avoid raising the question of deliberate treason." Welch also detected communist influence in the public schools, the mainline Protestant churches, the civil rights movement, and the campaign to fluoridate public water supplies. By his estimate, the United States was "50–70 percent Communist-controlled"—and the proportion was rising.[9]

Formed in 1958, "the John Birch Society resonated with many grassroots conservatives," observes historian Donald Critchlow, "and emerged as the first truly viable anti-Communist organization with a national membership and chapters throughout the country."[10] Along with Los Angeles, the largest of these chapters, according to Welch, was in Houston, and in Amarillo a Birch candidate for mayor actually received 42 percent of the vote.[11] In spring 1962, when Harris County Republican chair James Bertron resigned in advance of moving to Florida, the Birchers organized to replace him with one of their own. (They had come close to winning the previous county chair election.) Fearing that a Birch takeover would marginalize the GOP and stifle the party's growth, business-oriented Republicans approached Bush, who had recently co-chaired the county party's finance committee, and urged him to run. "The state party chairman said, 'How about your running for Harris County precinct chairman?'" Bush recalled.[12]

Bush welcomed the invitation: "This was the challenge I'd been waiting for—an opening into politics at the ground level, where it all starts." He agreed with his colleagues' assessment: "It was clear that a John Birch Society takeover of the Harris County party would mean that all the gains Republicans had made in recent years would be jeopardized."[13] Barbara Bush wrote in 1994 that the campaign for county chair was "the meanest political battle of his life," but Bush spent weeks paying nightly visits to the county's 207 precincts carrying the non-ideological message that Texas needed a viable two-party system.[14] After winning, he wrote a memo to some supporters, declaring, "We're not going to divide ourselves, calling anyone 'crazies' or 'nuts.'"[15]

The First Senate Campaign

In 1963, at age thirty-nine, Bush set his sights on the Senate seat occupied by the liberal Democrat Ralph Yarborough, who was up for reelection the following year. The seat seemed especially winnable for a Republican. President John F. Kennedy's diminishing support in Texas augured weakness at the head of the Democratic ticket, and Yarborough's severe unpopularity among conservative Democrats seemed likely to provoke a fierce primary challenge that would divide the party in the general election.

Kennedy's assassination on November 22, 1963, turned these calculations on their head. Instead of the Massachusetts liberal Kennedy, the Democratic ticket would be headed by Johnson, the first Texan president in history. Just as bad, from Bush's standpoint, was the new president's determination not to be embarrassed by the election of a second Republican senator from his home state. Despite his intense dislike of Yarborough, Johnson appreciated his vote for the Civil Rights Act of 1964—the only one cast by a southern senator—and felt pressure to support him from organized labor, an important national Democratic constituency for which the liberal Texan was a fierce advocate.[16] The president "'muscled' several conservative Democrats out of a primary challenge" to the incumbent, including close associate Representative Joe Kilgore and former representative Lloyd Bentsen.[17]

Yarborough still had to fight hard to defeat a much-less-credentialed conservative Democratic opponent for the nomination: Gordon McLendon, the owner of the Liberty Broadcasting System, a chain of financially troubled Texas radio stations. Yarborough prevailed in the primary by 904,811 (57.4 percent) to 672,573 (42.6 percent). Former governor Shivers was one of several prominent conservative Democrats to urge Texans to split their tickets in November between Johnson for president and the Republican nominee for senator.[18] Governor John Connally did not endorse his fellow Democrat and reportedly relished the prospect of seeing the liberal Yarborough defeated and no longer having to share federal patronage with him.[19] So fierce was the hatred between the two men that muting it in the interest of party unity was the main reason for Kennedy's visit to the state in November 1963.

Bush faced two serious challengers for the Republican nomination, both of them extreme conservatives who, unlike Bush, endorsed the Birch society's call to "get the UN out of the US and the US out of the UN." Jack Cox, a Texas native and erstwhile Democrat who converted to the GOP, had run a strong but unsuccessful race against Connally in the 1962 gubernatorial election. (Bush chaired the Jack Cox for Governor finance committee in Harris County.) Robert J. Morris was a lifelong New Jerseyan who moved to Texas in 1960 to become president of the new University of Dallas and was fired two years later for his ferocious outspokenness against communism and on other issues.

Birch society members and their allies in groups like the Texas Association for Political Action and the Conservative Action Committee were energized in 1964 by devotion to the presidential candidacy of Arizona Republican senator Barry Goldwater, a conservative icon, and trained their sights on Bush in the Republican primary. "BEAT THE BUSHES," read one far-right circular, linking Bush to his father, who in the Senate had supported foreign aid and civil rights and who, through his business association with Council of Foreign Relations member Averell Harriman, was alleged to be part of "the whole diabolical scheme of creating a ONE-WORLD FEDERATION of socialist states under the United Nations."[20] Cox was the main beneficiary of their efforts, in part because he had the active support of former army general Edwin Walker. Walker had achieved martyrdom on the right when he was removed from command of the 24th Infantry Division stationed in West Germany for using Birch and other far-right materials to politically indoctrinate his troops. Bush, who also endorsed Goldwater for the GOP nomination while calling himself a "responsible conservative," received 62,985 votes in the Republican primary, enough to outpace Cox (45,561 votes) and Morris (28,279).[21] But because Bush's share of the vote was 44.1 percent, less than the required majority, he had to face Cox in a runoff. Fending off his opponent's charge that he was the pawn of "Liberal Eastern Kingmakers," Bush prevailed by 49,751 votes (62.1 percent) to 30,333 (37.9 percent) votes.

As in 1962, Bush's intraparty victory was hard, even bitterly won: "I took on General Walker, The National Indignation Council, and the rest of those people," he wrote to Lud Ashley on June 22—"it got most unpleasant as you can imagine."[22] Bush resented that his efforts as Harris County chair to integrate Birch society members into the party leadership and even into his social circle had gone unappreciated. "His style was to charm them," recalls Henry Catto, a longtime friend who, like Bush, was working to build an effective Republican organization in Texas. "The right wing of the party, the John Birch wing—and they really were flat-earth types—they loathed him." Nevertheless, Bush did not attack the Birchers publicly (he thought Nixon had suffered by doing so in his 1962 California gubernatorial campaign) and tacked rightward in the general election, tying his candidacy to Goldwater's hoped-for presidential coattails in an effort to unite the party. Following Goldwater's lead, Bush opposed the Nuclear Test Ban Treaty with the Soviet Union, the Civil Rights Act of 1964, Medicare (he called it "socialized medicine"), and the "left-wing spending programs" that comprised Johnson's War on Poverty; he also supported U.S. recognition of an anticommunist Cuban exile government.[23]

Some of the positions Bush adopted as a candidate for the Senate in 1964 reflected his long-standing business conservatism and were comfortably held. For example, he said, "I support right-to-work laws" because "only unbridled free enterprise can cure unemployment." But issues that involved social policy left him torn. "What shall I do? How shall I do it?" Bush anguished in a July 28 letter to Marjorie Arsht, a friend and leader in Houston's Jewish community, about the Civil Rights Act. "I want to win but not at the expense of justice, and not at the expense of the dignity of any man—not at the expense of hurting a friend nor teaching my children a prejudice which I do not feel." On the other hand, because the incumbent Democrat he was trying to unseat had voted for the act, "the civil rights issue can bring Yarborough to sure defeat. I know this for certain." Goldwater, who was a member of the National Association for the Advancement of Colored People (NAACP) and had voted for the 1957 and 1960 Civil Rights Acts, himself opposed only two of the 1964 act's eleven titles, both because of constitutional objections grounded in legal advice from William Rehnquist and Robert H. Bork. "Goldwater's position is correct (and parenthetically so is mine)—for Texas and the USA," Bush wrote to Arsht. But "we must be sure we don't inflame the passions of unthinking men to garner a vote."[24]

Bush's moral anguish over the civil rights issue did not impede his otherwise full-throated attacks on Yarborough as a "Reuther-controlled radical of the left" and a member of "a militant, mean little band of left wingers" in the Senate.[25]

Yarborough "represents the labor bosses in Detroit," Bush told the voters of Texas in a paid broadcast. He is for every sweeping, high-spending New Frontier program."[26] (In truth, Yarborough's liberalism did not extend to opposing the oil depletion allowance and other federal benefits for the petroleum industry, favorite targets of other Senate liberals.) Meanwhile, Yarborough honed in on Bush's political vulnerabilities. The Republican was a northern "carpetbagger" representing Wall Street financial interests and, in moving to the right, had become "the darling of the John Birch Society."[27] He opposed the Nuclear Test Ban Treaty even though fallout from weapons testing was causing sterility and leukemia. "Big ole Daddy," Yarborough said scornfully of Bush's father, now retired from the Senate, "out to buy himself a seat in the United States Senate. Let's show the world that old Senator Bush can't send Little Georgie down here to buy a Senate seat."[28] Voters were repelled by Yarborough's ad hominem attacks and were increasingly drawn to the energetic, attractive young Bush. Ronnie Dugger of the liberal *Texas Observer* was struck by the "energy and sparkle" that Bush's campaign was receiving from "young Republican matrons who are enthusiastic about him personally and have plenty of money for baby sitters and nothing much to do with their time." Private Democratic polls showed Yarborough's lead shrinking from 15 points to 10 points to zero, a dead heat.[29]

Bush's superiority as a campaigner notwithstanding, he could not overcome Yarborough's greatest political asset: President Johnson's presence at the head of the Democratic ticket. With polls showing that his own victory in Texas was certain, Johnson nevertheless adjusted his late-October campaign schedule so that he could spend a full day touring the state on Yarborough's behalf.[30] "You have read that Senator Yarborough and I have had differences at times," Johnson told an audience in Stonewall. But "no member of the U.S. Senate has stood up and fought for me or fought for the people more since I became president than Ralph Yarborough." On Election Day, Johnson carried Texas with 63.3 percent of the vote—by far his best performance in a southern state (Arkansas was a distant second, with 56.1 percent). Bush ran nearly 200,000 votes ahead of Goldwater, receiving the highest vote ever won by a Republican candidate for any office in Texas history: 1,134,337. But Yarborough's 56.2 percent of the vote gave him a comfortable margin of 329,621 votes.

Election to the House of Representatives

Bush came out of the 1964 defeat with regrets that morphed into resolve. "I took some of the far-right positions to get elected," he told his minister in Houston. "I hope I never do it again. I regret it."[31] "I'm ashamed" for not taking on right-wing extremists in the party, he told an audience in the summer of 1965.[32] Looking forward, Bush wrote former vice president Nixon on November 10, 1964, to report that he had counseled Texas state party chair Peter O'Donnell that "the immediate job would be to get rid of some of the people in the Party who [permit] no difference, who through their overly dedicated conservatism are going to always keep the Party small."[33] On December 16, Bush wrote to O'Donnell and Senator Tower to argue that the GOP must oppose "Birchism . . . those mean, negative, super-patriots who give Texas Republicans the unfortunate image of total irresponsibility."[34] Invited to contribute to a forum on "The Republican Party and the Conservative Movement" in the December 1, 1964, issue of *National Review*, Bush dusted off a word whose usage he previously had forbidden and condemned the "'nut' fringe" that "pounced on" undecided voters, "pushed their philosophy in Goldwater's name, and scared the hell out of the plain average non-issue conscious man on the street."[35]

Beyond his resolutions for the party in the aftermath of Goldwater's landslide defeat, Bush also resolved personally to run for office again in 1966. In July 1965, with active support from O'Donnell and Tower, Bush and his allies narrowly beat back a Birch society–supported effort to win the Harris County Republican chairmanship.[36] Soon afterward, a wider door opened. Chase Untermeyer recalls in his oral history interview that in response to a series of recent Supreme Court decisions, "redistricting of congressional and legislative districts for that matter became required in the mid 'sixties. . . . The [Texas] legislature, which was totally Democratic, with reluctance, created a congressional district on the west side of Houston," the prosperous, growing part of town where Bush lived and where Birch society members, who were mostly working- and lower-middle-class, were less concentrated than in some other parts of the city.[37]

Bush was the presumptive Republican nominee for the new House seat. As Harris County chair in 1963 he had filed the lawsuit that forced the creation of the district (Houston's third), and as the party's Senate candidate in 1964, he won 56.6 percent of the vote there even as Johnson carried it against Goldwater. (Four years later Nixon outpolled Democratic presidential nominee Hubert H. Humphrey by nearly two to one, his best district in the state.) Far from being a "carpetbagger," Bush was among the three-fourths of the district's residents whom he estimated were newcomers.[38] Besides, Untermeyer recalled, Bush developed a good line to explain his birth in Massachusetts: "He felt that at a time like that he should be with his mother."

Although the Birchers and their allies continued their campaign to seize control of the Harris County organization, every other star that was aligned against Bush in 1964 was realigned in his favor two years later.[39] Nineteen sixty-six turned out to be an excellent year for the GOP, especially in House elections, where they added forty-seven seats nationwide and fourteen in the South, doubling their total in the region. The popular Senator Tower (who was seeking reelection), not Senator Goldwater, ran interference for down-ballot candidates as the head of the Republican ticket. Instead of facing a divisive primary, Bush sailed to his party's nomination. Media advisor Harry Treleaven, who later worked on Nixon's 1968 presidential campaign, ran commercials showing Bush with sleeves rolled up, jacket slung over his shoulder, walking the streets of Houston—all to convince the voters how hard he was working for their support. "People sympathize with a man who tries hard," Treleaven later wrote in an assessment of the campaign. "They are also flattered that anyone would really exert himself to get their vote."[40]

Bush's right-wing opponents, including the Conservative Action Council, endorsed his Democratic opponent, District Attorney Frank Briscoe. When, according to Bush, Briscoe "pitched his campaign way over in right field—near the Birchers—strongly anti-Lyndon and a subtle appeal to the back-lash," Bush was able to run as what author Richard Ben Cramer calls a "Main Street Republican."[41] One of Briscoe's attacks labeled Bush a liberal because he sponsored an African American girls' softball team instead of a white one.[42] This brand of conservatism still allowed Bush, like Briscoe, to support the war in Vietnam, reductions in federal spending, and the state's anti-union right-to-work law, but it did not drive him to adopt extreme positions like those that left him feeling somewhat ashamed after the 1964 election. And Bush was able to point out that if Briscoe were elected, his first vote would necessarily be for "that lifelong liberal Democrat," John McCormack of Massachusetts, as speaker of the House.[43]

In contrast to what he had done in his Senate campaign, Bush worked hard in 1966 to win votes from the district's relatively small African American population, remembering that just ten years before Eisenhower had won 39 percent of the black vote in his bid for reelection. In 1964, the African American turnout in Texas had more than doubled to about 260,000 voters, up from 105,000 in 1960, and the Democratic ticket received an estimated 95 percent of their support which gave Yarborough most of his margin of victory.[44] Bush's new outreach effort convinced National Negro Republican Assembly president Grant Reynolds of "the sincerity of Bush's desire to bring Negroes into the Texas Republican Party in meaningful ways."[45] Bush ended up with 34 percent of the black vote, a disappointment at the time "despite our making an all out effort to attract black voters" but a considerably better performance than he and most Republicans have earned then or since.[46] Bush cruised to victory in November, winning 53,756 votes (57.1 percent) to Briscoe's 39,958 votes (42.4 percent). In doing so, Bush became Houston's first Republican member of Congress since Reconstruction.

The House Years

Liberated, at least for a time, from pressures on his right political flank, Bush told his wife, "Labels are for cans." With greater insight, Barbara Bush added, "If I had to label George, I would say he was a fiscal conservative and a social liberal."[47] That said, Bush's voting record during his four years in the House of Representatives (eschewing pressures from some Republicans in 1968 to run for governor of Texas, he was instead reelected without opposition to the House) was consistently conservative by contemporary standards. One year it was the most conservative of anyone in the 23-member Texas delegation.

The liberal group Americans for Democratic Action (ADA), which focused largely on economic issues, gave Bush an average annual Liberal Quotient (LQ) of 5 percent for the period 1967–70, the four years he served in the House. Bush cast only four liberal votes in the seventy-four roll calls that ADA rated most important during the 90th and 91st Congresses: one for a 1967 bill making it a crime to injure, intimidate, or interfere with civil rights workers (it passed the House 326–93, with most Texas representatives voting for it); one for a 1969 bill forbidding a North Carolina presidential elector pledged to Nixon in the 1968 election to cast his vote for third-party candidate George C. Wallace; and two in 1970 for Nixon administration–backed proposals: the Philadelphia Plan mandating minority hiring in federal construction projects in ways designed to pit two Democratic constituencies, blacks and organized labor, against each other (Bush opposed a bill to kill it) and the Family Assistance Act, which proposed to abolish the federal government's main welfare program, Aid to Families with Dependent Children, in favor of a guaranteed income with a strong work requirement—the part of the bill that Bush emphasized as a remedy for "idleness" when defending his vote.[48]

Bush's somewhat misleading reputation in later years as a moderate Republican was forged at this stage of his career.[49] The reputation has two main origins, neither of them grounded in his conservative voting record in Congress or in his campaigns for political office in Texas. One was Bush's intense interest in issues related to population control—so intense that Representative Wilbur Mills, the powerful Arkansas Democrat who chaired the House Ways and Means Committee on which Bush served, referred to him as "rubbers."[50] Bush, like his father—but also like Senator Goldwater and many other conservatives of the era—was a strong supporter of the Planned Parenthood Federation of America at a time when that organization was mostly interested in making birth control devices available to women.[51] In November 1967, Bush lamented in testimony to the Senate Government Operations Committee, "My father, when he ran for the U.S. Senate in 1950, was defeated by 600 or 700 votes. On the steps of several

Catholic churches in Connecticut, the Sunday before the election, people stood there passing out pamphlets saying, 'Listen to what this commentator has to say tonight.' That night, on the radio, the commentator came on and said, 'Of interest to voters in Connecticut, Prescott Bush is head of the Planned Parenthood Birth Control League,' or something like that. Well, he lost by about 600 votes and there are some of us who feel that this had something to do with it."

As an organization whose primary purpose was to prevent unwanted pregnancies among the poor and foreign-born, Planned Parenthood and its predecessor, the Birth Control Federation of America, promoted what was then regarded as "a conservative program for social control," according to historian David M. Kennedy.[52] At a March 1967 meeting of the Ways and Means Committee, Bush told Planned Parenthood president Alan Guttmacher that his organization could do more "in the field of poverty and mental health and everything else than almost any other group that I can think of."[53] White, Protestant, upper-middle- and upper-class women formed the backbone of the birth control and, for many years, the broader population control movement.

The prominence of population control, a long-standing Bush family concern, was dramatically elevated in 1968 by the publication of *The Population Bomb*, by Stanford University biologist Paul R. Ehrlich. "The battle to feed all of humanity is over," began the pop-science book, which helped establish population control as a concern of the budding environmental movement. "In the 1970s the world will undergo famines—hundreds of millions of people are going to starve to death." Addressing the question of "what needs to be done," Ehrlich wrote, "We must rapidly bring the world population under control, reducing the growth rate to zero or making it negative. Conscious regulation of human numbers must be achieved."[54]

With *The Population Bomb* topping best-seller lists and prominent leaders such as United Nations secretary general U Thant saying that the world had only ten years to prevent an irreversible catastrophe, Bush accelerated his efforts in Congress.[55] In May 1969, he sponsored a bill in the House with New York Democrat James H. Scheuer and several dozen co-sponsors to create a National Center for Population and Family Planning within the Department of Health, Education, and Welfare. Another Bush-sponsored bill was designed to end the ban on mailing or transporting condoms across state lines; still another, which became law, repealed century-old federal anti-contraception statutes. In the international arena, in 1968 Bush "propose[d] that we totally revamp our foreign aid program to give primary emphasis to population control."[56]

Bush also headed the House Republican Research Committee Task Force on Earth Resources and Population, and on December 22, 1969, he issued a press release calling for federal assistance to "poor and near poor American

women . . . who want to avail themselves of family planning services in order
to have the knowledge necessary to make a personal choice of birth control
methods, whether it be the pill, an IUD, or the rhythm method."[57] According to
Untermeyer, who worked on population issues as a member of Bush's House
staff, "Planned Parenthood . . . viewed him as a great asset." In 1970, President
Nixon signed the Bush–sponsored Population Control and Research Act, which
among other things provided federal funding for the organization.

Nothing in Bush's record involved support for abortion, which did not
become a major activity of Planned Parenthood (either advocacy of abortion
rights or performance of abortions) until after the Supreme Court's 1973 *Roe v.
Wade* decision. Nor was the pro-life torch carried mainly by evangelical Christian Republicans, at least for the first several years after the decision. At its 1971
national meeting, for example, the Southern Baptist Convention adopted a resolution "call[ing] upon Southern Baptists to work for legislation that will allow
the possibility of abortion under such conditions as rape, incest, clear evidence
of severe fetal deformity, and carefully ascertained evidence of the likelihood
of damage to the emotional, mental, and physical health of the mother."[58] The
only significant organized opposition to legalized abortion came from the United
Conference of Catholic Bishops, and the most active opponents of abortion in
Congress were Catholic Democrats.

As a personal matter, Bush strongly opposed abortion, a position that John
Sununu traces in his oral history interview to "the death of his daughter," three-
year-old Robin, of cancer in 1953. According to Sununu, "He says that, 'You
know, if somebody had told us she was going to die early and we could have an
abortion and avoid it, I would not have given up the opportunity to have her.'"
To be sure, until joining former California governor Ronald Reagan as the vice
presidential candidate on the Republican ticket in 1980, Bush never took a position against the legality of abortions that was as strenuous as some on the right
began taking in the mid- to late 1970s. Bush later explained that he supported
Planned Parenthood "long before [it] began emphasizing abortion as a form of
family planning. At that point we had a parting of the ways."[59] But his and his
family's long alliance with the organization made it hard for him to move to the
right on abortion-related issues as far and as fast as other Republican politicians.

The second basis for Bush's reputation as a moderate Republican House member is the vote he cast for the Civil Rights Act of 1968, which was designed to
prevent racial discrimination in the sale or rental of housing. The House approved
the bill on April 10. The timing of the vote, less than a week after Rev. Martin
Luther King Jr.'s, assassination and the ensuing riots in urban ghettos across the
country, led some critics to argue that the action was unprincipled and politically
craven. But Bush attributed his aye vote—cast in the face of fierce opposition from

most of his constituents and the "seething hatred" (Bush's phrase) of some—to a source closer to conservative hearts than traditional civil rights concerns.[60] Facing a hostile open forum in his district, Bush explained, "In Vietnam I chatted with many Negro soldiers. They were fighting, and some were dying, for the ideals of this Country.... Somehow it seems fundamental that this guy should have a hope. A hope that if he saves some money, and if he wants to break out of a ghetto, and if he is a good character and if he meets every requirement of purchaser—the door will not be slammed solely because he is a Negro, or because he speaks with a Mexican accent."[61]

Bush's speech—a conservative, pro-military appeal to a conservative, pro-military audience—was greeted with a standing ovation. "More than twenty years later," he wrote in his 1987 autobiography, *Looking Forward*, "I can truthfully say that nothing I've experienced in public life, before or since, has measured up to the feeling I had when I went home that night."[62] Alarmed, however, by a report that twelve of the first 119 people arrested in the riot in Washington that followed King's assassination were federal employees, Bush also introduced a bill providing that any government worker who broke the law during a civil disturbance would be fired.

The Second Senate Campaign

Bush's record in the House as an economic conservative positioned him well for a potential rematch against Yarborough in the 1970 Senate election. Securing a seat on the powerful and prestigious Ways and Means Committee as a freshman representative—he was the only Texan member—had enabled him to fight increases in taxes generally and on the oil industry in particular.[63] According to former representative Edward J. Derwinski of Illinois, Bush's Republican colleague in the House, putting Bush on Ways and Means "was the Republican way of saying to the Texas economy, we're taking good care of your boy, send us more." In contrast, during each of Bush's four years in Congress, Yarborough had by far the most liberal voting record of any southern Democrat in the Senate. His ADA ratings ranged from 57 to 78 percent.

Presidential politics in 1968 also redounded to Bush's benefit as he considered a Senate race two years later. Johnson retired from the presidency, meaning that he had no political or personal interest in seeing the despised Yarborough reelected, and Republican nominee Richard Nixon elevated Bush's prestige in Texas by circulating his name as a possible vice presidential running mate in response to advice from Texas businessmen, younger Republican congressmen, and even the Rev. Billy Graham.[64] Bush and his supporters thought that in the youth-centered climate of 1968, Nixon might be open to choosing a young, attractive, conservative member of Congress for the ticket—an approach that apparently still seemed sound to Bush twenty years later when he chose the young, attractive, conservative Quayle to run with him in 1988. Nixon "confirmed that he gave it very serious consideration," Bush wrote in an August 20, 1968, letter to friend Bob Connery, "but decided against it because of my short service in the House."[65] Nixon did not want to invite the charge of inexperience that had been leveled at Goldwater's running mate, Representative William Miller of New York, four years earlier. He also worried about bypassing and thereby offending Senator Tower, Bush's senior Republican colleague in Texas politics.[66]

As president, Nixon strongly encouraged Bush to give up his safe House seat, which he was somewhat reluctant to do, and challenge Yarborough.[67] The Senate class that was up for reelection in 1970 included many liberal Democrats who, like Yarborough, had been elected in the very strong Democratic years of 1958 and 1964. Nationally, twenty-five Democratic-held seats were on the ballot, compared with only nine Republican seats. A gain of seven would give the GOP a de facto majority of 51–50, with Vice President Spiro T. Agnew providing the tie-breaking vote in his constitutional capacity as president of the Senate. Bush was one of several Republican office holders whom Nixon recruited to challenge Democratic incumbents, assuring them that if they lost he would have a job for them in the administration.[68]

Bush's strategy for victory in the 1970 Senate election was clear: build a coalition consisting of Republicans and conservative Democrats by attacking Yarborough from the right. Almost certainly this strategy would have succeeded. Although he had become the first Texan in fifty years to head a major Senate committee (Labor and Public Welfare), Yarborough "was [a] liberal, who was distrusted, even hated by a lot of conservative Democrats," recalls Untermeyer. Bush himself was right to conclude, "I could have beaten Yarborough."[69] Announcing his candidacy on January 13, he accurately claimed to represent "the majority of Texans [who] don't accept the old antidote of spend more money and let Washington do it all."[70]

But Bush's plan was thwarted when former representative Lloyd Bentsen—a banking and insurance millionaire whom New York Times columnist Tom Wicker described as "at least as conservative as the Republican George Bush, and probably hawkier, fat cattier, and oilier"—entered the Democratic primary.[71] Six years earlier Johnson had discouraged Bentsen and other conservative Democrats from challenging Yarborough. As president, he desperately wanted to avoid an intraparty bloodbath that would adversely affect his bid to carry Texas in the 1964 presidential election; he also wanted to keep his state's Senate delegation from becoming wholly Republican. By 1970, Johnson was out of office and largely out of politics.

Armed with what Jack Bass and Walter DeVries describe as "even by Texas standards—an unlimited supply of money," Bentsen slammed Yarborough for his opposition to the war in Vietnam; his votes against both of President Nixon's southern conservative Supreme Court nominees, Clement Haynsworth and G. Harrold Carswell; his refusal to support prayer in public schools and to oppose school busing; and, in general, for being "too liberal for Texas."[72] Bentsen won the hard-fought Democratic primary by 53.0 percent to 47.0 percent, earning a 92,519-vote majority. Meanwhile, Bush was cruising to an easy victory over one of his 1964 opponents, Robert Morris. Bush won the GOP nomination with 87.6 percent, which even in the much-smaller-turnout Republican primary represented an 83,142-vote majority. Certainty that Bush would be nominated prompted several anti-Yarborough newspapers to urge conservative Republicans to vote for Bentsen in the Democratic primary.[73]

Bush was flummoxed by Bentsen's nomination. As James Baker recalled in his political memoir, *"Work Hard, Study . . . and Keep Out of Politics!": Adventures and Lessons from an Unexpected Public Life*, "George, who had planned to run as the conservative alternative to the liberal Yarborough, found Bentsen portraying himself as the conservative alternative to an allegedly liberal Bush."[74] Bentsen attacked Bush as "a liberal Ivy League carpetbagger" who had voted for allegedly left-wing programs such as Nixon's Family Assistance Plan.[75] At the same time, the Democrat reached out to black party leaders like state senator Barbara Jordan, Latino leaders like Representative Henry Gonzales, and the Texas AFL-CIO, uniting them behind his candidacy by arguing that "Texas needs a Democrat in the Senate" and that Republican economic policies were a threat to poor and working-class people and minorities.[76] Bentsen even yielded to efforts to write an unprecedentedly liberal platform at the state party convention in September, ceding Senator Jordan virtual veto power over its contents.[77]

Some liberal Democrats supported Bush, calculating that a Bentsen defeat would drive more conservatives into the GOP and thereby leave the Democrats a more liberal party.[78] "Liberal Democrats would rather lose the election than control of the party," Nixon political aide Murray Chotiner confidently predicted after Bentsen won the Democratic nomination.[79] But most Texas liberals, remembering how Bush had attacked Yarborough in 1964, did not flock to the Republican's support as they had to Tower's candidacies against conservative Democrats in 1961 and 1966, when they calculated that as a member of the Republican minority, Tower would have less influence in the Senate than a conservative Democrat would. Even Yarborough endorsed Bentsen, albeit lukewarmly.[80]

Although Nixon had recruited Bush to run as part of a strategy to secure a Republican majority in the Senate, the ardency of his support flagged as the likelihood of achieving that goal diminished during the course of the 1970 campaign.

Mirroring the president's increasing disinterest, the Republican Senate Campaign Committee reduced its contribution to Bush from $72,879 through September, nearly double the amount given to any other Republican Senate candidate, to $1,100 in October, considerably less than other candidates received.[81] As far as Nixon was concerned, Yarborough's primary defeat by Bentsen meant that Texas would elect a conservative no matter who won the general election. Ham-handedly, Nixon aides leaked a story that the president might replace Agnew with Bush on the 1972 ticket if Bush won the Senate election, thereby giving pro-Agnew Texas conservatives another reason to vote for Bentsen.[82] Undeterred by (or unaware of) the rumor, Agnew campaigned for Bush, telling a Lubbock audience that a vote for Bentsen was "a vote to keep William Fulbright chairman of the Senate Foreign Relations Committee" because it would help preserve the Democratic majority in the Senate.

On Election Day, Bush's Senate bid fell short by 157,769 votes. Although he carried the state's eight largest counties, he lagged behind Bentsen everywhere else, earning 46.4 percent of the vote to the Democrat's 53.5 percent.[83] A liquor-by-the-drink referendum on the state ballot "brought out Democratic voters in rural Texas in record numbers," Bush concluded, as did another ballot measure to allow all undeveloped land in the state to be taxed as farmland. Turnout in 1970 was unusually high in Texas's rural areas, and Bentsen carried 161 of the 178 counties that voted against the "saloon amendment."[84] As in 1964, Bush's share of the vote rose by socioeconomic class, but Bentsen cut into his previous majority among upper-middle-class and upper-class voters.[85] Bush did better than he had in 1964 in the black and Mexican American communities, but he still lost them to Bentsen by about three to one.[86] Although Nixon's hopes for a Republican majority in the Senate were thwarted, he included Bentsen when he claimed after the election that he now had a "working" majority of conservatives in the upper chamber.[87]

Texan, Conservative

After abandoning his congressional career and with little interest in running for governor or any other state office, Bush spent the next six years representing the United States first at the United Nations (Nixon's consolation prize for running and losing in 1970) and then China, chairing the Republican National Committee, and serving as director of the Central Intelligence Agency. During this period, however, he was, more than in 1968, a finalist for the vice presidency. According to Richard B. Cheney, Bush was one of "three individuals—[former New York governor] Nelson Rockefeller and George Bush and [White House chief of staff]

Don Rumsfeld"—whom Gerald R. Ford considered appointing as vice president when he succeeded to the presidency in 1974. But in the end Ford "sort of looked on Bush and Rumsfeld as the future of the party. They were that younger generation." In contrast, Rockefeller, whom Ford appointed, was "an international figure. He was a major national figure."

At the end of the 1970s, Bush reentered elective politics at the national level, and from 1980 to 1992, he appeared on the Texas ballot four times as a candidate in his own right and twice as Ronald Reagan's vice presidential running mate. In 1980, Bush waged a long-shot candidacy for the Republican presidential nomination against the front-runner Reagan and several other credible contenders, including Senate Republican leader Howard Baker of Tennessee. With memories of his battles with the Texas Birchers apparently still fresh, Bush wrote to *Oak Cliff (Texas) Tribune* editor Ray Zauber on December 2, 1979, "I will get the vote of sound conservatives—not the conspiratorial ones."[88]

Bush's 1980 campaign is best remembered for his less-than-absolutist stance against abortion (he would allow it to remain legal in cases of "rape, incest, or when the life of the mother is at stake") and his offhand characterization of Reagan's proposal for major income tax cuts as "voodoo economics."[89] But "Bush was every bit as conservative as Reagan on virtually every issue that Republicans use as measuring sticks," observe journalists Jack Germond and Jules Witcover. They report that, when shown the text, but not the author, of a Bush campaign speech, Senator Orrin Hatch of Utah thought it had been delivered by Illinois representative Phil Crane—the most conservative candidate in the field.[90]

None of this prevented even astute observers of presidential politics such as Theodore H. White from characterizing Bush as "of patrician stock, of oldest New England heritage," with political views "somewhat to the center of center."[91] As a general rule, Bush's ability to win primaries and caucuses in 1980 was confined to a few northeastern and midwestern states, notably Iowa, Connecticut, Massachusetts, Pennsylvania, and Michigan. He lost every contest in the South and West to Reagan, nearly all of them by overwhelming majorities. But on May 3, weeks after it had become apparent that Reagan would be the Republican nominee and with, Bush later admitted, little organization on the ground ("in the South, not even Texas had been organized," he wrote), he held Reagan to an 18,979-vote majority in the Texas primary, losing to the Californian by only 51.0 percent to 47.4 percent.[92]

Eight years later, as Reagan's vice president, Bush faced similar doubts about his credentials as a conservative and a Texan when seeking the 1988 Republican presidential nomination. As Donald Critchlow notes, "Bush claimed to be a Texan, but many conservatives continued to see him as a representative of the elitist eastern wing of the Republican party—those internationalist, big government, 'me-too

Republicans'" whose support for population control in the 1960s had evolved into, in Bush's case, an ambition to become the "environmental president" twenty years later.[93] Yet in southern primaries that year, no state gave Bush a larger margin of victory over his chief rival, Senate Republican leader Robert Dole of Kansas, than Texas: 63.9 percent to 13.9 percent, or fully 50 percentage points. And when Democratic presidential nominee Michael S. Dukakis of Massachusetts, in a misguided bid to win Bush's home state, selected Senator Bentsen as his vice presidential candidate, Bush again prevailed easily, this time by a majority of 684,081 votes.

Bush appeared on the Texas ballot for the last time in 1992, as a reelection-seeking president. In the state's Republican primary, he unsurprisingly disposed of the pugnacious conservative pundit Pat Buchanan by a three-to-one margin. In the general election, which he lost to Governor Bill Clinton of neighboring Arkansas, Bush nevertheless ran better in Texas than in any other large state, carrying it by 40.6 percent to 37.1 percent.

Texans did not always vote for Bush, but they usually did. In three statewide contests—the 1964 and 1970 Senate general elections and the 1980 Republican presidential primary—they voted for someone else, sometimes veering to his left and more frequently to his right. In six other elections—the 1964 and 1970 Republican Senate primaries, the 1988 and 1992 Republican presidential primaries, and, most important, the 1988 and 1992 general elections for president—they voted for Bush. The state's largest city also voted to nominate and elect Bush to the House of Representatives in 1966 and 1968, a seat he almost certainly could have occupied for as long as he wanted it.

Bush's brand of conservatism, like conservatism generally, was inchoate when he first moved to Texas in 1948, centered on a New England patrician-style disposition to public service, the Republican Party, and gradual progress, however defined. As an independent businessman-turned-politician, Bush firmly embraced conservative economic doctrines, especially those centered on fiscal restraint and business-friendly government regulation. Beyond that, conservatism to Bush meant—and throughout his career continued to mean—what he wrote in his post-1964 election *National Review* essay: "moral fiber, prudence, love of country, the enlightened self-interest of the U.S., strength in foreign policy and freedom of the individual."[94] Nevertheless, Bush developed a reputation for moderation and even liberalism that far outstripped the reality.

One reason Bush gained this reputation was that certain policies that lay at the mainstream of conservatism in the 1950s and 1960s—notably a preference for balanced budgets over tax cuts and support for family planning as a strategy for lower-class population control and environmental preservation—fit uncomfortably with conservatism as it evolved during the 1970s and 1980s. In 1968, for example, Bush and several other Republicans on Ways and Means voted for a deficit reduction measure that paired $4 billion in spending cuts with $10 billion in tax increases. This position, which represented conservative orthodoxy at the time, would come to be regarded as conservative heresy a decade later.

As evidence of how much changed, consider the near-scriptural text for conservatives when Bush was running for office in Texas: Senator Goldwater's best-selling 1960 book *The Conscience of a Conservative*.[95] In it Goldwater called for ending farm subsidies, making Social Security voluntary, reducing the federal budget by 10 percent per year, affirming states' rights, and abandoning Cold War–era containment policies. The book's chapter titles featured farmers, labor, taxes and spending (with considerably more about the latter than the former), the welfare state, education, the Soviet menace, civil rights, and states' rights. Not a single chapter was devoted to—indeed, not a single mention was made of—any of the issues most prominently featured in late-century conservatism, such as abortion rights, homosexuality, gun control, prayer in public schools, and women's rights.

A second, perhaps more important, explanation for Bush's reputation as a moderate rather than a conservative was that he never got over his initial experience with right-wing extremists when he first entered politics in Houston. A recurring theme in Bush's political career from that point on was an aversion bordering on revulsion to the "nut fringe" he saw dominating nearly all grassroots conservative organizations. Bush "was never a movement conservative," says Quayle in his oral history interview. "He was always wary of the right wing of the party. He would always say, 'You can't get too close to them.'" Bush's experiences in Texas politics "colored his views on the conservative movement as such" for years to come, observes Untermeyer. Early in Bush's vice presidency, for example, Untermeyer recalls that when he would urge him to speak to conservative groups, "he would always dismiss these by saying, 'Those people have never been for me and they never will.'" Bush was, Untermeyer says, "disdainful of the kind of people who supported Ronald Reagan and imagining that's what all Reagan people, including the Reagans themselves, were like. And that experience . . . goes all the way back to when he was chairman of the Harris County Republican Party" in Texas. To some extent, then, those who have most loudly proclaimed themselves conservatives never fully trusted Bush because he never fully trusted them.

GEORGE BUSH AND AMERICAN CONSERVATISM

Hugh Heclo

The relationship between George H. W. Bush and American conservatism should be pictured as a prolonged dance of suspicion and courtship, of pandering and treachery. During the last half of the twentieth century, this political tango played out as the meaning and political practices of conservatism were undergoing fundamental transformations. The results manifested themselves in Bush's anomalous presidency. For four years, President Bush governed in a traditionally conservative manner but failed to live up to the standard demanded by the new form of conservatism. Seen from this historical perspective, and informed by the relevant Miller Center oral histories, a great many of the frustrations, failures, and hidden successes of the Bush presidency become more understandable.[1]

America's Exceptional Conservatism[2]

One might think that conservatism—being in the business of conserving— would be a fairly stable affair. In the latter half of the twentieth century, however, conservatism in America changed dramatically. It became a populist, ideological movement that grew to occupy the center of gravity in the Republican Party. Before considering the Bush presidency, we need to get a fix on this moving target of American conservatism.

In one sense, conservatism in America has always been exceptional. That is to say, it has had a distinctly non-European or—as followers of Louis Hartz would say—an unconservative flavor.[3] Traditionally understood, European conservatism emphasizes the importance of hierarchical order, especially as this order descends from the time-tested experience of the past. Political society is an ongoing concern organically stratified by the variations that arise naturally among human beings. Political efforts to impose any form of egalitarianism necessarily flatten and homogenize what it is to be human. Hierarchy trumps equality.

Once Great Britain lost the War for American Independence, this Tory element of conservatism largely disappeared from the American scene.[4] Tory Loyalists went home to England or fled to Canada and the Caribbean. The tragic exception to this generalization was the Tory-like American South, with its deeply stratified social structure grounded in slavery and racism.[5]

American Conservatism before the Revolution

In light of this history, it is fair to say that during the first half of the twentieth-century American conservatism was an essentially stable, if not stodgy, affair. It is a term that summons up memories of the Tafts of Ohio, the Lodges of Massachusetts, the Byrds of Virginia, and many lesser political figures in both the Democratic and Republican parties.

This traditional conservatism saw itself as principled but not greatly interested in the play of abstract ideas. It was more a disposition than an ideological package of doctrines.[6] It was, above all, a disposition firmly attached to what is familiar. It was disposed to prudent rather than hasty action, to incremental rather than large steps, to modest hopes rather than great expectations about overcoming the flaws embedded in human nature. It was the political faction of instinctive inertia.

Accordingly, traditional conservatism was also disposed toward a dour skepticism in public affairs. It was skeptical about society's capacity to manage and absorb big changes. It was skeptical about anything suggesting perfectionist politics. On the contrary, traditional conservatism held to the view that, rightly understood, politics is not concerned with truth or the plans of intellectual dreamers to perfect the human condition. Politics should be confined to the limited task of governing to reduce the occasions for conflict as individuals freely pursue their multiple interests. Governing should not impose substantive activities and directives on people. Rather, it should concern itself with enforcing general rules of appropriate procedure on everyone. In its purest form, conservatism cleaved to Disraeli's adage that "when it is not necessary to do something, it is necessary to do nothing."

In the essentially egalitarian American context, it would be wrongheaded to label this traditional conservatism as "elitist." But it did harbor an essentially patrician view of politics. Conservatives preferred to see themselves as more or less aloof from but honorably serving the sweaty masses and their passions. It was a worldview in which publicly spirited citizens (presumptively males) "stood" rather than crudely "ran" for public office and the attendant responsibilities of governing. A sharp mental line, implicit and thus all the more powerful, was drawn between electoral campaigning (a necessary evil in democratic times) and prudent governing (a positive duty of public service). At its most high-minded, traditional conservatism saw political activity as something resembling a sports competition, where the reward was the honor of public office.

The mechanisms for expressing this conservative disposition were well established and seemingly stable. Traditional conservatives served in the political arena primarily through personal relationships, not political organization. For purposes of political advancement, right character trumped right "ideology" on this or that policy issue. One's character was judged through personal networks with nodes in corporate board rooms, alumni groups, local chambers of commerce, country clubs, and small town service organizations such as the Rotary Lions and Elks clubs across middle America.

Insofar as conservatism took on a political cast in the first half of the twentieth century, it did so as an essentially negative and reactive force. It set itself against the growing power of "progressive" nationalism advocated by Herbert Croly and his political successors. From Woodrow Wilson's New Freedom on through FDR's New Deal and Truman's Fair Deal, progressives (in both political parties) championed new policy initiatives in Washington. Essentially this meant efforts to bring to bear a national consciousness, federal government power, and expert knowledge in solving America's social and economic problems. Progressives also sought to plan policies and create institutions that would bring order to America's growing role in the world.

Year after year, conservatives stood opposed to the statism that all these collective undertakings, both at home and abroad, necessarily entailed. True-blue conservatives were anti–New Deal, anti-union, anti–government planning, and anti-internationalist. What progressives promoted as hope for a better life, conservatives regarded as threats to constitutional government, to states' rights, free markets, individual responsibility, and American sovereignty. In G. K. Chesterton's phrase, the traditional conservative was a "permanent reactionary," someone who always seemed to be coming from somewhere rather than going anywhere.[7]

That said, we are talking about a conservatism in the first half of the twentieth century that was little more than a disposition in American politics. It was nothing like an organized political force advancing a clear policy agenda. Conservatives generally saw themselves for what they were—an unorganized minority protesting the forward movement of American politics, a worried corrective to the popular majorities that are always tempted to emotional excess and are always seeking government handouts at the expense of responsible budget-balancing. Looking back on the futile, sporadic efforts of Senator Robert Taft to win the Republican presidential nomination for the cause of conservatism in 1940, 1948, and 1952, we witness the maneuverings of a general without an army.[8]

The Making of a Movement

The Bush and Walker families, New England progenitors of first-born son George Herbert Walker Bush, were very much a part of the largely forgotten world of old-style American conservatism. Certainly not everything of this tradition was thrown overboard (which would have been a most unconservative thing to do). Nonetheless, the exceptional conservatism that Bush confronted in his four-year presidency was something quite different from what preceded it. By background and temperament, George Bush was of a conservative disposition, and his deportment and choices as president testify to that fact. But political time moves on, and Bush's traditional conservatism was distrusted by proponents of a newer form of American conservatism. This emerging presence on the American political scene was a passionate, popular movement. It was a movement eager to take the political offensive and to do so with immense intellectual firepower and organizational shrewdness.

The elements of this movement came together in a seemingly haphazard way during the Cold War years. Neither its intellectual nor its populist constituencies were univocal. And yet a coalescence occurred—however halting and rancorous—that eventually wiped out the liberal and most of the moderate elements of the Republican Party.[9] The morphology of this political formation is crucial for understanding the Bush presidency.

The earliest expression of the new conservatism was an intellectual resistance movement that opposed the powerful collectivist trends produced by the Great Depression and World War II. In both Great Britain and the United States, total war against Germany and Japan prompted ambitious visions of what all the horrendous suffering should achieve for the postwar world. From the necessarily collective nature of this massive societal war effort there emerged a correspondingly collectivist vision of "what we are fighting for." In Britain this was reflected in the government's Beveridge Report (which envisioned cradle-to-grave social insurance) and in the Labour Party's electoral pledge to reshape the British economy in a socialist direction (a promise that did much to defeat Prime Minister Winston Churchill's government in July 1945, even as Churchill stood at the pinnacle of public esteem as a wartime leader). This collectivist vision was also powerfully expressed in FDR's wartime declaration of the "four freedoms" that were to be secured in the postwar world, in large part through the policy guidance of his beloved National Resources Planning Board.[10]

Today we have mostly forgotten these grand Anglo-American visions of the postwar world as well as the domestic political realities in both countries that cut down these dreams into a more modest version of their original collectivist selves. What matters for present purposes is that the wartime dreams of a new "welfare" relationship between the national government and its citizens—and postwar efforts to implement this aspiration—produced a backlash, as such things do in democratic societies. The counterattack was proclaimed by intellectuals arguing against the conventional wisdom concerning what people were starting to call "the welfare state." The work of Frederick Hayek, Ludwig von Mises, and, at more popular level, Ayn Rand launched this libertarian element of the new conservatism on both sides of the Atlantic.[11]

At the same time, the onset of the Cold War unleashed anti-communism as a political passion at many different levels of American life. In 1947 congressional investigations of communist influences in Hollywood fired popular interest in anti-communism. So did the demagoguery of Senator Joseph McCarthy and others of his ilk. Vulgar nativism, a long-standing feature of the American political scene, clearly played a part in arousing the new conservatism. But that was far from the whole story. There were also thoughtful people inspired by Whittaker Chambers who, like him, saw the threat posed by communism as an existential moral struggle for the soul of Western civilization.

Year after year, the political drama of anti-communism played out before the American public. Liberal spokesmen decried the threat to civil liberties right-wing reactionaries posed. Their opponents, many of whom were not yet calling themselves conservatives, argued that American Communists were more than mere exponents of a more extreme form of leftist politics or nonconformists exercising their rights of free speech and association. They were conspirators directed from Moscow who were intent on subverting every political order they did not dominate. For Ronald Reagan and many other less-well-known but deeply concerned Americans, anti-communism became the path of conviction that led out of the Democratic Party and into what would be the new conservative movement.

Knowing an enemy when it saw one, the Catholic Church played a very important role after World War II in mobilizing many average Americans against the communist threat. Initially, this impulse came from the Church in Europe, as Pope Pius XII spoke out against Communists seeking political control of the fragile post–World War II democracies.[12] American intellectuals working within the Catholic tradition provided a sharp spear point for this nation's emerging conservative movement. First Russell Kirk's book, *The Conservative Mind* (1953), and then William F. Buckley Jr.'s founding of *The National Review* (1955) incubated and gradually mobilized thousands of young activists with a passion for conservative ideas.

It is also important that this young political movement found an attractive champion around whom to rally.[13] The 1964 Republican nomination of Senator Barry Goldwater of Arizona for president was a critical turning point for the young conservative movement. This was true for at least three reasons.

First, it clearly demonstrated conservative activists' raw political power in challenging the Republican Party's moderate/liberal East Coast establishment. The challenge was mounted by a principled, grassroots movement. It came out of thousands of neighborhoods in the booming suburbs of the American West and what people were beginning to call the New South. The young movement's activists were politically passionate, knowledgeable, and increasingly well organized.[14] Thus, it was fitting that Goldwater, coming out of the West, clinched the 1964 presidential nomination by defeating New York governor Nelson Rockefeller in California's winner-take-all primary.

The second implication of Goldwater's nomination was less obvious but of immense long-term significance. Goldwater was able to win the nomination while distancing the young conservative movement from the extremist conspiracy-minded groups on the far right.[15] This did not happen by chance. It was prudent work carried out by a handful of leaders who were shaping the new movement's claims on the American public. In 1962, as chapters of the John Birch Society were making ever deeper inroads in local politics, leading figures of the young movement entered into a secret arrangement with Senator Goldwater to expose the society's leader, Robert Welch, as a person who was (in Russell Kirk's phrase) "loony and should be put away."[16] Success in this effort gave Goldwater a fighting chance to become a credible presidential candidate while turning the society's grassroots membership toward an enlightened rather than a dark, conspiratorial version of conservatism. Although it was an uphill battle in subsequent years, success meant that the suburban backyard brigades of the new conservatism could surge forward in Republican presidential primaries with a fighting chance of countering liberal and media claims that they were right-wing nuts.

A final feature of the 1964 Goldwater experience was equally important for the future of Republican Party politics. The 1952 Republican convention fight between Taft and Eisenhower forces had been bitter, but Senator Taft and the new president were soon playing golf and enjoying each other's company. In 1964, something much different happened. As Goldwater supporters saw things, the fight for the nomination was between principled, true believers and political moderates and liberals. The hostilities became deep and visceral. By the time their convention began, some moderate Republicans leaders had branded Goldwater "as a fascist, a racist, a trigger-happy warmonger, a nuclear madman and the candidate who couldn't win."[17] In turn, Nelson Rockefeller was booed and drowned out on national television as he tried to address the delegates from the convention platform.

This bitterness only deepened during the months leading up to the November presidential election. Aided by the national press and television broadcasters as well as by candidate Goldwater's occasional verbal gaffes, leaders of the moderate Republican establishment seemed to work in tandem with Democrats to spread fears about the dangers of an extremist Goldwater presidency. The memory of the 1964 betrayal by moderate/liberal Republicans was burned into the soul of the conservative movement. This schism was carried forward in the 1976 nomination contest between President Ford and Ronald Reagan, which captured perfectly the struggle between Washington's Republican Old Guard and the grassroots insurgency of conservative activists. As we will see, conservative sensitivity to Republican Party leaders' betrayal of their cause endured and reached deep into the inner workings of Bush's presidency.

Meanwhile, in a backhanded way, the election of 1972 was as important as the 1964 Goldwater campaign in shaping the emerging conservative movement. Just as the conservative wing had captured the Republican presidential nomination eight years earlier, so now the Democratic Party's liberal wing captured its presidential nomination in the person of Senator George McGovern. McGovern's most vocal supporters epitomized the political and cultural insurgencies associated with the 1960s—feminism, campus radicalism, antiwar protesters, civil rights advocates, and all the rest.

This success of the McGovern forces in turn energized the conservative movement in unexpected ways. Heretofore, a liberal/conservative conflict had also been waged within the Democratic Party between the likes of McGovern and Scoop Jackson. By 1972, that conflict was sharpening into an ideological and cultural divide—an increasingly liberal Democratic party on one side and an increasingly conservative Republican party on the other side.

Other important consequences followed. The leftward shift in the Democratic Party's political center of gravity went a long way toward driving Democratic anti-communists and critics of New Left radicalism out of their party. Thus, as the 1970s unfolded, the conservative movement was infused with the considerable intellectual firepower of those who came to be known as "neoconservatives"—Cold War hawks whose sympathies with the New Deal did not inhibit their powerful critiques of the cultural disorders of the 1960s and the Great Society's schemes of social engineering. Among these new recruits to the conservative movement were a number of the philosopher Leo Strauss's students and his students' students. Now conservatives would not be confined to anti-communism, states' rights, and anti-collectivism. They were increasingly prepared to launch a thoroughgoing attack on the whole intellectual structure of liberalism, its utopian social imagination, and its simplistic secular view of human nature.

It remained for the Democrats to complete the conservative coalition. For almost fifty years, Protestant conservatives (who had become labeled as "fundamentalists") had mostly stayed out of public view. Their political disengagement stemmed from what was perceived as a series of ignominious defeats in the "culture wars" of the Roaring Twenties (the Scopes "monkey trial," the failure of prohibition, and many other crusades against "modern ways" of that time).[18] The cultural issues brought to the fore with McGovern's nomination and even the Supreme Court's legalization of abortion in 1973 did little to bestir evangelicals into political action. The 1976 election of Jimmy Carter, a born-again Southern Baptist who was not ashamed to speak of his religion, even reassured evangelicals that there was no need for rank-and-file Christians to leave the political sidelines. The four years of the Carter administration overturned that happy thought. The president's efforts to placate liberal activists in the Democratic Party convinced "evangelical" (the now preferred term replacing "fundamentalist") leaders that their concern for traditional family values was deeply threatened by public policies emanating from Washington. In return, political strategists in the emerging conservative movement welcomed America's evangelical spokesmen and their flocks of traditional "values voters" with open arms.[19]

The New Conservatism

Bringing these various threads together, American conservatism by 1979—when George H. W. Bush decided to run against former California governor Ronald Reagan for the Republican presidential nomination—was something quite different from what it had been when Robert A. Taft sought the White House decades earlier.

This new American conservatism was a multifaceted populist movement. It did not "serve" the masses from patrician heights. This conservatism (its champions proclaimed) was simply the political voice of most Americans. It expressed this people's moral convictions, their economic interests, their down-home common sense, their overriding love of freedom and of country. In short, conservatism was the American way of looking at public affairs.

Traditional conservatives saw populism as a threat to a stable political order. Movement conservatives eagerly enlisted popular passions, but they did so in the service of principles and doctrine. The new conservative movement saw populism as a corrective to the economic, social, and cultural disorder resulting from the designs of liberals. The new conservatism identified itself with ordinary Americans, the common people who had every reason to resist the desire of liberal elites to rule their lives from Washington.

Far from a politics of skepticism, this new conservatism was a politics of faith and hope. Far from being dour, it was a politics of sunny optimism about the future—if only conservatives could achieve power and put America back on track to a future of unlimited promise. The politician who emerged as the leading spokesperson for the movement delighted in quoting the democratic radical Thomas Paine: "We have it in our power to begin the world over again."[20]

Although populist in its appeal, the new conservatism was grounded in a deeply intellectual critique of Marxism and the new collectivist secular liberalism.[21] In foreign policy, it was radical, aiming not at a continuation of the status quo system of bipolar world powers but at the positive defeat of communism. In domestic policy, the new conservatism continuously attacked liberal schemes that claimed to use government to solve economic and social problems, plans that would smother individual liberty with a centralized collectivism that was dismissive of traditional Judeo-Christian values. In fiscal policy, traditional conservatism had urged little more than a "balanced budget." The conservative movement's new fiscal mantra was different—cut taxes to release private enterprise, cut taxes to reduce the deficit (in the cheery new supply-side view of economics), cut taxes to defund the liberal Left, cut taxes to stop feeding the beast and check the growth of Big Government in Washington.

On these and other matters, the new conservatism, far from playing defense, was eager to go on the offense. It did so not as in a sporting competition but as in a war for control of the public conversation, the power of government, and, ultimately, the culture itself. Thus, the new conservatism replaced old-boy loyalty to persons with a prior loyalty to principles. Being "one of us" by way of character was far less important than standing shoulder to shoulder on the barricades of ideological and cultural warfare.[22]

The political fate of Barry Goldwater serves as a case in point. In 1960, as the newly emerging conservative leader, Goldwater had proclaimed in glowing terms that conservatism was not an ideology but a shortlist of essential principles concerning human nature, American history, culture, and constitutional government.[23] Twenty years later, American conservatism had developed into a strict political ideology with programmatic givens. And so by the 1980s, Goldwater—who saw conservative principles as endorsing gay rights and a woman's right to choose an abortion and as opposing President Reagan's call for a constitutional amendment permitting public school prayer—was yesterday's man as far as the new conservative movement was concerned. Barry Goldwater died largely forgotten as a victim of Alzheimer's disease in 1998, while Ronald Reagan passed on from the same disease as a revered icon bequeathed to the nation by America's conservative movement.

Up to this point, I have tried to distinguish the essential differences between an old and a new conservatism in twentieth-century American politics. Gradually during the 1950s, 1960s, and 1970s, the new version was displacing traditional conservatism. And given this ongoing development, the question naturally arises: Where was George?

Where Was George?

After World War II, an imaginary journalist tasked with scouting the political landscape to find the next generation of conservative leaders who might succeed Robert Taft would very likely have spotted young George H. W. Bush. In the first instance, here was a true war hero. Graduating from Phillips Academy in 1942, the eighteen-year-old Bush abandoned the safe berth waiting for him at Yale. Instead, he became the youngest commissioned aviator in Navy history, a pilot of a three-man torpedo bomber who was shot down and miraculously rescued at sea after eighty-eight combat missions. Bush then took up his studies at Yale in 1945, carrying with him the Distinguished Flying Cross and three Air Medals.

Beyond that, this attractive young man had a traditionally conservative pedigree in the fullest sense of that term. His two parents, coming from the New England Walker and Bush families, represented a union atop the oldest and largest private investment house in New York (Brown Brothers Harriman). The Bushes were East Coast rich, which meant an extended world of family relationships that circulated through winter homes, summer residences, and a vast network of social and political friends. The paterfamilias, Prescott Bush, was a stern, steady, and loving presence throughout the first forty-eight years of George's life. Courtly in manner, disdainful of Joseph McCarthy's crude anti-communism, and a favorite golfing partner of President Eisenhower, Senator Bush epitomized the internationalist, moderate, and pro-business mainstream Republicanism of his time.

The Bush and Walker families immersed their son in a deeply held ethos. Insofar as the rough and tumble world of American politics harbored any place for a pre-democratic sense of noblesse oblige, it was in such redoubts of family tradition. Achievement was a matter of fulfilling duties, a view captured in the Phillips Academy's school motto, *Non Sibi* (Not for Oneself). For men in the extended Walker and Bush families, duty meant public service in the form of community and political leadership. The family ethos honored intense competitiveness, but that fighting spirit was always to be expressed in a thoroughly sportsmanlike way. By words and, more important, by example Prescott Bush impressed on his son a fundamental orientation toward politics, one of "duty and service."[24] Running to achieve office was a necessary chore. In contrast, governing in public office was a noble responsibility. Personal ties, loyalties, and reputation were the essential ligatures of any political leadership worthy of the name. The important thing was not to desire respect, public honor, or fame but to deserve those things. In short, Bush was to the conservative disposition born.

From 1946 to 1948, while the fading Hollywood idol Ronald Reagan was absorbed in anti-communist trench warfare as head of the Screen Actors Guild,[25] the war-hero Bush established a stellar athletic and academic record at Yale, graduating Phi Beta Kappa in 2 1/2 years. At Yale, young George Bush showed no interest in the lively conservative movement on campus fomented by his fellow student and World War II vet William F. Buckley Jr. Nor did Bush take offense at the secular humanism of his professors that Buckley would denounce in his scandalous (for that time) book, *God and Man at Yale*.[26]

The next obvious and traditionally conservative move would have been for Bush to take his many assets to one of the leading financial houses or elite law firms and lay the foundations for his future political career as a New England Brahmin.

At this point, the first of many anomalies emerged in George Bush's engagement with conservatism. The day after graduating from Yale, Bush and his new wife, the New York debutant Barbara Pierce (a descendent of President Franklin Pierce and the daughter of the president of McCall's publishing house), jumped outside the world of conservative expectations and headed for the burgeoning wildcat oilfields of west Texas. Yet Bush's career gamble was not as reckless as it might appear. Although he broke with the family's expectations, Bush was no rebel going off on his own. His increasingly successful ventures in the oil business had the essential help of his family's financial backing and his father's personal business connections.

In 1952, as Taft was losing to Eisenhower, and as Bush's fortune and reputation as a public-spirited businessman was growing, the 28-year-old Texan threw his immense energy into a seemingly pointless cause. George Bush began organizing the first Republican precinct in the heart of this solidly Democratic state. By the end of the 1950s, Bush was a leading figure in the growing Republican Party's county and state organization. Disliked by the John Birchers, Bush presented himself as a moderate Republican who supported Goldwater for the Republican nomination but was not hostile to Nelson Rockefeller.[27] In 1964, he easily won the Republican primary nomination for U.S. senator.

Seen from this perspective, Bush appeared poised to emerge as one of the young western politicians who would help ignite the new conservative movement in American politics. Yet once again, the reality was more ambiguous. Bush ran his 1964 Senate race against the liberal Democratic incumbent Ralph Yarborough in a cautious manner. While flirting with endorsements from Goldwater activists, Bush kept his campaign at arm's length from any groups that might be perceived as part of the "nut fringe." Texas had its share of John Birch Society cells, and

Bush was at pains to defend himself against Yarborough's charges that he was a "Goldwater extremist." As the outcome of the presidential campaign became increasingly obvious, Bush did what he could to distance his Senate campaign from the sinking conservative ship. By contrast, in these bleak last days, "citizen" Ronald Reagan gave a powerful TV address to rally Americans to Goldwater's conservative crusade. Bush could not have given a speech like Reagan's "A Time to Choose," nor would he have wanted to.

Goldwater's overwhelming defeat yielded two revealing "instant analyses" in the December 1st issue of Buckley's *National Review*, one by the promising young politician George Bush and another by Reagan.[28] As Bush saw it, Goldwater's massive defeat showed the need for a big-tent Republican Party, though he did not use that term. He pointed out that "hyper-tensioned types" and anti-LBJ "fanatics" had turned off undecided voters. For the future, while leaning in a conservative direction, the GOP should welcome anyone who wants to be a Republican. It should reject the idea of screening out people whose philosophy fails to conform to some "guidelines laid down by 'true conservatives' or 'informed conservatives.'" Americans wanted leadership showing "moral fiber, prudence, love of country."

While Bush viewed the Republican Party as "the hope for the conservative in the future," Reagan saw conservatives as the hope of the Republican Party. According to Reagan, LBJ and other Democratic leaders had concealed their liberal agenda and disguised themselves as members of a conservative status quo that was resisting dangerous radicals. Soon enough the whole Democratic apparatus would show its true colors. As Reagan saw it, there was no great need to sell conservatism to voters. This was because conservatism, rightly understood, represented the American way of looking at things. Conservatives "represent the forgotten American—that simple soul who goes to work, bucks for a raise, takes out insurance, pays for his kids' schooling, contributes to his church and charity and knows there just '*ain't no such thing as a free lunch.*'"

Bush ended his article by calling for a conservatism that would be "practical and positive." Reagan ended with a conservative warrior's postscript: "I don't think we should turn the [GOP] high command over to leaders who were traitors during the battle just ended." Thus the difference. Throughout his political career, Bush kept 3x5 cards. They held the names and contact information of thousands of people with whom he would personally stay in touch through notes, letters, and phone calls. Throughout his political career Reagan kept 5x8 cards. But they were cards noting ideas for speeches and folksy examples of how those conservative ideas played out in Americans' lives.[29]

As the intellectual and populist conservative movement coalesced in the 1970s, George H. W. Bush's midlife political career was a sorry tale, one increasingly removed from the electoral politics that might make him appealing, or even known, to American voters. Essentially, it was the story of a high-minded Republican loyalist being pushed around by the power plays of Washington insiders.

Thus, in 1970, Bush became one of the promising fresh faces that President Nixon recruited for Senate races as part of his new southern strategy. In 1966 Bush had joined the new group of southern Republican congressmen, though his liberal internationalist views had nothing in common with movement conservatism.[30] Dutifully abandoning his promising two-term career in the House as a Republican moderate, Bush charged into the Texas Senate campaign expecting a replay of his 1964 race against Yarborough. Instead, the Democrats nominated their own war hero, former congressman Lloyd Bentsen, a moderate Democrat who held the distinct advantage over Bush of being a true, home-grown Texan. Rather than campaigning from the right of his opponent, Bush now found himself situated on the left.

Facing ruthless Democratic attacks on him as a liberal Ivy League carpetbagger, Bush's prospects dimmed and Nixon did little to help.[31] In fact, Nixon had become enamored with the dashing Texas governor, Democrat John Connally, who was appearing in anti-Bush ads but who also had secretly lobbied influential Texans of both parties to support Nixon's 1968 presidential campaign.[32] The plan now was that the retiring Governor Connally, while remaining a Democrat, would become Nixon's secretary of the treasury. As a condition of taking the treasury job, Connally insisted that Bush receive some sort of position in the administration as a reward for his loyal service to Nixon.[33]

Once again, Bush's political career was a cat's paw amid political intrigues far removed from the coalescing conservative movement of the 1970s. Shortly after losing his Senate bid, Bush accepted President Nixon's job offer and was unanimously confirmed as U.S. ambassador to the United Nations, a suicidal career move for anyone interested in Texas politics. Bush may have hoped to build a national reputation in the position, but Nixon had other plans. For the president, the appointment was a matter of finding a likeable front man to perform a ceremonial role in New York. President Nixon and his national security advisor, Henry Kissinger, made dramatic foreign policy moves in 1971 and 1972 behind the backs of both Ambassador Bush and Secretary of State William Rogers. The typical result was to undercut Bush's public statements and often embarrass him personally.

At the beginning of 1973, as the Watergate scandal began closing in on the White House, Nixon called on Bush to become chairman of the Republican National Committee. For the next eighteen months, the Nixon White House exploited Bush's reputation for decency. Week after week the RNC chairman publicly, loyally, and fruitlessly defended Nixon and his men from any and all Watergate charges. Finally, convinced of Nixon's hopeless position, Bush boldly spoke up at the August 6, 1974, cabinet meeting and urged the president to resign.[34]

The ascension of Gerald Ford to the presidency meant that a new vice president would have to be appointed and confirmed by the Senate. Bush and his personal network of supporters (including Barry Goldwater) lobbied Ford to pick Bush. But in the hard world of politics, Bush's loyal service chairing the Republican National Committee had left him too tainted by Nixon and Watergate for the vice presidency or even a cabinet position. Instead, President Ford chose the person championed by Henry Kissinger, and Nelson Rockefeller was appointed vice president.[35] Bush was offered a modest consolation prize as chief of the U.S. Liaison Office in communist China, which he dutifully accepted.

When appointing Bush, Ford told him to expect to stay in China for two years, but after one year Bush wrote the president that he was eager to return to the American political scene. By this time the Ford White House was preoccupied with withering congressional investigations of the Central Intelligence Agency. Bush, who hoped for a cabinet appointment, was shocked to receive a return cable asking him to come home to become director of the CIA. He would be in charge of an agency that was under investigation for everything "from lawbreaking to simple incompetence." Since the post was considered "nonpolitical," Bush rightly suspected that his rival Donald Rumsfeld, Ford's chief of staff, wanted to bury him so Bush wouldn't "be in the political game anymore."[36] Nonetheless, Bush felt a duty to accept. In October 1975, Ford nominated Rumsfeld to become secretary of defense and Bush to be CIA director.

But now there came another political price to pay for doing his duty. Bush's confirmation was stalled when Senate Democrats demanded that he promise not to run for vice president in 1976. "If I wanted to be Vice President," Bush argued, "I wouldn't be here asking you to confirm me for the CIA." The senators persisted until Bush finally asked Ford to exclude him from consideration for the vice presidency. "I know it's unfair," he told the president, "but you don't have much of a choice if we are to get on with the job of rebuilding and strengthening the Agency." After President Ford notified the Senate Armed Services Committee that Bush would definitely not be considered for the Republican vice presidential nomination in 1976, the CIA confirmation quickly followed.[37]

And so it was that Bush remained on the political sidelines in 1976 while Reagan and the conservative movement challenged Ford for the presidential nomination. As the Texas delegates known as "Reagan's Raiders" roiled the Republican convention, George Bush, the once-promising pioneer in establishing a Republican base in Texas during the 1950s and 1960s, was nowhere to be seen. After the election, Bush continued to give President-elect Carter CIA briefings and offered to resign if he wished to name his own director.[38] To Bush's regret, Carter accepted the offer and George Bush returned to private life in Texas. Soon he was planning his own run for the presidency.

Taken out of context, Bush's quest for the Republican presidential nomination in 1980 was more than just bold. It was a hopeless move by a politician whose name registered in the public mind as little more than a pollster's asterisk.[39] But from Bush's perspective, a presidential bid made good strategic sense at this moment in political time.

President Ford's defeat at the hands of Jimmy Carter made clear that the battle for the 1980 Republican nomination was going to be waged in terms of the ongoing division between the centrist Republican old guard and the populist conservative movement championed by Ronald Reagan. Both sides were still feeling bruised and resentful from the 1976 convention battle, and older warriors remembered similar hostilities from 1964. Still, the likely field of candidates presented an opening for Bush. However strenuously Senators Howard Baker and Robert Dole might try to position themselves as conservatives, both would be vulnerable to attack because of their extensive congressional voting records. On the left was Congressman John Anderson, by then a Rockefeller Republican, and on the right was the conservative insurgency represented by former California governor Ronald Reagan and Illinois congressman Phil Crane. Floating ambiguously in the crowd was the Nixon Democrat-turned-Republican John Connally. Entering this potential mud fight for the nomination, Bush could present himself as an attractive and even redeeming figure—a likable, politically seasoned, internationally experienced, common sense Republican who could unite the party. Prescott Bush would have been proud.

Having almost snatched the Republican nomination from the incumbent President Ford three years earlier, Reagan seemed the odds-on favorite. But Bush had learned from Carter's 1976 candidacy and poured all his resources into Iowa, the first contest on the nomination calendar. When the caucuses met in January 1980, Bush pulled out a narrow victory over Reagan (31.5 percent to 29.4 percent) and claimed to have the winning momentum—the "Big Mo" as he called it—going into New Hampshire. Polls now showed Bush and Reagan running neck and neck, with the rest of the GOP pack far behind.[40] But in New Hampshire a disastrous debate performance, Reagan's superior organization, and grassroots conservative enthusiasm for Reagan soon dashed those hopes. Reagan beat Bush by a lopsided 50 to 23 percent, effectively ending Bush's presidential campaign.

At that moment, by any reasonable political calculation, one would have judged Bush's political career to be finished. And it appears that George and Barbara Bush reached that conclusion. In the spring of 1980, the Bushes sold their home in Houston and purchased his grandfather's estate, Walker's Point, at Kennebunkport, Maine. The moderate, patrician-minded, internationalist, dutiful Republican public servant had finally come home to New England.

Conservatism and the Bush Presidency

To say that George H. W. Bush was not a movement conservative is to state the obvious. Nevertheless, it would be difficult to overestimate the importance of that fact for Bush's presidency. In 1979, George Bush presented himself as the centrist alternative to the conservative Ronald Reagan. In 1988, Vice President Bush tried to appear as Reagan's successor while naturally wanting to seem his own man. To win in 1988 Bush would have to tap into the power of movement conservatism without ever really having been a part of it.

At this point, it worth pausing to avoid the oversimplifications of hindsight. As we have seen, the conservative impulse that grew into a political movement in the decades after World War II was a complex coalition.[41] When Bush won the Republican presidential nomination in 1988, outgoing President Reagan was by no means the conservative icon that he has since become. Neoconservatives, libertarians, and members of the Religious Right all found reasons to severely criticize President Reagan during his tenure in office.[42]

Yet almost no one in the conservative movement doubted that Ronald Reagan, regardless of his shortcomings as president, was one of them. After World War II and during the next twenty years before seeking public office, Reagan associated himself with the intellectuals, journalists, and policy experts who were building the new conservative movement. He became a faithful reader of and public commentator on material published in leading conservative journals such as *Human Events* and *National Review* and could recite sections from Whittaker Chambers's book *Witness*.[43] Before he became a politician, Reagan became a conservative by conviction, and it was generally recognized that his election in 1980 meant that the conservative movement had finally succeeded in entering the mainstream of national politics. Conservative critics of his presidency demanded, "Let Reagan be Reagan," but it would never have occurred to them to raise the battle cry, "Let Bush be Bush."

Once Bush entered the Oval Office, intellectual conflicts between the old and the new conservatism were expressed—as such disagreements always are—in the particulars of the personality conflicts, symbolic policy arguments, back-stabbing, and ongoing squabbles that marked the Bush presidency. To be sure, these are the characteristics that human agents have expressed in making political history in all times and places. But the tensions between the old and new conservatism took their own distinctive toll on Bush's capacity for presidential leadership. Looking back, it was probably a fatal toll.

The presidency of George H. W. Bush had its beginnings in the summer of 1980, when Reagan chose his running mate. It is important to recall that by this time, as never before in American political history, the vice presidency had become the inside track to the presidency, or at least to a presidential nomination (as with Vice Presidents Nixon, Johnson, Humphrey, Ford, and Mondale). Thus, in 1980, Reagan's choice of a running mate put Bush on a glide path to a post-Reagan Republican presidential nomination. Reagan did so precisely because Bush, his main challenger in the primaries, was not a movement conservative and was the only other Republican with delegates at the convention.[44]

In choosing Bush as his running mate, Ronald Reagan continued a strategy of unification that he had pursued throughout his late-blooming political career. It was explicit in his 1964 interpretation of Goldwater's defeat in *National Review*, where Reagan envisioned a conservative core that would include other elements in the Republican Party. He took the same approach when first deciding to run for office. To run his campaign for governor, Reagan sought out the young political consultants who had recently managed Nelson Rockefeller's fierce California primary contest against the conservatives' hero, Barry Goldwater.[45] The same strategy reappeared in Reagan's 1976 run for the Republican nomination against President Ford, when Reagan announced that should he win the nomination, his running mate would be liberal Republican senator Richard Schweiker. Thus, in choosing Bush as his running mate in 1980, Reagan simply gave expression to his enduring vision of a conservative-centered but welcoming Republican Party.

The result was that President Reagan's opportunity—to broaden support outward from his conservative core—mirrored Vice President Bush's problem. If George Bush subsequently wanted to run for president, how could he draw the new conservative movement to his cause? Standing in the way was a cultural gap and deep suspicions that divided Reagan loyalists from the moderate, East Coast Republicanism symbolized by Bush—which is to say, divided movement conservatives from traditional blue blooded conservatives.[46]

By all accounts Bush's service as vice president was exemplary.[47] He was politically self-effacing—to the point of deliberately avoiding any effort to bring Bush loyalists into jobs in the new administration.[48] He was discrete in his relations with the press and extremely protective of his private communications with the president. Not least, Vice President Bush scrupulously avoided becoming publicly identified with the Byzantine struggles that continued to churn at the highest levels of the White House, feuds that pitted moderate Republican "pragmatists" against movement conservative "ideologues." In all this, and above all else, Bush was utterly loyal to his president.[49]

Because Bush's service as vice president was so exemplary, it was of little value to him politically speaking. Such faithful service to the president did nothing to establish Bush's own power base. As vice president, Bush chaired two special task forces for Reagan, one on deregulation and the other on controlling international drug smuggling. Both issues were important to conservatives, but the task forces were obscure bureaucratic operations that paid Bush few political dividends. Moreover, there were deep and enduring suspicions among movement conservatives that Bush did not share Reagan's economic views[50]—suspicions that had grown when Vice President Bush stumbled badly during the 1984 campaign on the issue of possibly raising taxes.[51]

During his presidency, Ronald Reagan grew personally fond of George Bush.[52] But although Reagan was comfortable with the idea of Bush as his heir apparent, he also scrupulously observed the line between his official presidential functions and actual campaigning for Bush.[53] As his second term drew to an end, President Reagan did not endorse any of the contenders for the 1988 Republican presidential nomination. If Bush wanted to run for president, there would be no Reagan anointment, only a hardscrabble fight for that nomination.

A few weeks after Reagan's election to a second term, Vice President Bush decided to try to become his successor in 1988.[54] This required an immediate action plan. The early years of his political career in Texas had taught Bush that his father's patrician approach to electoral politics was futile. After his loss in the 1964 Texas Senate race, Bush won two terms in the House by becoming one of earliest adopters of the new ways of doing politics. This meant selling political candidates as if they were products in a mass consumer market, using all the tools and strategies of the modern profession of public relations.[55] Personally, Bush greatly disliked this new politics of being "marketed" or otherwise managed by political handlers. Nevertheless, since it was all a matter of "just" campaigning and not the real business of governing, Bush the politician learned to hold his nose and do what he had to do.[56] From Reagan's campaign team Bush chose as his chief campaign strategist Lee Atwater, a young talent well known for his smashmouth approach to political competition.[57] By the end of 1985, almost all of the old personnel in the Office of the Vice President had been replaced with people who were regarded as more competent and hard-charging staffers from the Reagan White House.

By then, too, Atwater had set up a campaign headquarters outside the White House that was staffed largely by young Reagan political operatives. It was not ideology but the pull of power and personal relations that brought these young Reagan loyalists to the task of devoting their immense energies to winning the presidency for the preppy New England moderate whom some of these same Reaganites had once jokingly called "the anti-Christ."[58] To support their efforts, Atwater established a Republican leadership PAC (The Fund for America) that raised more than $2 million by the end of 1985. This PAC was simply a front for funding Bush's 1988 presidential campaign and for paying political operatives in Atwater's shop who were working to derail Bush's potential rivals in the process of seeking 1988 convention delegates. Meanwhile, the vice president traveled the country trying to convince state party officials that he would be the strongest candidate to carry on after Reagan.[59] As the primary contests got under way, the centerpiece of Bush's strategy for winning the nomination became increasingly clear. It had everything to do with taxes.

The Tax Thing

As a presidential candidate, Ronald Reagan never pledged that he would not raise taxes, even as he consistently advocated cutting federal tax rates. As president, Ronald Reagan signed five tax increases in eight years, and at the time his actions were vigorously criticized in leading conservative circles.[60] But Reagan could always count on the underlying belief of the conservative movement that "he's one of us." Conservatives were likely to criticize not the man himself but his continuingly feuding advisors.[61] By contrast, for a non-movement conservative like Bush, there was no such reservoir of trust and goodwill to draw upon. As the 1988 primary season approached, there was good reason for the Bush election strategists to have their man appear more Catholic than the pope on taxes.

By the summer of 1987, Bush's campaign operatives had concluded that Senate Majority Leader Robert Dole was likely to be their main rival for the nomination. Staff members at Bush campaign headquarters set to work preparing for an all-out attack on Dole as the "tax collector for the welfare state." Although Bush's top campaign strategists were not convinced that their candidate believed in the no-new-taxes mantra, they urged it as a central theme throughout the primary debates and ad campaigns.[62]

Doubting that they could win in Iowa against the Kansan Dole, Bush's campaign machine focused on New Hampshire. When the results of the Iowa caucuses left Bush in a dismal third place behind Dole and televangelist Pat Robertson, the New Hampshire campaign took on do-or-die significance. At Atwater's headquarters the issue of a no-new-taxes pledge now became the decisive weapon against Dole.

An unexpected opportunity occurred during one of the New Hampshire debates when contender Pete DuPont pointedly challenged Dole to sign his name to a no-new-taxes pledge. Dole refused, and after some hesitation on Bush's part, Atwater unleashed a blistering negative ad campaign charging "Senator Straddle" with being on both sides of the tax question and on virtually every other public issue he had ever faced. Bush would continue the anti-tax mantra throughout the rest of his journey to the nomination.[63]

From his strategy in the primaries, it was a short but momentous step to Bush's tax pledge during his nationally televised acceptance speech at the Republican convention. Bush's campaign-focused advisors were convinced that the promise of no new taxes would be essential to carry movement conservatives with Bush through the general election. Bush's policy-focused advisors, led by Richard Darman and Nicholas Brady, considered the promise a foolish constraint on future policy making. They also believed that tax increases in a Bush presidency were likely and even desirable.[64] From their perspective, it was fortunate that even though Bush had frequently repeated his no-new-taxes pledge in his primary campaign appearances, it had not been etched in the public mind on prime-time television.[65]

As the Republican convention began, polls showed Bush trailing Democratic nominee Michael Dukakis by ten points. The felt need to do much more to reassure Bush skeptics in the conservative movement won out. Bush not only repeated the no-new-taxes pledge, he deliberately sank it deep into the rhetorical concrete of a dramatic, unqualified, Clint Eastwood-like promise on prime-time TV.[66] Bush's "read my lips" language went against the grain of anything resembling traditional conservative prudence. But in a political world increasingly driven by media images, public relations, and pandering, the dramatic pledge fit with a traditional Bush mindset that sharply compartmentalized the ugly necessities of campaigning from the noble duties of governing.

The same mindset was at work two years later when President Bush broke his promise. For conservatives the no-new-taxes pledge had become a guiding principle. To his senior domestic policy advisors, especially Budget Director Richard Darman, it was a problem to be worked around.[67] At an informal post-election gathering at the vice president's residence, Quayle was shocked to hear Darman, Brady, and Baker chatting amiably about raising taxes and waiting for an opportunity to make the recommendation.[68] When Quayle reported to the president-elect that his closest advisors were going to press him to raise taxes, Bush replied, "I know. But I can't do that."[69] Still, once Bush was in the Oval Office the no-new-taxes pledge began disappearing from presidential speeches.[70]

The opportunity Darman and his allies were waiting for came in 1990. It took the form of a perceived crisis in the federal deficit. Reagan's strategy of starving the government through tax cuts had not worked. Taxes as a share of GDP did stabilize and then decline slightly during the 1980s, but government spending continued to consume a larger share of the nation's output. By 1990, projections showed an accelerating rate of spending growth; the inevitable result was ever-larger federal deficits. At the same time, since Democrats now controlled both houses of Congress, President Bush was in a much weaker bargaining position than Reagan had been in his first term.

Unlike movement conservatives, Bush had always maintained a traditional conservative focus on deficit reduction and balanced budgets, not simply tax cuts. While running for the nomination against Reagan, Bush made it abundantly clear that he did not believe in the cheery supply-side theory that cutting taxes rates would produce larger revenue flows. To him that was "voodoo economics." Bush and his senior advisors intended to put their emphasis on long-term deficit reduction through enforceable caps on spending.[71]

In seeking a budget agreement, Bush relied heavily on men whose careers, like his own, were built outside the conservative movement—Darman, Brady, and Sununu—and Republican congressional leaders Bob Michel and Dole. Of his senior advisors, only Quayle was alert to the danger posed by conservative movement activists waiting in the tall grass, ready to pounce on Bush for breaking the no-new-tax pledge.[72]

The first sign of the political disaster to come appeared in June 1990. Quayle had left Washington assured at a meeting with Darman, Brady, and Sununu that preliminary negotiations with Democratic congressional leaders on a budget deal would not involve taxes. To the vice president's great surprise, the next day there were news reports that the president had agreed to raise taxes.[73] In fact, what had happened was a little more complicated. Treasury Secretary Brady, who always thought that the president was going to have to raise taxes to get a budget deal, had offered to put taxes "on the table" if the Democratic negotiators thought that would help get the budget-making process started. And the president had said he would not object to putting taxes on the table on that basis. Democrats were delighted to tell reporters that President Bush had courageously decided to consider raising taxes in order to achieve a budget agreement.

Officially, White House aides continued to put out the word that the president remained opposed to raising taxes. Privately, however, there were leaks and spins from Darman and others to the effect that in considering raising taxes, Bush the statesman was going to do what was right for the country. Conservatives began to smell betrayal in the Washington air. Instead of fighting tooth and nail to keep his pledge until the bitter end of negotiations, Bush appeared ready to break it before serious negotiations even started.

As the budget negotiations passed from summer into fall, Bush's bargaining position was increasingly weakened by virtue of a principled stand he took with regard to the approaching Gulf War. Following Saddam Hussein's invasion of Kuwait at the beginning of August, Bush believed that the properly constitutional and politically prudent course of action was to gain congressional backing for the war, both its preparation (Desert Shield) and execution (Desert Storm).[74] Accordingly, as budget negotiations reached a climax at Andrews Air Force Base, Bush was not in a position to push Democrats to the wall with a government shutdown. If he failed to get the agreement, the nation would be fighting a war with a divided government and no budget.[75]

In return for a budget deal with future spending caps, the Democratic negotiators demanded that Bush pay a price. He would have to break his no-new-taxes pledge. Bush was persuaded by his negotiators that it would be the largest spending-restraint budget in history. In the end, the president was willing to pay the price.[76] The final budget agreement was passed and signed by President Bush in late October 1990.

It quickly became clear that the political price of agreeing to a tax increase had been gravely underestimated. Bush and his senior advisors, apart from Quayle, simply did not take seriously enough Bush's precarious position with the conservative movement. Darman had argued that since Reagan raised taxes five times, why should doing so hurt President Bush? The answer should have been obvious. In the eyes of movement conservatives, George Bush was no Ronald Reagan.

The firestorm reaction caught the White House by surprise. When House Minority Whip Newt Gingrich walked away from the budget deal he had first agreed to, the Republican base exploded.[77] Public denunciations of the president ricocheted around the conservative landscape. As the influential conservative Richard Viguerie put it, Bush had "betrayed the Reagan Revolution." It would be "one of his legacies that he will have to carry always, that he lied and betrayed, because he didn't raise taxes kicking and screaming."[78] A dramatic revolt by House Republicans led by Gingrich defeated the first budget deal struck by congressional leaders and Bush officials. Conservative pundit Pat Buchanan was encouraged to think the president was vulnerable to a primary challenge in 1992.

Throughout this turmoil, Bush and his senior aides appeared oblivious to the need to sell his position to the American public, much less to outraged conservatives. Of course for those such as Quayle who took Bush's no-new-taxes pledge at face value, there was no need to prepare the public or conservatives for something that was not going to happen. After all, when warned that his top domestic advisors would press him to raise taxes, Bush had replied, "I know. But I can't do that."

But the larger question remains: Why did some of the shrewdest political minds in Washington do so little to prepare the public and Bush skeptics for his decision or to explain it afterwards?

The obvious answer is probably the truest one. By the fall of 1990, President Bush was preoccupied with the classic work of statesmanship. He went about the business of building a domestic and international coalition to secure the vital interests of the United States against the threat to world order posed by Iraqi aggression. Although Bush did express concerns about how appearing to break his word would affect public assessments of his character, he was also convinced that a budget agreement with spending caps was the right thing for the country. And he was determined to get this issue off his plate so he could move on to the larger threat facing America and the world. After that, the people could judge.[79]

Therefore, once again, Bush's traditional conservative framework was at work: the onerous chore of campaigning could wait until Labor Day 1992, after the noble work of governing had occurred. Over the years, Bush had adapted his patrician ethos to the new realities of postwar American politics. The 1988 campaign against Dukakis proved that. But in the end, governing well was the important thing. As one close friend and advisor put it, Bush was "not the kind of guy who's going to stand up there and act, and bite his lip, and put on a charade . . . not even to stay as President of the United States."[80] Looking back, Bush observed, "My most heroic compromise cost me my job. I was turned on by the right wing of my own party and, yet, we handed President Clinton a growing economy, an economy growing over five percent in the last quarter of 1992. So the economics proved to be okay, but the politics killed me."[81]

The Vision Thing

Vice President Bush's 1988 presidential campaign was designed to implement Atwater's view of political warfare while expressing the yearning among many Americans for a de facto Reagan third term. As the managers of Bush's campaign decreed, the only issues to be highlighted were the ones that were being pushed at the end of Reagan's second term—lower taxes and a strong defense. Thus, until he secured the Republican nomination, candidate Bush carefully avoided doing anything that would differentiate him from President Reagan.[82]

Entering the fall campaign, Bush's team employed the same tactics they had used against Dole in the New Hampshire primary, this time against the Democrats' hapless presidential nominee, Michael Dukakis. Bush's 1988 campaign for the presidency deliberately offered very little by way of a positive agenda. Instead, it launched a virulent attack that was designed to demonstrate that Dukakis was not fit to be president, combined with a reassuring Reaganesque message that George Bush's no-new-taxes pledge would curb the growth of Washington's ever-expanding welfare state.[83]

Bush's acceptance speech at the Republican convention demonstrated the general strategy. On the one hand, there was the very specific, Dirty Harry–style promise of no new taxes. On the other hand, there were the graceful but vacuous phrases about a "kinder, gentler nation" shining forth with "a thousand points of light." Regarding a Bush domestic policy agenda, his words could mean anything. Thus, with a domestic agenda enveloped in intentional vagueness, George Bush took up the duties of chief executive in what would become America's first post–Cold War presidency.

Once the election was behind him, Bush and his senior advisors began the delicate and necessary task of showing that the new president was his own man and not just a stand-in for Ronald Reagan's third term. The differentiation soon appeared in staffing decisions. Sununu had performed superbly during the political ground war leading to Bush's victory in the New Hampshire primary and was highly regarded for his decisiveness and managerial effectiveness. He would become Bush's chief of staff.[84] But in making this early and important personnel decision, undertones of the split between traditional and movement conservatism were already apparent. Although Sununu was a Reagan supporter in the 1980 New Hampshire primary contest with Bush, he was not a movement conservative. On the contrary, Sununu's late-blossoming political career took off in the early 1980s in a New Hampshire political culture where the ideological division between liberal and conservative Republicans had not developed into sharp animosities.[85] In 1982, Vice President Bush's fund-raising support had been instrumental in securing Sununu's nomination and election as governor.

Similarly, there was no White House plan for getting rid of Reagan people in the bureaucracy after the 1988 election. But there was a concerted effort to give political appointments to individuals who had been personally loyal to George Bush over the years. All of these staffing changes were guided by old-school personal loyalty, not by an effort to pursue any particular policy or ideological agenda.[86] Given Bush's approach to domestic policy issues, it could hardly have been otherwise. Ronald Reagan adhered to a few very clear, basic tenets about the role of domestic government, defense, and foreign policy. His appointees were expected to understand and follow those guidelines without his supervision. Bush held a more complex view of the world. He relished the details of problem solving, especially in foreign policy and in his personal relations with foreign leaders.

At the same time President Bush was in a far weaker position than Reagan to promote whatever legislation his vision entailed. In contrast to Reagan, who had the benefit of a Republican-controlled Senate (until 1987) and friendly aid from conservative "blue dog Democrats" in the House, Bush faced a Democrat-controlled Congress. More than that, Democratic leaders, particularly Senate majority leader George Mitchell, were eager for partisan warfare that would cut the president down to size in a new post-Reagan era. In short, the smudgy lines of compromise were a necessary feature of getting anything done after 1988.[87]

So it is not surprising that Bush's domestic policy agenda was an emerging phenomenon, recognizable mostly in retrospect. In contrast to the forward-leaning ideological program of a movement conservative, Bush's domestic initiatives were conservative in the traditional sense. They expressed a disposition that was suspicious of radical changes. They developed gradually, through a predictable and slow-moving policy development process managed from the White House. They proposed careful small steps rather than bold leaps. Looked at in this way, Bush's "vision" was one of conserving the achievements of the past, taking modest steps to reform America's welfare state in a careful, incremental way.

The achievements of incrementalism come into focus only in history's rear-view mirror, but they are no less real on that account. Thanks to Bush's leadership, the financial and moral crisis of the savings and loan industry was cleaned up and not allowed to fester into a long-term problem that threatened the economy as a whole.[88] The Clean Air Act brought the new tool of emissions trading to America's pollution problem. The Americans with Disabilities Act gave disabled persons enforceable ways of gaining access to places and opportunities other Americans took for granted. With these and other publicly underappreciated policy enactments, the Bush domestic agenda, with its necessarily compromised objectives, crept along. In short, it turned out that candidate Bush's "kinder, gentler nation" meant modest, prudent domestic reform, not ideological confrontation.

None of these "small-bore" achievements impressed movement conservatives.[89] On the contrary, the piecemeal domestic policy reforms that gradually emerged from the convoluted bargaining process between various units of the Bush administration and Congress were political poison. Any one item might make sense in isolation and at the moment. But once in place in the bureaucracy, each new Bush "reform" laid new foundations for erecting new regulations, new federal spending, new self-seeking interest group coalitions, and then new policy "improvements" in the next round of legislative initiatives. From this perspective, Bush's supposedly prudent, incremental reforms were nothing more than a series of open invitations to expand big government in Washington. Thus, as movement conservatives viewed the administration's gradually emerging domestic policy agenda, the central fact seemed clear. Bush didn't believe in Reaganism. Their outrage simmered before boiling over with the budget agreement of October 1990.

The Reelection Thing

As Bush's approval rating reached 91 percent in the aftermath of the Gulf War, a degree of complacency in the White House was understandable in 1991. Still, compared to the preparations for his 1988 run for the presidency, Bush's campaign mobilization for the 1992 election was by all accounts languid, bordering on the comatose. Why was that?

As noted earlier, left to his own devices George Bush would have happily left the start of any political campaigning until Labor Day 1992. Before that, one attended to the more important business of governing. This was simply a carryover of the traditional conservative view that consigned campaigning and governing to separate compartments of public life.[90] When Bush looked at his watch during a debate with Clinton and independent candidate Ross Perot, he apparently meant to signal to the debate moderator that the pre-agreed time limits on speakers were being violated by Perot's long-winded answers. The deeper truth is that as a traditional conservative Bush despised the whole process. By his own account, he viewed the presidential campaign debates as nothing more than "ugly . . . contrived . . . show business."[91] Prescott Bush could not have said it better.

Bush's traditional conservative disposition was given room to express itself when the hard-driving Lee Atwater, whom Bush appointed as chair of the Republican National Committee, suddenly collapsed with a terminal brain tumor. After March 1990, Atwater began fading from the president's political world. The consequences for Bush's reelection effort were momentous. Atwater was the central figure in Bush's relation to the American voter—his nerve end into ordinary Americans' thinking about politics, his chief campaign strategist, his prod to acting ruthlessly in the new politics, and, most importantly, the friend Bush trusted in the uncomfortable, post-patrician world of "selling" candidates to voters while cutting opponents off at the knees. Atwater, it turned out, was irreplaceable, and without him, Bush's reelection effort was headed toward feckless drift.[92]

Or was it? After the triumph of the Gulf War, Darman, Quayle, and others urged Bush to mount a dramatic "Domestic Storm" policy offensive. They argued that such an initiative would throw the Democratic Congress on the defensive and provide a focus for building the 1992 campaign against a do-nothing Congress.

As Bush's senior advisors debated the idea, objections mounted.[93] The substance of such a grand vision was murky at best. The president's towering standing in public opinion polls meant there was no need for high-profile initiatives in domestic affairs. One could wait, elect more Republicans in 1992, and then pursue a well-thought-out Bush domestic agenda in the second term. Moreover, the president could rightfully take credit for the important pieces of domestic legislation that had already passed. At least as important, neither President Bush nor Darman cared anything for the "New Paradigm" empowerment ideas being pushed by Jack Kemp and his allies in the administration.[94]

Kemp had entered politics after a stellar career in professional football and served nine terms as a congressional representative from New York. In the run-up to Reagan's 1980 election, Kemp was a leading advocate of supply-side economics and co-sponsored the law that eventually resulted in President Reagan's 1981 tax cut. Moreover, Kemp was the first national lawmaker to promote tax-favored "enterprise zones" as a way of encouraging economic development in underserved urban neighborhoods. President Bush appointed Kemp as his secretary for housing and urban development, but he and his inner circle soon came to regard Kemp as a self-promoting loose cannon in the administration who had radical ideas of "empowerment" that harkened back to the 1960s. Secretary

Kemp and his renegade allies in the Bush administration waged a largely fruitless campaign for Kemp's new conservative domestic policy agenda.[95]

In the end, what mattered most was that George H. W. Bush did not think it was "good governance" to pound Congress in the way Darman and other advisors were urging. Instinctively, at something approaching a visceral level, Bush disliked the political blame game.[96] As he had learned to regard such things, blaming other people for the challenges you faced and should rise to overcome was a tawdry, unworthy way to win anything, whether in sports or politics. Again, Prescott Bush would have been proud. Thus, by the time John Sununu resigned as chief of staff in December 1991, the president was locked into a State of the Union message the following month that contained nothing resembling a dramatic domestic agenda. On that front, there would be very little upon which to build a 1992 Bush reelection campaign.[97]

All this being said, looming in the background was probably the most important reason for Bush's slow-motion engagement with the 1992 election campaign. Bush knew that he had performed admirably as commander-in-chief and as the nation's chief diplomat. He believed that a leader deserved the respect of voters for trying to do the right, if unpopular, thing about taxes. Surely voters would reward such meritorious public service.[98]

Compared with such world-scale statesmanship, Bush's possible Democratic challengers appeared small. Democratic heavyweights such as New York governor Mario Cuomo and Senator Bill Bradley had decided not to take on the popular president. As the election drew near, the smallest challenger of all in terms of character was Bill Clinton, the eventual Democratic nominee. Could it be that the nation would prefer a draft-dodging, womanizing "bozo" (Bush's term) to a World War II hero and president who had brilliantly defended the world against a Middle Eastern dictator's aggression? At least one senior advisor reminded Bush that British voters had thrown out Prime Minister Winston Churchill at the pinnacle of his wartime success. Still, President Bush and his senior advisors found it incredible that the American public and the media would not care about the character issue.[99]

Likewise, movement conservatives had no interest in responding to Bush's patrician faith in the rewards due for good character and meritorious service. George H. W. Bush's long and troubled dance with the conservative movement was now reaching its dénouement. In the beginning, during the 1950s and 1960s, the political discrepancy between the old and new conservatism had appeared as a tiny hairline crack in young George Bush's first ventures into Texas politics. This disconnect had been expressed in the *National Review* when Bush and Reagan had offered differing interpretations of the meaning of Barry Goldwater's defeat in 1964. By 1992, that hairline crack had become a chasm dividing Bush and the conservative movement. It was given expression in the New Hampshire Republican presidential primary that year. Bush had every right to feel battered by this conservative challenge to his renomination. Pat Buchanan, who won 37 percent of the New Hampshire primary vote, damaged Bush's standing in the Republican Party and with the general public.[100]

In response, Bush strategists sought reconciliation with movement conservatives by giving Buchanan a featured appearance during prime time at the Republican national convention. Buchanan's trumpet call on national TV to "take back America" thrilled many conservative activists. As with Barry Goldwater's similar convention language in 1964 ("extremism in the defense of liberty is no vice"), however, Buchanan's harsh militancy spooked moderates and independents across the nation. In the end, the Bush team's effort to placate conservatives was all for naught. The Buchanan and Gingrich wings deserted the president in the 1992 election, mostly by not showing up at the polling stations.

As the 1992 campaign drew to a close, a Wagnerian, Götterdämmerung aura permeated the Bush campaign operation. Always loyal to those he worked for, Bush was also exceptionally loyal to those who worked for him, even when that loyalty was not reciprocated. This virtue inhibited Bush from inflicting the punishments and personnel changes that could have strengthened his 1992 campaign machine. As one old friend and senior advisor put it, "He's a gentleman of the old school. . . . He doesn't seek scapegoats or chop heads off at the first sign of trouble. . . . He stuck with certain people too long."[101]

At the same time, loyalty to Bush within his own campaign operation was disintegrating. The malaise was expressed in messageless speeches, rounds of indecisive meetings, leaks, and half-hearted efforts by self-serving staffers intent on building their resumes. An aide to Vice President Quayle captured the general condition of things when he described a Bush aide in a neighboring office at the Old Executive Office Building: "The quintessential Bush underling, he was a man in whom vanity ran far deeper than conviction. He brought to public service the greedy zeal of a hobbyist, a loyalty dependent on the next presidential favor or keepsake. . . . How did an honorable, loyal man like George Bush wind up dependent on men so devoid of both virtues?"[102] Answering that question would yield material fit for a Greek tragedy.

The Paradox Thing

Bush may have been the best thing to happen to the populist conservative cause since the election of Ronald Reagan. Bush's one-term presidency ended up giving a powerful boost to the conservative movement, energizing its offensive strategy for the remainder of the 1990s.

As we have seen, in breaking his no-new-taxes pledge in 1990, the president provoked a dramatic revolt among House Republicans and grassroots conservatives. Before this, the leader of the conservative revolt, Congressman Newt Gingrich, was a fiery but rather lonely minority whip whose 1990 bid for reelection was in major trouble in Georgia.[103] Redistricting by the Democratic state legislature had eliminated his old seat, leading Gingrich to sell his home and move to a newly created district in the Atlanta suburbs. The fierce battle between conservative House Republicans and the Bush White House threw a new national spotlight on Newt Gingrich, and the congressman took full advantage of it. A little over a month after walking out of the budget deal, he managed to be reelected to Congress, winning by only 978 votes. Gingrich then mounted a successful challenge to displace moderate and bipartisan Robert Michel as House minority leader. Out of this came the 1994 Contract with America, followed by the Republican takeover of the House, Gingrich's speakership, two federal government shutdowns, and, eventually, the reelection and subsequent impeachment of President Clinton.

What is one to make of all this in assessing the broader meaning of George H. W. Bush and American conservatism? The truth is that if Bush had possessed the ruthless and dissembling character of a Richard Nixon or John Connally, odds are that he would have had greater success in walking the political tightrope stretched across his presidency between the old and the new conservatism. If Bush had not remained loyal to the standards of success embedded in his family's ethos, in traditional conservatism, and in his own character, he would not have been so easily exploited by his fellow Republican leaders. More specifically, he would not have been as vulnerable throughout his political career to being continually used and pummeled by more ruthless, less principled political figures.[104]

Yet amid all the power plays plotted by more ruthless competitors, George Bush not only survived but succeeded in reaching the presidency. There he performed as a leader of personal integrity who gave outstanding service to his country. Even more, Bush emerged as a man of profound republican virtue in the classic sense of that term. Under the Constitution, Americans have a system of representative self-government that is designed to discover and operate from the political center. By contrast, the new political system that evolved in the decades after World War II—our modern unwritten constitution—has created a regime that demands and rewards political polarization. It is a politics in which integrity, personal character and honest compromise count for little. In fact, they are much more likely to count against a person. Such polarized politics translates into "pseudo-governing." This disfigurement of our Constitution's design for a representative democracy achieves very little in terms of accomplishments through governing. But it does produce big short-term returns for ambitious individuals seeking to gain and then hold onto the privileged plums of public office. Still, the long-term consequences of such a political regime have become increasingly clear—the alienation of ordinary American citizens who are rightly disgusted by the short-sighted political manipulation of slogans and symbolic media events.[105]

Understanding Bush requires us to understand how his political career straddled this transition between the old and the new politics, between the old and the new conservatism. Bush was the last president to govern without the "permanent campaign" mindset that has become mandatory in modern American politics.[106] Given his family ethos, character, and political career, it could hardly have been otherwise. If tragedy is defined as a drama in which the outward failure of a person is compensated for by the dignity and greatness of his character, then Bush's 1992 defeat can truly be called tragic.

In trying to judge the success or failure of Bush's one-term presidency, it is at this point we come to the essence of things. What standard is to be used? Any such standard is not a proposition to be proved. It is more like a self-evident truth that would be accepted by any reasonable person at the beginning of an argument. If the standard of political success is measured by long-term institutional values and moral competence, then George Bush earns a very high grade. Or, as Prescott Bush might have said, "quite worthy . . . well done, son." This standard, although wholly secular, was well-articulated by Cardinal Joseph Ratzinger (later Pope Benedict XVI):

> It is or course always difficult to adopt a sober approach that does what is possible and does not cry enthusiastically after the impossible. The voice of reason is not as loud as the voice of unreason. The cry of the large-scale has the whiff of morality. In contrast, limiting oneself to what is possible seems to be renouncing the passions of morality and adopting the pragmatism of the faint-hearted. But in truth, political morality consists precisely in resisting the seductive temptation of the big words by which humanity and its opportunities are gambled away.[107]

Part II

WAR AND STATECRAFT

ORGANIZING SECURITY

How the Bush Presidency Made Decisions
on War and Peace

Bartholomew Sparrow

George Bush's handling put just enough tension on the line. You know,
it's like catching a 10-pound bass on a 3-lb line, you've got to keep
the tension in there because if you let it go too slack its snaps the
first time there's a pull, and if you have too much tension you can
snap it. He handled it exactly right and that was the art at the time;
to give them encouragement, to drag them along slowly, but not to
pull too hard because you can break the string. It was really an artful,
artful dance. And everybody's conventional wisdom was that it would
have happened anyway. I don't believe it. I don't believe it at all.

—John Sununu[1]

[The president and I] talked about it many times . . . and how fortunate
it was that we were on the right side of history in what we were doing.
We were not bucking a tide. We were trying to mold it and guide it into
channels that would produce the right outcome and be peaceful. Yes,
there was a sense of amazement through the whole administration.

—Brent Scowcroft

George Bush engaged the U.S. military in several conflicts during his single term
in office: the invasion of Panama (December 1989), the forcible eviction of Iraqi
forces from Kuwait (1991), and, at the end of his tenure, the intervention in
Somalia (December 1992–January 1993). Equally significant was what the president and his advisors did not do. They did not occupy Iraq after successfully
counterattacking and devastating Iraq's infrastructure and air defenses. They did
not go into Kosovo, Bosnia, or elsewhere in the former Yugoslavia. And they did
not have to use force to effect the extraordinary reunification of Germany within
NATO; the democratic transitions in Poland, Hungary, and elsewhere in Eastern
Europe; and, ultimately, the dissolution of the Soviet Union.

The Bush administration conducted its foreign policy very successfully.[2] Even critics of the Bush presidency acknowledge that the president and his advisors achieved almost all of their objectives and that the Bush White House managed national security perhaps as well as it could have been managed in a momentous era of world history. Their success was in large measure the product of the policy process—the administration's comprehensive attention to the means of organizing national security affairs. "Process" included focusing on the personnel nominated and appointed to cabinet and subcabinet positions; President Bush, Secretary of State James A. Baker III, and National Security Advisor Brent Scowcroft all believed in the fundamental importance of getting the right people in the right slots. It meant paying close attention to the role of the national security advisor as the manager of the interagency procedures for formulating national security policy. Finally, the president and Scowcroft emphasized the organization of the bureaucracy—specifically, determining the venues and the ways in which decisions were made.

The consequence of the Bush White House's comprehensive attention to the policy process was that outsiders could discern little daylight between the foreign policy principals and Bush's policy positions. Nor were there many leaks from within the administration or much embarrassing publicity about Bush's foreign policy (news and commentary on U.S.-China relations after the Tiananmen Square massacre were a notable exception). Because of its tight focus on process, the Bush administration was able to act surely and quickly on pressing issues once they arose.[3]

Personnel

George Bush's first move as president-elect, which he announced the day after his election in November 1988, was to choose James A. Baker as his secretary of state. A former Marine, an able and successful attorney, a campaign manager, and treasury secretary and White House chief of staff under President Ronald Reagan, Jim Baker had been friends with Bush for thirty-five years. The two were as close as brothers, Bush the older and Baker the younger, and they often competed as if they were brothers.[4]

Bush's next personnel decision, which he made just after Thanksgiving, was to select Brent Scowcroft as his national security advisor. Scowcroft was a retired air force lieutenant general, who had worked as deputy to National Security Advisor Henry Kissinger (1973–75) and served as national security advisor under President Gerald Ford. He had known George Bush since the Nixon administration, when Bush had been U.S. ambassador to the United Nations (1971–73) and chairman of the Republican National Committee (1973–74). The two became further acquainted during the Ford presidency, when Bush was U.S. liaison to China (1974–75) and director of central intelligence (1976–77). In the Reagan years, Scowcroft headed the president's Commission on Strategic Forces, also known as the Scowcroft Commission (1983), and was one of three members of the Tower Board that investigated the Iran-Contra affair (1986–87) when Bush was vice president.[5] Scowcroft and the president-elect were friends as well as peers, and they shared many of the same views on the substance and the conduct of foreign policy. Bush, although slightly older than Scowcroft, treated his national security advisor like "a beloved older brother."[6]

Scowcroft had witnessed the friction between Secretary of State William Rogers and National Security Advisor Kissinger in the first years of the Nixon administration, when Richard Nixon chose to work closely with his national security advisor rather than his secretary of state, thereby cutting Rogers out of high-level decision making. He had observed the clashes between Zbigniew Brzezinski and Cyrus Vance under President Jimmy Carter, when Carter allowed Brzezinski as national security advisor to dominate foreign policy making, notwithstanding Vance's senior position as secretary of state. As a member of the Tower Board, Scowcroft had to clean up the damage done domestically and internationally to the American presidency and repair the national security policy process after the harmful conflict between Secretary of Defense Caspar Weinberger and Secretary of State George Shultz. As vice president, Bush had witnessed the feuding first-hand.[7]

Bush and Scowcroft sought to get the personnel right; they wanted people of ability who could get along with each other. From late November through late December, Scowcroft and Bush worked on personnel issues during long walks around the perimeter of Camp David. Not only did they discuss who would be on the National Security Council (NSC) and NSC staff, the president-elect also asked Scowcroft for his views on other key appointments and the two mulled over how they would proceed once in office. (The NSC's statutory members are the president, the vice president, the secretary of state, and the secretary of defense; as a practical matter, its members include the national security advisor, the director of central intelligence, the chairman of the Joint Chiefs of Staff, and sometimes the treasury secretary, other cabinet secretaries and agency heads, and often their seconds.)[8]

One of the first steps Scowcroft took to gain control of the national security process was to appoint Robert Gates as his deputy. Gates had served in the air force, had worked as a young staffer in President Ford's NSC, and, most recently, had served as deputy director of central intelligence under President Reagan. Scowcroft had followed Gates's career, knew him well, and thought he would make an ideal deputy, one who could be his alter ego. He wanted someone who could step into his shoes when needed, whether for a meeting with the president, the vice president, the secretary of state, the secretary of defense, the director of central intelligence, chairman of the Joint Chiefs of Staff, or others. Arnold Kanter, who worked with closely with both men while on the NSC staff, said he was not aware of anything that Scowcroft knew that Gates did not. Gates, who was a half-generation younger than Scowcroft and Bush, also had a good rapport with the president.[9]

With Gates effectively serving as his double, Scowcroft formed a de facto partnership for running the NSC. By building redundancy into the national security advisor position, he helped to ensure that the processes he set up would be followed and the president's decisions would be carried out. By elevating Gates to the position of his near equal—similar to how Kissinger had treated Scowcroft from September 1973 through October 1975—Scowcroft departed from the usual relationship between the national security advisor and his deputy. "The first thing that Brent arranged that conveyed a different sort of status for me at the deputy assistant to the president level that was unique was that I would have portal-to-portal secure transportation," Gates remarked. A White House car picked Gates up in the morning at his house, brought him to work, and took him home at night. "That was never done for a deputy assistant before."

Not long after, less than two months into President Bush's term, Scowcroft appointed Gates as "assistant to the president," thereby making Gates Scowcroft's equal in seniority. This was another unprecedented step; Gates now officially outranked all of the president's deputy assistants and special assistants, and it was rank that determined where someone could sit on Air Force One and ride in the presidential motorcade. "These little status things conveyed a message within the White House and throughout the government that this was a different sort of arrangement than had ever existed before," Gates remarked. He "had an access to the president and a role in the White House that had no parallel" with the previous ways the deputy national security advisor position had been operationalized. The "little status things," in other words, were not so little.

Scowcroft's second hire was Condoleezza Rice.[10] Scowcroft had been a mentor to Rice since meeting her at a 1985 dinner at Stanford and thought she was "just outstanding." He proceeded to promote Rice's career by inviting her to Aspen Strategy Group meetings and introducing her to other policymakers and foreign policy experts. Like Scowcroft, she was self-confident, poised under pressure, and good on her feet. She also had very strong powers of exposition and was extremely articulate. A superb teacher, Rice could communicate complex ideas in an accessible manner, again like Scowcroft, who had taught at West Point and the United States Air Force Academy.[11] She was analytical, unemotional, and non-ideological and like Scowcroft saw the Soviet Union more in shades of gray than in black and white.[12] And they both spoke Russian. Although Rice could have worked in the State Department—Dennis Ross, who was head of policy planning, wanted her to join his office—she chose to become the Soviet expert on the NSC staff.

Other selections by Scowcroft and Gates included Bob Blackwill as head of the European desk and Philip Zelikow as the director for European security affairs. Some of their appointees they knew, others they only knew of by reputation or came recommended. Whatever the case, Scowcroft and Gates wanted self-starters who would not require much supervision. Significantly, none of their personnel decisions was based on party affiliation and none was in response to a request by President Bush. Two areas were particularly sensitive: the Middle East and defense policy and arms control. Scowcroft chose the very capable Richard Haass for the former and Kanter for the latter. The resultant NSC staff—which was about 25 percent smaller than it had been in the preceding Reagan White House—required minimal supervision and exhibited little bureaucratic drama.

Because Scowcroft wanted to make a clean break with his predecessors, he told Reagan's national security advisor, General Colin Powell, to let the staff know that they should not plan on remaining in office. In fact, the president and his national security advisor treated all Reagan appointees this way, even though most of them, understandably, expected to stay at least for a short while since Bush had been Reagan's vice president. Instead, the few who kept their positions were the exceptions. Everyone else was shown the door. The sudden transition struck some outgoing officeholders as abrupt, even callous. Both the outgoing secretary of defense, Frank Carlucci, and the departing secretary of state, George Shultz, for instance, thought that the incumbent officeholders had been dismissed gracelessly and without proper recognition of their contributions.[13]

In the Department of State, James Baker assembled his own management team. His inner circle consisted of Robert Zoellick, Dennis Ross, Margaret Tutwiler, Robert Kimmitt, Larry Eagleburger, and Janet Mullins. Eagleburger, a career foreign service officer who former president Nixon described as "utterly loyal" and "smart as a shithouse rat," played a particularly important role.[14] As deputy secretary of state, Eagleburger was the chief operating officer of the State Department and was responsible for managing day-to-day business and attending meetings when Baker was out of town. Eagleburger also coordinated state department operations with the White House and smoothed out differences between State and Scowcroft and his NSC staff.

Had Baker not chosen Eagleburger as his deputy, Scowcroft probably would have done so. Eagleburger and Scowcroft were old friends who had both worked under Kissinger in the Nixon and Ford administrations and then joined him at Kissinger Associates, Inc., in the 1980s. In fact, Bush, Baker, and Scowcroft had all known each other for decades; had little to prove to each other, to the Washington policy community, or to the national press; and all got along. Scowcroft also worked well with White House Chief of Staff John Sununu—for fun, they would take turns insulting each other—and Sununu respected Scowcroft for his knowledge of national security policy and the bureaucracy. Although Sununu was typically forceful and outspoken, he was happy to leave foreign policy to the president, Baker, and Scowcroft.[15]

Sununu did not interfere with the memos Scowcroft sent to Bush and did not attempt to block Scowcroft's unlimited access to the president. Scowcroft was the only one besides Sununu who could go into the Oval Office and interrupt the president at any time (Baker could as well, but his office was at Foggy Bottom and he was often abroad). As Richard Haass observed, Sununu "knew not to get in the way of Scowcroft's relationship with the President." The same held true with respect to the secretary of state. The one time Sununu treaded on his turf, Baker exploded and chewed him out—with the president there as witness, Baker recalled.

The careful selection of personnel and attention to personal chemistry extended to two later additions to the Bush White House: Dick Cheney, who became secretary of defense two months into the administration after the Senate refused to confirm Senator John Tower's nomination; and Colin Powell, who replaced Admiral William Crowe as chairman of the Joint Chiefs of Staff on September 30, 1989. Cheney, who had been chief of staff under President Ford and then House minority leader, and Powell, who had been national security advisor under Reagan after serving as an assistant to defense secretaries Caspar Weinberger and Frank Carlucci, were both self-assured, on friendly terms with President Bush, and familiar with the ways of the Washington bureaucracy. They, too, had established reputations and little to prove.[16]

American presidents usually do not know how their appointees will interact with their each other and therefore cannot anticipate the backbiting and other bureaucratic battles that will occur in their administrations. President Bush, however, because of his deep foreign policy experience and his careful selection and matching of personnel, was able to form a foreign policy team of unusual loyalty, capability, and coherence. As Chase Untermeyer, the president's personnel director, remarked, "George Bush was probably the first president since Franklin Roosevelt or even before who was acquainted with all of the members of his cabinet before he named them. . . . Various presidents, famously John F. Kennedy, or Bill Clinton, were given names of people who on paper looked good and either proved to be great winners, like McNamara was for Kennedy, or losers in more cases."

The close friendship, mutual respect, and frequent levity that prevailed among the principals and top aides of the Bush administration served to deflate tensions in times of crisis and eased the handling of the inevitable disagreements when they arose. There "was an element of trust that made it a delight to go to work every day," Cheney noted. "You never had to worry that the secretary of state or the NSC Advisor was going to take something you said, use it out of context, leak it to the press, or take advantage somehow in the bureaucratic wars. There was the concept that it was a team." For Haass, the Bush White House was the most collegial of any in the four administrations in which he had worked. Working there "was actually fun. It sounds bizarre, but it was by far the most enjoyable experience a lot of us had had before or since in government. There was a lot of camaraderie and kidding around . . . it was very relaxed."

What helped matters immensely was the fact that George Bush cared about foreign policy. He enjoyed diplomacy and personally knew many foreign officials and most heads of state and government as a result of his experiences as vice president, liaison to China, director of central intelligence, and ambassador to the United Nations. He also liked keeping up with national security affairs and reading intelligence briefings. A practical man, Bush thought that smart people should be able to reach reasonable agreements. And his top White House appointees and other personnel choices in the government reflected his personality and tone. Because of the priority Bush assigned to foreign policy, in fact, he insisted that either Scowcroft or Gates be available at all times. Scowcroft therefore traveled with the president when he went overseas, and Gates accompanied Bush on most domestic trips.

The National Security Advisor Role

Bush and Scowcroft wanted to be sure that national security policymaking functioned smoothly and was not dragged down by bureaucratic battles. As a result of the Iran-Contra affair, for instance, Shultz had been "traumatized by the NSC and wanted to reduce the NSC to an executive secretariat," Carlucci reported.[17] Yet if the new Bush administration were to successfully manage national security policy, the policy process had to be as thoroughly thought out as personnel selections were.

Accordingly, Scowcroft designed the structure of the NSC system to maximize the chances of success.[18] Scowcroft had explicitly spelled out the role of the national security advisor in "Part V" of the *Tower Commission* report, the section he had drafted. The national security advisor's responsibility, Scowcroft wrote, was to "ensure that matters submitted for consideration by the [National Security] Council covered the full range of issues on which review was required; that those issues were fully analyzed; that a full range of options was considered; that the prospects and risks of each were examined; that all relevant intelligence and other information was available to the principals; that legal considerations were addressed; and that difficulties in implementation were confronted." The job of the national security advisor was to manage the national security process with skill, sensitivity, and integrity. And ideally, the national security advisor should operate behind the scenes with a "passion for anonymity."[19]

In Scowcroft's view, the national security advisor had to be an honest broker: fair when representing the views of the president's other principal advisors, impartial when offering competing policy options to the president, and straightforward when presenting his or her own advice to the president if asked to do so. Serving as an honest broker meant more than neutrally determining what the common positions were on national security issues and then presenting the president with distinct policy options. It meant giving the president unvarnished advice when solicited—advice "unalloyed by department responsibilities and interests," in Scowcroft's words. Although the secretary of defense and secretary of state had to represent their departments and could not stray too often or too far from the strongly held views of their staffs, the national security advisor had no client other than the president. Scowcroft acknowledged that he had his biases, but they were not institutional biases.

Even so, Scowcroft understood the importance of not steering the president's thinking, since a "lot of times you can get the answer you want by the way you ask the question." This, he believed, was how the Iran-Contra affair had happened. Scowcroft also knew that care had to be taken when interpreting the president's guidance. If he had any doubt after a meeting about what the president had decided, Scowcroft would write down his understanding of the conversation and take it back to the Oval Office, thereby ensuring "that this [was] exactly what [the president] had in mind." Miscommunication was surprisingly common, Scowcroft found. Many times after an NSC meeting "he would write up the decision and others would say, no that's not what happened."[20]

If Scowcroft as national security advisor was to realize the objectives stated in the *Tower Commission* report and give the president the best advice possible, he had to keep his eye on the ball—that is, on the near-term and the long-term security interests of the United States. He had to be able to act as a check on and serve as an extra resource for the president and his principal advisors, if need be, so as to safeguard the nation's security interests, whether military, political, or economic. As a practical matter, this meant that the national security advisor might have to challenge the options that a secretary of state or chairman of the Joint Chiefs brought before the National Security Council and the president, as happened in October 1990, when Scowcroft challenged the Joint Chiefs' plans for how to attack Iraqi forces in the Gulf. In other circumstances, the national security advisor might have to persuade the president to consider certain implications of a policy that the secretary of state, the defense secretary, or another official had not considered when proposing it. In other words, the job of the national security advisor went beyond brokering—contrary to what the term "honest broker" might connote—to include being responsible for the quality of the political choices and policy options made available to the president.[21]

Scowcroft followed his own prescriptions. He fostered the intellectual atmosphere and emotional pitch he wanted in the NSC through his personnel appointments, through his (and Gates's) rules of behavior, and through leading by example. He was thereby able to create an efficient, informal, and remarkably cordial atmosphere within which the work of foreign policy making could be done. He was further able to get the other chief foreign policy advisors—Baker, Cheney, Powell, Vice President Quayle, and others—to accept his vision of how the national security policy-making process would be managed. Trust was at the core of the atmosphere he wanted to foster: the belief that the principals could rely on and were accountable to each other and that the interests of the president and the greater interests of the United States came before any personal or bureaucratic interests.

With his cordial and self-effacing manner, Scowcroft made this easy. He was "as abrasive as a silk scarf," as Fred McClure, the president's assistant for congressional relations, described him. Early in 1989, for instance, Scowcroft reassured Secretary of State Baker that there would be no repeat of the hostile Kissinger-Rogers relationship or Brzezinski-Vance conflict and that he would not speak to the press or go on any talk shows without first informing Baker. Neither he nor any other member of the NSC staff would meet with or visit a foreign leader without first notifying Baker. Similarly, Gates recalled that although he could have easily kept the chief of staff out of the loop, Scowcroft sent Sununu copies of national security memos and otherwise kept him informed.

Scowcroft also let Baker know that he saw the president and secretary of state as the main spokespersons for the administration. Since as national security advisor he was not subject to Senate confirmation and could not be called to testify before Congress, Scowcroft felt it appropriate that he remain in the background. He appeared on television or allowed himself to go on record in the press only infrequently. Happily, the "passion for anonymity" that Scowcroft recommended in the *Tower Commission* report fit his personality. To the extent that he worked with the media, it was typically on background. Whenever possible, Scowcroft deflected attention to Baker, Cheney, Powell, or others, such as General Norman Schwarzkopf.

By the same token, if the national security process was to work there could be only one message coming from the White House. So when one of Scowcroft's NSC staff members was found to be the source of a news leak, he was out of a job.

Likewise, when Defense Secretary Cheney said in early 1989 that "Gorbachev's going to fail," Baker called Bush, and the president subsequently "cut the ground out from Dick quicker than you can imagine," as Baker described it. And when the General Michael Dugan, the air force chief of staff, made unapproved statements in September 1990 about the Pentagon's war plans for Iraq, Cheney immediately asked for Dugan's resignation. With precedents such as these, others in the administration were loath to make statements or release information without clearance from the president's top advisors. As a consequence, leaks about national security issues—except for those made strategically by Secretary of State Baker—were relatively few.

Organizing the Bureaucracy

In order to manage national security affairs effectively—including not requiring any more of the president's time than absolutely needed—Scowcroft, with permission from Bush, established a series of formal and informal bodies for handling information and making decisions.

The Deputies Committee, which consisted of representatives from the State Department, the Defense Department, the CIA, the NSC, the Joint Chiefs of Staff, and, depending on the issue, other agencies, served as the administration's workhorse. Although previous presidential administrations had relied on the Deputies Committee, what distinguished the Bush White House was the degree to which the deputies were trusted by their principals. As a result, the Deputies Committee was effectively able not only to make policy but also to handle crises. The meetings of the Deputies Committee enabled Gates (and then his successor, Admiral Jonathan Howe) and his number two or number three counterparts in Defense (Paul Wolfowitz), State (Robert Kimmitt), CIA (Richard Kerr), and the Joint Chiefs (Admiral David Jeremiah)—each of whom had decision-making authority—to consult regularly and sort out issues face-to-face. These interagency meetings, which Gates usually chaired, facilitated agreement before the issues went to the principals and then, if necessary, to the president. The Deputies Committee met frequently to discuss pressing issues and new events, and any of the deputies could call a meeting if he thought one was necessary. Often there would be more than one Deputies Committee meeting per day.[22]

Gates described the importance of the Deputies Committee in the context of the Persian Gulf War: "I'm not sure that before a war was ever launched that there was a precedent in our government for sitting down and articulating very explicitly what our war aims would be, what our objectives in the war would be. But that's what we did with the Gulf War, and the Deputies Committee did that." The

Deputies Committee looked at three options, Gates said: "one was destroying the Republican Guard, the second was throwing Saddam out of Kuwait, and the third was bring[ing] about a change of regime in Baghdad. Well, we agreed on the first two in about ten minutes and we spent two weeks debating the third one." What made the Deputies Committee work was that the debates about going to war against Iraq—"Is this a realizable objective? How do you actually make that happen? . . . Do you have to occupy Iraq to get it?"—were waged not on paper, with memos going back and forth, but in real-time and in person, Gates remarked. The administration had "just gone through the experience in Panama of not being able to find Noriega, eight or nine months before, and we had a hell of lot more information and a hell of a lot more presence in Panama than we were going to have in Iraq. To what degree are we likely to shatter the coalition if we try to bring out a change in regime?"

The Deputies Committee worked consistently well because Gates and the other deputies had the confidence of their respective principals. Thus empowered, everyone showed up at the meetings, even if by videoconference. "There were really very, very few substitutions," Gates noted. "Very rarely would somebody not be able to come."

Because of the effectiveness of the Deputies Committee, full NSC meetings were infrequent after the administration's first few months; the several that occurred in the immediate aftermath of the Iraqi invasion of Kuwait were among the few exceptions. Only occasionally were Baker, Cheney, and Scowcroft compelled to step in to resolve persisting disagreements personally; even more infrequently did they have to take issues to President Bush for his decision.

Operating at a level beneath the Deputies Committee and admittedly of less significance were the NSC Policy Coordinating Committees, which were established for the purpose of sharing information and coordinating action in particular regions of the world such as Europe and Latin America or in different functional areas, such as defense and international economics. These committees, which were renamed the Interagency Working Groups in the Clinton administration, either dealt with issues mid-level officials could handle, those below the rank of the deputies and principals, or prepared issues for referral to the Deputies Committee.[23]

Above the Deputies Committees, Scowcroft created the Principals Committee, a meeting of the foreign policy principals except for the president. Scowcroft had noticed that in President Reagan's NSC meetings a lot of time had been wasted on debates over issues that did not involve presidential-level decisions. He wanted to establish a smaller decision-making body that consisted of the secretary of state, the secretary of defense, the director of central intelligence, the chairman of the Joint Chiefs of Staff, the White House chief of staff, and himself.

Because he saw his role as national security advisor as arbiter, intermediary, and facilitator, Scowcroft chaired the meetings.

Forming the Principals Committee gave Scowcroft a forum in which to discuss issues and clarify positions with the other foreign policy principals. As a result, when Scowcroft went to the president with a policy proposal, he had "crisp" positions to present. Although the Reagan administration had established a Principals Committee near the end of its second term when Colin Powell was national security advisor, that committee never convened because Shultz, who outranked Powell, refused to allow the national security advisor to chair a meeting at which he was in attendance.[24] It was "with temerity," then, that Scowcroft proposed the idea to Baker, who was very much aware of his predecessor's views. But Baker said, "Fine, let's do it."

Scowcroft also formed the Core Group. Because of the frustration he experienced when there were press leaks after the first National Security Council meeting (a meeting that could include as many as thirty persons, since the principals could all bring their seconds and various "straphangers"), Scowcroft formed the smaller and less formal Core Group, which consisted of the foreign policy principals plus the president—essentially the National Security Council as originally designed in 1947 plus the national security advisor. The Core Group was formed in March 1989, when the White House was reviewing the studies Scowcroft had assigned for the purpose of reevaluating U.S. foreign policies—especially those that were relevant for Europe and the Soviet Union—and Scowcroft held an open session among the principals to promote candid discussion. The meeting, which took place without notes, without debriefings, and without prepared remarks, was very productive. Afterward, President Bush said, "Gee, I liked that," and the format stuck.

A series of three meetings held in January 1990 to discuss the Intermediate-Range Nuclear Forces Treaty and troop reductions in Europe exemplified the effectiveness of the Core Group. The Defense and State Departments were both opposed to troop reductions and were worried about the anticipated European reactions, while Scowcroft and others supported the treaty and the force reductions. With the group at an impasse, Scowcroft proposed that they ask the Europeans what they wanted. When the Europeans agreed to the reductions, the force deductions were then implemented. The advantage of the Core Group setting was that each principal could have his say in an uninhibited discussion. It freed the meetings from the restraints imposed by the attendance of backbenchers and others who might inhibit open discussion, leak self-serving information, and provoke a political backlash. With its restricted membership, informality, and effectiveness, the Core Group resembled Ex-Com, the group that was formed in the Kennedy administration to handle the Cuban Missile Crisis.[25]

Smaller, even more informal meetings also proved fruitful. During weekly lunches Scowcroft talked things over with President Bush and Secretary of State Baker, and in their 7:00 Wednesday breakfast meetings Scowcroft sorted things out with Baker and Cheney (and sometimes Powell) in his West Wing corner office. Over breakfast, Baker, Cheney, and Scowcroft were able to discuss whatever issues had arisen and were able to work out any interagency differences that had not already been resolved by the Deputies Committee. Because of these weekly meetings, relatively few issues ("four or five," Baker reports) had to be taken to President Bush for resolution. They "work[ed] them out in Brent's office" instead. Other administrations had similar informal meetings, but what made the Bush administration's meetings noteworthy was the degree to which these forums succeeded at settling interagency differences.

Still other decisions were made by Bush and Scowcroft themselves. Bush did nothing in foreign policy and little in domestic matters without first talking to Scowcroft. Although Baker also met privately with the president on a weekly basis and although the two men had their own special relationship, Bush and Baker did not discuss much policy in their meetings, which were generally occasions for the old friends to catch up.

Defense Secretary Cheney described President Bush's style of decision making during crises, as during the Persian Gulf War:

> Much decision making took place around the fireplace in the Oval Office, might be upstairs in his residence, in his office up there. He was comfortable in that kind of a setting. It was not a formal sort of arrangement. It would involve Baker and [Cheney,] Powell and Scowcroft, Quayle, Sununu usually. Sometimes Bill Webster, Bob Gates—Bob Gates would be usually involved. That's where a lot of the management of a crisis would actually take place. . . . Separate, apart from that, if you move off that to more normal peacetime operation, he did an awful lot in the diplomatic arena and the State Department arena, between himself and Jim and Brent, that I wouldn't be directly involved and didn't need to be directly involved.

These informal and formal decision making processes allowed for close, sustained interactions among the principals on issues of importance and sensitivity. This, of course, is where the principals' collegiality and mutual trust particularly mattered. Although some of the Bush administration's success was because of the groups Scowcroft set up, the NSC system depended on much more than formal meetings and specialized committees, as NSC staff member Robert Hutchings has pointed out.[26] If the national security policy-making system was to be successful, it had to be flexible and allow for creativity. The organization Scowcroft set up and Bush approved facilitated such flexibility and creativity.

One of Scowcroft's other innovations was to establish a special version of the Deputies Committee to handle the many issues that arose from Europe's transformation in 1989 and 1990, especially German reunification and the restructuring of military forces. Baker wanted four State representatives to be working on European issues, Ivo Daalder and I. M. Destler report in *In the Shadow of the Oval Office*. Scowcroft obliged by establishing the ad hoc European Security Strategy Group, which included four members from State—Zoellick (counselor for the State Department), Kimmitt (undersecretary for political affairs), Dennis Ross (head of policy planning), and Reginald Bartholomew (undersecretary for international security)—as well as representatives from Defense, the NSC, and other agencies.[27]

In another important move, Scowcroft established the ad hoc "Un-Group" to deal with the profoundly important and highly technical issues of strategic weapons and arms control—issues that President Bush and most of the principals knew little about but which were Scowcroft's area of expertise. The Un-Group handled negotiations with the Soviet Union over START II, chemical and biological weapons, open skies, and conventional force levels in Europe. Later, it dealt with the threat of loose nuclear weapons, nuclear proliferation, and the fate of top Soviet scientists and engineers. What would happen to the Soviet equivalents of Wernher von Braun and the 118 German rocket scientists who came to the United States after the Second World War, for instance?

The genius of the Un-Group was that it included experts who were senior enough to get their principals' buy-ins and were also specialized enough to have strategic weapons and arms control as their sole or their dominant portfolio. Arnold Kanter, the NSC's senior director for arms control and defense policy, chaired the Un-Group, which also included the head of the now-defunct Arms Control and Disarmament Agency, an assistant secretary in the Office of the Secretary of Defense, and representatives from the CIA and the Joint Chiefs. Because it included personnel at different levels of seniority, however, the Un-Group could not officially exist the way the Deputies Committee or the Policy Coordinating Committees could—hence its name.[28]

The lack of equivalence among personnel ranks did not hinder the effectiveness of the Un-Group. On the contrary, the team's members hung their organizational hats at the door, as Kanter put it. Its ad hoc, even rogue quality may actually have made it more effective by serving to encourage innovation in the cause of solving real and serious problems. Among its accomplishments, the Un-Group succeeded in getting Ukraine, Belarus, and Kyrgyzstan to give up their nuclear weapons

(Russia retained its weapons). At least one observer thought the Un-Group was the single most successful interagency group of the Bush presidency.[29]

It is easy to forget the absoluteness with which people perceived the political, economic, and ideological divisions that separated the United States from the Soviet Union. It is also easy to forget how quickly things happened when the Soviet empire and then the Soviet Union dissolved. Soon after leaving the Bush administration in the spring of 1991, for instance, Condi Rice said of the Soviet Union's prospects and its longevity: "People ask me, 'Well, what are you going to do now?' as if it's all over. The Soviet Union is still going to be there. It's not like studying the Ottoman Empire—the Soviet Union is going to be around for a long time to come."[30]

Within months of Rice's statement the Soviet Union ceased to exist, and the Bush administration deserves immense credit for its management of relevant national security policy. Largely because of the attention Bush, Scowcroft, and Baker paid to process—to the personnel staffing foreign policy issues and the interactions among those persons, to the critical role of the national security advisor as the manager of the process, and to the coordination of information and decision making among the departments and agencies—the administration was able to oversee the peaceful reunification of Germany within NATO, to successfully prepare for and wage the remarkable victory in the Persian Gulf War, and to manage the essentially peaceful dissolution of the Soviet Union. The processes put in place by Scowcroft and, by extension, President Bush, greatly facilitated the smooth conduct of national security policymaking.

Not every element of Bush's foreign policy went so smoothly. The administration could have done a better job of dealing with Panama and Manuel Noriega, especially with the coup attempt of October 2, 1989. It could have handled U.S.-China relations more adroitly after the Tiananmen Square massacre, particularly with the handling of Congress and the Pelosi Amendment. It is also possible to second-guess how the Bush White House dealt with the complex and centrifugal forces in the former Yugoslavia. And the Bush administration has come under criticism for insufficiently preparing the ground for a new grand strategy in the aftermath of the Cold War. One of the drawbacks to the NSC system set up under Scowcroft was that the careful selection of personnel and the well-organized and tightly coordinated processes led to a degree of insularity. It may be that the policy process produced fewer alternative perspectives and a narrower set of policy options than under a less controlled and less organized decision-making process. Yet considering the immense challenges Bush's foreign policy team faced and how quickly events came at them, their balance sheet is distinctly in the black.

Organizing Security under George Bush and George W. Bush

The George W. Bush administration had many of the same people working in it (Cheney, Powell, Rice, Wolfowitz, Haass, Stephen Hadley, and others) and faced many of the same problems (Iraq and Saddam Hussein, U.S.-China relations, and others) as the George Bush administration did. A comparison of the national security decision-making processes of the George Bush and George W. Bush presidencies thus offers an instructive contrast in the organization of national security. The ways top personnel were selected, the roles played by the national security advisor, and the operations of the NSC system loom large in accounting for the two administrations' diverging experiences.

President George W. Bush picked his top aides on the basis of talent and political stature rather than on the basis of their abilities to work well together. Although Bush was acquainted with Colin Powell, Donald Rumsfeld, Dick Cheney, and Condoleezza Rice, his foreign policy principals did not have particularly good chemistry, as their personal accounts of their times in office, the writings of historians, and journalists' reports have made clear. Secretary of State Powell had perhaps the greatest public reputation of all of the Bush administration's foreign policy principals, yet Vice President Cheney and Secretary of Defense Rumsfeld were able to undermine Powell's effectiveness and otherwise operate around the State Department. Ultimately, they succeeded in getting a reluctant Powell to go along with the president's and their plans to attack Iraq by making an important speech on February 3, 2003, to the United Nations General Assembly.

Rumsfeld also had strained relations with General Hugh Shelton, chairman of the Joint Chiefs of Staff, and other top military leaders. Former defense secretary William Perry observed that the relationship between Rumsfeld and military leaders was as bad as he had ever seen, according to David Rothkopf, a former NSC staffer. Neither Rumsfeld nor Cheney greatly respected Rice. A generation younger and with only three years of previous government experience, Rice usually deferred to the two older, more experienced men in meetings and in public (at least during Bush's first term in office) and was reluctant to confront either of them on issues on which she differed. Rather than hashing out agreements or insisting on her own position when there were disagreements—and Cheney often worked in tandem with Rumsfeld, his former boss, thereby making Rice's work that much harder—she was more comfortable papering over the differences among the foreign policy principals. Only later would she then discuss her thoughts and reactions with the president, since she was much closer personally to Bush than was Cheney, Rumsfeld, or any other official. Thus, in stark contrast to the interactions among George H. W. Bush's top advisors, the interaction of

George W. Bush's foreign policy principals was characterized by a marked absence of affection, trust, and camaraderie.[31]

National Security Advisor Rice did not see her role in the same way as did Scowcroft, her mentor, former boss, and friend. Initially, Rice said that she wanted to emulate Scowcroft's model—that is, she wanted to return to a smaller and organizationally flatter NSC staff, to attend to process, and to keep a lower profile than had her predecessor in the Clinton White House, Sandy Berger.[32] Once in office, however, Rice departed from Scowcroft's model and his prescriptions in the *Tower Commission* report. Rice did not, as a routine matter, systematically integrate and analyze the information collected by the various agencies and departments. She did not, as a rule, compensate for other principals' blind spots by offering the president a fuller set of policy options (or, if she did, she kept such recommendations and such conversations private). And she did not remain in the background, instead becoming a public figure who often spoke publicly for the Bush presidency, especially after the events of September 11, 2001.

As a result, the George W. Bush administration made serious mistakes in foreign policy, the two most noteworthy being its lack of response to the evidence of an impending terrorist attack in the summer of 2001 and its repeated assertions that Iraq possessed weapons of mass destruction. The evidence pointing to an airborne terrorist attack in mid-2001 was never fully integrated, it was not carefully analyzed, and it was not clearly communicated to the president, as Richard Clarke and others have noted.[33] Neither was there a thorough and impartial assessment of the evidence about Iraq's possession of weapons of mass destruction, which was the premise for the war against Iraq.[34] Instead of coordinating information and decision making, instead of monitoring the quality of information relevant to national security policy, and instead of ensuring that the president received a range of policy options, Rice sought to bridge the differences among Bush's foreign policy advisors, to anticipate the president's preferences, and to please him.[35]

As for establishing the bureaucratic organizations necessary for directing national security policy, President Bush and Condi Rice established the hard and soft organizational wiring within the government for the coordination and centralization of information flows and decision making. There was a Deputies Committee, there were temporary groups set up for planning the war against Iraq and for the postwar occupation, and other organizations were formed for handling particular national security issues. Yet the Deputies Committee and other interagency organizations were not reliably able to coordinate interagency action. Rather, the NSC policy process often revealed sharp differences among the departments and agencies that were simply passed up to the foreign policy principals for their resolution. The national security advisor would then try to reconcile the differences, usually between the State and Defense departments, as best as she could. But Rice did not—or perhaps could not—exercise the tight discipline and control over the national security process that would have enabled the administration to act effectively and with common purpose. The national security advisor was in over her head, as Elizabeth Bumiller, Marcus Mabry, and other writers point out.[36]

Because of the breakdown of discipline, meetings that should have taken place did not occur. No single NSC meeting or other meeting was convened so that the foreign policy principals and their top aides could discuss what the United States hoped to achieve by invading Iraq and deposing Saddam Hussein.[37] No consistent interagency process was put in place for determining the military's post-invasion plans for Iraq.[38] And sometimes the defense secretary and vice president simply did not bother to attend Principals Committee meetings called by Rice; they just sent their deputies instead.[39]

As one former senior official from the first Bush administration said about Rumsfeld, he had "never seen more high-level insubordination in the US government in almost thirty years." When a White House meeting failed to resolve several key issues related to Iraq, for instance, L. Paul Bremer went to Baghdad and proceeded to declare and implement policies that had not been agreed to. Presumably—this was the State Department's view—"Bremer had simply cleared it with his boss: Donald Rumsfeld." Rumsfeld was inclined to ignore process and do as he pleased. "People on the NSC staff believe that the secretary of defense has four points of entry into the White House," the official remarked. "He can go to Condi for the easy stuff; he can go to [White House Chief of Staff] Andy [Card] for the staff that's a little tougher; to Cheney, if it's really difficult; and then, for the ace in the hole, direct contact with the president if necessary."[40]

Meanwhile, organizations and relationships existed that should not have. Within the Office of the Vice President, for instance, Dick Cheney established what amounted to a second NSC. The vice president typically has too small a staff to allow him to participate much, if at all, in high-level foreign policy meetings. As a result, vice presidents usually have only one or two issues in their portfolios. But Cheney circumvented the NSC system by enlarging the Office of the Vice President so it had enough staff to "work the paper"—that is, to draft documents for the president's consideration and to mark up and respond to other documents sent to the White House by various departments and agencies. Furthermore, Cheney gave Scooter Libby, his chief of staff, the rank of presidential assistant (similar to what Scowcroft had done for Gates). Libby was therefore equal in seniority to Rice and was able to attend all top-level meetings.[41] Cheney also set up his own sources of intelligence within the government—including the NSC staff—as well as in Iraq and elsewhere and created separate channels through which to operate with Rumsfeld and other officials, such as Paul Wolfowitz (deputy secretary of defense),

Douglas Feith (the undersecretary of defense), and John Bolton (the undersecretary of state for arms control). With a much-expanded staff at his disposal and with briefings on all the research and information that was thus available to him, Cheney was able to fully participate in almost all high-level policy discussions.[42]

This enabled the vice president to form a shadow NSC and to some extent direct and coordinate national security policy. Like the national security advisor, Cheney had an office in the White House close to the Oval Office. Like the national security advisor, he had did not have a large bureaucracy with a huge budget and clearly identifiable major clients; therefore he, too, could claim to be above any narrow bureaucratic interests. Also like the national security advisor, Cheney had ready access to the president.[43] During the first few months after September 11, it was often Cheney (and Donald Rumsfeld)—rather than National Security Advisor Rice—who was Bush's leading advisor on national security matters.[44]

Presidents get the advice they deserve, to be sure, and the two George Bushes were clearly quite different persons. George W. Bush did not come into office with the diplomatic and bureaucratic experience of his father. Neither did he share his father's personality and disposition. Nonetheless, George W. Bush and the United States were poorly served by the national security policy process that he and his top advisors put into place—or, to put it perhaps more accurately, did not put into place. The "National Security Council was dysfunctional," one member of the 9/11 Commission observed, a view, this official added, that was shared by all of the commissioners.[45]

What drove George W. Bush's deeply flawed national security policy during his first term in office may thus have been something considerably more mundane than Republican partisanship or neoconservative ideology, contrary to what many have written. The chief cause of Bush's foreign policy missteps may simply have been his and Condi Rice's insensitivity to process: to the importance of personnel and the interactions among their appointees, to the role the national security advisor must play in order to safeguard American interests, and to the significance of coordinating and directing the national security bureaucracy. It is virtually impossible to imagine such developments taking place under George H. W. Bush.

WHEN GEORGE BUSH BELIEVED THE COLD WAR ENDED AND WHY THAT MATTERED

Jeffrey A. Engel

George H. W. Bush governed during remarkable times. The Berlin Wall fell. Germany reunited. The Soviet Union ceased to exist, Eastern Europe turned to democracy, and the Cold War ended. Simultaneously, bloodshed in China's Tiananmen Square proved the resilience of authoritarian rule. Violence in Rumania, Latvia, and Yugoslavia demonstrated that the new democratic age would not necessarily be a peaceful one. Indeed, the post–Cold War peace was remarkably short lived: the Gulf War was waged and won even as final plans for German unification were being drawn. Nearly forgotten in this cacophony of events are the American military interventions in Panama and Somalia, the former to root out a drug-dealing despot, the latter to deliver humanitarian aid. George Bush led the most powerful nation on earth at a time when it was arguably at the pinnacle of its strength, despite lingering fears of imperial overstretch. It was quite possibly the most powerful state in all of human history, making all the more remarkable his administration's self-restraint in the face of unprecedented change and uncertainty.

American policymakers believed themselves to be unrivaled in the international system. "When we ended up, everybody wanted to be friends with the United States," Secretary of State James Baker recalled in his oral history. "We had the best foreign policy situation that this country's seen in a long, long time. Everybody wanted to embrace free markets. Everybody wanted to embrace democracy, with the sole exceptions of North Korea, Cuba, Iran, Iraq and Libya. Everybody was ours."[1]

Baker's recollection of near-universal admiration can be factually disputed, but not his memory of widespread enthusiasm for the broad American project at the Cold War's end. American history is replete with similar statements. John Winthrop famously called his new Massachusetts home a "city upon a hill," an example of righteousness to the world, and a potential example of the Lord's rejection should colonists fail in their grand experiment. Three centuries later President Woodrow Wilson declared that "the force of America is the force of moral principle," and as World War II wound down, Secretary of State Cordell Hull believed that American morality and practices were synonymous. American "principles and policies are so beneficial and appealing to the sense of justice, of right and of the well-being of free peoples everywhere," Hull explained, that global peace would come when they were the universal norm.[2]

Baker's statement was at once consistent with earlier descriptions of American exceptionalism and profoundly different from them. Winthrop had a vision, Wilson the outlines of a plan, Hull a recipe for global success. Baker, on the other hand, described not a plan for victory but victory itself. In his view, Americans at the close of the 1980s had inherited what they previously had only promised or hoped for: the fruition of America's global project to accrue power and peace through active replication of the American system of government and values. Put simply, they had won. Humanity had arrived at the "end of history," political scientist and State Department staffer Francis Fukuyama famously declared in 1989.[3] After millennia of struggle, he argued, democracy had triumphed as the ideal form of human society. The United States, by extension, had triumphed because of its tremendous Cold War expenditures and its clear role as leader of the world's democratic alliance against fascism and communism.

Fukuyama's idea struck a chord (even though close reading of his treatise suggested that the end of history would prove unsatisfying). The West had triumphed: freedom was an idea whose time had come and whose superiority appeared to have been proven by the decisive conclusion of the Cold War. As Baker said, "everybody wanted to come on board." Indeed, amid apparent triumph, Fukuyama's provocative thesis was debated less for its veracity than for the extent of its revealed wisdom. The question for most was not whether American power and values had triumphed, which seemed obvious, but how one might best harvest the fruits of victory. As historian Bruce Cummings wrote of this period, "There are many ways by which we might come to understand the demise of authoritarian regimes, but in the U.S. the dominant tendency was to turn these events into a celebration of ourselves."[4]

George Bush lived and worked comfortably in the long line of American leaders who believed, most without question, that their country had a special mission in the world. "We do have principles, and it is time we stood up for them," he had written in his diary while serving as a diplomat in Beijing in the mid-1970s.[5] He rarely questioned the wisdom of those principles and was not one to spend hours contemplating a nuanced definition of "freedom" or "democracy."[6] Having enjoyed throughout his life the fruits of American wealth and power and indeed having lived his entire adult life during the pinnacle decades of what some termed the "American Century," he instead enthusiastically encouraged others to accept as gospel the values he'd been weaned on. "We know what works, freedom works," Bush declared after taking the oath of office, months before Fukuyama's book appeared in print. "We know what's right: freedom is right. . . . For the first time in this century, for the first time in perhaps all history, man does not have to invent a system by which to live. We don't have to talk late into the night about which form of government is better. We don't have to wrest justice from the kings. We only have to summon it from within ourselves."[7]

Bush and his advisors therefore perceived by 1990 an opportunity to remake the world in the American image just as previous generations had long dreamed— provided the world did not stumble in its moment of democratic triumph. As much as Bush believed his nation and its system of governance was triumphant at the end of the Cold War, he also feared the possibility of chaos and tumult in a world suddenly free from the geopolitical restraints of that war. The story of his time in office is a story of his administration's effort to balance the hope of their moment in history with trepidation about the possible downsides of the new world to come.

Hope and fear ran in tandem throughout Bush's policymaking circles because few in this group, and certainly not the president himself, considered American power to be unlimited. Bush believed that Washington drew strength from the foundational elements of democratic rule that triumphed during his presidency, which meant the country could only remain powerful by acting within the framework of Western solidarity. The United States could influence global events as no other power on earth, but it could not bend the rules of global order to its will except at great cost and with limited long-term success. Even as the world's most powerful state, the United States could merely influence the global stream of history rather than truly direct it; it lacked absolute hegemonic power. Thus, it acted cautiously even as so many around it celebrated the heady optimism of the times.

The search for that safe middle passage between hegemony and chaos ultimately produced a remarkable transformation in the highest levels of the administration, specifically in the way the Bush team sought to implement change, their tolerance for change, and their explicit global goal in the face of unprecedented change. Bluntly stated, Bush and his inner circle learned to trust that other global actors, and not just intimate allies, would act in accord with the liberal democratic tenor of the times. The group collectively entered office in January 1989 as hawks. They preferred the term "realists," although that term carries its own intellectual baggage. The foreign policy advisors Bush convened around him, universally critical of détente in the 1970s and skeptical of subsequent Soviet promises of reform, were more pessimistic than their immediate predecessors in the Reagan administration about the paramount issue of the day: dealing with a declining Soviet Union. Referring to Mikhail Gorbachev's reform, Baker asked the head of Reagan's European policy team "Don't you think you all went too fast?" soon after Election Day in 1988.[8] Indeed, although Bush's election assured a continuation of Republican rule in the White House, in concrete foreign policy terms continuities were few and far between. "This is not a friendly takeover," Baker reminded political friends and foes alike, and he demanded presigned resignation letters throughout the upper echelon of the executive branch. As he explained twenty years later, in politics, the appearance of change matters. "The new President has got to be seen to be the new leader, and in running for office," Baker explained, "he—and particularly one who has been an incumbent Vice President for two terms to a successful President, like Bush was to Reagan—has got to continue to support the policies of his predecessor, but also has to carve out a niche for himself and carve out an identity for himself and a persona for himself."

Optimism and trust were out as a new cast of characters took up the reins of American foreign policy in 1989; prudence and skepticism were in. Yet led by Bush, this group in time learned to trust that former adversaries such as the Soviets could join what the president called the "family of nations" that shared democratic values with sufficient depth that small ripples in international relations need not become global waves capable of disrupting the peace. Bush's team left office four years later still claiming realist credentials but in truth far more optimistic about the prospects for a truly transformed post–Cold War international system. As National Security Advisor Brent Scowcroft described their collective mentality in 2007, the term "enlightened realism" best fit, which he defined as the belief "that the world could be a better place ... but don't get carried away."[9]

Hypochondriac realism better describes the group's worldview at the start of 1989, when every opportunity for positive change was thought to contain the germ of destruction. As Scowcroft was fond of saying at the time, "there may be, in the saying, light at the end of the tunnel. But I think it depends partly on how we behave whether the light is the sun or an oncoming train."[10] His views evolved, demonstrating in microcosm the transformation of Bush's team. Put in the bluntest terms, they entered office skeptical that the Cold War was over. Because of widespread and arguably unprecedented changes in the international system, they left office assured of the Cold War's demise and speaking, if only vaguely, of a "new world order."

This alteration in strategic perception is notable. It is axiomatic among international relations scholars that policymakers rarely change stripes while in office. The demands of power are simply too great and too time-consuming to afford the kind of relaxed reflection that is necessary for transforming a leader's overarching worldview. Diplomat and scholar Henry Kissinger concluded that "high office teaches decision making, not substance. It consumes intellectual capital; it does not create it. Most high officials leave office with the perceptions and insights with which they entered; they learn how to make decisions but not what decisions to make."[11] Bush aide and future secretary of defense Robert Gates made a similar point during his time as dean of a public policy school. Gates said that he expected new government hires to arrive fresh from the classroom armed with the latest theories and ideas, because he and his staff had no time in their packed daily schedules for academic reading, and the only way they could stay near the cutting edge of research was to learn from recent students.[12] In short, policymakers rarely think hard about the world while holding power and they rarely change their views; instead, they base their actions on prior knowledge and experience.

The Bush administration largely defied this common logic. Responding to the scale of the global change they encountered, they did think and change while in office, and by the end of their terms in office their worldviews had changed. But this led to the criticism that they acted too lethargically at critical moments, pausing too long in search of an ideal response rather than simply an immediate one. Surely this criticism hindered Bush's 1992 reelection bid, though domestic rather than international issues played the critical role in his defeat. Still, internal embrace of Bush's "new world order" in his policymaking circles—a term unveiled only in late 1990 and only then in response to the brewing crisis over Kuwait, not the end of the Cold War—proved politically insufficient. His team also needed to convince the public of the need for a forward-leaning American global presence, even in an age of democratic multilateralism. With the Cold War over and a recession under way, many voters hoped their nation would assume a more limited global presence. They longed for a substantial "peace dividend" and for a return to a narrow global role bordering on isolation that arguably never existed. "We, too, no less than the Soviets, need to draw down the cold war," historian Ronald Steel stated in a widely circulated article in mid-December of 1988. "While we build arms for our competition with the Soviets, our factories no longer produce goods the world wants to buy, our cities are deteriorating and our social fabric is unraveling." As Steel concluded, global engagement had been costly, perhaps too much so. "If anyone has 'won' the cold war, it has been our allies: Japan, which chose to sit it out and concentrate on getting rich, and Western Europe, which kept military spending within tightly controlled limits.

Today, many of the allies are richer than we and steadily drawing ahead of us in productivity, competitiveness and standard of living."[13]

Bush and his cadre, internationalists to the core, believed their new world order required no less of an American international presence than before. A political battle over the new world order's meaning and its wisdom thus ensued, because as Brent Scowcroft privately preached to Bush and throughout the White House's West Wing, peace and stability demanded American global engagement. "The basic lesson of two world wars was that American power is essential to any stable equilibrium on the [European] continent," he wrote. "The postwar era's success is founded on recognition of this fact."[14] The president supported this view. "We must never forget that twice in this century American blood has been shed over conflicts that began in Europe," Bush explained in May of 1989, with French president Francois Mitterrand at his side. "That is why the Atlantic alliance is so central to our foreign policy. And that's why America remains committed to the alliance and the strategy which has preserved freedom in Europe. We must never forget that to keep the peace in Europe is to keep the peace for America." Secretary Baker echoed the point, publicly noting that same month that although "the burdens were—and indeed, the burdens still are—very difficult to bear. . . . we prevented for 40 years war in Europe." Baker's use of the collective pronoun should not be lightly dismissed. He spoke of the Atlantic community. But his "we" was in fact the United States as keeper of Europe's peace.

The story of the relationship between domestic and international politics in the Bush administration therefore has two intertwined narratives: the transformation of a foreign policy elite and the selling of their global vision to a doubtful public. This chapter presents both narratives by focusing first on the end of the Cold War and the development of Bush's new world order and then on the difficulties his administration faced as it sought to win widespread public acceptance of an American-led post–Cold War world. It explores how they learned to trust. As Baker reflected long after leaving the State Department, the Bush team learned in office to enlarge its comfort zone, to embrace former enemies, and to accept change without succumbing to fear of the unknown. "If you have the trust," he said, "you can get a hell of a lot more done than if you don't. If you and I are trying to negotiate something and I know I can trust your word, we've got a better chance of getting there than we do if—and if you think the same about me. So it's not so much friendship as it is a relationship, knowing that you can trust your interlocutor." When asked how one knew if trust really existed among international allies and competitors, in particular in the context of a world in flux such as existed at the Cold War's end, Baker answered: "You test it." The story of the Bush administration, the end of the Cold War, and the dawn of something new is about how they weathered those tests.

This story begins before Bush took office. During Reagan's second term, a remarkable transformation took place in the Soviet-American relationship. In 1983 Reagan had famously termed the Kremlin the head of an "evil empire" that was full of "aggressive impulses" and wholly at "fault" for the Cold War.[15] By 1988, dramatic changes in the Soviet leadership, marked most vividly by the transfer of power from a series of aged and infirmed conservatives to the (relatively) youthful and reform-minded Mikhail Gorbachev, led not just to promises of détente but also to open talk of ending the superpower conflict itself. Eager to modernize Soviet society through wholesale reforms wrapped up in the terms glasnost and perestroika—openness and reconstruction to diffuse centralized state power to the people—Gorbachev promised an equivalent transformation of Soviet foreign policy.[16]

American policymakers questioned Gorbachev's sincerity, and with good reason. Some believed his rhetoric of reform merely concealed an old-style allegiance to the party; others feared that Gorbachev wanted to save Soviet communism, not destroy it. No one in the West could truly assess Gorbachev's heart, but the skeptics seemed at least to have a valid point. Gorbachev never disavowed communism or the Soviet state. He instead assessed that a decrease in East-West tensions was not only politically prudent but also financially necessary for his overburdened economy. "We can't go on living like this," he told his wife the night he assumed power in 1985. "The [Soviet] system was dying away; its sluggish senile blood no longer contained any vital juices."[17] Saving communism meant adopting some of the more positive aspects of the West, Gorbachev told the Politburo in late 1988, reminding them that Franklin D. Roosevelt had saved American capitalism by "borrow[ing] socialist ideas of planning, state regulation, [and] . . . the principle of more social fairness."[18] Gorbachev would save the Soviet Union, he implied, by following Roosevelt's lesson that ideological rigidity was often the enemy of practicality. He would also save communism, according to Robert Gates, who was a consistent skeptic in the Reagan administration's Central Intelligence Agency and then as Bush's deputy national security advisor—by relying on American statistical analyses of the Soviet economy, recognizing that Washington's published and classified studies of his state were more reliable than its own.

Gorbachev believed that saving communism required ending or at least decreasing Cold War tensions. "The only rational way out of our current situation," he explained to the Soviet Central Committee that elected him, "is for the opposing forces to agree to immediately stop the arms race—above all, the nuclear arms race."[19] Razor-sharp tensions were not only expensive and potentially dangerous, he argued, but also intellectually and politically stultifying. As foreign policy advisor Anatoly Chernyaev noted, "We understood that if nothing was changed in our foreign policy, we would get nowhere with regard to the internal changes we had in mind."[20] Thus, only months into his tenure, Gorbachev announced a moratorium on Soviet nuclear testing and offered new plans for parity in East-West military spending. He authorized Foreign Minister Eduard Shevardnadze to publicly declare that "in order to carry out its large-scale plans" for reform, "the Soviet Union needs a lasting peace in Europe, [and] a lasting peace all over the world."[21]

These promised changes were well received in the West, especially in Western Europe, where Gorbachev became more popular than he was in his homeland. Foreigners enjoyed his rhetoric; Soviet citizens endured increasing hardships as the nation's overall standard of living—never high by European or American standards—began to plunge. British prime minister Margaret Thatcher referred to the new Soviet leader as "someone we can do business" with and helped convince her fellow conservative Ronald Reagan that she was right. Ever suspicious of nuclear posturing and fearful of nuclear Armageddon to a degree that shocked even some of his closest advisors, Reagan was willing to try a new approach for peace in his second term. An unusual friendship blossomed between the Soviet apparatchik and the former actor turned anticommunist zealot, and a series of remarkable Soviet-American agreements regarding trade, cultural exchange, and nuclear reduction followed. When asked during a mid-1988 visit to Moscow if he still considered the Soviets an "evil empire," Reagan bluntly replied, "No. I was talking about another time and another era."[22]

Other world leaders were even more direct. The Cold War was over, Thatcher famously declared in December 1988, one day after a long private meeting in Washington with Reagan and President-elect Bush. "We are not in a Cold War now," she said; instead, we were enjoying "a new relationship much wider than the Cold War ever was." Eager to demonstrate that her international influence would not wane with Reagan's departure, Thatcher was happy to give the impression that her words enjoyed Bush's implicit endorsement. For Reagan's friends and allies, the campaign to attribute victory in the Cold War to their leader had begun. The long-standing East-West conflict was, Secretary of State George Shultz concluded, "all over but the shouting."[23]

Gorbachev clearly agreed with Thatcher and Shultz. He went a step further on December 7, 1988, little more than a month before Bush's inauguration. In a speech to the United Nations General Assembly, Gorbachev announced unilateral cuts in Soviet military forces of more than half a million troops, including the withdrawal of tens of thousands from their once-seemingly-permanent stations in Eastern Europe. He repudiated Moscow's claim of a right to deploy force within its own sphere of influence in order to save communist states at risk (commonly referred to as the Brezhnev Doctrine). He even declared that "freedom of choice is a universal principle" that "knows no exceptions."[24] Gorbachev was scheduled to meet with Reagan and President-elect Bush the day after this speech, and his words carried great hope that the transition at the White House would not disrupt the general trend toward better East-West relations. He had earlier directed his staff to write a speech capable of being "Fulton in reverse," rescinding the Iron Curtain speech Winston Churchill had delivered four decades earlier.[25]

These were remarkable statements for a Soviet leader. Senator Daniel Patrick Moynihan called the speech a Cold War capitulation, referring to it as "the most astounding statement of surrender in the history of ideological struggle."[26] The *New York Times* editorial page was hardly less ebullient. "Perhaps not since Woodrow Wilson presented his Fourteen Points in 1918 or since Franklin Roosevelt and Winston Churchill promulgated the Atlantic Charter in 1941 has a world figure demonstrated the vision Mikhail Gorbachev displayed yesterday at the United Nation."[27] Thatcher said that all Gorbachev required to continue his remarkable transformation was a willing partner in the White House. "I expect Mr. Gorbachev to do everything he can to continue his reforms," she concluded, and the Western powers, London and Washington especially, needed be ready to help him whenever the need arose, "both verbally and in practice."[28]

Bush's team disagreed. He and the foreign policy aides closest to him feared that Soviet overtures of friendship masked a deeper plan to win a new phase of the Cold War by reinvigorating the reeling Soviet system, much as Brezhnev had done (in their interpretation) in the 1970s. Because reinvigoration was Gorbachev's stated goal, such fears were not unfounded, but they also represented a deep-seated distrust of communist promises. "When we came into office in 1989," Scowcroft recalled, "we had a new General Secretary of the communist party, a very different kind of person. Gorbachev was not the old Brezhnev type individual. But I had détente very much in mind. What I was afraid of was that Gorbachev—as he had actually done with the Reagan Administration at the end—was seducing us, with kindness rather than with new missiles."

Bush was among those who were less trusting of Gorbachev's promises and reforms. He rarely disagreed with Reagan while serving as vice president, believing that loyalty was his primary job requirement. But throughout the 1988 campaign he increasingly distanced himself from Reagan's pro-Gorbachev attitude in order to shore up his conservative credentials and firmly establish his own vision of the presidency. Reagan and Bush worked collegially, James Pinkerton recalled of this period, but "at the macro level, there was plenty of tension. Look," he continued, "Reagan was a wonderful optimistic guy, and Bush was a decent optimistic, not so optimistic, but decent enough guy so they got along fine." Diplomat Dennis Ross, who headed the State Department's Policy Planning Staff under Baker, was more blunt in his own recollection. "One of the things that is striking as I think about this, the Vice President before the nomination and after it in some ways was two different people. Not dramatically so, but before the nomination he was bound by propriety. He was the Vice President for the President and the President had responsibilities and he couldn't separate himself in any way. Not just from the responsibilities, but there couldn't even be a tonal difference between the two in public. After the nomination he stood on his own. At least he felt he stood on his own and he was freer to be able to go and say things in terms of what he would do if President."

The 1988 presidential campaign, the last of the Cold War, also offered what the Bush camp portrayed as a contrast between an experienced foreign policy expert and, in Massachusetts governor Michael Dukakis, an international neophyte. Bush had already run on his foreign policy credentials in the Republican primaries. When told that Reagan had abandoned his own "evil empire" term, Bush retorted, "I don't agree that we know enough to say that there is that kind of fundamental change." He conceded that Gorbachev was "stylistically different, obviously generationally different" from the Soviet leaders that preceded him. But when it came to Gorbachev's ultimate intentions, Bush said that "my view is, the jury is still out."[29] He repeated that phrase during a debate with Dukakis, after the Democrat praised Reagan's open embrace of Gorbachev's reforms: "Where I differ from my opponent is I am not going to make unilateral cuts in our strategic defense systems or support some freeze. . . . I'm not going to do that, because I think the jury is still out on the Soviet experiment."[30] Even Bush's choice of the word "experiment" emphasized his fundamental view that Gorbachev's promises were temporary at best, insincere at worst. As Jack Matlock, Reagan's and then Bush's ambassador to Moscow, later remarked, "He did not want his administration to look like a continuation of the Reagan Administration."[31]

As Bush distanced himself from Reagan, he also sought to demonstrate that his aides engaged the key foreign policy issues of the day with fresh eyes. As Scowcroft explained, "One of the problems we had at the outset of the Bush Administration was, to what extent were we a new administration and to what extent were we a continuation of the Reagan administration. The press seemed to take it for granted that we were simply a continuation of the Reagan administration. I thought that was a mistake." After hearing Bush repeatedly downplay the heady optimism of perestroika and glasnost, it is hardly surprising that Gorbachev privately told Nancy Reagan, "I wish your husband could stay on for another four years."[32]

Bush's team wasted little time after the election before revealing a reassessment of Soviet-American relations. In December 1988, he announced a "pause" in relations that was designed to provide the new administration time to catch up with events.[33] Bush's advisors found the exercise disappointing. As Scowcroft explained, "I set in motion a whole review of foreign policy, from start to finish, of the policies that were in place. Were they doing what we wanted? Should they be changed? It turned to be pretty much a failure. The bureaucracy just came back with what you'd expect: everything's fine." Baker later called the results of this top-to-bottom foreign policy review "pablum" and "mush," but he insisted that the process was worthwhile even though the final product proved deficient. "It showed that we were deliberate, that we were thoughtful, that we were not just going to jump in here and say everything is going to go exactly the way—a new President has to carve out his own identity.

By late spring the president began to reveal the direction of his policy. Scowcroft, with typical self-deprecation, recalls in his oral history interview that this process largely emanated from the Oval Office, noting that "we had a series of speeches with the President, which laid out our relations with the Soviet Union, with Western Europe, with arms control, to set a pattern of 'this is what the Bush administration is.'"

In truth, the passage of time seems to have slightly clouded not so much Scowcroft's recollection of events—the speeches did occur—but rather their detail, because in recollection those events seem to have been compressed in time. Indeed, people typically emphasize continuity when recalling past events, obscuring and ignoring details that detract from their overall understanding of events and their larger meaning. Psychologists theorize that memories are embedded in schema that are useful for organizing disparate facts. As time passes, the overall power of the schema grows—that is, the point or overall lesson of a series of events becomes increasingly clear and increasingly paramount. One result of this process is the excising of facts and events that do not neatly conform to the schema. Put simply, we recall the overall lesson more than the way we learned it; we recall where we ended up more than how we got there. Scowcroft, Gates, Baker, Dennis Ross, and others all recall in their oral histories a fervent desire to distance Bush's foreign policy from Reagan's. How long that process took matters less to them, in retrospect, than that they all agreed that it occurred.

Bush delivered those speeches throughout the late spring of 1989, but the White House wasted no time in publicly distancing itself from Reagan's legacy. Scowcroft, long a public, albeit polite, critic of Reagan's overtures to Gorbachev, told the *Washington Post* in a lengthy interview published two days after Bush's inauguration that "the Cold War is not over." This was more than semantics designed to temper enthusiasm. It was a warning to Gorbachev that he would not find so willing a partner in the Oval Office as he previously had enjoyed. Gorbachev "badly needs a period of stability, if not definite improvement in the East-West relationship so he can face the awesome problem he has at home," Scowcroft said. He added that Gorbachev was "interested in making trouble within the Western alliance, and I think he believes the best way to do it is a peace offensive, rather than to bluster the way some of his predecessors did."[34]

Gates concurred with this assessment in his oral history. "I think Brent and I both believed, and I think maybe the President believed, that the Reagan administration had gotten out ahead of itself in the last six or eight months of 1988 in dealing with the Soviet Union, that their aspirations had outrun reality and had outrun the capacity of the government to absorb and deal with what they were trying to do." Ultimately, Gates recalled, the purpose of the administration's strategic pause and reassessment was at once simple and profound. "There was a sense of 'let's see where we are' and if we think that the Reagan administration in its last six months or so was on the right track. There was never any idea that we would depart in any significant way in terms of going backward, in terms of the relationship with the Soviet Union. I think what we were trying to see is what's the right way forward and how do we respond to some of the things that are going on in Europe, and the President's and Brent's desire to get out in front of these events that began during the transition clearly was a part of this."

Scowcroft's post-inauguration warning that the West needed to beware of Soviets bearing gifts was public and blunt, revealing that the policymakers Bush assembled were more hawkish about Soviet intentions than those they were replacing. For example, Gates, who had studied Russian history throughout his career, said in the fall of 1988 that he was wary of the Soviets in general and of Gorbachev's reforms in particular. The Soviet Union was too unwieldy to be easily turned, he argued, and its bureaucracy too entrenched and archaic to be saved. Too rapid a change would likely bring a conservative counterrevolution. More ominously, Gates warned, Gorbachev's reforms would lift the lid from the cauldron of long-simmering ethnic and nationalistic tensions deeply embedded in Soviet society and throughout Eastern Europe. Moscow's centralized power had long kept potential interethnic violence at bay, whether through the force of a Czar or the power of a hard-fisted leader like Joseph Stalin. Gorbachev's promise to diffuse power augured something different and dangerous. "While Gorbachev's bold political moves and radical rhetoric have shaken the Soviet system, " Gates said, "he has not yet really changed it," and "it is by no means certain—I would even say it is doubtful—that Gorbachev can in the end rejuvenate the system."[35]

Gates's true divergence from Reagan's central conclusion was his warning that Gorbachev's success might not be in Washington's best interest. America might suffer whether Gorbachev's reforms succeeded, and thereby enhanced Moscow's power, or failed, leading to an aggressive anti-Western stance or a splintering of the entire Soviet system in a wave of violence not seen since World War II. "We see no slackening of Soviet weapons production or programs," Gates warned, and no reduction in Soviet aid to anti-American forces throughout the Western Hemisphere. In the end, he concluded, "Whether Gorbachev succeeds, fails, or just survives, a still long competition and struggle with the Soviet Union lie before us." "The most dangerous time for a bad government is when it starts to reform itself," Gates said, quoting Tocqueville's famous judgment of the French Revolution, which began with utopian hopes of universal fraternity and solidarity and ended in a wave of executions, terror, and war.[36]

Gates found a fellow skeptic about "Gorbymania" in Condoleezza Rice, another Soviet expert, who was on leave to the NSC staff from Stanford University. Perhaps Gorbachev himself was not to be trusted, they worried, or perhaps he was sincere but his efforts would fail, leading to a conservative crackdown and a renewed Cold War, or worse. "We did not disagree with the dominant administration position that they had to deal with Gorbachev and that he was a productive interlocutor for the United States government," Gates recalled. "But, I think Condi and I were much more pessimistic about Gorbachev's prospects for success, particularly when it came to economic reform and managing ethnic conflict, than others. In fact, I think we were pretty confident that he'd fail. So, we thought, the question was, how much can you get done, how much business can you get done with Gorbachev, how much can you get out of him that serves our interests before he crashes and burns? On that the administration was all agreed."

Secretary of State George Shultz could barely contain his anger, in late 1988, when he read Gates's words in the newspapers. "CIA Aide Says Gorbachev Is Likely to Fail," the *New York Times* blared. The *Washington Post* headlined more simply "Gorbachev Faces 'Struggle' on Reform, CIA's Gates Says." Shultz and Gates had sparred for years behind the scenes over the best course for dealing with the Soviet Union. Their feud was now laid bare for the world to see. The secretary called Gates early the next day to dispute the CIA's conclusion. More to the point, he reminded Gates that it was not an intelligence analyst's place to make public statements on the direction of American foreign policy. That was the president's job, Shultz said, or his chief diplomat's. Shultz followed this conversation with calls to the CIA director, the secretary of defense, the national security advisor, and ultimately Reagan himself, demanding Gates's immediate dismissal. Hardly one to engage in bureaucratic dust-ups and personnel decisions during his long tenure as president, Reagan was loath to feed such a firestorm during his last weeks in office. Shultz steamed, but Gates survived.

Gates not only survived but was promoted. He became Scowcroft's principal deputy and was given a West Wing office and easy access to the president. In time he would head the Deputies Committee, the semi-formal policy deliberation body that included the second-in-command of every significant national security and foreign policy department and organization in the executive branch. Rice followed him into the Bush White House. "Condi and I felt very strongly that we ought to be opening up and talking to other reform-minded people, and, of course, above all [future Russian President Boris] Yeltsin," Gates recalled. "And so the biggest issue on which we spent a lot of time on in '89, was in trying to figure out how to get Brent and the President to at least be willing to talk to Yeltsin and to begin a dialogue with the guy. Not to denigrate Gorbachev or anything else, but just the understanding that it was dangerous to pin everything on one guy and one guy who was walking a tightrope."

Gates's elevation sent a clear message throughout the national security bureaucracy that the Cold War was not yet over, a message that was reinforced in late March of 1989 when Representative Richard Cheney of Wyoming became Bush's secretary of defense following the aborted nomination of Senator John Tower, who failed to receive Senate confirmation. A hawk among hawks, Cheney used the occasion of his swearing-in to remark that "there are those who want to declare the Cold War ended . . . but I believe caution is in order . . . . We must guard against gambling our nation's security on what may be a temporary aberration in the behavior of our foremost adversary."[37] President Bush's beaming smile as Cheney spoke reinforced the image of White House skepticism about Gorbachev's intentions and likelihood of success.

Gorbachev reacted first with bewilderment toward the Bush administration's strategic pause, then with frustration, and ultimately with barely concealed fury. "What were they waiting for?" he privately fumed as the pause continued through the spring of 1989. Bush clearly "wasn't drawing the proper conclusions from his U.N. speech," Chernyaev recorded Gorbachev as complaining, "and even has in mind a Western effort to undermine the Soviet Union's international initiatives."[38] It was not until May that Bush formally announced a modest new way forward, promising merely to move "beyond containment."

This call was hardly a warm embrace of perestroika and glasnost. "The United States will challenge the Soviet Union step by step, issue by issue and institution by institution to behave in accordance with the higher standards that the Soviet leadership has enunciated," Bush declared. Specifically, if it wanted to win the Bush administration's trust, the Soviet Union would need to reduce its military posture, allow self-determination in Eastern and Central Europe, work hand-in-hand with the West to solve regional disputes, permit greater pluralism and human rights at home, and work with the West to address global problems such as the environment, terrorism, and the international drug trade. "In an era of extraordinary change," Bush reiterated two weeks later, this time with French president François Mitterrand at his side, "we have an obligation to temper optimism—and I am optimistic—with prudence," because "it is clear that Soviet 'new thinking' has not yet totally overcome the old."[39]

Looking for signs of sincerity, American policymakers initially focused on signs that the Soviets were willing to end aid to communist groups in Central America and the communist government of Cuba. As long as the Kremlin continued to assist those interested in undermining the Western Hemisphere, Scowcroft and others reasoned, its words could hardly be trusted. Gates explained the divergence between the Soviets' pledge of new behavior and their persistence in aiding their allies in Latin America as basically habit. "You sort of had the feeling, in contrast to during the mid '80s, that by 1989 the Soviets' heart really wasn't—that they really didn't give a shit about Latin America and it was sort of just a bureaucratic inertia in terms of continuing to be involved in Cuba . . . and also in Nicaragua. Their reaction was always really lame. There was no heart to it. It was sort of, 'What am I going to do? I have all these bureaucrats whose jobs depend on continuing to ship this stuff' and so on.'"

Although Bush's team met Gorbachev's promise of reforms, and with it the larger question of the Cold War's end, with great skepticism, their attitude was not fixed in stone. One of the most fascinating documents to emerge from recent declassification at the Bush Library is a speech that was intended for delivery in May 1989 that Cheney did not give. The draft he sent for White House approval was hawkish in the extreme. "President Gorbachev wants to be understood as the leader of a new generation of Soviet officials who have put behind them the rhetoric, propaganda, and aggressive intent of the past," Cheney proposed to say. "And this Administration wants to take seriously Mr. Gorbachev's pronouncements about Soviet military reform and 'new thinking.'" But, Cheney planned to conclude, "our problem comes when we try to compare the rhetoric with reality"—that is, Gorbachev's hopeful words with the limited if not imperceptible decline in Moscow's military posture. "These mismatches between rhetoric and reality have to make us wonder about the seriousness of Mr. Gorbachev's new thinking."[40]

Scowcroft concluded that the secretary of defense's rhetoric was too caustic and not in line with the administration's slowly evolving hopeful approach toward Soviet reforms. As one of Scowcroft's deputies explained, "Our reading of the speech is . . . [that] it serves too well its intended purpose—strongly suggesting that no major changes are needed in US defense policy vis-à-vis the Soviets." Bowing to White House pressure Cheney instead delivered boilerplate remarks that were unlikely to make any headlines.[41] The significance of the speech he never gave is that it demonstrates how far Bush and Scowcroft were leaning toward cautiously embracing Soviet change by May of 1989. Nothing Cheney proposed to say was in any way distinct from statements the president had made throughout 1988 and the early spring. But by late spring the secretary was behind the curve.

Even as the Bush administration paused in the spring of 1989, the world did not. Democratic movements surged throughout Eastern Europe. Poland's government agreed to open negotiations with reform groups as the year began, and Hungary allowed open elections in May. More than 300,000 citizens turned out in Budapest for a belated public funeral for Imre Nagy, the prime minister executed on Kremlin orders in 1956. Soon after that, Hungarian officials stopped protecting their border with Austria from Eastern Europeans who longed to emigrate westward, opening a pipeline out of the Soviet Bloc. Poland's June elections proved more detrimental for the communist government than anyone expected; they turned effective power over to the long-suffering Solidarity labor movement. Only in Rumania and East Germany did change seem to be on hold. "We took power in order to keep it forever," East German leader Erich Honecker simultaneously boasted and warned. He earlier had declared that the Berlin Wall "will be standing in fifty or a hundred years!" When Gorbachev visited East Berlin in October, crowds made their desire for change and their lack of faith in their own leaders abundantly clear. "Save us, Gorby!" they yelled.[42]

Democracy seemed to be sweeping the world, extending even to China, where protests against corruption and entrenched influence grew throughout the spring into the largest civil dissent in the nation's recent past. In April, students began to march in Beijing. Teachers and workers soon followed their lead. By the end of May, tens of thousands were encamped in Beijing's central Tiananmen Square. As luck would have it, Gorbachev was scheduled to arrive in Beijing at that very moment for the first Sino-Soviet summit in more than thirty years. Protestors complicated his plans, embarrassing China's party leadership. Tensions mounted, even as the first group of student protestors grew weary of their work and were replaced by fresh arrivals from the hinterland. Whatever had activated China's youth and populace, it was growing.

It is easy, although ultimately incorrect, to draw a direct line between the roughly simultaneous protest movement in China and calls for democracy in Eastern Europe. Such an elegant global interpretation diminishes the domestic origins of the Chinese movement. Recent scholarship suggests that the Chinese protests originated in pent-up frustrations over the growing inequities of the economic reforms Deng Xiaoping initiated in the aftermath of the destructive Cultural Revolution of the 1970s. By the late 1980s students believed enough time had passed to warrant results, and their leaders proved savvy enough to publicly link their movement with those occurring behind the Iron Curtain, especially when Western cameras arrived in Tiananmen Square eager to find signs in English. "We salute the Ambassador of Democracy," one poster read when Gorbachev visited. Another asked, "In the Soviet Union they have Gorbachev, but what do we have in China?" In truth these visible links between Tiananmen and perestroika were more show than substance, demonstrating above all else the media savvy of Chinese protesters eager to rally global support for their cause. Most protesting Chinese student leaders sought less to join a global movement than to align themselves with the revolution begun by students in their country generations before.

"Today, in front of the symbol of the Chinese nation, Tiananmen," one student manifesto read, "we can proudly proclaim to all the people in our nation that we are worthy of the pioneers of seventy years ago."[43]

American officials clearly saw protestors in Europe and China as part of the same democracy movement. More to the point, they interpreted Chinese calls for "freedom" and "democracy" and symbols such as the goddess of democracy that arose amid the cacophony of Tiananmen Square as further validation of Western values and policies. "They may have that name [Gorbachev] on their lips," James Baker told the president in late May, "but they have the policies of the West in mind. It is the philosophy of the West that they are advancing, and it is the values of the West that they are seeking."[44] Bush went a step further, explicitly equating China with Poland and Hungary as part of the same phenomenon. "Glasnost and the Beijing demonstrations proved that the democratic way is on the march," he declared, "and it is not going to be stopped."[45]

Even the ever-cautious Scowcroft was inclined to think big in the face of such global change. Newly released documents demonstrate that he was far more forward-leaning toward the Soviets behind the scenes than either his public statements at the time or his oral history interviews would suggest. In an early spring 1989 memo, even as the administration's strategic review continued, Scowcroft privately advised Bush that it was time to begin thinking about change in a new way. Scowcroft reminded Bush that "in his memoirs, *Present at the Creation*, [former secretary of state] Dean Acheson remarked that, in 1945, their task 'began to appear as just a bit less formidable than that described in the first chapter of Genesis. That was to create a world out of chaos; ours, to create half a world, a free half, out of the same material without blowing the whole to pieces in the process.'" Scowcroft wanted Bush to think in just such global, historical, and even biblical terms. "When those creators of the 1940s and 1950s rested, they had done much," he said. "We now have unprecedented opportunities to do more, to pick up the task where they left off, while doing what must be done to protect a handsome inheritance."[46]

The Bush administration was clearly deep in thought by mid-1989, even if it was unsure of its next step. In this regard, Scowcroft's deep influence with Bush, and in particular his plea to think in Achesonian terms, takes on particular weight. "They [Scowcroft and Bush] spent a lot of time together, just the two of them," Gates recalled, "and that began in the transition. . . . For example, in the transition, Brent was the one that kind of put forward the notion that we really need to take some bold initiatives to try and get the Soviet troops out of Eastern Europe. But it was also the President, particularly as the administration went along, who would be saying, 'We have to take an initiative to get out in front of this. We can't be seen as being reactive. The world has changed and we have to get out in front of these events and lead and here are some things that I want to do.'"

The Bush administration's equation of the protests in Europe with those in China is vital to an understanding of its collective mindset in the summer of 1989. Just as the president and those around him were beginning to warm to the idea of truly embracing global change and openly embracing Gorbachev's reforms, the crackdown at Tiananmen occurred. Chinese leaders, scarred by the violent Cultural Revolution, feared turmoil and instability above all else. Deng Xiaoping's son had been crippled by overzealous Red Guards demanding reform during the Cultural Revolution, and Deng was himself subject to internal exile twice for allegedly failing to follow the party line during this tumultuous time. Needless to say, these were not happy memories for Deng and those veterans of the 1970s who surrounded him, each of whom believed that civil disobedience, however well intentioned, could slip all too easily into mob rule and chaos. Thus, when students would not disperse as commanded, even after leaders promised to heed their calls for reform, they threatened a level of societal disruption that Deng and his cadre could no longer tolerate. On the night of June 3, 1989, troops and tanks moved through the square, dispersing the crowd and killing hundreds. The bloody crackdown at Tiananmen seemed to validate Tocqueville's warning that governments are most dangerous when they begin to reform. As Michael Dobbs, the *Washington Post's* Moscow Bureau chief, reminded his readers, Tiananmen "reminds us how readily communist leaders can still resort to brute force when their power is threatened."[47]

The crackdown at Tiananmen reinforced Bush's natural caution. On the very night tanks rolled over Chinese students, Polish voters unexpectedly turned out their communist government. No one could predict the reaction in Moscow, or for that matter the consequences in Warsaw. As China's premier caustically reminded the American ambassador soon after the crackdown, "No government in the world would tolerate this kind of disorder in the middle of its capital."[48] Whenever crowds gathered throughout Eastern Europe in the months that followed, particularly in East Germany, where by October weekly demonstrations grew into the tens of thousands, Bush feared the truth of these words. It was only after visiting Poland and Hungary in the summer of 1989, after the Tiananmen crackdown, that Bush publicly held a piece of the barbed wire used until recently to protect the Hungarian-Austrian border and declared, "Let Berlin be next!"[49] This was also the moment the president decided to meet with Gorbachev face-to-face; he realized that he could pause no longer or events might spiral beyond even minimal control. On the way home from Europe, Bush wrote a letter to Gorbachev requesting a meeting. There could be many more Tiananmen massacres if change was not managed, he realized. Thus, he implored Gorbachev to meet "without thousands of assistants hovering over our shoulders," in order to "reduce the chance that there could be some misunderstanding between us."[50] The two leaders agreed to meet in Malta in early December.

By the time Bush and Gorbachev met, much had changed. The Berlin Wall was down. Gorbachev had refused to intervene to save the East German state, although he did place urgent calls to Bush (and to West German chancellor Helmut Kohl and Thatcher as well) to ask them to downplay celebration of the moment lest crowds gather too massively and local authorities respond with force. Bush obliged, promising, as he described in his memoirs, not to "dance on the wall," even though he was pilloried in the press for supposedly failing to grasp the historic nature of the change swirling around him. Other Western leaders were less circumspect. Kohl surprised both Moscow and Washington by endorsing full unification of his divided country in advance of any substantive discussions of the matter with the victors of World War II, who retained legal authority to refuse, or at least retard, rapid unification.[51]

Bush eventually sided with Kohl on German unification, but he still rebuffed the idea that the Cold War was over. In truth, he simply did not know what would come next. If the Cold War was over, what was America's global vision? Indeed, what was the central purpose of his career? Asked once too often if the Cold War was over after his December 1989 meeting with Gorbachev in Malta, Bush lost his temper in response, less because of the repetition of the question than because he did not know the answer to the next obvious question: What would come next? "Is the Cold War the same?" he stormed. "I mean, is it raging like before in the times of the Berlin Blockade? Absolutely not. Things have moved dramatically. But if I signal to you that there's no Cold War, then it's 'what are you doing with troops in Europe?' I mean, come on!"[52]

Bush knew that the end of the Cold War eliminated the most stabilizing aspect of the post–World War II international system, and he above all was a man enamored of stability. Time and again during the spring and early summer of 1990, Bush told global leaders that their alliances required an enemy to survive, and in his words, the new enemy was instability. He told Kohl, "The enemy is unpredictability, apathy, and destabilization." He told Thatcher that "when I am asked who our enemy is now, I tell them apathy, complacency." As for America's military needs, "It is premature to speak about a 'peace dividend'—to take a lot of money out of defense and put it into other worthy causes," Bush said as 1989 came to a close. "I don't want to hold out to those that want to rush out and spend a lot more money [on domestic needs] the hope that this is going to happen."[53]

By February of 1990, Bush was convinced that his country needed to remain engaged globally if peace were to be maintained amid such change. But he did not know how to make that case politically at a time of triumphant euphoria and increasing calls to bring the troops home and refocus on domestic needs, including the declining economy. "As Americans have always believed," Bush argued that month, "our foremost goal is to prevent another world war. To do so, we will still need to remain fully engaged. European security, stability, and freedom, so tied to our own, require an American presence. Western Europeans all want us to stay there—every single country—want us to avoid pulling back into an uninvolved isolation. I have the feeling that when the dust settles, the new democracies of Eastern Europe will feel exactly the same way. We must remain in Europe as long as we are needed and wanted." In the final analysis, Bush maintained, "the prospect of global peace depends on an American forward presence." Aware that the foundation of post-1945 American prosperity also rested to no small extent on the combined effects of defense spending, financial stimulus, and scientific research, Bush was also clearly of no mind to restructure his entire budget prematurely. As late as July of 1990, he vigorously warned his staff against declaring any end to superpower tensions. "Do NOT use words 'Cold War is over' in any draft statements," he told his national security team. It was still too soon for such public utterances. As Undersecretary of State Robert Zoellick summed up the meeting, Bush's point was clear: "Gradualism . . . that's the key."[54]

Bush finally found a post–Cold War purpose when Saddam Hussein invaded Kuwait. In a speech delivered on September 11, 1990, Bush envisioned a "new world order" in which the international system, newly bonded across former Cold War lines, would unite against aggression. He described a world system "where the United Nations, freed from Cold War stalemate, is poised to fulfill the historic vision of its founders. A world in which freedom and respect for human rights find a home among all nations." Bush thought that the end of the Cold War offered his generation a "rare opportunity to move toward an historic period of cooperation," one that was "freer from the threat of terror, stronger in the pursuit of justice, and more secure in the quest for peace."[55] The full scope of Bush's global vision was revealed in the midst of the Iraq War, even as bombs and missiles rained down on Baghdad, when he and Gorbachev argued about a potential quick end to the conflict mediated by the Soviets. "Don't let us fall out over Iraq," Bush warned. "There are things far bigger than this conflagration, which is going to be over very soon."[56]

Bush never envisioned the new world order as being devoid of conflict and strife. Optimistic but no utopian, Bush believed it within his generation's grasp to "move toward" a more cooperative global system. A close reading of Bush's September 11 speech reveals his hope for an international system that was "freer" and an international community that was "stronger" in the pursuit of justice than during the Cold War; he was not envisioning a fully free and just world in that moment. Ultimately, he hoped for a world in which humanity was, at the least, "more secure in the quest for peace." For Bush—a man who had seen combat and lost friends in World War II, lived through the difficulties of the half-century-long Cold War, thought words like Munich and Yalta meant appeasement and disgrace, and occupied a front-row seat in government during the tribulations of Watergate and Vietnam—change was best pursued cautiously. Criminals and tyrants would forever seek to exploit cracks in the international order, and the rule of law so fundamental to democratic societies would have to be enforced. The new world order was a step in the right direction, because it was in many ways a step back to the founding vision of the modern world developed at the end of World War II, before Cold War tensions pulled it off course. As he had said earlier, "In an era of extraordinary change, we have an obligation to temper optimism—and I am optimistic—with prudence."[57]

Bush failed to make his vision clear to the voting public, because in truth the "new world order," by harkening back to 1945, did not appear all that new. Even Bush's press secretary, Marlin Fitzwater, later conceded that his team, and in turn the president, did a poor job in enunciating anything more than the broad outlines of the president's vision. "Well I don't think it ever really got defined," he said. "He [Bush] never tried to lay it out. The problem with that, of course, is that it leaves a vacuum of definitions and that others can jump in and fill."[58] Bush's critics from the left and especially from the right quickly occupied the political and strategic void he inadvertently created by using but never fully defining his understanding of the new world order. In challenging Bush for the Republican nomination in 1992, conservative pundit Patrick Buchanan derided the president as too willing to forsake American interests for his internationalist vision. "He is a globalist and we are nationalists," Buchanan charged. "He believes in some Pax Univeralis [sic]; we believe in the Old Republic. He would put America's wealth and power at the service of some vague New World Order; we will put America first."[59] Buchanan's far-right presidential campaign echoed the far-left George McGovern's "Come home, America" slogan from 1972, which the Democratic candidate had offered at the height of the Vietnam War. Clearly the Vietnam syndrome had not been fully ended by victory in the Gulf; rather it returned to haunt domestic electoral politics. Indeed, McGovern briefly reentered the political fray in 1992 to cast liberal aspersions on Bush's new world order. Quoting Gorbachev's notion that "the long years we spent plunged in the Cold War made losers of us all," McGovern rebuked the central triumphalism that marked the ending of the Cold War. "I share these sentiments," he said. "The Cold War has devoured much of the physical, financial, scientific, industrial, and human resources of the Soviet Union and the United States. It has cost the United States $12 trillion in tax funds, and has helped to create a national debt of $4 trillion. It has drained off so much of our research and development resources to the military sector that we have lost our civilian industrial productivity edge." Although Bush hoped that the end of the Cold War would not simultaneously end Washington's global role, from both ends of the American political spectrum came cries for the very retrenchment he feared.[60]

Bush feared American isolationism, in fact, more than he feared the once-provocative ideas of perestroika and glasnost. He learned over the course of his administration to trust Gorbachev, and of equal importance in his world-view, learned to view the communist leader as a friend. He entered office wary of Gorbachev's reforms and intents, but by 1991 Bush had come to rely on his Soviet counterpart and to see him—and a reformed Soviet state—as a global partner, not a strategic competitor. In the midst of the Gulf War, in fact, when Gorbachev attempted an eleventh-hour intervention to maintain peace and save his former ally in Baghdad, Bush, wearied by events and frustrated by Soviet diplomacy, reached his saturation point. He began to yell at Gorbachev in the midst of a multi-hour phone call. Typically it is difficult to discern when someone is yelling by reading an official transcript. In this case, however, the transcript reveals Gorbachev saying over and over, "Calm down George, calm down."

The reason for Bush's anger was not just the stress of the moment but also his fear that Gorbachev's intervention might wreck his broader plans for the post–Cold War order. Gorbachev listened and effectively ended his diplomatic intervention, prudently calculating that relations with the world's most powerful state, and most powerful man, mattered far more than Saddam Hussein's fate. He trusted in Bush, having little choice to do otherwise. Bush, in turn, came to see in Gorbachev possibilities for partnership he had never imagined possible with a devoted communist leader. Indeed by the late summer of 1991, as Soviet hardliners attempted a last-ditch effort to thwart reform by removing Gorbachev from office in an attempted coup, Bush's affection for his Soviet counterpart was palpable in their first post-crisis conversations. "Oh my god, that's wonderful. Mikhail!" Bush declared when first hearing his counterpart's tired voice. He was thankful, of course, that stability had (somewhat) returned to a nuclear-armed superpower. And he was thankful, no doubt, that hardliners had not retained power. But he was also grateful, ultimately, that he still had his partner, whom he had learned to trust.[61]

Even at the moment of triumph, with the Cold War over, the Berlin Wall down, and the Gulf War won, many Americans failed to share Bush's optimism about the future, a sure sign that he had failed to convey to the electorate the transformation he experienced in conceding that the Cold War was finally over. Bush had learned and changed, retaining faith in the centrality of America's global role even as he incorporated former adversaries, the Soviets chief among them, into his vision of the future. He failed, however, to transmit the nuanced character of his transformation to the American people, and this undoubtedly contributed to his 1992 electoral defeat. After finally conceding that the Cold War was over, Bush sailed into retirement along with it.

CHARACTER AND CONSEQUENCE
The John Tower Confirmation Battle

Robert A. Strong

In December 1988 when George Bush announced his choice for secretary of defense, he appeared to be making a conventional cabinet nomination. Like many of his other early appointments, the nominee for the Pentagon was an old friend and political ally. He was a former senator from the president-elect's home state. He had served as chair of the Senate Armed Services Committee, as the senior member of a high-profile commission that investigated a foreign policy scandal in the Reagan White House, and as leader of a delegation that negotiated arms control in Geneva. He was an acknowledged expert on the defense budget and national security issues. As a former member of the legislative body that would vote on his nomination, John Tower seemed likely to win an easy and early confirmation. In the history of the republic, only eight cabinet-level nominees had ever been rejected on the floor of the Senate. None had suffered that fate since 1959. No newly elected president had ever lost a Senate vote on a cabinet nomination.[1]

John Tower became the ninth cabinet nominee rejected by the Senate and the first to be denied his post at the outset of a new administration. The confirmation battle that took place in the honeymoon weeks of the Bush administration was a media circus dominated by salacious accusations about the nominee's private life. Although there was no doubt some truth in the observations that Tower, at various points in his career, drank hard liquor and enjoyed the company of women, many of the accusations that garnered the most media attention were demonstrably false or came from obviously unreliable sources. Senator John McCain called the Tower confirmation a "witch trial."[2] NBC anchor Tom Brokaw concluded that the coverage of Tower's nomination had been "unconscionable," involving the frequent airing of "very damaging allegations without documentation or confirmation."[3] Despite this lack of documentation and confirmation, or perhaps because of it, the newly elected president suffered a significant defeat in his dealings with the Democratic majority in the Senate and his nominee suffered a public humiliation from which he never recovered.[4]

The Tower nomination is often studied by those who are interested in the politics of scandal, the breakdown of collegiality in Congress, and issues related to media reporting on the personal lives of public servants.[5] But students of the Bush administration also have a number of lessons to learn from this episode. The Senate battle over John Tower served as a preview and a prelude to the even more politicized Supreme Court confirmation conflict involving Clarence Thomas, when once again the private behavior of the nominee and what constituted appropriate evidence to judge that private behavior were controversial matters. The episode may also be important for the clues it gives to the character of the forty-first president.

Although Tower's rejection on the Senate floor was an unusual event, it was not unheard of for a presidential nominee to encounter difficulties in the confirmation process. When such difficulties arose, other presidents tended to cut their losses and move on. In 1977, Jimmy Carter abandoned Ted Sorensen as his choice for director of the CIA. Bill Clinton, serving in the term immediately after Bush, had a series of problems with his Justice Department appointments and withdrew his support from three prominent nominees who encountered confirmation controversies. George Bush took a different path. He stuck with Tower, even after the prospects of winning on the Senate floor became dim and even after the nominee expressed some interest in withdrawing. Bush did so at some expense to his political reputation at the outset of his presidency and to his relations with the Democratic Senate majority. Why did the president steadfastly support his wounded nominee when there was an easy, obvious, and conventional way out? The answer to that question tells us something important about George Herbert Walker Bush.

The President's Choice

John Tower may initially have been seen as a likely nominee for George Bush's cabinet, but earlier in his career he was a most unlikely United States senator. The son and the grandson of Methodist ministers, Tower was an obscure college professor and a sometime polemicist for the Texas Republican Party when he was asked to run for the Senate in 1960. Apparently no one else could be found to stand against Lyndon Johnson, then the majority leader of the Senate and the Democratic candidate for the vice presidency. Tower garnered 41 percent of the vote, a respectable showing for a Republican in Texas, and lost the Senate race to Johnson. But because the Kennedy-Johnson national ticket won, a special election was called to fill Johnson's seat. A large field of Democratic hopefuls entered the open primary. The Democrats fought bitterly among themselves, and in the run-off election, in which Tower faced conservative Democrat William Blakley, liberal Democrats voted for Tower as the lesser evil or stayed away from the polls completely. Tower, to nearly everyone's surprise, won a narrow victory and became the first Republican Senator since Reconstruction to be elected in a former Confederate state.

When he first went to Washington, Tower behaved as if he would only have one term in the Senate, a reasonable assumption for a southern Republican who had won his seat by a narrow margin. Tower enjoyed his newfound fame. He was celebrated by conservative audiences across the country and became an outspoken opponent of the New Frontier legislation of the Kennedy administration and, after Kennedy was assassinated, of Johnson's Great Society legislation. He voted against the Civil Rights Act of 1964 and the Voting Rights Act of 1965 and supported conservative Barry Goldwater for the presidency in 1964. He also began to acquire a reputation for a liquor-lubricated social life. Such a reputation did not make him distinctive in the nation's capital in the 1960s.

After the unlikely senator won a second term in 1966 against a still-divided Texas Democratic party, he began to moderate some of his political positions and focus more of his attention on the issues that came before the Senate committees on which he served. Over the years, Tower demonstrated that his early political career was not a fluke; he won two more terms in 1972 and 1978 despite personal problems that led to a divorce, a second marriage, and eventually a second and much more bitter and public divorce. Always a staunch anti-communist and proponent of a strong national defense, Tower moved away from the ideological conservative movement. He took a pro-choice position on abortion and in 1976 campaigned for the moderate Gerald Ford, not the conservative Ronald Reagan, in the contest for the Republican presidential nomination.

In his home state Tower remained an unusual success story. Lacking the stature of Lyndon Johnson, the wealth of Lloyd Bentsen or George Bush, or the flare of John Connally, Tower nevertheless led the Republican Party (which Connally eventually joined) to a position as a consistent competitor in statewide races. Throughout these years he was an important mentor for up-and-coming Republicans, including Bush, who was elected to the House of Representatives in Houston and tried twice to win the other Texas Senate seat. In Bush's 1970 Senate race, Tower, then the chair of the Republican Senate Campaign Committee, provided him with almost twice as much financial support as was given to any other Republican candidate.[6] When Bush got into trouble in his Houston congressional district for a vote in favor of fair-housing legislation, Tower defended him to Texas conservatives.[7] In 1980, and again in 1988, Tower supported Bush in his campaigns for the presidency.

When Reagan, with Bush as vice president, was elected in 1980, Tower lobbied to become secretary of defense. It was a job he had wanted for some time, but the new president told the Texas senator that his leadership would be more important as the chair of the Armed Services Committee. From 1981 to 1984 Tower pushed for dramatic expansion of the defense budget and the Reagan military buildup. As a powerful committee chair and throughout his later years in the Senate, Tower was acknowledged for his intelligence and determination to move an agenda, but he made few close friends and was thought by many to be arrogant, imperious, and uncompromising. His critics would later say that he had "never seen a weapons system he did not like."[8] But he was a genuine expert on Pentagon projects and, like many other such experts, was never an enthusiastic advocate of Reagan's strategic defense initiative (the so-called Star Wars missile defense system). After leaving the Senate in 1985, Tower worked as a consultant and held two major presidential appointments as head of an arms control delegation in Geneva and as the leader of the presidential commission that investigated the Iran-Contra scandal. The *Tower Report* on Iran-Contra was highly critical of President Reagan for his loose administrative style but placed most of the blame for the failures that took place on certain National Security Council staff members who were fired, investigated, and indicted. George Bush, who publicly said that he "was out of the loop" on the decisions that led to Iran-Contra, was not seriously criticized in the *Tower Report*.

Very few knowledgeable observers were surprised by President Bush's decision to name Tower to the top Pentagon position. The president's first cabinet appointment had gone to James Baker as secretary of state. Baker was a long-time friend from Houston, an experienced member of the Reagan administration, and the campaign manager of Bush's unsuccessful run for the White House in 1980 and his successful one eight years later. Some of the other senior cabinet appointments also went to people Bush had known and trusted for many years, including Nicholas Brady as treasury secretary, Robert Mosbacher as commerce secretary, and Brent Scowcroft as national security advisor.[9] The president was clearly assembling a team of advisors, particularly in the area of foreign affairs, that included friends and associates he had known for a long time. John Tower fit the profile.

Tower met with the president-elect on November 19, 1988, and outlined the case for naming a secretary of defense, like himself, who would not need on-the-job training. In the talking points he prepared for this meeting, Tower argued that the administration's leading critics on defense-related issues were likely to be Democratic senators Sam Nunn, Charles Robb, and Al Gore, who had all served with Tower on the Armed Services Committee that Nunn now chaired. The president needed a secretary who knew the issues and the players on Capitol Hill, not someone from industry who would have a lot to learn about Washington and could easily be captured by Pentagon bureaucrats. Tower admitted that budgets would have to be cut and outlined his hope that cuts might be accompanied by the implementation of a two-year defense budget that would allow for more coherent planning.[10] John Sununu, who participated in some of the meetings with the prospective secretary of defense in the fall of 1988, reports that he was highly impressed by Tower's command of defense matters and satisfied that he had workable strategies for managing the department in austere times. Tower "really was excellent on identifying the approach that could be taken to make reductions in defense spending without severely impacting the defense readiness of the country," says Sununu. "Really was very, very impressive in his understanding of how to do this. So the President really wanted John Tower as Secretary of Defense."[11]

Although President Bush appears to have made up his mind about the nomination in mid-November or earlier, the announcement of the Tower choice was delayed to allow time for an extensive FBI background check. Such checks were routine but in Tower's case would obviously include investigation of the old complaints about liquor and ladies that had circulated in Washington for nearly two decades. Those complaints may have been fueled by new and specific accusations emanating from the bitter divorce that had ended Tower's second marriage. While the FBI did its work, newspaper stories critical of the likely nominee appeared in the *Atlanta Constitution*, the *Los Angeles Times*, and the *New York Post*. The last of these appeared on November 25 and carried the headline "Tower Facing Sex Scandal." The story reported claims from the divorce proceedings that Tower had had affairs with three women in the 1980s, including a maid in Geneva when he was serving as an arms control negotiator.[12]

Other issues also kept the FBI busy. Some people raised questions about how the former Senator had used his campaign war chest after he decided not to run for a fifth term in 1984 and wondered exactly what he did as a consultant to various defense contractors in the years after his Senate career. Although it was commonplace and perfectly legal for former members of Congress to sell their expertise to corporate clients after leaving office, it was almost always difficult to prove full compliance with the complicated set of regulations that governed such activity or to avoid the appearance of improper ties and conflicts of interest for anyone returning to government service. President Bush was broadly concerned about such issues and appointed a bipartisan commission to review the laws and ethical standards governing former and future government appointees. The president declared a National Ethics Week shortly after his inauguration, and in this climate, several members of the new administration, including Secretary of State Baker and White House counselor C. Boyden Gray, were under scrutiny about which of their assets constituted possible conflicts of interest and which had to be put into blind trusts.[13]

While the FBI was investigating Tower, some of the president's closest advisors, reportedly including Robert Teeter, Nicholas Brady, Greg Fuller, and Boyden Gray, argued against the nomination.[14] Bush was not moved by whatever objections his advisors raised or by any of the evidence that the FBI uncovered. In mid-December the president was briefed on what became Tower's first FBI report. That document was based on interviews with seventy-nine individuals and noted that one anonymous source said that Tower abused alcohol.[15] Other witnesses reported sexual indiscretions by the nominee, but the FBI investigators could not substantiate these allegations. When the nomination was made public on December 16, the president-elect was asked about the rumors that had appeared in the press and publicly pronounced that he was satisfied with what had been learned in the FBI investigation and speculated that it would also satisfy "the most inquisitive members of the Senate."[16] Senate hearings were scheduled for January, after the holiday recess and the president's inauguration.

The initial hearings went reasonably well. Tower reassured the members of the committee, as he had earlier reassured President Bush, that he understood the budget realities of the late 1980s. The president had promised no new taxes and had inherited a large and growing budget deficit. In that environment, there would be pressure to reduce defense spending, and Tower was prepared to consider procurement reforms to improve the efficiency of the department he would lead. He answered detailed questions about his use of residual campaign funds after leaving the Senate and about his work as a consultant to various defense contractors. He promised to remove himself from any decisions that might involve those former clients. Senator Edward M. Kennedy reflected the tone of the early proceedings and their likely outcome when he observed that "I didn't always agree with Senator Tower, but I respected him and am looking forward to working with him as Secretary of Defense."[17] The Massachusetts Democrat apparently expected, as many observers did, that his former colleague would win confirmation despite the negative news stories about his personal life. Republican senator Richard Shelby of Alabama was even more dismissive of the media accounts of Tower's private behavior when he suggested in an off-the-record comment that he would "never trust a man who didn't drink a little and chase a little."[18] Whatever the initial expectations of Senators Kennedy and Shelby may have been, the dynamics of the confirmation process changed dramatically with one of the final witnesses heard by the Armed Services Committee.

Tower's Inferno[19]

Paul Weyrich was neither a close friend nor a professional associate of John Tower. He was a political activist and fund-raiser with close ties to the religious right in the Republican Party. In what *Newsweek* identified as "one of the most extraordinary moments in the history of confirmation hearings," Weyrich testified on January 31, 1989, that over many years he had seen the nominee in a condition involving a "lack of sobriety" and "with women to whom he was not married."[20] The Weyrich accusations were not much more specific than that, but because they conformed to what many members of the Senate and press corps already knew to be long-standing stories about Tower's personal behavior, they had an immediate and powerful effect. When the committee went behind closed doors to hear more from Weyrich and one other witness who gave testimony about the prevailing rumors, a number of senators were not impressed. In particular Senator McCain, who earlier in his career had worked for Senator Tower, was appalled to discover that Weyrich's testimony was based on one occasion when he saw Tower "coming on" to a woman who was not his wife at the Monocle, a restaurant and bar close to the cluster of Senate office buildings. "What do you mean by 'coming on'?" McCain asked. Weyrich replied that he had seen Tower and the woman in question holding hands. According to McCain, Weyrich made "an ass of himself behind closed doors."[21] Nevertheless, his testimony was damaging. The public portion was brief and included tantalizing references to inebriation and infidelity. It played well in various media outlets that were already carrying stories about Tower's personal life. Weyrich's inability to provide any convincing corroborating detail was known only to the committee members who attended the confidential closed session.

The next day Tower returned to the witness chair to deny Weyrich's allegations. When Senator Nunn asked the nominee directly if he had a drinking problem, Tower responded, "I have none, Senator. I am a man of some discipline."[22] That direct denial did not end the issue. Though Nunn publicly predicted that his committee was likely to endorse the nominee, he postponed the committee vote that had been expected to take place immediately after the hearings. The Weyrich testimony guaranteed that there would be further FBI investigation of the Tower nomination and additional delays in any formal action by the Armed Services Committee.

Two days after the first round of committee hearings, Republican congressman Larry Combest of Texas met with Senators Nunn and John Warner. Combest had been a staff assistant to Tower before he ran for Congress and wanted to reassure his Senate colleagues that there was no serious question about his former boss. He wanted to convey to the senators two conclusions from his personal observations: Tower drank more in the 1970s than he did today, and even in those earlier days his drinking had not been a serious problem. Instead, and inadvertently, the congressman provided the two senior members of the Armed Services Committee with a reliable eyewitness report, by someone favorable to the nominee, that confirmed the existence of a drinking problem.

Nunn came away from the conversation with information that Tower used to consume a bottle of Scotch in one evening and occasionally had to be helped to bed by an aide. Combest's later and much more detailed testimony to FBI investigators was more balanced and nuanced than his brief conversation with Nunn and Warner. Combest told the FBI that he had seen Tower "drink to excess" on perhaps two occasions in the mid-1970s when the Senator was particularly distraught about the divorce proceedings ending his first marriage.[23] Since 1978, Combest reported, Tower had apparently given up hard liquor and Combest had not seen him consume anything stronger than a glass of wine. He told the FBI that he considered Tower to be a first-rate statesman but a lousy politician. He was not a "back slapper," "a chew the fat politician," or a "bullshitter." Tower was, in reality, "a shy person, whose shyness is frequently misconstrued as 'aloofness.'"[24] The scotch he drank at the end of the day in the 1970s helped him overcome his shyness and relax with friends and staff. On the question of womanizing, Combest speculated that this was more a matter of perception than reality. The senator dressed in expensive suits and may have cultivated a reputation as a ladies man to boost his ego and to demonstrate that a man of modest stature could be attractive to women. Combest reported that he never saw Tower behave "inappropriately" or in an "ungentlemanly" fashion in the presence of women.[25]

Combest's testimony, like Weyrich's, had two sides, but only the side that did damage to the nominee had real consequences. After the congressman's conversation with Nunn and Warner, the two senior senators wrote a memo arguing that the accusations involving alcohol against Tower would have to be seriously examined. Tower believed that the Combest conversation, more than the Weyrich testimony, was crucial to Sam Nunn's eventual decision to oppose the nomination, although Nunn made no public indication of how he would vote for several days after meeting with Combest.[26] Throughout this period the FBI conducted additional interviews of Combest and others whose names had come forward in connection with new accusations about Tower. Public reporting on the growing controversy made it open season for anyone who wanted to discredit the former senator. Tower remembered feeling as if he were living in a Kafkaesque world in which the cycle of investigation-allegation-investigation would never end. But if the cycle continued, "enough mud would be thrown on my reputation—for whatever reason, be it malice, politics, kookiness, the vindictiveness of an ex-wife—that it would be impossible to scrape it off in a month or a year or a lifetime."[27]

Some of the accusations that were reported in this period were genuinely bizarre. One story had the senator and a former Russian ballerina dancing and disrobing on top of a piano at a Texas country club. It turned out that the only Russian ballerina living in Texas who had ever met Tower was seventy years old and she told the FBI that the story was preposterous. She had never danced on a piano with any member of Congress, with or without clothing, and, furthermore, if the story involved some other Russian émigré, she was confident that she would have heard about it. It wasn't true.[28] But the story was broadcast on the *NBC Nightly News*. Another accusation about a drunk-driving incident involved a car that Tower had never owned. Yet another concerning sexual harassment in his Senate office came in a telephone tip from an individual who had no discernible connection to Tower. That accusation could not be corroborated by anyone with actual knowledge of the senator's staff. On February 7, a White House lawyer working on the Tower confirmation briefed the Republican Senate caucus about the failure of the FBI to find any credible evidence about either the new or the old accusations. This was a preliminary report and did not reflect all of the investigations that were still under way. The final FBI report would not be completed until February 20. The fact that the Republicans got this early information and received it before the same information was officially delivered to the Armed Services Committee did not please Senator Nunn, who continued to move toward open opposition. Nunn postponed the committee's official vote on the nomination until after the February congressional recess. This left more time for rumors to fly.

And fly they did. Throughout the deliberations on the Tower nomination, information from the FBI investigations was leaked to multiple media organizations. According to John McCain, "the shortest trip in Washington was the distance traveled by details from the FBI reports in committee files—no matter how salacious, absurd, or provably false—to the front pages of the nation's newspapers."[29] This was unusual in confirmation cases, since FBI files were usually treated by all who officially saw them with some sensitivity. They were often raw documents that included transcripts of investigator meetings with unreliable witnesses and no accompanying analysis of the witnesses' veracity. If the FBI talked to someone, a summary of the conversation became part of the file. It is, of course, nearly impossible to prove that a particular person was responsible for leaking FBI material to a particular news organization. Tower notes that Nunn's senior staff assistant on the Armed Services Committee, who may not have been treated well when Tower chaired the committee, was allowed to see the FBI material, something that had not happened in the past. Tower expressed his suspicion that Nunn or his staff was directly responsible for news stories based on FBI interviews.[30] As interest grew in the confirmation controversy, it is also possible that individuals who were making allegations about incidents in Tower's past to the FBI and to other government officials were passing the same information to journalists. Several people report that Tower's second wife was the source for a number of the early press accounts of his private behavior. However they got there, the allegations made good copy and the Kafkaesque cycle that Tower feared filled the month of February.

As senators were returning from the February recess, a second FBI report was delivered to the White House and to the Armed Services Committee. The president and his staff found the report reassuring since it contained no concrete evidence that any of the various accusations about alcohol abuse or sexual misconduct were true. The report also cleared the senator of direct involvement in an ongoing investigation of contractor problems in Pentagon procurement. Despite the White House's optimism about the new report, Senator Nunn and the Democrats on the Armed Services Committee read it in a different way. Although there was no convincing confirmation of alcohol abuse, there were plenty of allegations. "There is no smoking gun," said Senator Tim Wirth, a Democrat from Colorado. "But the ground, it seems to me, is littered with a substantial number of empty cartridges."[31] In public statements by Nunn and some of the other Democratic members of the committee, concern was expressed about the particularly sensitive role of the secretary of defense in the military chain of command and the possibility that Tower's judgment might be impaired by alcohol at a time of crisis. These concerns were connected to the long list of allegations about alcohol abuse and not to any recent eyewitness reports concerning Tower's behavior. Combest's testimony about a few occasions of excessive drinking in the 1970s are the only ones Nunn is known to have heard from a reliable source. Other Democratic senators, who did not share Nunn's concerns about alcohol or may not have wanted to publicly criticize Tower's private life, couched their reservations in comments that harkened back to old issues involving conflicts of interest and questions about Tower's behavior as a consultant.

In a straight party-line vote of 11 to 9, the Armed Services Committee recommended against the Tower nomination on February 23. Three days later the nominee appeared on a popular Sunday morning news program and pledged not to drink any form of alcohol while serving as secretary of defense. The "pledge," as it became known, did not help the senator's prospects for confirmation. It may actually have made matters worse since the promise not to consume alcohol in the future suggested that the concerns about Tower's drinking in the past had some validity. Even if the pledge did some good, it was too little and too late to stem the tide of opposition to the nomination that had been growing throughout the month of February. Senator Nunn, a moderate Democrat respected for his defense expertise, was now leading the campaign to defeat the nomination, and the administration had to consider whether it was wise to confront a powerful committee chair by forcing a floor vote and a likely defeat. Throughout the month of February, President Bush rejected all suggestions to withdraw the nomination, including one from the beleaguered nominee, and continued to privately and publicly praise John Tower.

A few Senate Democrats, including southerners Howell Heflin of Alabama and Lloyd Bentsen of Texas, broke with their party and announced that they would support the nomination. Christopher Dodd, a liberal Democrat from Connecticut, remembered that Tower had been one of only five members of the Senate to support his father in a 1967 censure vote. The younger Dodd announced that he would vote for Tower's nomination. No other Democrats broke ranks.

A few days before the scheduled floor vote, the *Washington Post* ran the most damaging news story that had yet appeared concerning Tower's conduct. Bob Woodward's front-page story described incidents that allegedly occurred in the mid-1970s when Tower, as a member of the Armed Services Committee, made two visits to an air force base in Austin, Texas. According to a witness, retired sergeant Bob Jackson, the senator was visibly drunk during his inspection tours and, on two separate occasions, fondled a female employee and a woman among the enlisted personnel on the base. One of Woodward's sources for the story was clearly the FBI file that many senators were reviewing in preparation for the upcoming vote.[32] That night an abbreviated version of Jackson's allegation was included on the CBS evening news.

By the next day the story had been largely discredited. Senator McCain, rushing to the defense of his former boss, discovered that the witness cited in Woodward's account had retired early from the air force as a result of psychological problems. According to McCain's air force sources, Jackson suffered from "mixed personality disorder with antisocial and hysterical features."[33] Moreover, and more importantly, Jackson had not even been stationed at the air force base near Austin when Tower made his one and only official visit in 1975.[34] Air force officers who were present when the senator toured the base uniformly reported that his behavior had been professional and without incident. The *Washington Post* printed a second front-page story on March 3 with all the evidence that McCain had used on the Senate floor to undermine the original account. Years later, in a footnote in one of his books, Woodard expressed regret for publishing the Jackson story.[35]

Whatever regrets Bob Woodward may have had came far too late to help John Tower. When the Senate floor debate ended, only three Democrats—Heflin, Bentsen, and Dodd—voted to support the Republican nominee, and one Republican, Nancy Kassebaum of Kansas, voted with the Democratic majority. The final tally was 47–53, with Republicans supporting the nomination by 44–1 and

Democrats opposing it by 3–52. The president had been dealt a historic defeat, John Tower's reputation had been destroyed, and new standards had been set for the evaluation of the private conduct of public officials. Those new standards were clearly higher than they had been in the past regarding the kind of personal behavior that would be tolerated, but they were also vague about what evidence could be used to assess the behavior in question. The nation would struggle with these issues in the years ahead, up to and including the impeachment proceedings against President Clinton.

Loyalty

George Bush quickly named Richard Cheney, another longtime friend and associate with experience in Congress, to the post of secretary of defense. This time the nomination was overwhelmingly approved in a matter of days without any possibility for an exhaustive FBI background investigation. Cheney became an integral part of the administration's tightly knit national security team and a highly regarded secretary of defense during the Gulf War. The president was no doubt pleased with Cheney's selection and performance, but he never expressed any regret in public or private about his first choice for the Pentagon position. Bush remained loyal to John Tower at every stage of the long, drawn-out confirmation ordeal and in every public comment he made about Tower for the remainder of his administration.[36]

In a diary entry on February 9, 1989, Bush recorded his frustration with the controversy that had arisen concerning his original choice for secretary of defense. "It's so damn ugly," he wrote. "Rumor after rumor, insinuation after insinuation, investigation after reinvestigation. And it's damned unfair."[37] Just before the Armed Services Committee vote, the president wrote a letter to a friend, Charles Bartlett, expressing his determination to stick with his nominee and complaining, "I have never seen such a campaign of innuendo, vicious rumor and gossip in my entire life."[38] On the same day the president wrote to Bartlett, he wrote in his diary. "No one has ever questioned his [Tower's] ability to run the department and his knowledge of defense matters, but he has been tested by fire and he's earned my support. And he damn sure has got it."[39] It was evidently difficult for President Bush to comment on what was happening to John Tower without using the word "damn."

The next day the president left Washington to attend the funeral of Emperor Hirohito. The news of the negative vote in the Armed Services Committee dominated his press conference in Japan and when the presidential party went on to visit Beijing, Bush spent time late at night in China calling Democratic senators back in Washington and asking them to support Tower. The president made no progress, but he refused to "knuckle down to the idea that allegations and rumors should bring down a man whose qualifications are unchallenged."[40]

On at least three occasions, John Tower considered withdrawing his name from nomination. On February 7, in a late-night conversation with Boyden Gray, he reportedly offered to withdraw.[41] Near the end of the month, after Bush returned from Asia, Tower talked to Gray again about the slim prospects for success on the Senate floor and this time made his offer to withdraw directly to the president. Bush rejected the offer without giving it serious consideration and reportedly said, "To Hell with it. Let's fight this one out."[42] Between those two conversations, Tower made another offer to drop out of the nomination process to his former staffer Fred McClure, who was working in legislative affairs for the new administration. McClure reports an emotional encounter with his former boss in the Jefferson Hotel at the height of the media attacks that followed the committee hearings. Alone in the hotel room, Tower "turned to me and he said, 'Fred,' and he had tears in his eyes, 'I've decided I'm going to call the President this afternoon and ask him to withdraw my name as Secretary of Defense because it's taking too much of a toll on him. It's going to affect his ability to be the leader that I'm confident that he can become and is, and I don't need to be this kind of distraction, and I'm tired of this.'" McClure convinced Tower not to back out and to continue the fight.

And, of course, the president fought with him. On February 28, President Bush spent the whole day, from 8:30 a.m. to 6:00 p.m., talking to senators about the Tower nomination.[43] Whether he called long distance from China or talked to them in Washington, the opposition could not be moved. Democrats had, for the most part, decided to support their chair of the Armed Services Committee, and the Democratic majority leader, George Mitchell, helped produce a party-line vote. According to some observers, toward the end of these legislative deliberations the Tower nomination was no longer merely about the nominee. As the issue moved to the Senate floor, it became a test of partisan strength with "at least a whiff . . . of resentment over what the recent campaign had done to the character of Governor Dukakis."[44] The Democrats held their ground with just as much tenacity and determination as the president showed on his side of the question. In the end, party discipline carried more weight than the president's personal pleas on behalf of his friend from Texas.

The story of the John Tower nomination involves a complicated set of personal and partisan motives among a variety of people. In some cases, it is difficult to fully explain the behavior of principal participants. For example, it is not clear why Paul Weyrich chose to testify against the nominee with accusations about Tower's personal behavior that he could not corroborate behind closed doors. Weyrich was critical of Tower for his position on abortion and other social issues, but there were other members of the Republican Party with similar views and Weyrich had to go out of his way to get on the witness list and push the committee to public discussion of alcohol and infidelity. Exactly why he chose to do that remains unclear. There are also problems explaining the motivations of Sam Nunn. The senator from Georgia had a well-earned reputation as a moderate and serious member of the Senate. On this issue he became the leader of a highly partisan and controversial vote against a former colleague on the Arms Services Committee. There are some reports suggesting that Nunn agonized about what to do with the mixed information his committee received about Tower's personal behavior.[45] In his public statements, Nunn said that he was worried about a secretary of defense who had a problem with alcohol even if the best evidence about that problem involved periods of time in the past. The nation should not take chances with an important cabinet post. Was that the whole story? Were there incidents in Nunn's earlier committee service under Tower's chairmanship that led to animosities or rivalries that came to full fruition in the nomination process? Did the senator from Georgia want the new president to appoint a less-experienced secretary of defense so that his committee could exercise more influence over the important defense budget issues that lay ahead?[46] Questions about Nunn's decisions and actions remain. However important they may be, they are probably less important than the questions about why George H. W. Bush made the Tower nomination in the first place and why he stuck with it.

Why did President Bush insist on the selection of an individual for a sensitive senior cabinet post when the early publicity about the prospective nomination made it perfectly clear that there was likely to be some airing of unpleasant material about the nominee's personal behavior? Why did Bush ignore the advice of aides and counselors who warned him about the potential for controversy? And why did he continue to fully support his troubled nominee, even after Tower was ready to throw in the towel and the head counts in the Senate made it clear that the nomination was lost? The best answer to all of these questions is the simplest one—loyalty. John Tower was George Bush's friend and political mentor and the president never gave any public or private indication that he would consider abandoning his first choice for secretary of defense. Gregg Fuller, a senior advisor to Vice President Bush, tried to convince the president not to make the Tower nomination and quickly saw the futility of his position. According to a reporter who interviewed him, "Fuller knew loyalty was a core value for Bush, and there was no budging him."[47] There were costs associated with that loyalty and not just the obvious ones involved in the loss of an important congressional vote at the outset of the administration.

The efforts of the president to make the elevation of government ethics a theme early in his administration were overwhelmed by the Tower controversy. So were many other things. The president's first major trip abroad, which included an important meeting with French leader François Mitterrand at the Hirohito funeral and sensitive negotiations with the Japanese about the joint development of a new fighter aircraft, were hardly reported in the aftermath of the Armed Services Committee vote against Tower. The president's press conference in Japan was dominated by the news from Washington and questions about his controversial nominee. Later in his Far East trip and when he returned to the White House, the president devoted a significant amount of time and energy to the unsuccessful effort to win some Democratic support for his nominee, time and energy that might have been spent on other administration priorities. These costs must have been obvious to the president, but they never altered his decisions about the nominee.

Bush entered the White House calling for a "kinder and gentler" version of the Reagan revolution and better relations between the executive and legislative branches. The American people "didn't send us here to bicker," he told the nation, including the assembled members of Congress, in his inaugural address. "They ask us to rise above the merely partisan."[48] The media stories on John Tower were neither kind nor gentle. The deliberations about the president's nominee rarely rose above the partisan and were accompanied by a souring of the political atmosphere on Capitol Hill. Investigations of Democratic house speaker Jim Wright, publicity about suspicious overdrafts for members allowed by a congressional credit union, scandals involving meetings between prominent senators and a notorious savings and loan executive, and a variety of ethical issues would do considerable damage to the reputations of both individual legislators and Congress as a whole. Neither the president nor the members of Congress wanted this result, and even though the Tower controversy was only a small part of the larger deterioration in congressional collegiality and public esteem for legislators, it was a small part that mattered. A timely withdrawal of the Tower nomination after it was clearly in trouble would have meant one less instance of sustained national publicity damaging a public figure and the political profession.

Such a quick withdrawal would arguably have been the wise course of action for a new administration seeking better relations with Capitol Hill and would certainly have been better for Tower's personal reputation, which suffered more with each passing day in late February and early March. But as the president kept insisting to anyone and everyone who urged withdrawal, that result would not have been fair. Whatever Tower's personal problems may have been, many of the published accounts of his behavior were not true and were printed and broadcast without adequate checking of facts. Reporters were no doubt able to verify that what they were reporting about Tower came from the confidential FBI file, but they could not verify whether the material in that file deserved public dissemination. Much of it did not. Tower said that the staff of the Armed Services

Committee sorted accusations against the nominee into separate categories depending on the reliability of the source and the likelihood that the accusation might be substantive. One category was referred to as the X file. It contained accusations that were so bizarre and unsubstantiated that they did not deserve further investigation. Bob Woodward's damaging front-page story about alleged episodes of sexual harassment at a Texas airbase, published just before the Senate vote, came from that file.[49] The treatment of John Tower was unfair. And the president of the United States did not like it and did not want to see it succeed.

Although Bush wanted to establish high ethical standards for his administration, he also understood that a cumbersome clearance and confirmation process could get in the way of finding and appointing high-quality nominees. Throughout recent administrations the confirmation process has been getting longer, increasingly intrusive, and more highly politicized. Nominees for positions that require Senate confirmation are asked to answer sixty-four pages of questions about every stage of their careers and personal lives. Those who have previously served in government have to resubmit the same information for each new appointment and reopen the investigation of any questions that may have been raised in previous confirmations. Today, almost all cabinet officers, one leading scholar notes, feel that they are "innocent until nominated."[50] Once subjected to the kind of FBI investigation that has become common in the review of senior appointees, anyone would have to worry about what such a file might contain or what the readers of that file might do with the information collected. These problems would have emerged even without the Tower controversy, but his nomination clearly raised the bar on acceptable personal behavior and lowered it on what evidence could be publicly discussed regarding that behavior. There were clearly issues of fairness and even larger issues about how to structure a humane review process for prospective public servants that could have justified the president's continued support for his nominee.

Moreover, a case can be made that it was politically wise for the president to stick with his first choice apart from any considerations of personal loyalty or procedural fairness. John Sununu was convinced that staying the course would not "hurt George Bush one iota." On the other hand, withdrawing a nomination quickly on the basis of charges that were partly trumped up would have been taken as a sign of weakness in a president who faced large opposition majorities in both houses of Congress. Forcing a difficult vote arguably hurt Democrats almost as much as it hurt the president. Surely among the senators voting against Tower were a few whose private lives could not have withstood the kind of scrutiny that Tower received. Forcing those senators to cast an unpleasant— and perhaps hypocritical—vote had to have some costs within the Democratic caucus. On the Republican side there was genuine appreciation of the way the president stood his ground and stuck with the former Republican senator who had chaired an important committee. Some members of the party outside Congress—Paul Weyrich, Phyllis Schlafly, Pat Robertson, Kenneth Adelman, and Strategic Defense Initiative advocate General Daniel Graham—openly opposed the nomination, but in the Senate there was solid Republican support for the president's nominee. Even Nancy Kassebaum would have voted for the nomination if her vote had been decisive.[51] John McCain took particular pride in fighting this losing battle and would not have been happy about the withdrawal of a nominee he genuinely admired. This was an issue on which the Republican minority in the Senate was united.

Very little evidence exists to suggest that President Bush made his decision to force a Senate vote on the basis of either a principled defense of legitimate standards in the confirmation process or a political calculation that the Democrats might suffer for their action while the Republicans might benefit by standing up for one of their own. Everything the president recorded in his diary, everything he said in lobbying for his candidate, and certainly everything he said in public paints a clear and simple picture of a friend supporting a friend and of a president utterly dismissive of any advice to abandon that friend.

According to James Baker, loyalty was a "defining strength" in George Bush's character.[52] And by loyalty, Baker meant loyalty to people, not to ideas. The Tower nomination was a complicated case in which some politicians might have found their loyalties divided. If the president genuinely wanted to emphasize the highest standards for government officials in his administration, John Tower, or at least the publicity that he attracted, would not have helped his cause. If the president felt fully committed to both the idea of high ethical standards and the appointment of his friend to a cabinet post, the Tower controversy should have pulled him in opposite directions. It did not. George Bush never wavered in his support for John Tower. At one point a reportedly teary-eyed Tower told the president, "I can never thank you enough for standing at my side."[53] The president apparently gave very little consideration to doing anything else. He appears to have thought about the issue almost exclusively in terms of how it was affecting his friend. That was the loyalty that George Bush both practiced and preached.[54]

Of course, all presidents preach loyalty. They generally have in mind the faithful support they expect from those who work in the White House and in the cabinet and measure it by the absence of leaks and by a willingness to stick with the administration in controversial decisions. It goes without saying that genuine loyalty has to be reciprocal and must also involve acts of support for subordinates beyond naming them to their posts. Although that principle may go without saying, the reality is that costly acts of loyalty by senior officials on behalf of their friends and subordinates are somewhat rare. Harry Truman's decision as vice president to attend the funeral of Tom Pendergast, a notorious Missouri Democratic boss who had helped Truman in his early career and was subsequently convicted of corruption, would be one famous example. Jimmy Carter's long support for his budget director, Bert Lance, might be another. In both of those instances, the president, or future president, suffered considerable criticism and was utterly unable to bolster or rescue the reputation of his troubled associate.

Nevertheless, the test of loyalty comes in hard cases, and although it must be a two-way street, presidents obviously pay the higher price when they are called upon to travel very far along that street. George Bush paid some hard-to-measure price for his loyalty to John Tower at the outset of his administration. He paid another high price at the end of his administration for a controversial decision to pardon some of the government officials involved in the Iran-Contra affair. It is significant that in both of these cases he did not appear to agonize over the decisions or regret them at a later time. Observers, even friendly observers, see this loyalty as both a strength and a weakness in the president's character. According to Robert Gates, who served as deputy National Security Council advisor, Bush "was at times too patient and too forgiving of the ambitions and game-playing of both foreign leaders and some of his own people. He was at times loyal to some who did not deserve it or return it."[55]

The Bush administration had an unusually talented and close-knit team of senior foreign policy advisors. They often disagreed on the policies that should be adopted, but they seldom aired those disagreements in public and worked together with remarkable effectiveness during the international upheavals that accompanied the end of the Cold War and the building of a complex coalition for the conduct of the Gulf War. The level of camaraderie and collegiality that characterized the Bush foreign policy team was rare. It is often observed that these relationships were mostly a matter of fortunate circumstances. The president's team was made up of people who had known each other for many years and had held positions of responsibility in both the Ford and Reagan administrations. All of this is true. But the team did not succeed merely because of these long associations or common political experiences. It succeeded, in part, because the president took positive steps to cultivate friendship and loyalty. The Tower nomination mattered to this group. A powerful demonstration of presidential loyalty at the outset of the administration made it clear to everyone in the president's service that they worked for a chief executive who would stand by his subordinates in hard times. The value of that lesson, like the costs that President Bush paid in delivering it, is hard to measure.

Part III

DOMESTIC POLITICS AND POLICY

THE OFFERED HAND AND THE VETO FIST

George Bush, Congress, and Domestic Policy Making

Barbara Sinclair

George H. W. Bush became president in a context not conducive to domestic policy making on a heroic scale. A number of analysts have argued that in any case he was not much interested in domestic policy. But whether that assessment is accurate or not, he faced some domestic problems that had to be dealt with and the likelihood that he would need at least modest domestic policy accomplishments to win reelection. In addition, as problematic as the political environment was, the prospects for bipartisan cooperation were in some ways better that they had been in a number of years. How did these various strands come together to shape the Bush domestic presidency?

This chapter examines the political context and the character of the Congress Bush faced. It then considers Bush's domestic agenda and his administration's routines and strategies for dealing with Congress. It argues that in response to the constraints under which the Bush administration operated in the domestic sphere, it developed and deployed a combination of strategies that can be labeled the offered hand of bipartisanship and the fist of veto threats. A survey of major legislative efforts on domestic policy with special attention to the Clean Air Act and the 1990 budget deal illustrates these strategies and their limitations.

A Constraining Political Context

George H. W. Bush began his presidency in a weak strategic position vis-à-vis Congress.[1] Democrats controlled both chambers, the Senate by a margin of 10, the House by 85. Although Bush was elected with a respectable 54 percent of the national popular vote in 1988, Republicans lost seats in both houses of Congress.

In his campaign for the presidency, Bush had faced a problem of perception. Was he running for Ronald Reagan's third term or his own first term? Bush could not and did not want to repudiate Reagan, but he needed to give voters a reason to vote for him. Much of the Republican base was fervently devoted to Reagan, but in the general electorate there was some Reagan fatigue. Bush was thus threading the needle between maintaining fidelity to the Reagan legacy and offering something new. During the campaign he promised a "kinder, gentler" domestic policy and mentioned education and the environment as issues requiring particular attention. But he offered few specifics; instead, campaign rhetoric about patriotism and crime dominated media coverage and the average voter's perceptions. The most memorable "promise" to come out of the campaign was Bush's "Read my lips: No new taxes."[2]

The rare loss of seats by the party winning the presidency and the relatively issueless character of the campaign meant that the election carried no policy mandate. Consequently, Democratic members of Congress felt they had nothing to fear by defying Bush. In 1981, in the wake of an issue-oriented campaign in which significant numbers of incumbent Democratic members of Congress were defeated and Republicans won control of the Senate, many Democrats believed that their constituents wanted them to support Reagan's policies and that they risked defeat if they opposed him.[3] The 1988 election carried no such message, thus depriving Bush of a key resource for eliciting support from Democrats beyond that based purely upon policy agreement.

TABLE 2   Strength of the Congressional parties during the Ronald Reagan and George H. W. Bush presidencies

PRESIDENT	CONGRESS	DATES	HOUSE		SENATE	
			REPUBLICANS	DEMOCRATS	REPUBLICANS	DEMOCRATS
Ronald Reagan	97	1981–82	192	243	53	46
	98	1983–84	167	268	54	46
	99	1985–86	182	253	53	47
	100	1987–88	177	258	45	55
George H. W. Bush	101	1989–90	175	260	45	55
	102	1991–92	167	267	44	56

Source: Norman Ornstein, Thomas Mann, and Michael Malbin, *Vital Statistics on Congress: 2001–2002* (Washington, D.C.: AEI Press, 2002), 57–58.

A More Formidable Congress

If Bush seemed to be in a weak strategic position as he started his presidency, congressional Democrats appeared to be in an even weaker position. House Democrats underwent a series of traumas—an extremely bitter and divisive fight over a pay raise that in the end failed, a protracted ethics investigation of Speaker Jim Wright culminating in his resignation in June of 1988, and ethics charges against Democratic whip Tony Coelho that led him to resign as well. The new leadership team of Speaker Tom Foley, Majority Leader Richard Gephardt, and Whip Bill Gray, which was completed with the election of the latter two on June 14, 1989, included only one member with experience in the top ranks of House leaders. Foley had served as majority leader in 1987–88 and as whip from 1981 to 1986. The Senate too saw leadership turnover. After a vigorous three-way contest, Senate Democrats elected a new majority leader, George Mitchell, in late 1988. Mitchell understandably required some time to consolidate his political position and become conversant with the job.

Yet this turmoil obscured a more consequential truth: Congress and the Democratic majority with which Bush would have to deal was a more formidable force than his Republican predecessors had faced. The Congress of the late 1980s was a very different institution from the one in which Bush had served in the 1960s.[4] Bush's two House terms (1967–70) were in a decentralized Congress still largely dominated by powerful and autonomous committee chairmen. Although the Democratic Party held sizeable majorities in both chambers, its membership was ideologically divided between mostly conservative southerners and mostly liberal northerners. Many of the committee chairmen who attained and retained their positions based on seniority were conservative southerners and were little beholden to the party leadership or the party caucus as a whole.

The Congress of the late 1980s was a transformed institution. A major expansion in both personal and committee staffs in the 1960s and 1970s made members of Congress much less dependent upon the executive for information and enhanced members' and committees' legislative and oversight capabilities. The upgrading of the Congressional Research Service (CRS) and the General Accounting Office (GAO) and, most importantly, the establishment of the Congressional Budget Office (CBO) gave Congress access to independent expertise.

In the 1970s, House Democrats altered chamber and party rules in ways that eroded committee autonomy and fostered stronger party leadership. Committee chairs no longer attained their positions automatically on the basis of seniority but instead had to be approved by a secret ballot of the full Democratic membership. The speaker was given greater say in the appointment of members to committees and the power to choose Democratic members of the Rules Committee, conferring true control of floor scheduling.

The split in the Democratic Party decreased as the proportion of southerners in the membership steadily declined. Many conservative southern Democrats were replaced by Republicans. To be elected as a Democrat in the South, a candidate had to win the black vote by a large margin, which led to moderation among the remaining southern Democrats. The increasing success of Democrats in the North, especially the Northeast, brought in new liberal members.

In the 1980s, under pressure from a conservative, confrontational president who threatened its policy and election goals, the more ideologically homogeneous Democratic Party became increasingly willing to allow its leaders to make aggressive use of the resources conferred by the 1970s reforms.[5] During the 100th Congress (1987–88), the House Democratic leadership put forth its own policy agenda and, using the Rules Committee to advantageously structure members' floor choices and the party's large and increasingly effective whip system to mobilize votes, it passed the party's entire agenda, often over Reagan's objections and sometimes over his veto.[6] Thus, when Bush became president he confronted a more cohesive Democratic Party whose leaders were better equipped and more experienced at building majorities in opposition to the president than those Reagan and Richard Nixon, Bush's Republican predecessors, had faced.

Still, congressional Democrats were inclined toward cooperation and compromise with Bush. Some resentment still lingered about the campaign Bush had waged—especially about the Willie Horton ads linking Democratic nominee Michael Dukakis with a felon who had committed rape and murder when on a furlough from a Massachusetts prison. Yet the Democrats' dominant emotion was relief that the new president was not Reagan but rather someone who believed that sometimes government could contribute to the solution of societal problems and who appeared to acknowledge that Congress had a legitimate role to play in policy making.[7] Furthermore, many Democrats believed that the public wants any new president to be given a chance and that a confrontational attitude would only hurt them politically.

Bush's Domestic Agenda

On February 9, 1989, President Bush gave his first address to a joint session of Congress. Presidents typically use their first address to enunciate their agendas, and as a result the speech is scrutinized by members of the Washington policy community to ascertain what the president really wants. Bush began with a careful nod to the Reagan legacy: "I don't propose to reverse direction. We are headed the right way." He then added, "But we cannot rest. . . . My plan has four broad features: attention to urgent priorities, investment in the future, an attack on the deficit, and no new taxes." Bush labeled education his top priority, but the new educational programs he proposed were fairly modest. He advocated increased funding for the war on drugs and a tax credit for child care, endorsed making disabled Americans "full partners in America's opportunity society," and called for legislative action on the Clean Air Act. Specifically, Bush announced: "I will send to you shortly legislation for a new, more effective Clean Air Act. It will include a plan to reduce, by date certain, the emissions which cause acid rain— because the time for study alone has passed, and the time for action is now." He advocated a decrease in the capital gains tax and emphasized the need to cut the federal budget deficit.[8]

A president's agenda is a combination of what he wants to do and what he has to do. Crises and past policy decisions constrain presidential choices. Thus the debacle in the savings and loan industry that Bush inherited had to be dealt with quickly.[9] He not only called for swift action in his address but had already announced support for a plan to restructure and refinance the thrift industry and its deposit-insurance system. The large budget deficits that were the legacy of the Reagan years severely constrained Bush's choices. The massive 1981 tax cut and the enormous defense spending increases of the early Reagan presidency had produced a sizeable gap between revenues and expenditures even in the midst of healthy economic growth. In the succeeding years, some of the tax cuts were rolled back and discretionary domestic spending was trimmed, but nowhere near enough to solve the deficit problem. The fundamental differences in budget priorities between Reagan and congressional Democrats had produced stalemate on the deficit by the middle of Reagan's presidency. Congress did pass the Gramm-Rudman-Hollings Act, which mandated a phased reduction in the deficit over several years and automatic spending cuts if the specified reductions (labeled targets) were not attained by policy decisions.

Dealing with the deficit was the most problematic domestic issue forced onto Bush's agenda by previous policy choices. It constrained what he could propose in the way of new domestic programs, as he acknowledged. "We have more will than wallet," Bush said in his inaugural address. Of course, his "no new taxes" pledge made the straitjacket that much tighter; reducing the deficit and meeting the Gramm-Rudman-Hollings targets without any tax increases would make a difficult task a great deal more difficult.

The Washington policy community, at least as reflected in coverage in the *New York Times* and the *Washington Post*, received Bush's address to Congress quite favorably. He proposed no bold new programs, but he had promised none during the campaign. Bush's vow of a "kinder, gentler" domestic policy was reiterated in his proposals, although the requests for increases in domestic programs were modest.[10] The news stories emphasized his conciliatory tone and his offer to work with Congress. And all the accounts noted the warm welcome Bush received from Congress and its frequent and enthusiastic applause.

Dealing with Congress

Presidential success in domestic policy making depends on Congress. Because presidents lack constitutional authority to force Congress to do their bidding, they need to develop strategies and routines for dealing with legislators that maximize their chances of getting Congress to do what they want. For a president as poor in political resources as George H. W. Bush, effective strategies are important but can only compensate for a lack for resources to a limited extent. Congress is an independent body and its members pursue their own goals and interests.

With both chambers controlled by Democrats, Bush would need bipartisan "buy-in" for legislative success. Thus, "the offered hand," as he phrased it in his inaugural speech, was a key strategy. Bush would cultivate members of Congress of both parties and would of necessity compromise on matters of substance with Democrats. Bush had reason to believe that the strategy could work. He knew Democrats were glad to be dealing with him rather than Reagan and that they believed they had to be perceived as cooperative. Furthermore, considerable overlap existed between the Bush agenda and that of congressional Democrats. Education, child care, rewriting the Clean Air Act, and legislation guaranteeing rights to the disabled were all Democratic priorities.

Yet the Bush administration also knew that there were significant differences between the president's policy preferences and those of congressional Democrats even when the issues they wanted to address were the same. If Bush was to meet his policy and electoral goals, some very tough bargains would need to be struck. The threat of vetoes to extract concessions became a central strategy.

Cultivating Members

Cultivating members of Congress personally was both strategy and second nature for Bush. A longtime Washington insider, Bush had a broad circle of acquaintances that he had nurtured over the years by sending handwritten notes and making personal phone calls. Although Congress had changed greatly since he served in the House, Bush knew many of the members and had as vice president done considerable lobbying on behalf of Reagan's legislative priorities. Vice President Dan Quayle was also a Hill veteran. "There were a number of times where we'd choose to call the Vice President into service telephoning and lobbying members of the Senate and the House . . . with whom we knew he had good relationships," explained Fred McClure, a congressional liaison aide for Reagan and later head of congressional liaison for Bush. "We used him quite often in that capacity."[11] As vice president and president, Bush continued to use the House gym, an excellent venue for informal contact with members. A few old friends from his years of House service were now in positions of great influence, particularly Democrat Dan Rostenkowski, chair of the tax-writing Ways and Means Committee.

"With high hopes for the new year, the 101st Congress convened Jan. 3, [1989] in an atmosphere filled with talk of bipartisanship and improved White House relations," began *Congressional Quarterly's* article on the new Congress.[12] To be sure, new presidencies tend to bring high hopes. And for Democrats the improved atmosphere was, in part, due to relief that Reagan no longer was president. But Bush's efforts also contributed to the positive atmosphere.

As soon as the 1988 election campaign was over, Bush began a second campaign to build and rebuild bridges to members of Congress. He made a special effort to cultivate the Democratic leaders, even traveling to Capitol Hill to confer with them. In his inaugural address, Bush declared:

> A new breeze is blowing—and the old bipartisanship must be made new again.
>
> To my friends—and yes, I do mean friends—in the loyal opposition— and yes, I mean loyal: I put out my hand.
>
> I am putting out my hand to you, Mr. Speaker.
>
> I am putting out my hand to you, Mr. Majority Leader.
>
> For this is the thing: This is the age of the offered hand.[13]

Bush continued to meet frequently with Democratic congressional leaders over the course of his presidency. A study of in-person and over-the-phone contacts between presidents and opposition party Senate leaders from John F. Kennedy through Bush found that Bush's contacts with Mitchell far outstripped those of his predecessors with Mitchell's counterparts, averaging about seventy minutes per week.[14]

Bush's attentions were by no means restricted to congressional leaders. Unlike the Reagans, the Bushes invited members to the White House residence, not just its public spaces. McClure recalls the president telling him during his first days in the White House, "Okay, I want you to develop a plan, McClure, to get all these members of Congress down here. Just start working on them, get time on my schedule, and we're going to do stuff up in the residence." A routine was also developed whereby every week McClure would bring members and "five carefully selected constituents" of each one into the Oval Office for pictures and brief conversation.[15]

White House Lobbying

The White House Office of Legislative Affairs, the president's in-house lobbying shop, was headed during most of the Bush presidency by Fred McClure, who, although relatively young, had extensive experience as a congressional aide and in Reagan's Legislative Affairs office. Initially the office consisted of seven professionals, all of whom had considerable Hill experience as aides or as private sector lobbyists, backed up by twenty staffers.[16] As had become standard, the professionals were assigned to either the House or the Senate and, within their chamber, to specific committees.

As lobbyists for the president, senior Legislative Affairs staff members are tasked with counting and persuading. They serve as information conduits, providing strategists in the administration with readings on where members of Congress stand and making sure that members know the administration's positions. Ideally, they also help get the votes needed to pass the president's programs and prevent proposals he opposes from passing. By most accounts the Bush liaison operation performed its information-gathering function well. It saw cultivating members through small favors as central to its job and worked at that assiduously. McClure and his senior staff were well liked on the Hill, where they spent most of their time.

McClure was effective at deploying the "big guns" when that seemed advisable. He asked President Bush and Vice President Quayle to make calls to members of Congress to request their votes on important pieces of legislation at key moments in the process. Both were willing to do so. Of course, the president as the "biggest gun" cannot be squandered, McClure explained:

> Number one, there is a strong, strong bias against using the President unless you have to. . . .
>
> So you do have to conserve the President's capital. A lot of times we did it in meetings. He said, "Okay, let's just get 30 minutes of time and get these guys in a room." And you put together a group of guys who are going to totally support the President and are just gung-ho cheerleaders and get a few guys who are in there wavering, and make them start putting pressure on each other there in front of the President. Get a couple of Cabinet members or right guys there on a particular issue and you create a dynamic, a group-think kind of a deal that herds them along.

The liaison staff during the Bush administration did suffer from a perception on Capitol Hill that it lacked clout in the White House.[17] McClure insists that he had excellent access to Bush. But because his influence on legislative strategy seemed to be limited, members of Congress did not see him as a significant conduit for influencing the president. This perception in turn reduced his effectiveness as a persuader.

Payoffs and Limitations of the Strategy

"Most everyone [on the Hill] knows George Bush, the former Houston congress-man who still breaks a sweat in the House gym," concluded a *CQ* story in late 1989. And, added a senior member, "Everybody liked George Bush personally."[18] Bush's cultivation of members made a difference. The senior member argued:

> It is remarkable how much difference that makes. . . . A likeable guy can still influence a lot of people. George Bush did, he called and talked to members personally. He had a very engaging personality. He was likeable. That gave him, I think, more influence than he otherwise would have had.[19]

By virtue of the prestige of the office, a president's attention is valued by members, which sometimes means that he can gain credit without giving a quid pro quo. McClure provided an example:

> There are a lot of members of the House of Representatives who serve their time over there in relative obscurity. And every now and then you say, "Let's go call on one of these dudes who's never been called on before by the White House," and you get all sorts of blessings that flow from those kinds of things.
>
> Or occasionally you say, "Hey, why don't we get the President to call Congressman X. He's a freshman, just got here from so-and-so. He's going to be okay on this vote, but we're going to need him six weeks from now on this other vote, so why don't we get the President to call him." We find out that so-and-so is going to be firmly in our corner and we get the President to call—use a little capital. And he tells X member, whom he's never talked directly to before in this kind of way, how happy he is that he's going to be able to support him on this issue and he looks forward to working with him in the future on some other mutual issues, even though you know you're going to have disagreements. And you kind of go through all that crap. It's wonderful. And they get a big kick out of it and they issue a press release and the President gets kudos out in western Oregon.

The translation of personal goodwill into legislative support, however, is distinctly limited. Members of Congress have their own interests and goals and, especially if they are of the opposition party, these will often conflict with those of the president. By the late 1980s, the ideological polarization of the parties was well under way and the conflicts were often sharp. Perhaps because of his congressional service in an earlier era or because of the enormous value he placed on friendship, Bush seems to have expected friendship to trump interest. According to Chief of Staff John Sununu:

One of the problems we had in congressional relations is that George Bush thought that his friends cared about him as much as he cared about them. I think he thought Don Riegle would be more constructive on savings and loan than he turned out to be. . . .

I think he expected more from Rosty [Daniel Rostenkowski] in terms of supporting the budget agreement and didn't get it. He hoped that John Paul Hammerschmidt could have done more for him on some of the budget issues than he did. . . .

Sununu and Darman

Sununu and Office of Management and Budget (OMB) director Richard Darman were, by all accounts, the Bush administration's chief architects of strategy on major domestic policy.[20] Roger Porter, head of the White House Office of Economic and Domestic Policy, who reported to Sununu, also played a central role on a few high-priority bills. On the Clean Air Act, Porter was the central administration participant, "meet[ing] constantly with House and Senate committee members to rewrite various parts of the legislation and rally[ing] constituent groups to support the president's point of view."[21] Experienced and well liked on Capitol Hill, Porter became so enmeshed in specific legislative efforts—clean air and then civil rights—that his influence was lessened on other issues.

The dominance of Sununu and Darman affected the direction of domestic policy as well as the tenor of relations with Congress. Although highly intelligent, both were often perceived as arrogant in their dealings with members. "John is a very smart guy," McClure says. "But John also could sometimes be abrasive and basically tell members how dumb they were, and there are reported incidents of that."[22] Some commentators have suggested that because Bush was "too nice," Sununu of necessity had to play the role of Bush's "son of a bitch."[23] In any case, his and Darman's dismissive attitude rankled members of Congress.

More significantly, Darman and Sununu's "shared commitment to fiscal conservatism ensured that policy initiatives that cost money were shelved and that departmental budget proposals were focused on reducing spending."[24] The emphasis on deficit reduction through budget cutting to the detriment of "kinder and gentler" policy initiatives was, in considerable part, dictated by fiscal reality— "the facts on the ground." But the president's hard line on the budget certainly made reaching agreements with the congressional majority party more difficult.

Veto and Veto-Threat Bargaining

The Constitution gives the president the veto and thus a potent weapon in the legislative struggle. So long as he can muster more than a third of the vote in either the House or Senate to uphold his veto, the president can prevent a bill from becoming law. The Bush administration knew from the beginning that with the Democrats in control of both chambers the veto would of necessity be a major weapon.

During the course of his presidency, Bush cast 46 vetoes—29 of which were regular vetoes and the other 17 pocket vetoes—and he was overridden only once.[25] Although not a record, Bush's success rate is nevertheless impressive. Furthermore, most of these vetoes were cast on significant legislation, not minor bills. Most scholars would consider at least 37 of the 46 bills Bush vetoed to be significant.

A presidential veto, even if it is sustained, need not be the end of the legislative story. Of the 45 vetoes that were not overridden, 22, according to political scientist Charles Cameron, were links in a "veto chain";—that is, after the veto Congress passed another bill, usually incorporating concessions to the president.[26] For example, in 1989, Congress passed a bill raising the minimum wage. The administration had made clear that it opposed the sizeable increase congressional Democrats wanted and tried to reach an acceptable compromise. The Democrats, however, persisted with the higher increase and Bush vetoed the bill. After the House tried but failed to override the veto, both sides returned to the bargaining table and a compromise was reached.[27]

As this example illustrates, the president may use the veto to force a better bargain. In Bush's first Congress, the 101st, he vetoed 21 bills; one was very minor, another was moot, and, in one case, he vetoed two different versions of the same legislation. Of the 18 remaining vetoed bills, seven subsequently became law in some form, and, on at least six of those, Bush obtained significant concessions. In many cases, the provisions he objected to were removed. District of Columbia appropriations legislation, which Bush vetoed twice, provides an example. Bush objected to abortion language in the first bill. The House had just failed to override his veto of the Labor, Health and Human Services, and Education appropriations bill over a similar disagreement. So, knowing they could not override the veto, congressional Democrats removed one of the abortion-related provisions Bush opposed and passed the altered legislation. He vetoed this version too. Democrats then capitulated and sent Bush a bill without either of the offending provisions.

Of the bills killed by Bush's vetoes, he unequivocally opposed nine. He regarded as unacceptable a bill amending the Hatch Act to allow federal workers to engage in more political activities, a bill mandating that large employers give their employees parental leave, and a bill imposing textile quotas. Some others, such as an intelligence authorization bill, Bush supported but only without certain provisions he found objectionable. In only one case, however, was a veto that killed legislation he would have liked to have signed politically costly. Bush very much wanted to sign a civil rights bill passed by Congress. A conundrum confronted him on the issue, however. Much of his business constituency opposed the bill as written by congressional Democrats and the Republican Party base saw it as a "quota" bill, but many others favored the bill, which would overturn Supreme Court decisions that made proving employment discrimination extremely difficult.

Presidents often do not actually have to veto legislation in order to gain concessions. A bill's supporters may know that overriding a veto is not possible and so be willing to compromise with the president earlier in the legislative process. A president who maintains a sterling record of sustaining vetoes has a strong hand in such bargaining.

Although Bush is certainly not the first president to use veto threats to extract concessions, his administration did refine the strategy. As Fred McClure explained:

> Dick [Darman] early on established these levels of veto threat. . . . I can't remember the correct terminology we used, but it's probably something to the effect of, "We don't like what you're doing." And then the next step was the President's senior advisors would recommend that he veto it, and the next step was the Secretary of the Treasury, the Secretary of State, and the Secretary of so-and-so would recommend that he veto. And then ultimately it was, "He will veto.". . .
>
> If they used it previously, I didn't know about it, but we used it in such a fashion that it allowed us to send the kind of signals that we needed during the development of legislation at the committee level such that we would set the stage for what our voting would be like when we—because you could always back away until you got to the real big one.

Since the mid-1970s, administrations have sent Congress formal Statements of Administration Policy, known as SAPs. These letters, which are vetted by the OMB, lay out the administration's position on pending legislation.[28] Frequently a SAP includes detailed administration objections to provisions in the legislation and may include a veto threat. For example, a SAP sent to the Senate on April 25, 1990, stated, "If Congress presents the President with a bill that contains the abortion language that was approved by the Senate Appropriations Committee in H.R. 4404, his senior advisors will recommend that he veto the bill, and it is virtually certain that he would do so."[29]

During the Bush presidency, members of Congress and other interested parties quickly became aware of the variations in language and their importance. As CQ reporter Janet Hook explained, "Official policy statements from the Bush administration regarding legislation have to be scrutinized carefully because there are subtle but important differences in language that tell a sharp-eyed legislator how much the administration hates a bill. The varieties of 'vetospeak' range from narrow objections raised by agency officials to unequivocal veto threats straight from President Bush's mouth."[30] The SAP targeting H.R. 4404, an emergency supplemental appropriations bill that contained the strong veto threat quoted earlier, also included this much weaker statement: "The Administration also opposes a provision that makes mandatory the interest equalization program of the Export-Import Bank."[31]

According to political scientist Samuel Kernell, the Bush administration issued 114 SAPs containing veto threats in the 101st Congress and 195 in the 102nd Congress.[32] In a number of cases, a bill was the target of multiple SAPs containing veto threats. For example, a SAP was sent to the House and another to the Senate concerning the first minimum wage bill. In the 101st, 87 separate bills were targeted with veto threats and in the 102nd 140 were.[33]

As with vetoes, some veto threats are unequivocal and others are invitations to bargain. The statement "The Administration opposes enactment of S. 2203. If S. 2203 were presented to the President, the Attorney General would recommend that the bill be vetoed" left no room for negotiation.[34] In contrast, an August 2, 1990, SAP on the defense authorization act threatened a veto (of the "Secretary of Defense would recommend" variety) if the bill "does not contain proper funding and flexibility . . . for SDI" and a few other items. But it also began, "Although the Administration has several objections to S. 2884 as reported by the Senate Armed Services Committee, the bill would make a substantial positive contribution to our vital national defense needs within current fiscal constraints." And after issuing the veto threat, the SAP continued, "The Administration urges the Senate to adopt the following amendments to correct the present shortcomings of the bill."[35]

How successful was the Bush administration at veto-threat bargaining? Did the threats influence Congress to make concessions? My data set of major legislation in the 101st Congress provides some basis for answering these questions. I defined major measures as those listed by *Congressional Quarterly* in its list of major legislation and added any legislation not so captured on which key votes as chosen by CQ occurred.[36] This definition yielded 57 major measures in the 101st Congress. The administration threatened vetoes on 27—47 percent—of these major measures and, in 8 cases, it actually cast a veto.

Not all of the 57 measures reached the president, either because they failed earlier in the process, possibly because of a veto threat, or, in a few cases because the president lacked the veto power (primarily on budget resolutions). Of those that did reach the president, did the veto threats cause Congress to revise the bills to make them more to the president's liking? I coded on a five-point scale how close the House floor bill, the Senate floor bill, and the bill at final disposition was to the president's position and then examined the change that occurred from the chamber floors to final disposition. Certainly the coding contains an element of subjectivity, but what is at issue here is not absolute scores but whether bills under veto threat were more likely to move toward the president's position. In fact, they were: 46 percent of major measures moved toward the president's position between the House floor and final disposition when no veto threat was issued and 80 percent did when the bill was under a veto threat. The comparable figures for the Senate were 8 percent and 40 percent, respectively. The large differences between the chambers were attributable, in part, to the fact that the president did better initially in the Senate and to the fact that the House tends to act first.

The effectiveness of the veto-threat strategy depended on the president's ability to consistently muster the votes needed to prevent overrides. Until late in his tenure, Bush maintained a perfect record—all of his vetoes were sustained. "He's had an extraordinary batting average," said Senator Richard G. Lugar (R-Ind.) in late 1990. "His threats have credibility."[37] In fact, the administration was usually quite astute at picking its shots. Reagan had developed a reputation for being quick to issue veto threats but often not following through or casting vetoes that would be impossible to sustain.[38]

Nevertheless, maintaining Bush's near-perfect record often required pressuring Republican congressional allies. "On FS-X, I thought he was wrong; on China students, I thought he was wrong; then comes the Hatch Act," complained Senator Trent Lott (R-Miss.), who switched his vote from for passage to against override on all three bills. "I don't want to embarrass him, but there's a limit to where you'll bite that bullet."[39] But as Lott fully understood, it was in congressional Republicans' own interest to preserve Bush's legislative influence. "If he loses that leverage, we lose that leverage," Lott said.

Legislative Battles

The Financial Institutions Reform, Recovery and Enforcement Act of 1989 offers a clear example of the "open hand" strategy working well. A snowballing financial crisis in the savings and loan industry made action imperative, and although there were differences of opinion about a number of specific issues, these differences did not fall uniformly along partisan lines. The administration offered a draft bill quickly and that provided a focal point for the congressional effort. Democrats opposed Bush and congressional Republicans on whether the bailout should be on or off budget (Bush prevailed in keeping it off), but in the House, Democrats provided greater support than Republicans for certain tough provisions that Bush requested and the savings and loan industry opposed. The administration worked closely with members of Congress on both sides of the aisle throughout the process, and the bill Bush signed on August 9 closely resembled the proposal he had unveiled on February 6.[40]

On a number of Bush's other high-priority domestic legislative requests, however, the president's policy preferences and those of congressional Democrats were much farther apart. The increasing ideological homogeneity of the Democratic membership and the resulting greater sway of the leadership and caucus meant that picking off just enough majority party members to form a winning coalition with minority Republicans was difficult. In 1981, Reagan had successfully gotten enough conservative southern Democrats to support his initiatives to defeat the Democratic leadership in the House. When the number of such Democrats decreased and Reagan became a lame-duck, second-term president who could no longer defeat them at the polls, that strategy rarely succeeded. For Bush, whom congressional Democrats did not fear, it was seldom a feasible approach. To get legislation, Bush often had to accept language he thoroughly disliked.

Obtaining legislation to bar discrimination against and provide greater access for people with disabilities was a priority of both Bush and congressional Democrats. Yet this general agreement obscured a yawning disagreement on how strong the protections should be. "The first bill [considered by the Senate] was terrible," according to Sununu. But, he continued, "how could you vote 'no' for a piece of legislation called the Americans with Disabilities Act?" So "almost anything would have gotten 90 votes [in the Senate] and we're struggling to build into it provisions that the business community was desperately coming to us with concerns about." The administration did manage early in the process to negotiate a deal with Senate sponsors on remedies, one of the president's primary concerns. With some reduction in the penalties for violators, the bill passed the Senate Judiciary Committee with a unanimous vote and the Senate by 76–8.[41]

The remedies issue surfaced again in the House, and there the administration was less successful.[42] Administration-supported amendments failed in the Judiciary subcommittee, the full committee, and on the floor.[43] Without the filibuster, the House minority lacks the leverage its Senate counterpart commands, so the majority has less incentive to offer concessions.

The conference committee did not alter the remedies language to the administration's liking. Nevertheless, Bush proclaimed himself "delighted" with the final version of the bill and said he looked forward to signing it and that it would "serve as a declaration of independence for millions of persons with disabilities in this country."[44] A number of Republicans believed that the administration gave up too much on remedies and on other provisions. But, as Representative Jon Kyl (R-Ariz.), pointed out, "The other side always had the main bargaining leverage because they knew the president was going to sign the bill."[45] Furthermore, the White House knew that the overwhelming vote in favor in both chambers meant a veto threat was unlikely to be persuasive.

The political dynamics were similar on Head Start reauthorization and child care legislation in the 101st Congress. Both Bush and majority Democrats wanted bills, but their preferences about the bills' contents were different. Bush had promised full funding for Head Start during the 1988 campaign, and Democrats knew he had a major stake in getting a bill. Because a veto was not an option, they wrote a bill much closer to their own preferences than to his.[46] On child care, the administration wanted only tax credits, and Bush did issue a veto threat if a grant program was included. Negotiations with congressional Democrats caused them to modify their initial bill, but, in the end, Bush was forced to accept a substantial grant program in order to get a child care bill.[47]

Clean Air

The premier example of the president's agenda-setting power and its limits in determining outcomes is the Clean Air Act of 1990. Congress had been in stalemate on rewriting the act for over a decade. President Reagan opposed any strengthening of the law; his administration had, in fact, attempted to weaken it. Democrats were split. On many components of the bill, geography, not party, was the overriding determinant of a member's position. Until 1989, Robert Byrd, who was from the coal-producing state of West Virginia and was a staunch opponent of stronger clean air requirements, was the Senate Democratic leader. Throughout the 1980s, attempts to update the law had ended in failure. Without a strong push from Bush, it is unlikely that Congress would have tried again in the 101st Congress. When a president puts his prestige on the line by making an issue a legislative priority, however, even a Congress controlled by an opposition party seldom ignores it.

Bush followed his campaign promise to emphasize the environment with a June 12, 1989, unveiling of the outline of his clean air proposal.[48] The outline had been developed in numerous meetings led by Roger Porter, who had assembled a staff from the Energy Department, the Office of Management and Budget, the EPA, and the White House and had made the Clean Air Act his top priority.[49] After the Porter group worked out most of the issues, several major ones were presented to the president to decide. The Bush proposal was greeted with widespread praise, even from those who believed it was too weak. The president had guaranteed that clean air would receive serious attention on Capitol Hill. Porter's group then drafted legislative language, a complex process that took another six weeks.[50]

Porter and other administration officials began consulting members of Congress in March 1989 and continued these consultations and negotiations for the almost two years it took to enact the bill. Once Congress began its work, however, the administration could no longer control the process. The strongly environmentalist Senate Environment and Public Works Committee reported a bill in November 1989 that the administration abhorred.[51] The bill went too far for Senate Republicans and for some Democrats as well. Majority Leader George Mitchell, who brought the bill to the floor in early 1990, was unable to amass the 60 votes necessary to overcome a threatened filibuster. This gave the administration new leverage. Mitchell, a strong environmentalist, very much wanted a bill. He took the lead for Senate Democrats and negotiated directly with an administration team headed by Porter. After a month of intensive private negotiations in Mitchell's office, a deal was reached.[52] Mitchell, Minority Leader Bob Dole, and the administration fended off all "deal-breaker" amendments on the floor, and the Senate passed the compromise on April 3, 1990.

The administration had less leverage in the House. John Dingell, chair of the Energy and Commerce Committee, which has predominant jurisdiction over environmental issues, represented Detroit and was a fierce defender of the auto industry. He had been instrumental in blocking action in the past and preferred enacting no bill. Henry Waxman, who chaired the Energy and Commerce subcommittee, represented smoggy Los Angeles and was as wily a legislator as Dingell. Waxman wanted a bill much stronger than the administration's. These two key players did agree that administration officials should not be in the room when the deals were cut.[53]

The White House, of course, continued lobbying, in one embarrassing case sending conflicting signals about its position.[54] But the real deal-making took place among House members, especially Dingell and Waxman. Convinced that Bush's interest made a bill inevitable and concerned that he would lose on the House floor, Dingell gave considerable ground.[55] With frequent pressure from Speaker Tom Foley to move the process along, the Energy and Commerce Committee reported a strong bill by a 42–1 margin. The House passed the bill with several modestly strengthening amendments on May 23, 1990, by a vote of 401–21.

The bill that emerged from the conference committee "set up an ambitious program to reduce smog and toxic emissions from industry, including pollutants that cause acid rain, to clean up motor vehicles and fuels, and to phase out chemicals, particularly chlorofluorocarbons, that harm the Earth's protective ozone layer."[56] As *CQ* wrote at the time, "Congress ended up approving a conference report that in many areas goes far beyond what the administration had envisioned. Industry lobbyists said the bill would hit consumers with increased prices for automobiles, fuel and electricity, and small businesses with complex and costly permit requirements."[57] The administration had expressed concerns over too much regulation and at too great a cost from the beginning of congressional consideration, but it failed to prevail.[58]

Strategic mistakes contributed to the outcome. In spring 1990, Mitchell had offered the administration an agreement: the participants to the Senate deal would bind themselves to stick by it in the conference committee. The administration, believing it could do better in the House, refused. That turned out to be a miscalculation. Dingell and Waxman agreed to adhere to their agreement throughout the conference.[59] The result was that where the House bill was stronger, especially on the mandates concerning how and when cities must meet clean air standards, the House position prevailed.

The administration did attempt to deploy the "fist" of veto threats on several aspects of the bill. In a January 1990 letter to Minority Leader Dole, Bush wrote that he would send back any proposal that would cost the economy more than 10 percent above the administration bill. He also issued a veto threat against including any program to financially aid workers displaced because of the bill.[60] Congress simply did not believe that Bush would veto a bill he himself had placed at the top of the agenda. The bill Congress presented to Bush contained a worker assistance program, albeit a weakened one, and, far more significantly, it "in many cases [imposed] tougher and far more costly controls on industry." As Henry Waxman exulted, "In almost every title we have provisions that are stronger than those we were advocating through the years."[61]

Bush scored a major political win on the issue. He had broken the long-standing congressional logjam and signed a highly significant clean air bill; he could claim to be an—if not the—"environmental president." In terms of achieving his policy preferences, the verdict is mixed. The bill went considerably beyond what the administration preferred. As one journalist wrote at the time, "Bush has had trouble controlling the ball once he puts it into play."[62] That is frequently the fate of a president faced with a Congress controlled by the other party, especially early in his term when he needs to get legislation passed to accomplish his aims.

The final, usually routine and symbolic, steps in the Clean Air Act's enactment showed the extent to which relations between Bush and congressional Democrats had become strained. Democrats held up the enrollment of the bill until after the 1990 midterm elections so that Bush could not hold a splashy signing ceremony in California, where it might help Republican candidates. When Bush signed the bill he did not invite the key congressional Democrats to stand behind him, where they would be in the news photographs, as was traditional, nor did he hand out pens.[63]

Budget Politics and the 1990 Budget Deal

Budget politics during the first two years of the Bush administration illustrate the constraints on domestic policy making in the environment Bush found himself in.[64] To be sure, one important constraint—the "no new taxes" pledge—was of his own making. Many Bush administration officials argue that serious tactical mistakes were made and some contend that Bush was victimized by highly partisan Democratic leaders and betrayed by House Republican whip Gingrich. But, in fact, Bush was confronted with congressional parties that were changing in ways he and his aides seem not to have understood.

The first year of the Bush presidency yielded only a "slide-by" budget agreement and no cut in the capital gains tax that Bush had strongly advocated. It also set a tone of mistrust between Bush and congressional Democrats on budget issues that should have sent him a warning. In early 1989, unwilling to abandon the tax pledge, seeking to avoid blame for unpopular program cuts and yet wanting to influence congressional budget decisions near the start of the process, the administration presented to Congress a list of additions it wished to make to the outgoing Reagan budget but refused to specify where the cuts that were needed to avoid the Gramm-Rudman-Hollings across-the-board spending reductions should come. Many Democrats interpreted the proposal as a continuation of the blame-avoidance budget games of the Reagan years. As Democratic representative Charles Schumer said, "He picks the increases and lets us make the cuts—that's not very bipartisan."[65] After a Republican campaign that had tarred them as the party of high taxes, Democrats had no intention of playing into GOP hands by advocating a general tax increase. But without a substantial tax increase, the Gramm-Rudman-Hollings deficit reduction target could be met only through draconian cuts in defense or domestic spending or through accounting gimmickry.

Talks between the administration, led by OMB director Darman, and congressional leaders ensued, and on April 14, 1989, Bush and a bipartisan group of leaders announced that a budget agreement had been reached. "This is not a heroic agreement," Speaker Jim Wright conceded.[66] Indeed, as *Congressional Quarterly* pointed out, the deal was based on the administration's overly rosy economic assumptions and a large share of the spending cuts were attained by "one time windfalls or other accounting gimmicks that would not carry over into future years."[67] In addition, the agreement called for at least $5.3 billion in new revenues from unspecified sources that Bush insisted could be achieved without reneging on his "no new taxes" pledge. The participants hoped that the modest agreement was only the beginning and would lead to a more significant deal later in the year. Darman was talking about making the "deal of the century," one that would tackle the deficit in a serious and comprehensive fashion.

Any good feelings generated by reaching an agreement dissipated in the battle over the capital gains tax. When the House Ways and Means Committee went to work drafting tax provisions to meet the budget agreement's new revenue figures, conservative Democrat Ed Jenkins proposed a cut in the capital gains tax, and when five other Democrats and all committee Republicans joined him, the committee voted for such a provision over the objections of its chair. The Democratic leadership opposed the cut and believed that Bush had agreed as part of the budget pact not to pursue it in 1989. Yet now the administration put on a full-court press to enact a capital gains tax cut. Because this change in tax law would actually increase revenues for the first year or two, its appeal to Bush was enormous. Passing it would enable him to keep two of his major campaign pledges simultaneously. On September 28, President Bush won a major victory on the House floor when the Democratic leadership's alternative was defeated and the Jenkins provision passed the House.

In the Senate, however, the Finance Committee reported a bill without the capital gains tax cut, thereby giving opponents a procedural advantage on the floor. Supporters needed 60 votes to cut off a filibuster before the tax cut could come to a vote, and Majority Leader Mitchell rallied enough Democrats to prevent this from happening. Eventually the administration and congressional Republicans capitulated and the modest deficit reduction package was enacted just before Thanksgiving. Not only had no progress toward the "deal of the century" been made, but any spirit of cooperation had been badly frayed. The administration publicly accused Mitchell of abusing Senate rules and privately seemed shocked by his intransigence on capital gains. Over and over in later commentary, Bush administration officials accused Mitchell of being ultra-partisan. Even McClure called him an "extremely partisan individual."

In 1990 a minimalist deal was no longer a viable option. The economy was slowing, and by midyear, the projected Gramm-Rudman-Hollings sequester if deficit cuts were not made had, Darman argued, "grown to a size that would not prove sustainable politically."[68] Because serious deficit reduction would entail making highly unpopular decisions, neither Republicans nor Democrats wanted to lay out their plan first and thus receive the blame for originating painful policy proposals. Darman had been pushing to get serious talks started for months but Democrats feared that the administration was attempting to set them up as the fall guys. Democrats had been tarred as high taxers by Republicans too often; they agreed among themselves that any proposal for higher taxes would have to come from the GOP. Only if Bush publicly put everything—including taxes—on the table would serious talks become feasible, they insisted.

After the president stated that there were "no preconditions," Democrats agreed to talk. But the negotiations went nowhere, and in late June, Democratic congressional leaders told the president that unless he was willing to make a stronger statement on taxes, there was no hope of the talks succeeding. With the economy looking increasingly shaky and the size of the automatic spending cuts that would occur in the absence of a deal soaring, the price the president would pay for a breakdown rose sharply. The health of the economy, Bush's high popularity, and even his reelection were potentially at stake.[69] On June 26, 1990, Bush issued a statement that read, in part, "It is clear to me that both the size of the deficit problem and the need for a package that can be enacted require all of the following: entitlement and mandatory program reform; tax revenue increases; growth incentives; discretionary spending reductions; orderly reductions in defense expenditures; and budget process reform. . . . The bipartisan leadership agree with me on these points."[70]

The reaction to this statement made clear why Bush stuck with his initial budget strategy as long as he could. The media played the concession on taxes as a huge story and stressed that Bush was reneging on his campaign promise. Some editorials commended the president for finally recognizing fiscal reality, but headlines, lead paragraphs, and TV news stories emphasized that he had broken his promise. Editorial page editor Lynn Ashby of Bush's hometown *Houston Post* asked, "Was he lying or did he just not understand the situation?"[71] A significant number of Republican members of Congress vowed to vote against any deal that included new taxes.

Bush administration officials agree that major strategic mistakes were made in the budget battle, and most argue that releasing the statement was a significant turning point. Bush should never have reneged on his "no new taxes" pledge, some argue.[72] But if he did have to break his pledge, he should have gotten a significant quid pro quo from Democrats and have done it only after a major deal had come together. All agree that the communications effort surrounding the statement was seriously mishandled.

In fact, the statement did get talks going, but the negotiations remained difficult because of the parties' differing priorities. A frustrated Bush castigated Congress, saying that legislators deserve "an editorial pounding to get them to do what they ought to do—support the President as he tries to move the country forward . . . and not let them dominate debate by blocking everything I try to do."[73] Finally, on September 30, the president and the congressional leadership announced that an agreement had been reached. The deal included neither a capital gains tax cut, as Republicans wanted, nor an increase in income tax rates for upper-income groups, as Democrats preferred. It relied instead on spending reductions and excise tax hikes, including increased taxes on gasoline and home heating oil. A large proportion of the domestic spending cuts would come out of Medicare and required sharply higher payments by the elderly.[74]

None of the principals to the negotiated agreement were enthusiastic. It was an unpalatable package, but given the deep policy differences between the two sides, they all said it was the best they could do. And it was better, they contended, than the alternative: severe, automatic across-the-board spending cuts. Ominously, on October 1, Republican whip Gingrich, one of the original group of negotiators and a leader of his party's right wing, came out against the package because it included new taxes. Democratic liberals were upset by the Medicare cuts and the regressive nature of the new taxes.[75]

From early in the talks, it had been understood that for an agreement to go into effect, support from majorities of all four party-chamber groups—House and Senate Republicans and House and Senate Democrats—would be required, thus spreading the responsibility and the blame for the controversial decisions that would have to be made. Securing a majority of House Republicans would require an extraordinary presidential effort: in July, the House Republican Conference had passed a resolution opposing new taxes by a 2–1 margin. The president began working the phones on October 1, calling individual House Republicans and asking for their votes. In the succeeding days, groups of Republicans were brought to the White House to meet with Bush. At the administration's request, former presidents Reagan and Ford made some calls. Overly vigorous lobbying by high administration officials may, however, have backfired. Sununu, never known for his tact, offended members when he threatened retaliation for a negative vote. Bush would come into their districts and embarrass them in front of their constituents, Sununu warned.[76]

At the urging of both Democratic and Republican supporters of the budget agreement, Bush went on television to attempt to sell the package to the American people. The speech backfired: constituent opposition to the accord swelled instead of receding. Even high presidential popularity ratings cannot automatically be translated into policy support, Bush learned. When the House voted on October 4, the budget resolution failed by 179 to 254; majorities of both parties voted against it.

The defeat reduced Bush's leverage drastically, and in the end, he had little choice but to accept a revised plan drafted primarily by Democrats that included no gas tax, significantly decreased the Medicare cuts, and raised tax rates on the wealthy. For Bush, signing off on the deal may have been better than any alternative, but it was a major defeat both substantively and politically.[77] Public opinion polls suggested that the budget imbroglio took a toll on Bush's job approval rating: it fell by 19 points between mid-September and mid-October, according to the ABC News-Washington Post poll.[78]

The budget fight suggests that the Bush administration did not understand the Congress with which it was dealing. Bush and his staff believed that Democrats would be unable to stick together on the tax issue. When Democrats did stick together, Bush officials labeled the congressional leadership's behavior as at best borderline illegitimate. "Foley and Mitchell . . . were the most partisan congressional leaders the country has ever seen. Absolutely partisan," Sununu said years later. "No question in my mind that George Mitchell created an environment that allowed Bill Clinton to win by being so partisan." Gingrich's behavior was interpreted as a betrayal by many—and a surprising one at that.[79] Yet there had been many warnings that conservative Republicans were unwilling to vote to raise taxes. A great many of them believed that not only was "no new taxes" good policy, it was also the party's best hope of securing a majority in the House and Senate. The underlying political reality was that the congressional parties had become considerably more ideologically homogeneous and moved much further apart than in the past, which made reaching bipartisan budget deals enormously difficult under conditions of divided party control. Reaching and enacting a deal that was both a substantive and political victory for Bush may simply have been impossible.

Although many commentators and some administration officials attribute Bush's 1992 reelection defeat to the budget deal, the evidence points to the economy more generally. In retrospect, most analysts credit the deal with beginning the process of getting the deficit under control that Clinton and Congress accomplished in the 1990s. But the political legacy of Bush's reneging on the "no new taxes" pledge and his ensuing 1992 defeat is a core conviction among Republicans that raising taxes in any form and under any circumstances is a kiss of death politically, a conviction that is still prevalent today.[80]

Bush in the Domestic Policy Sphere

The battle of the budget deal, like those fought on many other Bush domestic policy priorities, illustrates the difficulty that presidents have getting their priorities enacted when the other party controls Congress. Presidents have formidable negative powers, especially the veto. When the president unconditionally opposes legislation, he can kill it with little fear of an override, especially with the parties so ideologically polarized.

Bush was most successful at preventing Democrats from accomplishing policy goals such as parental leave legislation and Hatch Act revision. But when presidents want Congress to enact new laws, legislators hold the upper hand. And when the opposition party's preferences are dramatically different from those of the president, the president may have to choose between accepting legislation in a form he really does not like or getting no legislation at all. Bush used veto threats effectively to extract concessions, but when it came to his own agenda, veto threats could only affect the outcome so much. In many cases, members knew that Bush really did not want to veto and that he was willing to pay a considerable price in substantive terms to get a bill.

Bush and his aides appear to have lacked understanding of how much Congress and the congressional parties had changed. Certainly they were blindsided by the House Republicans' revolt on the budget agreement; "movement conservatism" with its harder ideological edge and its deep commitment to an anti-tax stance caught them unaware. Similarly, they failed to understand how much the Democratic Party had changed as its more conservative southern wing withered away. Peeling off enough Democrats to support conservative Bush policies was seldom a viable strategy, and committee chairmen were no longer free agents who could make deals with the administration in opposition to a majority of their own caucus. Yet in the end, the Bush administration's misreading of the Congress it faced probably had limited consequences. Under the circumstances, there were no really good strategies available to Bush.

FROM ORAL HISTORY TO ORAL ARGUMENT

George Bush's Supreme Court Appointments

Barbara A. Perry and Henry J. Abraham

President George H. W. Bush's chief of staff, John Sununu, who had appointed state judges as governor of New Hampshire before joining the White House staff, observed about judicial nominations in his oral history interview for the University of Virginia's Miller Center "that when you appoint people, of course they fit what you're looking for in terms of discussions and interviews and what they said [before their nomination]. It's so hard to get what you think you're getting."[1] Sununu's statement that it is difficult for chief executives to determine exactly what they are "getting" in a judicial appointment perfectly summarizes President Bush's two U.S. Supreme Court appointments: David Souter in 1990 and Clarence Thomas in 1991.

Republicans and Judicial Politics

The 1988 Republican Party platform did not mention the Supreme Court explicitly, but it "applaud[ed] President Reagan's fine record of judicial appointments" and reaffirmed the party's "support for the appointment of judges at all levels of the judiciary who respect traditional family values and the sanctity of innocent human life." The platform also touted Reagan's nomination of "judges who have been sensitive to the rights of victims [of crime] and law abiding citizens."[2]

In accepting his party's presidential nomination, Vice President Bush likewise did not mention the nation's highest tribunal or its justices, but he did describe the conservative planks in the party's civil rights and liberties platform. He took an implicit swipe at judicial activists in his reference to "social planners." "I respect old fashioned common sense," he explained. "I like what's been tested and found to be true." He then spelled out an illustrative list of how conservatives would like federal judges to rule and contrasted his positions with those of his Democratic opponent, Massachusetts governor Michael Dukakis:

- Should public school teachers be required to lead our children in the pledge of allegiance? My opponent says no—and I say yes.
- Should society be allowed to impose the death penalty on those who commit crimes of extraordinary cruelty and violence? My opponent says no—but I say yes.
- And should our children have the right to say a voluntary prayer, or even observe a moment of silence in the schools? My opponent says no—but I say yes.
- And should, should free men and women have the right to own a gun to protect their home? My opponent says no—but I say yes.
- And is it right to believe in the sanctity of life and protect the lives of innocent children? My opponent says no—but I say yes. You see, we must change, we've got to change from abortion—to adoption. . . .
- I'm the one who believes it is a scandal to give a weekend furlough to a hardened first degree killer who hasn't even served enough time to be eligible for parole.
- I'm the one who says a drug dealer who is responsible for the death of a policeman should be subject to capital punishment.[3]

In the fall campaign, Bush questioned Dukakis's patriotism for his position on the Pledge of Allegiance. Dukakis had vetoed the requirement that Massachusetts schoolchildren recite the pledge, based on the Supreme Court's 1943 invalidation of mandatory flag salutes in public schools.[4] "And we were criticized for that, for crying out loud," Bush's campaign manager James A. Baker III complained in his oral history interview. "Unfair campaign. Pledge of Allegiance. Go into flag factories. But it works. I mean, if you're patriotic, you like the flag. Most Americans are patriotic."

Baker also helped construct a political ad attacking Dukakis's furlough policy of releasing state convicts, including those in prison for first-degree murder. "We pointed out that this guy had a prison furlough program when he was governor of Massachusetts that let killers out on furlough," Baker recalled. "People don't like that. That is a legitimate policy issue. We never ran pictures of a big black guy with a beard looking very menacingly at the viewer. We never did that. We had a prison furlough ad that we constructed around my table that was quite legitimate. It had a rotating door—" and through it, the silhouetted figures of prisoners passed.[5] An independent group, Americans for Bush, aired an even more menacing ad that told the story of African American Willie Horton, a convicted murderer who slashed a man to death and raped his wife while out of prison under the Massachusetts furlough program.[6] Even more damaging to Dukakis's hopes than these ads was his dispassionate answer to the hypothetical question of whether he would change his anti–capital punishment stance if his wife were raped and murdered. Vice President Bush swept to victory on November 8, 1988, winning forty states, their 426 electoral votes, and 53 percent of the national popular vote.

Two Supreme Court Vacancies

Four U.S. presidents (William Henry Harrison, Zachary Taylor, Andrew Johnson, and Jimmy Carter) had no opportunities to make a Supreme Court nomination, and ten presidents had but one opportunity.[7] As a one-term president, Bush was fortunate that two vacancies occurred on the nation's highest tribunal in the first two years of his presidency.

On July 20, 1990, Justice William J. Brennan Jr., suddenly announced his retirement from the Supreme Court. At age eighty-four, Brennan had been in declining health, but he had remained a vigorous member of the Court and a formidable creator of majority coalitions through its 1989–90 term. Indeed, he had fashioned narrow majorities for the dwindling liberal bloc in recent cases involving flag-burning and affirmative action. Brennan, who had served as an Eisenhower appointee since 1956, suffered a slight stroke early in the summer of 1990, and his physician urged him to accept the inevitable. He reluctantly announced his retirement, citing the burdens of the Court on his fragile health.[8]

A year later, in June 1991, an aging, tired, and frail Justice Thurgood Marshall announced his retirement from the Supreme Court, where he had served as the tribunal's first and only black member since his appointment by President Lyndon Johnson in 1967. The high court would be without its two liberal lions of the past several decades. In addition, African Americans viewed the Marshall position on the Court as the "black seat," in the long tradition of seats informally designated for Catholics and Jews. George Washington had reserved seats on the high bench for geographic constituencies. In fact, this so-called representative criterion for geography, religion, race, and, most recently, gender and ethnicity is only one of a quartet of factors presidents have used to place 112 justices on the Court.[9] The other three are objective merit, ideological compatibility, and personal friendship.[10] "Representativeness" may seem an oxymoronic term when applied to an unelected judicial body whose members ideally should serve as neutral arbiters of the law. Presidents have nominated justices as passive representatives who mirror societal characteristics, but they have also appointed jurists who actively pursue the interests of racial, religious, gender, or geographic constituencies.[11]

David Souter's Appointment

David Souter's strong New Hampshire ties served him well in the Bush administration's consideration of a replacement for Justice Brennan. The geography criterion had disappeared from presidential consideration in Supreme Court appointments after FDR. Yet Souter's New England roots matched those of President Bush and those of two key players in the decision about Brennan's replacement. The Granite State's Republican senator, Warren Rudman, was a close friend and mentor to Souter, who during Rudman's days as attorney general of New Hampshire had served as his deputy attorney general in Concord. Rudman was not shy about advocating federal judicial appointments for his New Hampshire colleague. Souter, who had a stellar scholastic record at Harvard (for both undergraduate and law degrees) and Oxford (as a Rhodes Scholar), was thought to be a moderate conservative. Bush had nominated him to the First Circuit Court of Appeals, where he had begun serving in May 1990. When the Brennan seat opened up a few months later, Rudman lobbied hard for Judge Souter to fill it. Rudman phoned Sununu and then the president, telling Bush, "Mr. President, you have just appointed this man to the First Circuit Court of Appeals, and he can easily be confirmed for the Supreme Court. I can guarantee you that he has no skeletons in his closet, and he's one of the most extraordinary human beings I've ever known."[12] Rudman alerted Souter that the White House would probably contact him. When asked how much opportunity administration outsiders like Rudman had to "weigh in on" the Supreme Court nomination, former attorney general Richard Thornburgh responded, "You know Warren Rudman? . . . To ask that question answers it." Bush was grateful for Rudman's recommendation but made no commitments to him over the phone. Nevertheless, the president publicly vowed to make quick work of the selection process for Brennan's replacement.

Souter, who had been confirmed unanimously by the Senate for his federal circuit judgeship, had yet to write a circuit court opinion at the time Brennan retired. When Sununu was governor, he had named Souter to the New Hampshire Supreme Court in 1983 and thought highly of him. "David had a very good record [in his home state]," Sununu remembered. "He became known as a very strong, for lack of a better term, law and order judge, a very academic judge in the sense that his decisions were not only a decision but he took great pains to create a legal structure for the decision that frankly a lot of the court admired."

The Department of Justice and the White House Counsel's office worked together to develop a list of potential nominees, which at one point included Solicitor General Kenneth Starr and U.S. Court of Appeals Judge Clarence Thomas, who had recently been appointed to the prestigious Washington, D.C., Circuit. According to Sununu and Thornburgh, eventually the names were winnowed to two: David Souter and Edith Jones of the Fifth Circuit Court of Appeals. "The one that was really pushing very strongly for David was [White House Counsel] Boyden [Gray]," Sununu recalled. Gray's assistant counsel Lee Lieberman "had read his decisions and if anybody who is a conservative goes back and reads his decisions, in spite of his history [of] adjustments to the contrary, David was a very conservative New Hampshire State Supreme Court judge. The issues were not the issues he would run into at the federal Supreme Court but on the issues that he did deal with, he was a strict constructionist. . . . No legislating from the bench and very meticulously tightly written [opinions], you know these are nice, classic—if you're a historian of the law, David Souter's decisions, even when you disagree with them, are written very nicely."

Nevertheless, Sununu did not initially support Souter as President Bush's first Supreme Court nominee. As he explained in his oral history interview:

> Frankly I was leaning slightly towards the advantage of appointing a woman to the Court because I didn't want the president to have to appoint a woman to replace a woman; it was possible that the next one who was going to leave was Sandra Day O'Connor and I did not want the president to be looking like he was slotting seats. Also Thurgood Marshall was about to leave, and I knew that there was going to be a strong pressure for the president to appoint a black. It was going to be Clarence [Thomas] and I didn't want him to be stereotyped as a president who was slotting seats. I thought if he was going to appoint a woman it would be better to appoint a woman now and a man later rather than a man now and a woman later. So I had a slight instinctive preference for Edith Jones. As close as I felt to David I thought David was going to get his chance very quickly because Marshall was quite ill. . . .[13]

Journalistic and scholarly sources[14] as well as some of the Bush oral histories indicate that when President Bush took a straw poll of his judicial selection team (Sununu, Gray, Thornburgh, and Vice President Dan Quayle), the result was a split decision. Thornburgh recalls that he and Gray supported Souter, while Sununu and Quayle preferred Jones. As noted above, Sununu took a tactical approach to the selection criteria he considered, including preserving the president's options for future nominations. He also wanted to avoid reserving seats for various groups on the high bench. Souter's lack of a paper trail on federal judicial issues constituted a distinct point in his favor among some members of the president's team, Sununu reported. As he observed in his oral history interview, "We know, [President Ronald Reagan's nominee, Robert] Bork, was rejected. That was the environment in which the next Supreme Court appointment came up for George Bush, and the president obviously wanted to make a positive impact on the court and yet, at the time, really did not want to go through a contentious hearing process on his first Supreme Court nomination."

Just as his predecessor had brought in Arizona Court of Appeals judge Sandra Day O'Connor for an interview before her nomination as the first woman justice in 1981, Bush met with Souter at the White House. Souter was skeptical of the process and his chances of landing the nomination. He was perfectly happy with his life in Weare, New Hampshire, living with his elderly mother in a ramshackle cabin in the woods. Moreover, he had been thrilled to accept the federal circuit court judgeship a few months earlier. Why go all the way to Washington to interview for a position he did not want and did not think he would get? Friends encouraged him to accept the interview request, if for no other reason than it would generate a lifetime's worth of interesting cocktail-party anecdotes—not that the introverted Souter attended many such soirees. A supportive Rudman drove Souter to the Manchester airport for his flight to Washington and even loaned his famously parsimonious friend $100 when the future justice discovered that he had only $3 in his wallet.[15]

Bush and Souter had a productive discussion in which the two gentlemanly, Ivy League–trained, Episcopalian New Englanders compared notes and philosophies. "Souter came in, and as usual Souter in his own New Hampshire dry charm made the president feel very comfortable," Sununu recalls. In Souter, the president saw a perfect nominee for the times: a brilliant jurist who represented the best of American virtues and exhibited no vices or controversial positions on judicial issues. He had written more than 200 opinions while on the New Hampshire Supreme Court, but they reflected a state docket rather than the divisive federal constitutional issues that reach the U.S. Supreme Court. A computer search of law review articles turned up only one example of Souter's published work, a eulogy for a New Hampshire judge. Because Robert Bork had been foiled by his own extensive paper trail of conservative commentaries on virtually every major constitutional issue of the day, Souter's obscurity became the deciding factor in his favor and gave him the nod over Jones, whose opinions on the federal bench were more controversial.[16]

With a stunned candidate at his side, Bush announced Souter's nomination on the same day he met him for the first time, a mere seventy-two hours after

Brennan announced his retirement from the bench. The president stressed that Souter was "a remarkable judge of keen intellect and the highest ability, one whose scholarly commitment to the law and whose wealth of experience mark him of first rank." Refusing to speculate about Souter's positions on legal issues, Bush tried to situate him as a conservative, using the coded language that Souter had "a keen appreciation of the proper judicial role rooted in the fundamental belief in separation of powers and the democratic principles underlying our great system of government."[17]

Called to the lectern at the president's news conference in the press briefing room, Souter humbly thanked Bush and then offered the media these few words in rather jumbled syntax: "If it were possible for me to express to you the realization that I have of the honor which the president has just done me, I would try, and I would keep you here as long tonight as I could do to get it out."[18] After the press conference and in the privacy of the White House, Bush offered the future justice a drink to calm him and called the nominee's aged mother in New Hampshire to tell her the surprising news.

In the weeks leading up to his Senate confirmation hearings, the media subjected Souter to probes into his personal life that were painful for the nominee and fruitless for the journalists. For an intensely private man, the scouring of his life and habits (especially his bachelorhood) was nearly more than he could bear.[19] Judge Souter even worried that the press would come to his cottage in the New Hampshire countryside and peer into the windows. Bush's assistant for legislative affairs, Fred McClure, thought the future justice's worry was unfounded:

> I'll never forget. [Souter] called me up one day and he says, "Fred, I left so quickly to come down to do this deal that I don't have the slightest idea what people can see through the window into my house and what magazines and books are there." Then he says, "Oh, I know one in particular though," because he was reading it at the time or had read at the time and he knew it was on top of his desk—because he's a prolific reader. What is it—*Drawing With the Left Side of the Brain* or something like that. He's saying, "They're going to think I'm weird." And I'm saying, "You're just creative, David, just creative. We can get through that one." Every time I see that book now, it brings back laughter. And I think, too, there was one other. I think he had bought a somewhat pornographic magazine at a book store, and he couldn't remember whether it was on the top of his desk or not, and he's saying, "Oh, my God." And I said, "Which book was it? It may be good on this side as opposed to on the other."

Senator Rudman, Souter's friend and mentor, introduced the quiet New Hampshire judge on the first day of the Senate Judiciary Committee's confirmation hearings. Rudman angrily declared, "It is remarkable that there are some people here in Washington who view a man who has a single-minded dedication to this chosen profession, the law, and possesses great qualities of humility, graciousness, frugality, charity, reverence to his faith and to his family as . . . an anomaly and somehow out of touch with life." Rudman later wrote, "If David Souter is odd, our society is in big trouble."[20]

Souter received the severest grilling from the Judiciary Committee's leading liberal Democrat, Senator Edward Kennedy of Massachusetts, who had successfully mustered the opposition to Bork's nomination. Kennedy endeavored to have the articulate but cautious Souter respond to a plethora of specific questions that reached into every conceivable area of public and constitutional law. To the surprise of many observers and commentators, the nominee proved to be much more forthcoming in his responses than had been predicted, even acknowledging the existence of a constitutional right of privacy and providing a ringing, touching tribute to Justice Brennan. But Souter drew the line at the insistent and repetitive questions on how he would vote in a challenge to the seminal abortion case of *Roe v. Wade*. Soft-spoken and even-tempered, Souter remained polite, almost courtly, throughout five days of testimony.[21]

Rudman and Souter need not have worried. "The nomination went up [to the Senate] and sailed through," Sununu explained. "So the President got what he wanted, a confirmation that was well received publicly, well received at the Senate level, and a well processed confirmation. From the needs that he had at the time, it was the right decision."

McClure helped smooth the way for Souter's nomination on Capitol Hill: "One of the things I did with Souter was we went to see all these guys who had been AGs when he was attorney general in the state of New Hampshire to build a body of support amongst those individuals; that gets you the [Senator Joseph] Liebermans of the world, or people who had been prosecutors like [Senator Patrick] Leahy, or people who have had similar career experiences." "David's a very smart guy and my biggest concern about his confirmation, other than the personal side and how they were trying to portray him," McClure recalls, "was to keep him from getting into an intellectual discussion that he shouldn't be getting into with members of the Senate. That was a big challenge with him, but he was smart enough to listen to us and so it worked out well in that regard." Despite its Democratic majority, the Senate Judiciary Committee, which was chaired by Delaware senator Joseph Biden, voted 13–1 to send the Souter nomination to the floor. Only Kennedy dissented. Eight other liberal Democrats then joined him in the full Senate to vote "nay." David Souter garnered ninety votes to replace Justice Brennan and was sworn in on October 9, 1990, joining the Court for its fall term, which had just begun.[22]

Clarence Thomas's Appointment

In 1989, President Bush nominated Clarence Thomas, a prominent conservative African American lawyer in the Reagan administration, to the U.S. Court of
Appeals for the D.C. Circuit, a well-established professional stepping-stone to
the Supreme Court. Thomas took his seat on the appeals court in 1990 after Senate confirmation by voice vote, despite opposition from some House members
and civil rights organizations. A graduate of the College of the Holy Cross and
Yale Law School, Thomas had a compelling, up-from-poverty personal story. He
had served during the Reagan presidency as assistant secretary for civil rights
in the Department of Education and then as chairman of the Equal Employment Opportunity Commission. His tenure at the EEOC had provoked criticism, including from the General Accounting Office, for "lax enforcement" of
antidiscrimination laws.[23]

Nevertheless, Thomas secured the top position on the short list to replace Justice
Marshall. As former attorney general Thornburgh recalls, "Clarence, for obvious
reasons, jumped to the front because of the racial factor. It was very difficult to
avoid. . . . By that time he had had a degree of seasoning on the D.C. Circuit and
it was a pretty short meeting. We went through the usual suspects and I think the
consensus was that Clarence was the choice." Ironically, Thomas's race almost cost
him the nomination. "The president did not want it to look again like there was a
woman's seat on the court, a black seat on the court, a Northeast seat on the court,"
reports Sununu. Moreover, Thornburgh expressed concerns that the American Bar
Association might give Thomas a low rating. "Not for any deficiency on his part,
but the fact that his judicial experience was so limited, and that was a big factor [for
the ABA]. So, I just counseled some caution in the making the selection." Thornburgh's comment led to a "dust-up" with White House Counsel Boyden Gray.
"Boyden was very much afraid for some reason that I was out to torpedo Clarence," observes Thornburgh. "We had a short but intense confrontation over that."

The president's selection team phoned him at his summer home in Kennebunkport, Maine. According to Thornburgh, Bush suggested, "Look at the
Hispanic candidates and interview some of them." Choosing a Hispanic, thought
the attorney general, "would have some of the same appeal that Clarence would
have, but with a little less controversy" over maintaining a "black seat" on the
Court. U.S. Fifth Circuit of Appeals judge Emilio Garza flew to Washington for an
interview, and Gray talked to him for two and one-half hours.[24] Although "very
agreeable, very talented," according to Thornburgh, Judge Garza seemed even less
seasoned than Thomas.

The selection team quickly informed the president that Judge Thomas was
the best choice. Sununu, Gray, Thomas, and Thomas's wife, Virginia, headed to

the Bush compound at Walker's Point. Thomas seemed unusually nervous at the thought of confronting hordes of journalists. Sununu suggested that he wear the chief of staff's glasses so that perhaps the press might think Thomas was the former governor of New Hampshire. That quip prompted one of the future justice's famous belly laughs and settled his nerves.

Bush asked Thomas two questions as they chatted in the president's bedroom: "If you are appointed to the Court, could you call them as you see them?" When Thomas responded that he could, the president queried, "Can you and your family make it through the confirmation process?" Thomas observed that he had successfully navigated four confirmation processes in the previous decade. Bush assured him that he would never publicly criticize any decisions he might make on the high court. Then the president said, "At two o'clock, I will announce that I will appoint you to the Supreme Court. Now let's go and have lunch." Thomas was so stunned that he had trouble rising from his chair, but he made a call to his wife to calm himself. In announcing his choice to replace Thurgood Marshall, Bush argued that "the fact that he [Thomas] is black has nothing to do with the sense that he is the best qualified at this time."[25] "Even I had my doubts about so extravagant a claim," Thomas recalled years later.[26] Thornburgh remembered that "I kind of did a double take. I think what [the president] meant, *sotto voce*, or with a wink of the eye, was that this was the best qualified African-American candidate we could find. And I think he's right."

The new nominee stepped to the microphone outside the Bush summer compound and expressed the improbability of his appointment. Born into abject poverty in the tiny fishing village of Pin Point, Georgia, he had never dreamed of such an honor. With a catch in his voice, Thomas thanked his mother and his maternal grandparents, who had adopted him when his mother could no longer care for him and his brother. He also offered a word of gratitude for the Roman Catholic nuns who taught him in grade school that he could rise above his lowly origins.[27]

Thornburgh had correctly predicted a less-than-top American Bar Association rating for the inexperienced Thomas: the ABA gave him a merely "Qualified" grade. Comparing how Souter and Thomas were prepared for the initial Senate confirmation hearings, Fred McClure recalls that, unlike Souter, Thomas

> hadn't really been immersed in the intricacies of the law. And you're in a situation where you've really got to work with him on that because he hadn't spent a whole lot of time studying how the Court has dealt with *Baker v. Carr* or *Marbury v. Madison* or all those dudes because that has not been his life. He's been in a political world. So we had probably more what I would describe as educating and refreshing about

constitutional law principles and in taking those constitutional law principles and surrounding them with the political discussions of the day. He had a good awareness of the political discussions of the day, but how you connected those with constitutional law issues that the Court could potentially be in a position to decide was where we had to spend a lot of time with Clarence.

Fortunately for Thomas, he had a powerful personal advocate in the Senate, the widely respected Republican John Danforth, who had mentored Thomas in an early position in the Missouri attorney general's office and on Capitol Hill. Well aware of the problems that had plagued the outspoken and discursive Judge Bork at his unsuccessful Supreme Court hearings, Thomas attempted to use the evasion technique that had served Justice Souter and other nominees so well. The Senate Judiciary Committee divided 7–7 in its vote on the nominee and forwarded his name to the full Senate without the committee's endorsement. Before the Senate could vote, however, controversy ensued.[28] Journalists were leaked a sensational story about an FBI report the Judiciary Committee had received in which Anita Hill, a University of Oklahoma law professor, accused Thomas of verbal sexual harassment when she worked with him at the EEOC. The Judiciary Committee reconvened for several additional days of hearings. Hill, like Thomas, a graduate of Yale Law School, described in shocking detail the nature of the alleged harassment in front of a transfixed national television audience of 20 million households.[29] Thomas vehemently denied any wrongdoing and questioned the good faith of senators for putting him through such an ordeal, famously calling the proceedings "a high-tech lynching for an uppity black man."[30]

McClure explains Thomas's response: "Clarence is a very religious guy and I think he reached the point where, in our conversations then and afterwards, he kind of shifted it to somebody else's hands and responsibility—somebody much higher than either one of us. . . . And it was kind of, 'Now that I have the chance, I need to say this. And I need to say this because it's the right thing to do and if I don't do what I believe is the right thing to do now when they are attacking my character—which is an unfounded attack on my character—then I'm not living up to those things that I believe in. And if that costs me being on the Supreme Court, which I didn't ask for in the first place, then okay.'"

According to Sununu, "nothing had come up" about Anita Hill in the administration's initial scrutiny of Thomas's past. "But fiction never shows up in the vetting and I am absolutely convinced in my heart that Anita Hill had said something in the past, . . . and it just snowballed on Anita Hill and what was fictional became fact in her mind. There were enough other nonconfirmable incidents and events and data . . . which really absolutely convinced me in my heart that whatever might have been there was an absolutely trivial situation that she had blown into a monstrosity." After Hill's allegations, Sununu explains, "We sent people to Oklahoma, we sent FBI everywhere. This was absolutely vetted top to bottom as intensely as any—that process is automatic on one of these things. Absolutely automatic. Let me remind you of what really swayed us. When we talked to people who knew only Anita Hill, some of them supported Anita Hill. When we talked to anybody who knew both Anita Hill and Clarence Thomas, unanimously they supported Clarence Thomas. Not a single, single, person who knew them both, in the contest, supported Anita Hill." ("Before, during, and after" her testimony, Sununu added.)[31] In the end, Thomas's "second round of hearings failed to vindicate or determine the veracity of either Hill or Thomas."[32]

Vice President Quayle, a former Republican senator from Indiana, lobbied his erstwhile colleagues on Capitol Hill for Thomas's confirmation. "I worked directly with the senators, especially with Senator [Alan] Dixon [D-Ill.], who kept his word and voted for him. It probably cost him the election. Sam Nunn [D], Wyche Fowler [D], who [were] from Georgia, as was Thomas, and folks like that." Indeed, eleven Democrats (seven from the South) joined forty-one Republicans to confirm the beleaguered candidate, 52–48, the closest vote in the twentieth century for a successful candidate.[33] When his wife reported to Thomas that he had been confirmed, the disgusted appointee replied, "Whoop-dee damn-doo."[34] In 2007, the still-bitter Justice Thomas told a *60 Minutes* television audience that liberals had orchestrated the attack on his character because they feared he would vote to overturn abortion rights. The political atmosphere turned so poisonous after Thomas's confirmation that the U.S. marshals who were guarding him advised that he wear a bulletproof vest. On October 23, 1991, an emotionally battered but determined Clarence Thomas was sworn in as an associate justice of the Supreme Court in a ceremony on the sun-splashed White House lawn.[35]

Reflecting on the Thomas-Hill spectacle, former attorney general Thornburgh concluded, "'Some of the people who went to such lengths to discredit Clarence Thomas turned out to be the same people who supported Bill Clinton over much more egregious conduct, so you tell me who is kidding whom here. This is all partisan.'"

In perhaps the most striking aftereffect of any confirmation hearing in Supreme Court history, many women political writers, activists, and candidates made the all-male Judiciary Committee's arguably callous treatment of Anita Hill a major campaign issue in the 1992 Senate elections. When the political dust cleared, four more women had joined "the world's greatest deliberative body."[36] Two of them, Senators Dianne Feinstein (D-Calif.) and Carol Moseley-Braun (D-Ill.), were named to the Judiciary Committee.

Souter's and Thomas's Records on the Supreme Court

David Souter served ably and conscientiously for nineteen years on the nation's highest tribunal, consistently writing his intellectually consistent opinions in clear, elegant language. Before retiring from the bench in 2009, soon after Democrat Barack Obama assumed the presidency, Souter's participation in oral argument usually reflected his gentlemanly demeanor as well as his clipped New England brogue. He once apologized for confusing an arguing counsel by asking for the "floor" in his argument. Souter was trying to articulate the word "flaw," but, as he admitted, his "regional accent" had betrayed him.[37]

During his first term on the high bench, Souter felt inundated with the work that awaited him in an atmosphere, city, and context that were totally unfamiliar. He described the burdens that he faced at the Court as "walking through a tidal wave."[38] Historically, freshmen justices take a reserved role while they adjust to their new surroundings, but Souter was even less visible than most.[39] He wrote only eight majority opinions in his first term on the Court, none of which were of major significance, and he wrote just two concurring and two dissenting opinions. His initial votes aligned him with the Court's conservative bloc, but his highest level of agreement (89 percent) was with Justice Sandra Day O'Connor, a moderate conservative and often the Court's swing vote.[40] In criminal justice cases, Souter continued a tendency from his days on the New Hampshire courts to side with the government. Observers noted that his predecessor, Justice Brennan, a champion of criminal rights, would surely have voted in the opposite way from his replacement in these cases. Conservatives hailed Souter's decisive vote in *Rust v. Sullivan*, which upheld the constitutionality of regulations prohibiting federally funded family planning clinics from discussing abortion with their clients.[41]

After a refreshing summer in Weare, Souter returned to the Court for his second term in the fall of 1991 with much more confidence in his ability to handle the job at an institution he utterly revered. His charm, warmth, and good humor had won him friends among the Court's close-knit staff. More significantly, he struck up a friendship with his predecessor, retired Justice Brennan, who maintained chambers at the Court. By the end of the Court's 1993–94 term, it had become clear that Souter had moved leftward on the Court and was almost always aligned—more often than not in dissent, notably in affirmative action cases—with liberal Justices John Paul Stevens, Harry Blackmun, and Ruth Bader Ginsburg (and later with Justice Stephen Breyer after he replaced Blackmun in 1994).[42] Some believe that Souter's transformation resulted from his admiration, bordering on adulation, of Brennan, whom he saw almost daily at the Court until Brennan's death in 1997. Brennan was the marshaler of Court majorities par excellence, possessing incisive, if gentle, powers of persuasion.[43] In his moving eulogy for Brennan, Souter, the reserved, formal, Yankee judge, revealed how the gregarious Irish jurist embraced him in a warm bear hug, called him "pal," and taught him "how to count to five."[44]

The majority that Souter helped fashion in the 1992 case of *Planned Parenthood of Pennsylvania v. Casey* to uphold the core of *Roe v. Wade* was reminiscent of Brennan-led majority building in the past. Souter was influential in coauthoring a rare triple-plurality opinion with Justices O'Connor and Anthony Kennedy that validated a woman's right to terminate her pregnancy based on a constitutionally protected personal liberty. This position attracted the vote of *Roe*'s author, Justice Blackmun, as well as that of Justice Stevens. Both would have gone even further and simply reconfirmed all of *Roe*'s reasoning. Souter, Kennedy, and O'Connor, however, abandoned the 1973 decision's trimester system of determining that a woman had an unfettered right to choose an abortion in the first three months of pregnancy. Instead, they substituted O'Connor's "undue burden" test, which would invalidate a state restriction on abortion when it "has the purpose and effect of placing substantial obstacle in the path of a woman seeking an abortion of a nonviable fetus."[45]

Needless to say, conservatives, particularly members of the pro-life movement, were furious that Souter had not provided the fifth vote to overturn *Roe*. Nor would he do so in two subsequent cases involving bans on so-called partial-birth abortions. *Stenberg v. Carhart* (2000) found Souter in the five-justice majority that struck down Nebraska's ban. In 2007's *Gonzales v. Carhart*, however, Souter's vote to invalidate the federal prohibition on partial-birth procedures placed him in the minority. President George W. Bush's appointment of Samuel Alito to replace Justice O'Connor in 2006 had added a pro-life vote to the Court.[46]

Souter also participated in an escalating war of words with his conservative colleague Antonin Scalia.[47] In First Amendment Establishment Clause cases, Souter began to take the lead on the separationist side. He wrote for the Court in *Board of Education of Kiryas Joel School District v. Grumet* that the state of New York could not constitutionally carve out a separate school district for a village of Satmar Hasidic Jews so that they would not have to send their special-education and handicapped students to secular public schools. Scalia's dissent in the 1994 case repeatedly criticized Souter by name, violating the Court's usual norm of not singling out individual justices for reproach, especially when they are representing the Court as an institution in its majority opinion. Souter's passionate dissent in *Rosenberger v. University of Virginia* (1995) also argued the separationist cause by defending the university's decision not to fund a student-run Christian magazine with proceeds from the student activities fee. He authored another vehement dissent, this time from Chief Justice William Rehnquist's majority opinion in 2002's *Zelman v. Simmons-Harris*, the Court's 5–4 decision in favor of government vouchers that provided tuition aid for needy students in Cleveland to attend private schools of their parents' choice. In practice, parents receiving the vouchers chose Catholic schools 95 percent of the time. Souter accused the majority of promoting "divisiveness" through its "dramatic departure from basic Establishment Clause principles."[48]

In school prayer cases, Souter also supported a high wall between church and state. He contributed a strong concurrence with Justice Kennedy's majority opinion to prohibit clergy-led prayers at public school graduations in *Lee v. Weisman* (2002) and voted with the majority's ruling in *Santa Fe School District v. Doe* (2000), which banned student prayer over the public address system at public school football games in Texas. As Souter explained his vote to a group of high school students, "Although I am a religious person, I do not favor prayer at games because eliminating it doesn't prevent individuals from praying. When I was in school, I never had official prayer before math class, but I can assure you, I prayed before each and every math class."[49]

Souter reflected an equally staunch separationist position regarding religious displays in public buildings. He penned the Court's opinion in *McCreary County v. American Civil Liberties Union* (2005), arguing that two Kentucky counties' displays of the Ten Commandments in their courthouses served a religious purpose and, therefore, violated the Establishment Clause.[50]

Although Souter generally trended to the liberal side, he occasionally returned to his more conservative roots, particularly in criminal justice cases. One of his majority opinions, in a search and seizure ruling, *Atwater v. City of Lago Vista* (2001), seemed particularly harsh and drew criticism from the left by Justice O'Connor. Souter wrote for a 5–4 majority that the Fourth Amendment does not forbid warrantless arrests for minor criminal offenses, in this instance a misdemeanor seatbelt violation punishable only by a fine. What raised O'Connor's ire was that the police had hauled Mrs. Atwater off to jail in front of her two frightened young children because no one in her car was wearing a seatbelt.[51]

In contrast to Souter's jurisprudential odyssey, Clarence Thomas's two decades on the Supreme Court have been marked by his reliable membership in the tribunal's conservative bloc; his closest voting ally has been Justice Scalia. Thomas's embrace of the founders' original intentions is so complete that Scalia has said that his colleague "doesn't believe in *stare decisis* [following judicial precedent], period."[52] Thomas maintains a firm commitment to limited government, except, most notably, in regulation of abortion. He joined the majority, for example in *Gonzales v. Carhart*, in upholding the federal ban on late-term abortions. His insistence on strict statutory construction was evident in 2007's *Ledbetter v. Goodyear Tire*, when he voted with the majority. Led by Justice Alito, the Court narrowed the use of the 1964 Civil Rights Act in the case brought by a woman who claimed pay discrimination over the course of her entire career. (The act mandated that plaintiffs claim discriminatory pay no more than 180 days after its first instance.) Congress ultimately overturned the Court's ruling with an amendment to the civil rights law, expanding the time period for suits against companies that discriminate by small dollar amounts over a long period of employment.

Thomas is most notable for his determined opposition to the racial preferences inherent in affirmative action. In the 2003 University of Michigan cases, he voted against the race-based admissions policies used by both the undergraduate college (*Gratz v. Bollinger*) and the law school (*Grutter v. Bollinger*). His dissent in *Grutter* reflected his outrage that Justice O'Connor had marshaled a majority to uphold the use of race and ethnicity as a "plus" factor in admissions to the law school. As Thomas wrote, "Like [Frederick] Douglas, I believe that blacks can achieve in every avenue of American life without the meddling of university administrators." Not surprisingly, he voted with the majority in the 2007 Louisville and Seattle rulings that banned the use of race in assigning students to public schools to ensure diversity.[53] Thomas condemns what he calls the "intellectual slavery" that he asserts liberal black interest groups attempt to impose on him.[54] "The Constitution is what matters," he declares, "not my personal beliefs."[55]

Thomas's view of the Constitution has led him (in dissent) to uphold the application of capital punishment to mentally retarded murderers (*Atkins v. Virginia*), to defendants who were juveniles when they committed their offense (*Roper v. Simmons*), and to rapists of children (*Kennedy v. Louisiana*). He voted with the majority in 2008 to uphold the lethal injection method of execution (*Baze v. Rees*) as not constituting cruel and unusual punishment and wrote the majority opinion in a 2006 case finding constitutional a Kansas law under which the death sentence is automatic if the jury finds an equal number of reasons for and against execution (*Kansas v. Marsh*).[56]

Thomas is remarkably silent in oral argument, sitting through entire terms of the Court without posing a single question to the counsel arguing before the justices. He has been utterly silent for more than the last six terms, eschewing queries even in the hotly contested 2012 "Obamacare" case. "I don't see where that advances anything," he observed of his colleagues' intense questioning in the health care arguments. "Maybe it's the Southerner in me. Maybe it's the introvert in me. I don't know. I think that when somebody's talking, somebody ought to listen."[57]

Thomas's refusal to interrogate counsel is especially obvious because of the "hot bench" on which he sits. Justice Sonya Sotomayor, now the most active inquisitor, asked as many questions in her first day on the Court in 2009 as her colleague, Justice Thomas, had posed during the previous decade. Further explaining his reticence, Thomas has also cited his grandmother's advice to remain silent in order to listen and the stigma he felt in college from speaking English with a Gullah dialect, which he had acquired during his boyhood in coastal Georgia. In 2007 he boasted to the conservative Federalist Society, "One thing I've demonstrated in sixteen years [on the Supreme Court] is you can do this job without asking a single question."[58]

Entering his third decade on the Court, Thomas is (oral argument aside) a confident and comfortable participant in the high tribunal's work. His opinions evince considerable strength and resolve. He has demonstrated an increased willingness to express himself, both in his own judicial opinions, mostly in dissent and usually, but not always, in tandem with Justice Scalia, and before public audiences.[59]

Conclusion

In his Bush Presidential Oral History interview, former attorney general Thornburgh starkly summed up Justice Souter's record: "I think Souter turned out to be much more liberal than those involved in the selection process anticipated." Bush's chief of staff, Sununu, put it, with slightly more pith, "To this day, any time I go to a conservative meeting 15 people come up and hit me with a Souter two-by-four across the forehead." About President Bush's second Supreme Court nominee, Thornburgh uttered a blander truism, "I think Clarence is . . . [a] solid, conservatively oriented vote."

George Bush's administration was marked by a cautious, deliberate, moderate, controversy-shunning, compromise-prone ethos, which his thirty-seven courts of appeals appointees tended to reflect. In contrast, Bush's 148 district court judges, whose nominations were guided more by their senatorial sponsors, applied on the bench the "ultra-conservatism" of the Republican Party's base.[60] Movement conservatives from the Reagan era witnessed a mixed outcome in Bush's two Supreme Court appointees, who occupied positions closer to the left and right edges of the ideological spectrum than did their appointing president. In doing so, they illustrate compelling lessons about the politics of judicial appointments, particularly in the late twentieth century. Souter's nomination, for example, was a direct result of the 1987 Bork debacle over filling the Court's swing seat. The Bush White House had learned not to appoint a loquacious scholar-jurist who boasts volumes of controversial speeches and judicial opinions. With his quiet persona, first-rate credentials, thin paper trail, and sparse decisions on hot-button issues in federal litigation, Souter represented the epitome of a "stealth nominee." Yet his movement away from a genuinely conservative state court record illustrates the hazards of nominating a candidate to the U.S. Supreme Court who possesses a tabula rasa on federal judicial questions. On most of the issues where Bush advocated a conservative agenda in his 1988 acceptance speech at the Republican convention, Souter departed from his appointing president. In abortion, school prayer, and death penalty cases, he reflected Brennan rather than Bush.

Souter's ideological U-turn also influenced future nominations, especially those by President George W. Bush, who wanted to name Attorney General Alberto Gonzales, his longtime Texas friend and advisor, to the O'Connor seat in 2005. When conservatives protested that "'Gonzales' was Spanish for 'Souter,'" Bush relented.[61] The right side of the political spectrum simply did not trust Gonzales on affirmative action and abortion, matters on which they hoped to overturn years of liberal precedents. Bush finally settled on John Roberts and Samuel Alito as his nominees, after an abortive attempt to place another of his Texas friends, Harriet Miers, on the Supreme Court.

Conversely, Clarence Thomas's ideology is clearly conservative—arguably more so than that of the president who nominated him. Bush's brand of conservatism leaned more toward New England pragmatism than New Right orthodoxy. Thomas and Bush would agree that prayer is allowable in public schools, but Bush would probably not go as far as his second appointee to claim that the First Amendment's Establishment Clause should never be applied to the states. Indeed, Thomas's federalism jurisprudence harkens back to a pre–Civil War vision of the Constitution that believes states may act as long as no explicit bar to such action exists in the governing document. Although as vice president, Bush called for the death penalty in the hypothetical case of a drug dealer who murders a police officer, it is a stretch to envision him agreeing with Thomas that a mentally retarded person may receive capital punishment. Nevertheless, the president's appointment of Justice Thomas reflects the long American political tradition of "representing" constituencies on the nation's highest tribunal—both to bolster the tribunal's legitimacy and to court support from geographic, religious, racial, ethnic, and gender groups. Sununu remarked "that judicial appointments are the greatest nightmare any governor or president has." The Souter and Thomas nominations illustrate that the politics of naming Supreme Court justices can derail presidential dreams of finding ideological soul mates to inhabit the marble temple on Capitol Hill.

Conclusion

NAVIGATING THE CROSSWINDS OF MODERN POLITICS AND POLICY

Sidney M. Milkis

As the chapters in this volume reveal, George H. W. Bush was a pragmatic politician who entered the White House during extraordinary times. In chapter 4, Jeffrey Engel nicely summarizes the momentous international events that occurred during his presidency: the Berlin Wall fell, the Soviet Union imploded, the Cold War ended, China's political reform movement came to a bloody halt in Tiananmen Square, the Gulf War was waged, and the Bush administration intervened in Panama to dethrone a drug-dealing dictator and in Somalia to ameliorate the inhuman suffering that a ferocious civil war was imposing on its people. According to Hugh Heclo in chapter 2, domestic events were no less momentous. He describes Bush as a "traditional conservative" dedicated to upholding the constitutional sobriety that James Madison prescribed in the *Federalist Papers*. The president bravely resisted but ultimately was victimized by the emergence of a new political order that jarred if it did not undermine a Constitution that proscribed raw and disruptive partisan conflict. "Under the Constitution," Heclo writes, Americans have a system of representative self-government that is designed to discover and operate at the political center." Bush entered the White House when a "modern unwritten Constitution" was cresting; indeed, it was significantly advanced by the "new conservatism" of the Reagan administration that he loyally served as vice president. This "new political system," which emerged in the decades after World War II, did not result from formal constitutional change; instead, it joined American politics and government to raw and disruptive partisan conflict. In the wake of the Reagan "revolution," polarization, not moderation, was rewarded and demanded. Once in charge, Heclo argues, Bush tried to tack back toward the center, but the headwinds of a polarized party system—the leading feature of the period's de facto regime—overwhelmed him. Bush's cachet was prudence, yet the politics of the 1980s disavowed the qualities that defined his long public service: "integrity, personal character, and honest compromise."

Received wisdom has it that President Bush managed to navigate the choppy waters between traditional and new conservatism, and the polarization it contributed to, in foreign affairs but failed to manage successfully the domestic challenges he faced. Like all received wisdom, this characterization of the Bush presidency has much truth on its side. Any fair reading of the president's foreign policy would have to judge it a success. Prior to becoming vice president, Bush had held positions that deepened his interest in and knowledge of international affairs. He had served as ambassador to the United Nations, the director of the Central Intelligence Agency, and emissary to China. Moreover, he performed sensitive diplomatic duties for the Reagan White House that made him the most traveled vice president in history. As Bartholomew Sparrow notes in chapter 3, the value Bush placed on personal relationships served him especially well on the world stage. Before and during his presidency, he put considerable stock in cultivating a wide acquaintance with world leaders. He also chose strong policy advisors: former Reagan chief of staff and secretary of the treasury James A. Baker III as secretary of state; former Ford chief of staff Richard B. Cheney as secretary of defense; former air force general Brent Scowcroft as national security advisor (a position he also held in the Ford Administration); and former Reagan national security advisor and army general Colin Powell as chairman of the Joint Chiefs of Staff. These individuals, Sparrow observes, were forged into a cohesive team because Bush chose them not just on the basis of their talent and experience but also because of their ability to work well together—no mean achievement, given the palace intrigues that have afflicted most modern presidents' foreign policy staffs.

Bush and his collegial foreign policy aides pursued a policy that Engel, invoking Scowcroft, describes as "enlightened realism." Their prudence was most evident in the administration's deft management of the final stages of the Cold War. Critics variously charged that the president was either too reticent about publicly celebrating communism's fall or too willing to interfere in other countries' affairs. In truth, Bush adroitly avoided both extremes. A more assertive policy may well have provoked a defensive, even military response from the Soviets. A less supportive one could have turned the newly free and democratic governments of Eastern Europe against the United States. As Engel points out, the administration's measured response had its costs; indeed, Bush's reluctant embrace of the possibility of a new world order may have hurt his prospects for reelection. Nevertheless, the Bush foreign policy team's rare capacity to act deliberately and adjust to the facts on the ground—for example, coming to the realization that Soviet leader Mikhail Gorbachev could be a trusted partner in bringing the Cold War to an end—resulted in foreign policy accomplishments that spanned the globe.

And yet the same pragmatism and faith in personal relationships that served Bush so well in world affairs seemed to backfire in domestic matters. Barbara Sinclair notes in chapter 6 that the president thought his friendships with Democratic members of Congress would enable him to forge bipartisan agreements on sensitive issues like the Clean Air Act, civil rights reform of employment practices, and fiscal policy. In the end, however, the rising tide of partisanship trumped these personal ties. Sinclair records Chief of Staff John Sununu's lamentation that the chairman of the House Ways and Means Committee, Representative Dan Rostenkowski (D-Ill.), whom the president affectionately called "Rosty," did not do as much as he might have to help Bush elide the firestorm that engulfed the administration during the notorious 1990 budget controversy. Ironically, Sinclair argues, Bush's very pragmatism blinded him to the polarizing partisan climate. The president and his aides "seem not to have understood" the way the two congressional parties were developing into hostile camps.

These scholars' characterizations of the Bush presidency offer an important but incomplete portrait of a savvy politician and central figure in the rise of a decidedly right-of-center Republican Party. Michael Nelson's study of Bush's long-standing connection to Texas politics in chapter 1 shows clearly that he could hardly be described as a bystander to the transformation of party politics. Bush was far more conservative than his reputation for pragmatism suggested. More to the point, he played a leading role in developing the Texas Republican party—"a seemingly pointless cause" at the time, as Heclo describes it—that became a leading site of one of the most important political developments of the past half-century: the transformation of southern politics from Democratic to Republican dominance.

Bush's party building was not merely the work of an effective Republican apparatchik. Instead of standing fast against "movement conservatism," he embraced it, however unhappily, at critical moments during his long march to the White House, most notably when he handed over control of his 1988 campaign to Lee Atwater, a leading practitioner of the slash-and-burn politics that eventually engulfed the Bush presidency. Nor was this aggressive partisanship limited to domestic issues. As Heclo points out, the new conservatism was abetted considerably by the grassroots anti-communism Barry Goldwater and Ronald Reagan made central to Republican presidential politics. Bush's "enlightened realism" was joined uneasily to this aggressive partisanship, which extended the rancorous divide between Democrats and Republicans. As Engel points out, the 1988 presidential campaign—the last of the Cold War—highlighted these partisan differences over the role America should play in the world. The Bush camp not only offered "a contrast between an experienced foreign policy expert and, in Massachusetts Governor Michael Dukakis, a foreign policy neophyte"; it also sharply contrasted Republican strength with Democratic weakness in world affairs, unwittingly symbolized by a photo of Dukakis—grinning awkwardly and wearing a huge helmet—riding in a tank (satirists noted that he looked like the Peanuts character Snoopy). Bush's hard-edged speech accepting the Republican nomination began by sharply contrasting Democratic and Republican views of America's place in the world:

> My opponent's view of the world sees a long slow decline for our coun-try, an inevitable fall mandated by impersonal historical forces.
>
> But America is not in decline. America is a rising nation.
>
> He sees America as another pleasant country on the UN roll call, somewhere between Albania and Zimbabwe. I see America as the leader—a unique nation with a special role in the world.[1]

Bush's contribution to party polarization does not mean that he was a wolf in sheep's clothing. Rather, it suggests that like most presidents since the Reagan "revo-lution," he was torn between two competing visions of the executive office. One, forged in the Progressive and New Deal eras, exalted the president as a nonparti-san administrator of the welfare and national security states—the "steward of the public welfare," to use Theodore Roosevelt's beguiling phrase. The other was an emergent style of presidential leadership that featured vigorous efforts to draw dis-tinctions between Democrats and Republicans and to accomplish partisan objec-tives. From this perspective, Bush's remarkable achievements and stunning failures were only partly attributable to his dual political personality   a complex amalgam of his New England roots and adopted Texas conservatism. His record also mani-fested competing strains of American politics that came into full view during his presidency and have reverberated into the present. Bush was the first president to be tasked with navigating the complex terrain of a "new American party system," char-acterized by high expectations for presidential leadership in a context of widespread dissatisfaction with government, strong and intensifying political polarization, and high-stakes battles over the basic direction of domestic and foreign policy.[2]

Bush's Conservatism and the Republican Right

The chapters in this volume and the George H. W. Bush Oral History Project that they heavily rely on "illuminate the question of his conservatism," as Nelson writes, "while complicating it." That Bush, unlike Reagan, did not like rhetoric and struggled with "the vision thing" does not make the task of identifying his political principles any easier. Nelson and Heclo both acknowledge that Bush's conservatism, as the latter writes, "was a disposition more than an ideological package of doctrines." This "disposition"—toward prudence, incrementalism, opposition to statism, and above all toward duty, that is, "to public service in the form of community and political leadership"—had deep historical roots. Its origins lay in President William Howard Taft's resistance to Theodore Roosevelt's insurgent Progressive Party campaign of 1912. In opposing TR's crusade, a seminal historical episode in the creation of the popular nationalism that dominated American politics for much of the twentieth century, Taft stood for constitutional principles such as the separation of powers and federalism, embraced a settled body of law, upheld the right of property, and resisted progressive and populist solutions to political and social discontents. Taft recognized that the rise of the corporation and the threat of imperialist powers required an expansion of the role of government. Indeed, as a member of the cabinet, he supported many of the pragmatic measures Roosevelt pursued during his presidency, such as the 1906 Hepburn Act, a moderate railroad reform that was developed in cooperation with "stand-pat" Republican congressional leaders and left considerable discretion for interpreting the law to what was then a very conservative court. Taft's was a "progressive conservatism": his desire to subordinate private power to law made him a progressive, but his insistence that public power respect the law made him a conservative."[3]

Taft's progressive conservatism gained him the respect of his party and eventually the position of chief justice of the United States, but it was a political disaster. He won only two states in his 1912 reelection bid—Utah and Vermont—and just 23 percent of the popular vote. In contrast, Roosevelt won 27 percent of the popular vote and 88 electoral votes—the best showing of any third-party presidential candidate in American history—and the Democratic nominee, Governor Woodrow Wilson of New Jersey, who also ran as a Progressive, was elected president with 41 percent of the vote. Taft's pragmatic conservatism would live on—indeed dominate—American politics during the 1920s, but after the New Deal, as Heclo indicates, it was "essentially a negative and reactive force." Its leading figures, such as Dwight Eisenhower and Nelson Rockefeller, accepted the two new rights Franklin Roosevelt trumpeted in his 1941 Four Freedoms address—freedom from want, embodied by the welfare state, and freedom from fear, embodied by the national security state—while seeking to create boundaries for the expanding national state with reverence for private property, the constitutional system of checks and balances, and the rule of law. Eisenhower's pragmatic orientation toward the New Deal appeared to place it above party, thereby solidifying what Arthur Schlesinger Jr. characterized in the late 1940s as the "vital center."[4]

As Heclo suggests, Bush felt most comfortable with this pragmatic conservative tradition, which he inherited from his father, Senator Prescott Bush of Connecticut, a strong supporter of Eisenhower. There is a real sense, in fact, in which Bush dedicated his one-term presidency to pragmatic conservatism. His 1992 reelection effort was a disaster—his 37 percent of the vote was the worst showing for a Republican nominee since Taft's 1912 debacle. And yet Heclo concludes that Bush, like Taft, deserves honor for thinking and acting constitutionally. "By the standard of political success measured by long-term institutional values and moral competence," he writes, "George Bush earns a very high grade. Or, as Prescott Bush might have better said it, 'quite worthy . . . well done, son.'"

But Bush's Yankee disposition was uneasily joined to the "movement conservatism" that animated the rise of the Republican Party in Texas. This new strain of conservatism, Heclo observes, did not fear but instead eagerly enlisted popular passions for a full-scale assault on liberalism at home and communism abroad. What would Bush's father have thought of his son's invocations of Clint Eastwood in his best-remembered speech? Perhaps, as Heclo suggests, the red meat Bush fed the Republican base in 1988 and the polarizing politics his campaign strategist Atwater practiced on his behalf were necessary evils in an era when the Democrats and Republican had become more divided. By all accounts Bush agonized over the need to make concessions to the tawdry partisanship that arose from the culture wars of the 1960s, in which Democrats and Republicans not only disagreed over fundamental principles but also questioned the motives of their opponents. Nevertheless, Bush's migration to Houston, Texas, Nelson tells us, placed him at the "epicenter" of Republican politics in that state, a critical beachhead for the political realignment envisaged by "movement conservatives." No other modern president cut his teeth on the nuts and bolts of party organization as Bush did.

The story Nelson tells of Bush's election as the Harris County Republican Party chair, won in a bitter contest with the virulently anti-communist John Birch Society—"the meanest political battle of his life," according to Barbara Bush—is a fascinating prelude to the struggles he would have with self-styled Reaganites during his four years in the White House. Ironically, however, Bush and the other pioneers who planted the Republican flag in the South helped prepare the way for the "great sorting out" of parties.[5] Sinclair notes that as conservative southern Democrats were replaced in Congress by Republicans, Democrats had increasing success in the North, especially in the Northeast, a shift that led to a more unified and disciplined liberal party. More broadly, these changes in the Republican and Democratic parties resulted in a decisive shift from the localized, practical party politics that had prevailed through most of American history to the national, programmatic, ideological organizations that compose the "unwritten Constitution."

Bush's contribution to this development was not merely organizational competence. As Nelson points out, like John Tower, who would be the first Republican Senator elected in the former confederacy since Reconstruction, Bush, both as party organizer and candidate, did not resist movement conservatism in Texas; indeed, he played an important role in its incursion into the Lone Star State. As head of the Harris Country Republicans, Bush did not attack the Birchers publicly, lest he suffer politically, as Richard Nixon may have by doing so in his 1962 California gubernatorial campaign. Nelson shows that Bush moved hard right in his 1964 Senate campaign against the liberal Democrat Ralph Yarborough, the only southern Senator to vote for the recently enacted Civil Rights Act. Perhaps because he was a loyal partisan and foresaw the future of the Republican Party, Bush tied his campaign to Goldwater's. Like both the Republican standard-bearer and Ronald Reagan, who gave a well-received televised speech for the Goldwater campaign, Bush opposed the Nuclear Test Ban Treaty with the Soviet Union, the Civil Rights Act of 1964, Medicare (he called it "socialized medicine"), and the "left wing spending programs" of Lyndon B. Johnson's Great Society. Bush was equally strident in attacking Yarborough's pro-union record. Invoking United Auto Workers president Walter Reuther, he attacked Yarborough as a "Reuther-controlled radical of the left" and a member of "a militant little band of left wingers." Bush's actions in 1964 thus abetted rather than constrained the populist militant conservatism that was reshaping the Republican Party.

Nelson shows that Bush privately expressed remorse for his 1964 campaign, quoting a letter to his minister in Houston that he "took some far-right positions to get elected" and hoped he would "never do it again." And both Nelson and Heclo see tangible signs of this regret in Bush's postmortem of the 1964 election, an essay he wrote for a *National Review* forum on "The Republican Party and the Conservative Movement" to which Reagan also contributed. In their essays, candidate Bush and citizen Reagan agreed that LBJ's historic landslide victory over Goldwater was not a condemnation of conservatism; instead, both attributed the thumping to Johnson and the Democrats' effective, albeit distorted, view of Goldwater as a radical intent on dismantling the New Deal and advancing dangerous imperialism. Unlike Reagan, however, Bush believed that the far right of the Republican Party unwittingly gave the Democrats considerable help in selling this caricature. Ending his forbearance toward the Birchers and other extremists vying for control of the party, Bush, as Nelson writes, used the "n-word of the time." Goldwater's negative image, Bush wrote, was embellished by "the so-called 'nut' fringe." "Goldwater didn't want to repeal Social Security but some of his more militant backers did," Bush charged. "He didn't want to bomb the UN but these same backers did. They pushed their philosophy in Goldwater's name, and scared the hell out of the plain average non-issue-conscious man on the street."

And yet, Reagan, as he would show as governor of California and president, shared Bush's desire to portray conservatism as a positive understanding of government rooted in the shared values of the American people. Although Reagan stated this preoccupation differently than his more pragmatic fellow Republican, he did not take issue with Bush's position that it is necessary to "re-package our philosophy, emphasize the positive, eliminate the negative, warn of the dangers from the Left but do so without always questioning the patriotism of those who hold Liberal views." As Reagan wrote at the end of his essay, it is "time now for the soft sell to prove our radicalism was an optical illusion. We represent the forgotten American—that simple soul who goes to work, bucks for a raise, takes out insurance, pays for his kids' schooling, contributes to his church and charity and knows there just *"ain't no such thing as free lunch"* (emphasis in original). Bush thought this repackaging had mostly to do with building personal networks at the local and state level; Reagan put more stock in his well-crafted and effectively delivered speeches. But their views were different sides of the same coin—a top-down, bottom-up endeavor to build a center-right Republican Party that came to fruition during the Reagan-Bush administration.

Bush's dedication to building a competitive Republican Party is what clearly distinguished him from other pragmatists, like Rockefeller, who refused to support Goldwater. In a clear reference to the New York governor, Reagan ended with the harsh postscript: "I don't think we should turn the high command over to leaders who were traitors during the battle just ended." But Bush, too, gave no quarter to those who defected in 1964: "I have no respect for the Republican who quit his Party this year because he didn't get it all his way."

Considering their common sentiments about the future of the Republican Party and the conservative movement, it is not so surprising that Reagan and Bush shared the ticket in 1980. Nor is it surprising that their uneasy but effective partnership governed the country for twelve years. That this center-right coalition would eventually give way to the harsh partisan conflict that reverberates through our own time suggests that Bush contributed, however unintentionally, to long-developing forces that were beyond his control.

Bush's Place in History

Although Bush would remain a good party soldier as the Republicans became a decidedly right-of-center party in the 1970s, he retained his reputation as a moderate pragmatist who never overcame his fear that the "nut fringe" would take over the GOP. Even as Bush's adopted state of Texas warmed to him, Donald Critchlow notes, nationally "many conservatives continued to see him as a representative of the elitist eastern wing of the Republican Party—those internationalist, big government, 'me-too Republicans'" who prevented a full-scale attack on the liberal administrative state.[6] Nelson observes that Bush's unearned reputation as a moderate was advanced considerably during his four years in the House. Elected in the 1966 midterm election that registered the first strong reaction against LBJ's Great Society, Bush acquired the reputation, as Barbara Bush put it, of a "fiscal conservative and social liberal" by standing against the emerging southern wing of his party to support the Civil Rights Act of 1968, which was designed to prevent racial discrimination in the sale or rental of housing. That Bush was the first Republican Houston had ever sent to the House and a poster child for what came to be called the party's "southern strategy" makes all the more notable his standing firm at a hostile open forum in his district, where he won his conservative promilitary audience over by linking support for civil rights with a commitment to do right for the brave African Americans serving their country in Vietnam. This episode is a moving example of the pragmatic congressman's capacity for statesmanship and a sign that the remorse he expressed for his opposition to the 1964 civil rights bill was sincere.

Bush's reputation as a moderate, as both Nelson and Heclo note, also followed from the shifting tides of conservative opinion on positions such as birth control and fiscal policy. As Nelson writes, "Bush's support for certain policies that lay at the mainstream of conservatism in the 1950s and 1960s—most notably his preference for a balanced budget over tax cuts and support for family planning as a strategy for lower class population control and environmental preservation— fit uncomfortably with conservatism as it evolved during the 1970s and 1980s." Bush's long-standing support for Planned Parenthood never included acceptance of abortion on demand, although he did say during the 1980 campaign that he did not oppose it in cases of "rape, incest, or when the life of the mother is at stake." But even this limited concession condemned Bush as an ideological trimmer on the abortion issue in the aftermath of *Roe v. Wade*, the critical starting point of the GOP-Christian Right alliance that would be sealed during the Reagan presidency.[7]

The populist and aggressive conservatism that Reagan helped bring to fruition also had profound consequences for fiscal policy. Traditional conservatives since Taft had championed balanced budgets, a position that called not only for restraining spending but also for raising taxes if needed to pay for those limited government actions that even conservatives deemed necessary. But Reagan, who had been looking to "repackage conservatism" as a more optimistic movement ever since the Goldwater debacle, spied great potential in the "supply side economics" advanced by innovative thinkers such as Arthur Laffer and Paul Craig Roberts, who argued that a large tax cut would stimulate productivity so much that tax revenues would actually increase and allow the budget to be balanced in 1984. Yet, as Reagan's brilliant but reckless director of the Office of Management and Budget, David Stockman, admitted at the time, "None of us really understood what's going on with those numbers."[8] The administration later became saddled, contrary to supply-side projections, with the largest national debt in United States history.

This was an ironic and troubling legacy for a conservative president. But Reagan was determined to remake conservatism as a popular movement, and supply-side economics was an indispensable initiative for a successful makeover. Just as the Lyndon Johnson's policy innovations would become core Democratic commitments in the 1970s, Reagan's fiscal policy became an enduring rallying cry of Republican conservatism in the 1980s. Reagan reached out to anti-tax advocates such as Grover Norquist, whose militant advocacy would play a critical role in transforming supply-side theory into the anti-tax mantra that had become GOP orthodoxy by the time Bush ran for and governed as president.

During the 1980 primary contests, Bush famously dismissed Reagan's fiscal policy as the "free lunch approach," "economic madness," and, most famously, "voodoo economics," implying that it represented a radical innovation as dangerous as those liberal experiments that conservatives had been attacking since the Goldwater campaign. Reagan's willingness to name Bush as his vice presidential candidate in spite of this slight showed that the GOP standard-bearer recognized both the value of the balance that Bush would bring to the ticket and the continuing electoral appeal of pragmatic politics, even as the differences between Democrats and Republicans grew wider. Indeed, before settling on Bush as his choice, Reagan seriously considered former president Gerald Ford, with whom he had fought a bitter, losing contest for the 1976 presidential nomination. But Reagan and his top strategists eventually settled on Bush, viewing him as more sympathetic than Ford to Reagan's militant anti-communism and receiving Bush's assurance that he supported the most conservative Republican platform in forty years "with no exceptions," including its strong anti-abortion and pro–supply side provisions.

Bush vindicated Reagan's choice by proving to be a capable and loyal vice president. In chapter 5, Robert Strong quotes James Baker as stating emphatically that loyalty was a defining strength in Bush's character. This trait served Bush well as vice president, winning him the president's trust and positioning him as Reagan's heir apparent in the 1988 campaign. "Bush knew that his [loyalty] would reinforce Reagan's trust in him and allow him to be an effective confidant and adviser," Roman Popadiuk has written; "but it was also genuine."[9] Indeed, many scholars and pundits viewed Bush's easy victory over Dukakis in the 1988 election as a remarkable triumph for Reagan. Like Andrew Jackson, who in 1836 had aided Martin Van Buren, the last incumbent vice president to be elected president, Reagan proved to be unusually helpful to his vice president, both in his popularity and in his active support during the campaign.

Still, Bush's pragmatic past, especially his initial repudiation of Reagan's fiscal policy, continued to strain his relations with the conservative movement and, as Stephen Skowronek has written, "became emblematic of a much larger credibility problem that would define his presidency." As Russell Riley argues in the Introduction, it would have been difficult for anyone to fill Reagan's shoes; the anecdote Riley relates about Colin Powell's awe of Reagan's spit-and-polish footwear "is freighted with political significance." Just as Reagan seemed to be perfectly cast as the steward of a conservative political realignment, Bush seemed doomed to dwell in his successor's shadow. Riley makes note of Skowronek's theoretical explanation of the dilemmas of the "faithful son," the president who comes into office pledged to continue the work of a highly consequential predecessor. It is no coincidence that Bush and his political allies often compared his historical fate to that of Harry S Truman. Like Truman, Bush succeeded a president who seemed to play the critical role in creating a new political order, recasting the very terms of constitutional government. And like Truman, Bush inherited a "politically potent agenda but [found] the exercise of power on its behalf constrained by partisan divisions within the government" and disagreements within the new establishment over the true meaning of its core commitments.[10]

Still, Truman's surprising victory in the 1948 president election, the progress he made in strengthening New Deal commitments in domestic and foreign policy, and his honored place in history show that the role of what Skowronek calls the "orthodox innovator" can be performed successfully. Just as important, the leadership requirements of a worthy successor are not the same as those needed to initiate the founding of a new political order. Bush's campaign for the presidency in 1988 and the early days of his administration in 1989 suggested that his more pragmatic and conciliatory conservatism was well suited to shoring up the Reagan Revolution. As Kenneth Duberstein, who was Reagan's chief of staff, observed:

> If Reagan's was a "defining" presidency that in bold strokes and grand ideas set the tone of the present political order, Bush's promises to be a "refining" administration that in pastel colors and day to day steps will consolidate the gains of the Reagan years. Bush's task, although less dramatic, is every bit as important.[11]

Duberstein's view was endorsed by many other Republicans during Bush's first year in office. Even the militant conservative Newt Gingrich, who was elected GOP minority whip at the beginning of the 101st Congress (1989–90) and then abandoned the president during the critical budget battles toward the end of that legislative session, was initially optimistic about the Bush presidency:

> I do not think [Bush] needs to be another Ronald Reagan. Reagan laid the foundation for a new paradigm in American politics. Bush is well-suited to institutionalize the gains made over the last eight years. It takes different types of statesmen to build a regime, on the one hand, and to implement it, on the other hand. I think Bush can serve and benefit from Reagan, just as James Madison served and benefitted from Thomas Jefferson.[12]

These observations suggest the enduring power of an important dynamic of American politics—the rise and fall of governing political orders orchestrated by America's most consequential presidents. And yet by the time Bush ascended to the presidency, politics had been transformed dramatically—both by the expansion of national administration, especially as manifested in the departments and agencies of the executive branch and the Executive Office of the President, and by the growing partisan divisions over the direction this "big government" should take—that created new challenges for each new president. Of course, there was nothing new about partisan rancor. In a sense, "the unwritten Constitution" emerged very early, with Thomas Jefferson and the Democratic-Republican Party's mobilization against Alexander Hamilton's Federalists, culminating in what Jefferson termed the "Revolution of 1800." But the parties that arose from the conflict between the Democratic-Republicans and Federalists and became an enduring part of American politics and government during the Jacksonian period were highly localized and dependent on patronage. Compared to Europe, where parties have been divided by fundamental questions of religion and class, America has had "small" parties, to use Alexis de Tocqueville's description, which have divided over sectional interests and personal ambitions more than over fundamental principles. These "small" parties have gotten caught up in something big periodically—during so-called critical partisan realignments, most notably during the slavery controversy and the Great Depression—but the rancor has proved temporary when a new majority coalition and a broad consensus in support of a new regime has emerged.

In contrast, the new and polarized party system that arose after the 1960s has been characterized by partisan conflict that appears to be more structural and centralized than those that animated previous critical junctures in American democracy. With the emergence of nationalized and highly ideological parties, which focus political conflict on the activities and commitments of the federal government, the modern presidency plays an especially important and ambiguous role in contemporary partisan rancor. The Great Society and the Reagan

Revolution did not eliminate the "stewardship" role celebrated by Progressive and New Deal presidents but instead gave rise to a more partisan style of leadership that was layered on top of that role. On one hand, the president still is responsible for presiding over and administering an expansive federal government in an ostensibly nonpartisan fashion. On the other hand, as the nation's most prominent political figure and the occupant of its most powerful office, the president is almost by definition his party's leader. Because the president holds the impressive powers of the office, he can leverage these resources for partisan gain. Consequently, Republicans and Democrats have become more dependent on presidential leadership for mobilizing popular support and promoting party policies. Yet at the same time, presidents have reinforced many citizens' hostility toward partisanship through their recurrent appeals for unity and their repeated criticism of "politics as usual." This complex interplay between the modern presidency and party combat helps explain why many citizens have continued to decry partisanship and express alienation from government, even as they were becoming more partisan themselves.

Reagan's was the first presidency to fully reflect the political challenges presented by the emergence of what might be called the new American party system in the late 1970s and early 1980s. Whereas previous post–New Deal presidents—even LBJ and Nixon—had largely eschewed partisanship in office, Reagan embraced the role of party leader in an effort to bring about the partisan realignment conservative Republican activists had long desired. Reagan not only sought to advance a more appealing brand of Republican conservatism than had previously been articulated but also made unprecedented presidential efforts to raise campaign funds, stump for Republican candidates, and build his party's organization. These actions helped strengthen the Republican Party and extend support for conservative principles among the public. Nonetheless, Reagan's sometimes strident rhetorical attacks on the legacies of the New Deal were joined to administrative aggrandizement. Facing a recalcitrant Democratic House during his entire tenure in office and a Congress fully under Democratic control after 1986, Reagan pushed his administrative powers to the limit in order to advance Republican conservatism. Indeed, Reagan exercised unprecedented centralized authority over appointments and regulatory rule-making in order to bring the executive branch under presidential control. He routinely used executive orders, memoranda, signing statements, and other proclamations to make policy "with the stroke of a pen." In essence, Reagan's presidency showed that administrative aggrandizement could be used to accomplish conservative objectives.

To be sure, Reagan's ardent partisanship was not completely novel. All of the presidents who instigated a "paradigm shift" were either founders or refounders of political parties. But extraordinary party leadership prior to the 1960s served mostly to highlight the collective nature of great political transformations. Political parties kept presidents faithful to broader interests even as, episodically, they gave presidents the political strength to embark on ambitious projects of national reform. Moreover, prior to the New Deal, none of the programs that formed the core of a new political regime entailed a substantial expansion of executive power. The modern executive office forged during the New Deal stood apart from and even obscured party politics. But a new presidential synthesis has emerged since the late 1960s—one marked by an uneasy confluence of executive prerogative and partisan polarization. Reagan's presidency demonstrated both the promise and the perils of attempting to synthesize presidency-centered and partisan approaches to governing. Far from bringing about a decisive Republican realignment, Reagan's partisanship stimulated liberal activists to redouble their efforts, thereby intensifying partisan conflict in Washington and in the country. Moreover, although Reagan's presidency witnessed an impressive advance of Republican political and programmatic objectives, it was also characterized by serious administrative failures, culminating in the Iran-Contra affair during his second term.

Reagan did not transform Washington. But he did strengthen the Republican beachhead in the nation's capital, solidifying his party's long-standing dominance of the presidency and providing better opportunities for conservatives to become part of the executive establishment. Similarly, Reagan's two terms witnessed a revitalization of the struggle between the executive and the legislature that had flared during the Nixon presidency; indeed, his rhetoric and his program became the foundation for more fundamental philosophical and policy differences between the branches. Prior to the 1960s, the institutional arrangements created by the written Constitution provided for bounded conflict between the branches of government. Party politics, especially when crystallized by national emergencies and strong presidential leadership, enabled the president, Congress, and even the courts to work in harness—to govern. The new party system that formed afterward did not combine but instead divided in an unprecedented manner these separate branches. The result was not institutional competition, which the framers anticipated and celebrated, but institutional combat, which jolted the system of checks and balances and threatened the rule of law.[13]

The Bush Presidency and Divided Democracy

The results of the 1988 election did not seem to offer any way out of the conundrum created by divided government. If anything, it appeared to yield a more extreme manifestation of this puzzling and worrisome condition. Never before had a president been elected—by a landslide no less—while the other party gained ground in the House, the Senate, the state governorships, and the state legislatures. Never before had the voters given the newly elected president fewer fellow partisans in Congress than they gave Bush. Never, in short, had the American system of "separated institutions sharing power" been characterized by such partisan segmentation. By many indications, the Reagan Revolution had left the United States in a state of striking and unprecedented ambiguity with respect to its governing institutions. It also seemed to leave the American people in a funk. Unlike traditional partisan realignments, the split verdict of the 1980s did not result in a surge of democratic participation. Rather, the 1988 campaign signaled a new low in the deterioration of American electoral institutions. Less than half of the eligible electorate bothered to vote in 1988, the lowest turnout in a presidential contest since 1924. In fact, in the non-southern states, where three-quarters of the American people lived, the 1988 turnout was the lowest in 164 years—the most dismal showing since the United States became a mass democracy during the Jacksonian era.

In the face of this constitutional and partisan conundrum, the task George Bush set out for his administration was to negotiate his way through the competing tasks of harsh partisanship and responsible governance. As many of the chapters in this volume make clear, he saw campaigning as a necessary concession to the harsh partisan politics of the day, which, although not pretty, highlighted important domestic and foreign policy differences between Democrats and Republicans. His hope was to move toward a more pragmatic stewardship of the welfare and national security states, a strategy that would not ignore principled differences between the parties but would ameliorate the politics of destruction and make it possible for the president and Congress to rise above partisanship to solve critical problems. In many respects, Bush's attention to problem solving at home and abroad would reveal that pragmatic presidential leadership still resonated in American politics. At the same time, he learned that the modern presidency, partly through his own actions, had been pulled into the vortex of intractable partisan divisions that rendered responsible government, as traditionally understood, impractical.

Bush's presidential leadership did not so much attempt to reconcile as to tack between pragmatic management and hard partisanship. This was foreshadowed by his 1988 acceptance speech at the Republican National Convention. It begins, understandably, with a paean to the Reagan presidency and a promise to carry on the work of Reagan's two terms, expressing special pride in the economic prosperity that marked the administration's final six years. But rather than base his campaign on the Reagan-Bush management of the economy and world affairs or tout his impressive political résumé, burnished by loyal service to the administration,

Bush chose to fight his election battle on the field of the conservative movement. In chapter 7, Barbara Perry and Henry Abraham reprise the vice president's rendition of his differences with Dukakis on "movement" issues such as teachers' obligation to lead their students in the pledge of allegiance, the death penalty, voluntary school prayer, abortion, drugs, and, most prominently, the Massachusetts policy of furloughing prisoners. Perry and Abraham note James Baker's defense of the Bush campaign's attack on Dukakis's support for the furlough program, made so controversial when Willie Horton, an African American convicted of murder, brutally beat up a man and raped his wife during his temporary release from prison. Bush's detractors claimed that his law and order campaign was tinged with racism and that the vice president remained committed to the Republicans' "southern strategy." Baker rightly points out that the Bush campaign did not run the ad that displayed a menacing mug shot of Horton; instead, the official campaign spot showed "a rotating door" and, through it, the silhouetted figures of prisoners passing in and out. An independent group, Americans for Bush, aired the more menacing spot. Baker's account gives testimony of the early emergence of shadow parties that engage in the rancorous politics Heclo scorns without the candidate's consent. Indeed, many Bush and Republican strategists told me in private conversations that the attack on the furlough program would have been more effective if Willie Horton had been white. But it was the Americans for Bush ad, amplified by the heavy media coverage it received, that made the furlough issue so potent. Bush's reference to it in his nomination speech, arousing a roar among the delegates, fueled his critics' charge that his campaign had to take some responsibility for the issue's strong racial overtones.

Bush hardly stood like Horatius at the bridge against partisan polarization; his 1988 acceptance speech, which set the tone of his campaign, contributed to it. Indeed, the litany of conservative causes that Perry and Abraham quote culminated with the vice president's firm pledge to uphold the Reagan orthodoxy on tax policy. Hoping once and for all to dispel the Reaganites' suspicion that he disdained supply-side economics, Bush mimicked Clint Eastwood's bad cop, Dirty Harry, with a bravado performance that sent the delegates into a frenzy: "The Congress will push me to raise taxes, and I'll say no, they'll push, and I'll say no, and they'll push again. And all I can say to them is: Read my lips: no new taxes."[14]

Even as he championed the Reagan Revolution, however, Bush did not abandon pragmatism, nor did he abandon the hope that he might put his own stamp on Reaganism. Lost amid the excitement of his brash anti-tax pledge was the rest of the acceptance speech, which strongly hinted that, if elected, he would be his own man. Bush pledged that his administration would provide every child with a "first rate school," would grow LBJ's Head Start program, would "do whatever it takes to make sure the disabled are included in the mainstream," and would tackle environmental problems like acid rain and the pollution of the nation's waterways. These promises, he admitted, required exploiting the modern presidency's capacity for "gentle persuasion," and completing the mission would require preparing the executive office and the American people for "a kinder, gentler nation." These passages in the nomination speech, which were hardly acknowledged by the delegates or the press, recurred in Bush's inaugural address. Adding rhetorical flourish to his hope for a more harmonious nation, he exhorted the country on January 20, 1989, to "make kinder the face of the nation and gentler the face of the world." He called on Democrats and Republicans to find common ground on "crucial things" because the American people "awaited action." "They didn't send us here to bicker," the new president admonished. "They ask us to rise above the merely partisan."[15]

The mystifying mix of partisanship and pragmatism that marked Bush's most important rhetorical utterances characterized his four years as president. As Strong points out, the rejection of John Tower's nomination as secretary of defense, ostensibly because of the former Texas Senator's excessive drinking, "was a test of partisan strength with at least a whiff . . . of resentment [among Democrats] over what the recent campaign had done to the character of Michael Dukakis." And yet, like Sparrow, Strong claims that although the president's deep commitment to loyalty and personal friendship—demonstrated by his willingness to stand by Tower, past the point when it was clear that the Senate would not approve the nomination—failed to trump partisan rancor, it did succeed magnificently in cultivating the camaraderie and collegiality that characterized Bush's foreign policy team. Although Bush's faith in trust and personal relationships worked more effectively in foreign policy, Sinclair notes that for a time, Democrats in Congress, even as their resentment about the campaign Bush had waged lingered, were relieved that the new president "was not Reagan but rather someone who believed that sometimes government could contribute to the solution of societal problems and who appeared to acknowledge that Congress had a legitimate role to play in policy making." After intensive negotiations, Bush managed to reach agreements with the Democratic Congress on two of the most troubling issues he inherited from Reagan: aid to the Contra rebels in Nicaragua and the savings and loan crisis. The president won high marks from many legislators for his give-and-take approach to domestic and foreign policy and for the personal attention he paid to the political needs of Democrats and Republicans alike.

But the renewal of the "old bipartisanship" that Bush urged in his inaugural address was short lived. Several Republicans, especially the party's more conservative members, grew restless at Bush's disinclination to lead in a partisan style. Jeffrey Eisenach, who advised the 1988 presidential campaign of Delaware governor Pierre S. du Pont, expressed the widespread fear of conservatives that the Republican Party would not gain control of Congress in the 1990s if Bush "submerge[d] the difference between parties so it's impossible to create a set of issues to distinguish Republicans and Democrats."[16] Similarly, as Sinclair points out, the Democratic leadership in Congress, led ably by Senator George Mitchell of Maine and Representative Thomas Foley of Washington, was determined that any negotiations with the Bush administration concerning controversial matters of budget and regulatory policy would redound to their party's benefit.

Tasked with navigating this complex and divisive political terrain, Bush's conciliatory approach to Congress was joined uneasily to an aggressive partisanship aimed at extending the political gains of the Reagan Revolution beyond the presidency. Since his days at the vanguard of the Republican offensive in Harris County, Bush had shown a keen interest in party organization, even taking on the unhappy task of heading the Republican National Committee during the Watergate storm that engulfed the party. The first president to have served as national party chair, Bush, more than any other recent chief executive, came to the White House with a zeal for his partisan duties. He not only continued Reagan's practice of campaigning for his fellow Republicans—the one form of campaigning, former vice president Quayle reports in his oral history, that the president truly enjoyed—and raising funds for the regular party apparatus, but he also gave his party's national organization an unprecedentedly high profile in the era of the modern presidency. Bush placed his principal campaign strategist, Lee Atwater, the architect of the rougher features of the 1988 campaign, in the national party chair. Atwater, with Bush's approval, did not confine himself to the chair's customary role of presiding over the party's institutions. Instead, he sought to transform the Republican National Committee into an aggressive political organization that would highlight the differences between Republicans and Democrats on economic, social, and foreign policy issues at every level of the political system.

In part, Atwater's aggressive partisanship provided a balance to a presidency that otherwise favored consultation and compromise over confrontation—a felicitous union between the White House and the party that suggested Bush might be able to command the new party system. Political strategy during the Reagan years was conceived by assertive and influential presidential aides in the West Wing, who were prone to sacrifice the interests of the party to the ambitions of the president. In contrast, the Bush White House's political shop was run by a second-rank aide, former Atwater associate James Wray. Wray attended to Bush's long-term schedule and routinely reviewed administration appointments, leaving the party's big-picture strategy to Atwater. Atwater talked to Bush three or four times a week and had several conversations a day with White House Chief of Staff John Sununu in order to coordinate operations and mobilize the resources of the national party on behalf of the president's program.[17] In early 1990, the head of the research division of the Republican National Committee prepared a memo for Atwater that hailed the fortunate melding of president and party. Citing statistics suggesting that Bush's popularity had increased the number of voters who identified as Republicans, he wrote, "After a year of the Bush presidency and after nine years of Republican leadership in the White House, the Republican party is stronger than it's been since the 1940s and is poised to assume majority status." Although similar gains in Republican identification had occurred in 1981 and 1985 following Reagan's victories, what distinguished Bush's early tenure, the memo reported, was that "the gains following the presidential election still existed more than a year after the after the election." The 1980s was the first sustained period when the two parties were at virtual parity since 1946, the year Republicans had last won control of both houses of Congress in a mid-term election.[18]

In the end, however, the Bush administration's efforts to combine pragmatism with partisan leadership imploded. The episode that sealed the fate of the president's strategy was the 1990 budget deal. Sinclair's blow-by-blow account of this effort to fulfill the president's hope, stated in his inaugural address, that he could attain a bipartisan agreement on a balanced budget reveals the political maneuvers that eventually hoisted Bush on his own petard. Having promised "no new taxes" during the campaign, with such braggadocio, the president now found it impossible to reach bipartisan accord on an issue that fundamentally divided Democrats and Republicans, a division that his own campaign had widened. Not surprisingly, the first version of the compromise aggravated liberals, who abhorred the proposed cuts to Medicare, a core liberal entitlement, and infuriated conservatives, who felt betrayed by Bush's willingness to abandon his celebrated campaign pledge even to the extent of raising excise taxes. The defeat of this measure left Bush with little recourse but to accept a second version drafted primarily by Democrats that significantly reduced Medicare cuts and raised income tax rates on the wealthy, further infuriating the Republican base. As former vice president Quayle notes, Bush's reversal looked especially bad because the president put taxes on the table at the start of negotiations. If he at least had waited until the end of budget negotiations, when compromise might have looked like the only alternative to accepting deep and chronic deficits, his actions might not have made his dramatic campaign pledge look so disingenuous.

The Bush oral histories are full of recriminations against Gingrich for the seemingly underhanded way that he turned against the first budget plan after taking part in the bipartisan leadership meetings that crafted it. Gingrich certainly did not act forthrightly, but it is hard to imagine that he could have staved off the conservative House Republican rebellion against the White House. Conservatives believed that Bush not only had deserted his sacred pledge but had also forfeited the party's best hope of becoming the majority party in the House and Senate. By obscuring the differences between the parties, the budget agreement undercut Republican congressional candidates' chances to campaign in 1990 on what they considered their party's most effective issue.

In late October, Bush became embroiled in a feud with the co-chair of the National Republican Congressional Committee, Ed Rollins, who circulated a memo urging his party's House candidates to feel free to distance themselves from the president in their campaigns. This spectacle embarrassed the White House, which pressured Rollins to resign in early 1991. But the damage had been done: Republicans lost ground in the House and Senate. The Democrats added one seat in the Senate and eight seats in the House. Perhaps Bush would have better managed the explosive politics of the budget agreement or recovered from it politically had he not lost the services of Atwater, who collapsed in early March 1990 while delivering a speech. Physicians diagnosed a brain tumor, and although Atwater continued to occupy the party chair, he had to abandon his political responsibilities. That left the party headquarters without effective leadership for almost a year before Bush, after receiving several rejections, most notably from conservative intellectual William Bennett, finally tapped Secretary of Agriculture Clayton Yeutter to replace Atwater, who died in 1991. Since Yeutter lacked his predecessor's close relationship to the president as well as his strong ties to the party's activists, Atwater's absence returned the center of political strategy to the West Wing, leaving Sununu as Bush's principal political advisor. Sununu, who originally opposed the income tax increases, argues that Atwater's absence deprived the administration of its vital connection with the party base. Without the chair's ability to offer counsel and advocate for policy "with an edge," Sununu could not prevent the White House from veering in the direction of Office of Management and Budget director Richard Darman—and Darman disdained both the "read my lips" pledge, which he had tried to purge from the Bush's acceptance speech, and supply-side economics more generally. Atwater was "a magnificent buffer for the President," Sununu notes. "And that was gone. It's like Star Trek, when you knock down the shield, the photon tubes get through."

Without denying the significance of Atwater's loss, Bush found himself in a dilemma by the second year of his presidency that would have been very difficult to resolve under any circumstances. If Atwater had been involved in the budget machinations, the negotiations may very well have collapsed and the fiscal brinkmanship that has become a routine part of contemporary American politics might have arrived sooner and with even more damage to the American economy than what has transpired over the past two decades. Although politically disastrous for the president, the budget agreement included a procedural reform, the so-called PAYGO, that required all increases in direct spending or decreases in revenue to be offset by other spending decreases. These changes in the budget process were, as Heclo puts it, "conservative in a traditional sense." Expressing a disposition suspicious of radical changes, "they developed gradually, through a predictable and slow moving policy development process managed from the White House." And yet, save for a very brief televised speech to the nation before the first ill-fated vote on the budget compromise, Bush gave no defense of traditional conservatism or pragmatism. The address he did give, his first attempt to mobilize public opinion to pressure Congress, fell flat. Despite his personal popularity, Bush could not prevent a devastating intraparty feud that left him politically isolated.

What Woodrow Wilson called "extraordinary isolation" also well describes the president's political dilemma in the enactment of another major compromise with the Democratic Congress, the 1990 Clean Air Act Amendments.[19] Congress had been stalemated in its attempts to rewrite the law for a decade, and the Reagan administration's program of deregulation had focused heavily on loosening environmental standards. In contrast to the budget battle, however, this legislation marked the fulfillment, rather than the abandonment, of a campaign pledge. Bush had made clear during the 1988 campaign that he wanted to do something dramatic about clean air, even expressing his ambition to become "the environmental president." Democrats, who were energized when the environment-friendly Mitchell replaced Robert Byrd as Senate majority leader, also were anxious to get something done. Sinclair depicts the negotiations over and enactment of this law as a victory for the Democratic Congress; certainly the ardent environmentalist, Representative Henry Waxman (D-Calif.) was delighted with the final legislation, which contained provisions that imposed tighter regulations than the White House favored. Still, the president's aides, led ably by the director of the Environmental Protection Agency, William Reilly, were able to inject a market orientation into the law, most notably in the provisions dedicated to regulating acid rain. Instead of following the command-and-control model of regulation that Senator Mitchell and environmental advocates favored, the bill created a cap-and-trade system that established a market in pollution permits but capped at 6 million tons the amount of sulfate that the nation's utility plants could emit annually.

This compromise on acid rain, and the first overhaul of the Clean Air Act in two decades, was an important legislative achievement for Bush and seemingly a major political victory. But Sinclair's description of the unusual final step of the bill's enactment reveals how the compromise between environmental protection and market principles camouflaged significant partisan conflict between Republicans and Democrats on the issue. Democrats stalled the final passage of the bill until after the 1990 election, thus depriving the president of a splashy signing ceremony in California, an environmentally friendly state where the clean air amendments might have helped Republican candidates. In retaliation, Bush refused to allow key Democrats to stand behind him while he signed the bill, depriving Congressman Waxman and his colleagues of an important photo opportunity. Indeed, the president even refused to hand out pens to the sponsoring legislators.[20]

Besides losing Atwater, another major reason for the budget debacle and the disappointment over the clean air act was that by the fall of 1990, President Bush was preoccupied with the "classic work of statesmanship," as Heclo puts it—the business of building a domestic and international coalition to secure the vital interests of the United States against the threat to world order posed by Iraqi aggression. For a time, it looked as though this state of affairs would rescue Bush's presidency from the malaise that followed the budget controversy. As Quayle confirms, Iraq's invasion of Kuwait in August 1990 stirred Bush's deepest commitments and allowed him to display considerable skills as commander in chief. Assuring his impressive foreign policy staff that "this shall not stand," the president showed a deft and steady hand in the first major crisis in the post–Cold War world, and the United States–led forces rapidly triumphed over Saddam Hussein's troops, forcing Iraq to withdraw from Kuwait. Amid a national celebration that seemed to dispel the agonizing memory of Vietnam, Bush's popularity reached a historic peak: 89 percent of the American people approved of his performance as president. Nevertheless, Hussein remained in power, much to Bush's surprise and disappointment. The president had expected the military defeat to lead to Hussein's overthrow by the Iraqis themselves.

Besides the president's conservative (as traditionally understood) inclinations, the major reason that going to Baghdad to topple Hussein militarily was a nonstarter in 1991 was that the patriotic fever aroused by the Gulf War concealed significant differences between Republicans and Democrats about the appropriate role of America in the post–Cold War world. As the Iran-Contra affair revealed under Reagan, these differences tempted presidents to sidestep sharp partisan divisions in Congress by managing the national security state unilaterally. Quayle notes that Bush was uncertain about whether to seek congressional approval to fight the Gulf War, largely because he doubted whether the legislature would grant it. Although Bush ultimately sought the approval of Congress, the January 1991 votes on the issue revealed a legislature deeply divided along partisan lines. Not since the War of 1812 had Congress so narrowly approved the use of military force. Although Republicans lined up solidly in favor of the president (42–2 in the Senate and 165–3 in the House), Democrats voted against authorizing military action by large margins (45–10 in the Senate and 179–86 in the House). The especially close division in the upper chamber, which approved the Iraqi resolution by only 52–48, makes clear why President Bush, as well as Secretary of Defense Richard Cheney, were reluctant to seek congressional approval in the first place. After the vote, Democrats closed ranks behind the president as the nation prepared for war, but a broader partisan dispute over the conduct of foreign policy and constitutional powers lingered. Quayle reveals that Bush told his foreign policy team that he would send troops to expel Hussein from Kuwait even if the Senate did not authorize military action. For good measure, after the vote, the Bush administration issued a statement denying that the president needed legislative approval to fight the Gulf War because the United Nations had adopted a resolution authorizing the use of force against Iraq.

Bush's determination to uphold the president's prerogative in managing the national security state in the face of sharp partisan conflict continued even after he became a lame duck. Most dramatically, he outraged congressional Democrats by pardoning former secretary of defense Caspar Weinberger and five other Reagan administration officials for any crimes they may have committed during the Iran-Contra affair. The president's action sought to redress what he viewed as a blatantly partisan act during the final days of the 1992 campaign. Bush and his advisors were furious that Iran-Contra special prosecutor Lawrence Walsh handed down his indictment just four days before the election. Adding insult to injury, Walsh's announcement charged not only that Weinberger had lied when he denied taking extensive notes during Reagan administration meetings about ransoming hostages from Lebanon but also that as Reagan's vice president, Bush was present for at least one of those meetings. Bush had claimed that he was not in the "loop" when the arms-for-hostages deal was discussed. The president and his supporters cried foul, claiming that Walsh had engaged in improper politicking.

Bush offered no defense of his role in the Iran-Contra affair. But in his post-election announcement of the pardon, he criticized the Ethics in Government Act, which had been enacted in the wake of Watergate, especially its independent counsel provisions, for "a profoundly troubling development in the political and legal culture of our country: the criminalization of policy differences." Reflecting on nearly two decades of institutional and partisan combat, the president proposed that these differences be "addressed in the political arena" because "the proper forum is the voting booth, not the courtroom." Although congressional Democrats and the press attacked Bush for issuing the pardons, his own attack made Walsh the issue. Nevertheless, Bush's willingness to join presidential prerogative to partisan conflict in foreign affairs, even though often high minded and well intentioned, furthered the advance of a novel form of party combat. Consequently, the Gulf War did not establish the conditions for a restoration of bipartisan consensus but instead set the stage for additional bitter conflicts in domestic affairs that rivaled the ideological and institutional clashes of the Reagan years.

The most bitter of these fights occurred over Bush's second nomination to the Supreme Court, Clarence Thomas, a conservative black appellate judge and former chair of the Equal Employment Opportunity Commission. The Senate confirmed Thomas 52–48, the closest Supreme Court vote in more than a century. Ironically, Perry and Abraham conclude, in both of Bush's two Supreme Court appointments—David Souter in 1990 and Thomas in 1991—the White House's "cautious deliberate, moderate, controversy-shunning, compromise prone ethos" put justices on the bench who "occupied positions closer to the left and right edges of the ideological spectrum than did the appointing president." In truth, however, Bush's pragmatic conservatism unraveled in the polarizing political environment of the 1980s and 1990s. His ambivalent rhetoric and actions with respect to this raw and disruptive partisanship advanced a novel form of party politics that joined executive prerogative to high-stakes constitutional confrontations.

Heightened conflict over constitutional issues and the judiciary extended to legislative battles about court rulings, most notably the complicated partisan maneuvers that led to the passage of the Civil Rights Act of 1991. Although the landmark 1964 and 1965 civil rights acts were now honored by Democrats and Republicans alike and had strong support among the public, liberals and conservatives engaged in an ongoing disagreement about how these laws should be administered with respect to issues such as busing and affirmative action. The 1991 Civil Rights act, which was championed by congressional Democrats, nullified nine previous Supreme Court rulings in order to shift the burden of proof in antidiscrimination lawsuits from employees to employers. Most significantly, the legislation restored the standard established by the Supreme Court's 1971 ruling in *Griggs v. Duke Power Company,* which held employers responsible for justifying employment practices that were superficially fair but had an "adverse impact" on women and minorities. A 1989 ruling, *Wards Cove Packing Company v. Atonio,* had shifted the burden, ruling that workers had to show that companies had no legitimate basis for the challenged practices. The new legislation instructed the courts to follow the standard of *Griggs,* not *Wards Cove.*[21]

The enactment of the Civil Rights Act ended two years of acrimonious partisan debate over how much latitude businesses should have in defending insufficient diversity in their workforces. Bush had vetoed a similar bill in 1990, arguing that the burden of proof it imposed on businesses was so onerous that it would lead to quotas for minorities and women in hiring. The compromise legislation hammered out by congressional Democrats, moderate Republicans, and the White House included a far more flexible standard of "business necessity," essentially leaving the courts to decide what constituted discriminatory employment practices.

Beleaguered moderates of both parties hoped that the agreement, coming in the wake of the Willie Horton controversy and the explosive Thomas hearings, might, as Senator John Danforth, a moderate Republican from Missouri, stated, "reestablish the consensus on civil rights, which is so important to our Nation."[22] But any hope that the hard-won compromise "had taken race out of the political arena" was quickly disappointed. A draft presidential signing statement, prepared under the direction of White House Counsel C. Boyden Gray ordered the heads of all federal departments to review immediately their equal opportunity programs and eliminate many affirmative action programs. This order ignited strong protests in Congress, including a threat from the respected Danforth that he would boycott the signing ceremony. Bush modified the draft, but his signing statement proclaimed that a narrow interpretation of the statute that Republican Senate leader Robert Dole had introduced into the congressional record would "be treated as authoritative . . . guidance by all officials in the executive branch with respect to the law of disparate impact as well as other matters covered in the documents."[23]

Bush's revised signing statement appeased moderate Republicans, but it failed to head off a boycott of the signing ceremony by Democratic lawmakers. Before Bush's signature on the civil rights act could dry, therefore, the much-acclaimed compromise that had led to enactment of this legislation had dissolved into partisan combat. More broadly, Bush used a tactic to shape legislation that would become a very controversial feature of the partisan and institutional conflicts that roiled his son's administration a decade later. As energetically employed by George W. Bush, signing statements served partisan objectives by circumventing the veto provisions of the Constitution and declaring portions of certain congressional statutes null and void by executive fiat.[24]

The Pragmatist Leaps into the Fray

After a lengthy oral history interview, in which he candidly assessed the successes and failures of the Bush presidency, John Sununu was asked to address a final "macro question": How would Bush be considered in terms of the conservative movement? His answer was unequivocal: "This was a very conservative Presidency. . . . His stand on right to life. His position on legislation in terms of market economy and all that, fighting for the market rights on Clean Air and all those things. All the things that conservatives will enunciate as things they'd like to see in legislation, he got into legislation. . . . In terms of foreign policy and exercising power and standing up for what is strategically important to the U.S., they'll like that. . . . The one negative will be . . . the Souter nomination. Clarence Thomas will certainly be a big positive for him and I think they will eventually recognize that he thought he was appointing a conservative when he appointed Souter. So I think he's going to get good marks with future conservatives."

As the 1992 election approached amid a serious recession, Bush seemed determined to leave a conservative legacy, even if doing so meant campaigning against his own policies.[25] His administration turned its attention to "liberating the economy" from the regulatory explosion that was pending as a result of the legislative mandates enacted during his first term. In addition to the Clean Air Amendments and the Civil Rights Act, Bush also signed the Nutrition and Labeling Act, a major consumer protection initiative. Reagan had vetoed similar versions of these bills. As he promised during his 1988 campaign, Bush also strongly supported the Americans with Disabilities Act, enacted in 1991, which was dedicated to guaranteeing the civil rights of the disabled in gaining access to buildings and finding employment. Laudable and even popular as these laws and their objectives had been, signing them clearly veered off the path blazed by the Reagan revolution. Attacked from the right, getting no credit from the left, and seeing his poll numbers sink as the economy slumped, Bush repositioned himself in 1992 as the champion of core conservative causes and policies. The President's Council on Competitiveness, created in June 1990 and headed by Vice President Quayle, assumed increasing importance in White House policy deliberations, putting regulatory agencies on notice that the president expected them to justify the cost of existing and proposed regulations. "The impact of the President's proposal sends a chilling message to the agencies that the President is waging war on his agencies," the liberal public interest group OMB Watch lamented. "It is almost as if the President is choosing to run in this year's election as an outsider campaigning against the bureaucracy."[26]

Of course, Reagan had campaigned against the bureaucracy, but he did not have to run against himself to do so. Bush's position on abortion and taxes in the waning days of his term further revealed the degree to which he was willing to abandon his pragmatic credentials. In 1990, the president had joined Atwater in an effort to extend the GOP's appeal to middle-class suburban voters by asserting that the party "was a big enough tent" to welcome differing views on abortion.[27] But this inclusive strategy evaporated when the administration proceeded with plans formulated in the Reagan administration to bar employees of federally financed family planning clinics from providing clients with basic medical information about abortion. The Reagan administration was thwarted in this policy by the lower courts, which delayed the so-called gag rule for three years. But in late May 1991, the Supreme Court upheld the regulation in *Rust v. Sullivan* and the Bush administration prepared to carry it out. Although Congress quickly passed legislation to prevent the administration from enforcing rules barring abortion counseling in federally funded family planning clinics, the House failed by a dozen votes to override Bush's veto.[28]

The president's election-year right turn on taxes resulted in a dramatic mea culpa at the 1992 convention. In his acceptance speech, Bush pleaded for absolution from the delegates—and expressed bitter recriminations against the Democratic Congress. ""Two years ago, I made a bad call on the Democrats' tax increase," he told the delegates. "I underestimated Congress' addiction to taxes. With my back against the wall, I agreed to a hard bargain: One tax increase one time in return for the toughest spending limits ever.... Well, it was a mistake to go along with the Democratic tax increase, and I admit it."[29]

Bush's confession set the stage for a fall campaign in which he ran against the Democratic Congress more fervently than he ran against his opponent, Bill Clinton. Bush's reelection campaign was badly damaged by conservative pundit Pat Buchanan's insurgent assault on the president in the Republican primaries and the surprisingly strong general election campaign of independent candidate H. Ross Perot. Some hoped that Bush would duplicate Harry Truman's feat in 1948, when Roosevelt's beleaguered heir ran a spirited campaign against the Republican Congress and won a personal and party triumph.

But Bush was no Truman, and the circumstances he faced were dramatically different than those of the post–World War II years. The 1948 election ratified a political revolution that secured an understanding of rights and institutional arrangements in which party politics were subordinated to presidential politics—to the tasks, as FDR put it, of "enlightened administration." The Reagan and Bush administrations viewed the modern presidency as a sword that could cut in a conservative as well as a liberal direction. Their leadership hastened the development of a new presidential synthesis—one that exhibited an uneasy confluence of executive prerogative and partisan polarization. Rather than institutionalize the Reagan Revolution, Bush sought mightily to reconcile the two competing tasks demanded of presidents since the 1980s: stewardship of the welfare and national security states and party leadership in an emerging struggle over what role the state forged on the New Deal political realignment should play. As Riley points out, Bush's earnest, if sometimes awkward, efforts to subject partisan rancor to more prudent governance has worn well–indeed, his presidency now represents for many Americans an admirable interregnum in the ineluctable development of harsh partisanship that has both enhanced the public's interest in politics and alienated them from America's governing institutions.

And yet Bush's troubled four years in the White House did not temper partisan rancor; rather, it brought into stark relief the tensions between executive and partisan responsibility in the new party system. In fact, the remarkable successes and dramatic disappointments of the Bush presidency ensured that these divergent roles would share an uneasy coexistence after he left office. The stewardship role of the president is aided by the deep entrenchment of the institutions of the modern presidency, the popularity of many government programs (if not of government as a whole), and the disgust of many citizens with strident partisanship in Washington and, increasingly, in the state capitals. The partisan role of the president is succored by the rise of partisan and ideological polarization among elected officials and powerful interest groups as well as by the growing partisanship of the public, on both domestic and foreign policy issues.

Caught between pleas for nonpartisan stewardship and demands for partisan leadership, presidents since Bush have combined elements of both. At the rhetorical level, presidents mix paeans to public unity with strident attacks on their political opponents. In making policy, they both seek to build bipartisan coalitions and employ highly partisan maneuvers to achieve programmatic objectives. In campaigning, they combine personalistic appeals and candidate-centered campaign organizations with partisan get-out-the-vote efforts. And in administering the executive branch, they leverage the ostensibly nonpartisan administrative legacies of the New Deal to achieve partisan objectives that cannot be secured through the normal legislative process.

No president has combined these imperatives in the same way, and each president's choices have been constrained by the specific political opportunities and limits he faced. Nonetheless, each president since Reagan has sought to navigate a course between nonpartisan and partisan approaches in the pursuit of programmatic and political objectives. That George Bush was the first president to negotiate this treacherous political terrain speaks to the significance of his presidency—and to the lessons it holds for the opportunities and perils of our own political time.

Appendix 1

INTERVIEWEES FOR THE GEORGE H. W. BUSH ORAL HISTORY PROJECT

Date of interview	Name and location of respondent
5/10–11/2001	Lamar Alexander with Rebecca Campoverdi and David Kearns, Diane Ravitch, Bill Hansen, Bruno Manno and Jeff Martin via telephone, Charlottesville, VA
1/29/2000	James Baker III, Charlottesville, VA
3/17/2011	James Baker III, Houston, TX
4/5/2001	William P. Barr, Charlottesville, VA
9/22–23/2000	David Bates, College Station, TX
5/26/2011	Jean Becker, Kennebunkport, ME
8/2/2011	Robert D. Blackwill, Pacific Palisades, CA
7/30–31/2001	Michael J. Boskin, Stanford, VA
9/13/2001	Nicholas F. Brady with Hollis McLoughlin, Charlottesville, VA
2/22–23/2001	Phillip D. Brady, Charlottesville, VA
12/21–22/1999	Andrew Card, Charlottesville, VA
4/12/2000	Henry E. Catto Jr., Charlottesville, VA
3/16–17/2000	Richard Cheney, Dallas, TX
7/19/2001	James W. Cicconi, Washington, DC
12/2/2002	James W. Cicconi, Washington, DC
7/19/2000	Richard G. Darman, Charlottesville, VA
1/18/2010	David Demarest, Charlottesville, VA
5/3–4/2001	Edward J. Derwinski, Charlottesville, VA
5/15/2001	Marlin Fitzwater, Washington, DC

4/17–18/2001	Barbara Franklin with William Clark, Jr., Charlottesville, VA
5/12/2004	Craig Fuller, Charlottesville, VA
8/23–24/2000	Robert M. Gates, College Station, TX
2/3–4/2000	C. Boyden Gray, Charlottesville, VA
5/27/2004	Richard Haass, New York, NY
1/6/2004	Carla A. Hills, Charlottesville, VA
1/6–7/2000	Edith Holiday with Daniel Casse, Charlottesville, VA
11/15/2010	David E. Jeremiah, Charlottesville, VA
8/6/2003	Ronald C. Kaufman, Washington, DC
11/20/2009	Barbara G. Kilberg, Herndon, VA
8/19/2001	Robert M. Kimmitt, Washington, DC
12/4/2001	Robert M. Kimmitt, Washington, DC
7/13/2011	John Major, London, England
11/5/2010	Timothy McBride, Charlottesville, VA
9/20/2001	Frederick D. McClure, Washington, DC
12/16/1999	Robert Mosbacher with Michael Ferran, College Station, TX
6/24/2011	C. Gregg Petersmeyer, Charlottesville, VA
12/14/2010	Thomas Pickering, Washington, DC
2/6/2001	James P. Pinkerton, Washington, DC
6/28/2003	Roman Popadiuk, Washington, DC
12/11–12/2001	Roger B. Porter, Charlottesville, VA
3/12/2002	J. Danforth Quayle, Phoenix, AZ
3/8–9/2001	Sigmund Rogich, Charlottesville, VA
10/30/2000	Edward M. Rogers, Jr., Washington, DC
8/2/2001	Dennis B. Ross, Washington, DC
11/12/1999	Brent Scowcroft, Washington, DC
9/2–3/1999	Thomas Scully, Charlottesville, VA
10/21/2002	Samuel K. Skinner, Charlottesville, VA
11/17–18/2003	Louis Sullivan, Charlottesville, VA
6/8–9/2000	John H. Sununu, Charlottesville, VA
11/9/2000	John H. Sununu, Washington, DC
10/23–24/2001	Richard Thornburgh, Charlottesville, VA
4/5/2000	Margaret D. Tutwiler, Charlottesville, VA
7/27–28/2000	Chase Untermeyer, College Station, TX
1/19/2001	Clayton Yeutter, College Station, TX
1/21/2011	Robert Zoellick, Washington, DC
7/6/2011	Robert Zoellick, Washington, DC

INTERVIEWERS FOR THE GEORGE H. W. BUSH ORAL HISTORY PROJECT

Interviewer	Affiliation*
David Alsobrook	George Bush Presidential Library
James E. Anderson	Texas A&M University
Nancy V. Baker	New Mexico State University
Spencer Bakich	Sweet Briar College
Richard K. Betts	Columbia University
Henry William Brands	Texas A&M University
James W. Ceaser	University of Virginia
Jeffrey L. Chidester	Miller Center, University of Virginia
Martha Derthick	University of Virginia
Matthew Dickinson	Middlebury College
George C. Edwards III	Texas A&M University
John Fortier	American Enterprise Institute
Paul Freedman	University of Virginia
Erwin C. Hargrove	Vanderbilt University
Charles O. Jones	University of Wisconsin-Madison
John Karaagac	George Bush Presidential Library Foundation
Stephen F. Knott	Miller Center, University of Virginia
Paul S. Martin	Miller Center, University of Virginia
Tarek E. Masoud	Miller Center, University of Virginia
Ernest May	Harvard University
James H. McCall	George Bush Presidential Library Foundation

Daniel J. Meador	University of Virginia
Martin J. Medhurst	Baylor University
Sidney Milkis	Miller Center, University of Virginia
Timothy J. Naftali	Miller Center, University of Virginia
Bradley H. Patterson Jr.	National Academy of Public Administration
Barbara A. Perry	Miller Center, University of Virginia
James P. Pfiffner	George Mason University
William B. Quandt	University of Virginia
Russell L. Riley	Miller Center, University of Virginia
Leonard Schoppa	University of Virginia
Wilbur J. Scott	University of Oklahoma
Colleen J. Shogan	George Mason University
David Shreve	Miller Center, University of Virginia
Robert A. Strong	Washington and Lee University
Kathryn Dunn Tenpas	University of Pennsylvania
Maris A. Vinovskis	University of Michigan
Charles E. Walcott	Virginia Tech University
M. Stephen Weatherford	University of California—Santa Barbara
Brantly Womack	University of Virginia
James Sterling Young	Miller Center, University of Virginia
Philip D. Zelikow	Miller Center, University of Virginia
Fareed Zakaria	Council on Foreign Relations

*Interviewers' affiliations are from date of interview

Notes

INTRODUCTION

1. The term is sociologist Gary Alan Fine's. See his instructive "Reputational Entrepreneurs and the Memory of Incompetence: Melting Supporters, Partisan Warriors, and Images of President Harding," *American Journal of Sociology* 101, no. 5 (1996): 1159–1193. On the activist effort to promote Reagan's legacy, see http://www.ronaldreaganlegacypro ject.org, accessed April 9, 2012. To use Fine's language, Reagan's supporters decidedly did not "melt."

2. Washington's intentions are suggested by Barry Schwartz, *George Washington: The Making of an American Symbol* (Ithaca, N.Y.: Cornell University Press, 1987), 184.

3. Excerpts from Bush's 1988 acceptance address, http://www.presidency.ucsb.edu/ ws/?pid=25955, accessed June 3, 2013. On his aversion to the first-person singular, see Peggy Noonan, *What I Saw at the Revolution: A Political Life in the Reagan Era* (New York: Random House, 1990), 301–302.

4. David McCullough, "Introduction," in McCullough, *Affection and Trust: The Personal Correspondence of Harry S. Truman and Dean Acheson, 1953–1971* (New York: Alfred A. Knopf, 2010), xii.

5. See Roman Popadiuk, *The Leadership of George Bush: An Insider's View of the Forty-First President* (College Station: Texas A&M University Press, 2009), 7.

6. All quotations in this chapter relating to the Bush presidency are from the George H. W. Bush Oral Histories unless otherwise noted. The interviews are available on the Miller Center Web site, at http://millercenter.org/president/bush/oralhistory.

7. George H. W. Bush and Brent Scowcroft, *A World Transformed* (New York: Vintage Books, 1998).

8. See Bush's September 1, 2004 radio interview with Don Imus, http://www.msnbc. msn.com/id/5889684/ns/msnbc_tv-imus_on_msnbc/t/we-are-better-today-says-george-h-w-bush/, accessed April 9, 2012. President Bush did not contribute an oral history interview to the project from which this book arises, notwithstanding multiple attempts to schedule one. His son's presence in the White House during the main run of the project unquestionably contributed to his reluctance to participate.

9. Bob Woodward, *The War Within: A Secret White House History, 2006–2008* (New York: Simon & Schuster, 2008), 331.

10. Unless otherwise noted, all polling data reported here are taken from Gallup Polls, available at http://www.ropercenter.uconn.edu/data_access/data/presidential_approval.html.

11. "Little Support for Pardon," *USA Today*, November 13, 1992, A10.

12. See John M. Berry, "Could the Good News Have Helped Bush? Economic Gains Seen Unlikely to Have Altered Election if They Had Come Sooner," *Washington Post*, December 6, 1992, H1.

13. On Clinton's public commitment to tackling the issue, made shortly after his election, see John Barry and Daniel Glick, "Crossing the Gay Minefield," *Newsweek*, November 23, 1992, 26.

14. Quoted in "Historic Humanitarian Effort May Bolster Bush Legacy," *St. Petersburg Times*, December, 5, 1992, A8.

15. Peter Applebome, "Mission to Somalia: Seared by Faces of Need, Americans Say, 'How Could We Not Do This?'" *New York Times*, December 13, 1992, A16; Richard Benedetto, "Presidential Approval," *USA Today*, December 10, 1992, A6. Bush's public reputation was not noticeably scarred when that intervention later went badly on Bill Clinton's watch.

16. See David W. Moore, "Public Generally Tolerant of Presidential Extramarital Affairs," The Gallup Organization, http://www.gallup.com/poll/4246/public-generally-tolerant-presidential-extramarital-affairs.aspx, accessed November 18, 2011.

17. It can be fairly noted here, of course, that the Bush White House decided not to pursue a vigorous domestic agenda even after the success of Desert Storm, which left it fewer opportunities for the kind of victories at home from which a favorable legacy could be constructed.

18. A user-friendly table compiling these assessments can be found on the Wikipedia Web site, at http://en.wikipedia.org/wiki/Historical_rankings_of_Presidents_of_the_United_States. I have cross-checked the Wikipedia table against some of the original source sites (for example the C-SPAN and the Arthur Schlesinger surveys of scholars) to establish confidence that the table accurately conveys the information found in those studies.

19. There has been no case of a significant and persistent *drop* in historical evaluations of a former president in this interval, but there are three instances of major and lasting improvements in historical reputation: Truman, Eisenhower, and Reagan. Truman's resuscitation is largely the product of his memoir and the effect of Richard E. Neustadt's scholarship. See David McCullough, *Truman* (New York: Simon & Schuster, 1992), 947–949; Alonzo L. Hamby, "The Clash of Perspectives and the Need for New Syntheses" and Harvard Sitkoff, "Years of the Locust: Interpretations of the Truman Presidency since 1965," both in Richard S. Kirkendall, ed., *The Truman Period as a Research Field: A Reappraisal, 1972* (Columbia: University of Missouri Press, 1974). Fred I. Greenstein was the central figure in Eisenhower's reassessment. His *The Hidden-Hand Presidency* (New York: Basic Books) appeared in the fall of 1982, but by that date his argument was familiar to specialists in U.S. political history because he had telegraphed his case for Eisenhower in several journal articles, including "Eisenhower as an Activist President: A Look at New Evidence," *Political Science Quarterly* 94, no. 4 (1979–80): 575–599. See also Richard H. Immerman, "Eisenhower and Dulles: Who Made the Decisions?" *Political Psychology* 1, no. 2 (1979): 21–38. Reagan's case is less clear cut, but his historical reputation enjoyed a major turnaround between 1996 and 1999, probably because of a tipping point on the most contested issue of his legacy: responsibility for ending the Cold War.

20. Personal communication with the director of the George Bush Presidential Library and Museum, October 28, 2011. Approximately 25 percent of Bush's presidential records have been processed, but about a third of those have been kept out of the public domain for reasons related to national security or personal privacy restrictions.

21. Glenn Thrush, "Clinton Archive a Tough Request," *Newsday*, March 18, 2007, available at http://www.newsday.com/news/clinton-archive-a-tough-request-1.639969, accessed December 18, 2012.

22. National archivist Allen Weinstein has testified that because the Presidential Records Act governing the disposition of these materials privileges FOIA requests, the presidential libraries governed by it (those after Carter) "in practice open records almost exclusively in response to FOIA requests . . . and have less opportunity to conduct systematic processing of records." See Weinstein, "Statement on the Implementation and Effectiveness of the Presidential Records Act of 1978," Subcommittee on Information Policy, Census, and National Archives of the Committee on Government Oversight and Reform, House of Representatives, U.S. Congress, March 1, 2007, 3, at http://www.globalsecurity.org/military/library/congress/2007_hr/070308-weinstein.pdf, accessed December 18, 2012.

23. For an assessment of the strengths and weaknesses of this kind of oral history, see Russell L. Riley, "The White House as a Black Box: Oral History and the Problem of Evidence in Presidential Studies," *Political Studies* 57, no. 1 (2009): 187–206.

24. Colin Powell with Joseph E. Persico, *My American Journey* (New York: Ballantine Books, 1995), 333.

25. Quoted in Michael Nelson and Russell L. Riley, eds., *The President's Words: Speeches and Speechwriting in the Modern White House* (Lawrence: University Press of Kansas, 2010), 174.

26. Stuart Spencer Interview, Miller Center, University of Virginia, Ronald Reagan Presidential Oral History Project, November 15–16, 2001, 66.

27. Robinson's remarks appear in Nelson and Riley, *The President's Words*, 246.

28. In Skowronek's matrix of presidents, he styles Bush more generally an "orthodox innovator," which he defines as those who "galvanize political action with promises to continue the good work of the past and demonstrate the vitality of the established order in changing times" (41). Stephen Skowronek, *The Politics Presidents Make: Leadership from John Adams to George Bush* (Cambridge: Harvard University Press, 1993), 429–442.

29. Bush's personnel chief, Chase Untermeyer, was mindful of this problem from the outset and studied the friendly transition between the Coolidge and Hoover administrations (1928–29) for tips on managing the tensions.

30. Paul Laxalt Interview, Ronald Reagan Oral History Project, November 9, 2001, 53.

31. Jefferson's original quote was bilingual: "Every office becoming vacant, every appointment made, *me donne un ingrat, et cent ennemis.*" See William Safire, *Safire's Political Dictionary* (Oxford: Oxford University Press, 2008), 290.

32. "Most people have no idea how exhausting the White House can be for people in it, unless they've been there. People wear out quickly." Former Nixon speechwriter Ray Price in Nelson and Riley, *The President's Words*, 114.

33. Burnham, "Realignment Lives: The 1994 Earthquake and Its Implications," in *The Clinton Presidency: First Appraisals*, ed. Colin Campbell and Bert A. Rockman (Chatham, N.J.: Chatham House, 1996), 367.

34. John Quincy Adams might be added to this group, but his political situation is complicated by the fact that he rose to the presidency as a coalition candidate.

35. Figures calculated from tables of partisan control found in Robert A. Diamond, ed., *Congressional Quarterly's Guide to U.S. Elections* (Washington: Congressional Quarterly, Inc., 1975), 928–929.

36. See, for example, Susan Page, "History Not Kind to Presidents during Second Term," *USA Today*, January 20, 2005.

37. See David Halberstam, *War in a Time of Peace: Bush, Clinton, and the Generals* (New York: Scribner, 2001), 15.

38. Both quotes are taken from Robert J. Donovan, *Conflict and Crisis: The Presidency of Harry Truman, 1945–1948* (New York: W. W. Norton, 1977), 107, 125.

39. Only the broad outlines of this logic and its relationship to the forty-first presidency can be presented in this essay. I have developed the complete argument in a forthcoming book provisionally titled *American Regicide: The Troubled Fate of Postwar Presidents in the United States.* Two published works deal directly with post–Cold War pressures on the presidency: John Kenneth White, *Still Seeing Red: How the Cold War Shapes the New American Politics* (Boulder, Colo.: Westview Press, 1997), 199–285; and Anthony J. Eksterowicz and Glenn P. Hastedt, eds., *The Post-Cold War Presidency* (Lanham, Md.: Rowman & Littlefield, 1999). Thomas Langston's "Bill Clinton as Warren Harding: The Post-War President as a Problem in American Political Development," reproduced in the latter volume, merits special mention as the sole published work to make the connection between the immediate post–Cold War presidency and its relevant historical antecedents.

40. David Runciman, "Will We Be All Right in the End?" *London Review of Books*, January 5, 2012.

41. There is one case in American history that comports with this rosy picture of accommodation. During the American Revolution, Congress designated General George Washington as a powerful wartime commander in chief. When that conflict was won, he subjected himself to a formal ceremony in Annapolis to return his leadership commission. The particulars of that ceremony—which, importantly, Congress designed to display its restored primacy as a governing institution—are brilliantly described in Schwartz, *George Washington*, 137–143.

42. U.S. Senate, Special Committee on the Termination of the National Emergency, *Emergency Powers Statutes*, 93rd Cong., 1st sess., S. Rept. 93-549. See also Harold C. Relyea, *CRS Report for Congress: National Emergency Powers* (98-505) (Washington, D.C.: Government Printing Office, 2007). Ronald Reagan later succeeded in accomplishing something of a restoration in the standing of the office by asserting that the nation had been harmed by overdoing the reforms of the 1970s that sought to constrain what had come to be called the imperial presidency.

43. Representative Nicholas Mavroules (D-Mass.), quoted in Annetta Miller et al., "Peace Brings Tough Times," *Newsweek*, August 6, 1990, 44.

44. John Lewis Gaddis, *The United States and the End of the Cold War: Implications, Reconsiderations, Provocations* (New York: Oxford University Press, 1992), 18–19, 135.

45. Musallam Ali Musallam, *The Iraqi Invasion of Kuwait: Saddam Hussein, His State, and International Power Politics* (London: British Academic Press, 1996), 100; Joseph Nye, "Why the Gulf War Served the National Interest," *Atlantic Monthly*, July 1991.

46. David Halberstam suggests that the Somalia intervention also should be understood as a product of the new postwar environment. *War in a Time of Peace*, 74–75, 248–253.

47. The term is John Robert Greene's, *The Presidency of George Bush* (Lawrence: University Press of Kansas), 127.

48. "'I just want everyone to know, if they vote me down I'm still going to do what I have to do.' [The president] told us that pointblank." Dan Quayle interview.

49. See the account of internal White House deliberations over this matter in the William Barr interview.

50. *Congressional Quarterly Almanac, 102nd Congress, 1st Session, 1991* (Washington, D.C.: Congressional Quarterly, 1992), 3.

51. Ibid., 442. The quoted phrase paraphrases an assertion by Senator Paul Simon (D-Ill.).

52. See Daniel Patrick Moynihan, "A Return to Cold War Thinking," *Congressional Record,* January 10, 1991, available at http://thomas.loc.gov, accessed April 18, 2012; Daniel Patrick Moynihan, "Next Step in the Gulf—It's Almost Midnight; Restraint, Mr. Bush," *New York Times*, January 15, 1991, A19.

53. The first use I can find of the term "peace dividend" in this period is in William Safire, "Is Peace Bullish?" *New York Times*, June 8, 1989, A31.

54. *Aviation Week & Space Technology*, March 12, 1990, 7.

55. Bill Turque et al., "Warriors without War," *Newsweek*, March 19, 1990, 18.

56. White, *Still Seeing Red*, 214.

57. This uneven geographic distribution of defense benefits is highlighted in U.S. Congress, Office of Technology Assessment, *After the Cold War: Living With Lower Defense Spending, OTA-ITE-524* (Washington, D.C.: U.S. Government Printing Office, February 1992), 12, 14, 25. The resultant effect on Electoral College votes was calculated by the author.

58. Dennis S. Ippolito, *Blunting the Sword: Budget Policy and the Future of Defense* (Washington, D.C.: National Defense University Press, 1994), 49–58.

59. *Congressional Quarterly Almanac, 102nd Congress, 2nd Session, 1992* (Washington: Congressional Quarterly, 1993), 106.

60. Ibid., 104.

61. See Lorna S. Jaffee, *The Development of the Base Force, 1989–1992* (Washington, D.C.: Joint History Office, Office of the Chairman of the Joint Chiefs of Staff, 1993).

62. White, *Still Seeing Red*, 202, 330.

63. Author's calculations. Jimmy Carter's 1976 address, which was the first delivered after the Vietnam War, devoted a similar proportion to foreign policy, 8 percent.

64. On this topic, see the Quayle interview.

65. Robert Higgs, *Crisis and Leviathan: Critical Episodes in the Growth of American Government* (New York: Oxford University Press, 1987).

66. The seven instances are 1826, 1894, 1918, 1946, 1954, 1994, and 2006. The case of John Quincy Adams (1826) is muddled because of his coalition status and thus might be excluded. Woodrow Wilson's midterm occurred just days prior to the armistice, but the electorate clearly viewed his October efforts to nationalize that election as an illegitimate attempt to control the peace from the White House. George W. Bush's experience in 2006 in some ways is an odd fit, given the ongoing conflicts in Iraq and Afghanistan, but the nation by that time was reacting with weariness to over five years of the "war on terror," as no new homeland attacks had occurred to suggest that that war still justified Bush's "constitutional dictatorship." See Russell L. Riley, "Divided We Stand," *Politico*, January 30, 2007, htp://www.politico.com/news/stories/0107/2538.html, accessed December 19, 2012. Both 1866 and 1974 might be added to these five signature postwar elections. Partisan majorities in Congress did not change in either of those cases, but both brought to Washington famously oppositionist legislatures: the first impeachment Congress and the renowned class of "Watergate babies."

67. A brief version of the argument about Clinton's impeachment appears in Russell L. Riley, "The Presidency, Leadership, and Race," in *One America? Political Leadership, National Identity, and the Dilemmas of Diversity*, ed. Stanley A. Renshon (Washington, D.C.: Georgetown University Press, 2001), 80–83.

68. Quoted in White, *Still Seeing Red*, 256.

CHAPTER 1

1. All quotations in this chapter relating to the Bush presidency are from the George H. W. Bush Oral History Interviews unless otherwise noted. The interviews are available on the Miller Center Web site, at http://millercenter.org/president/bush/oralhistory.

2. Quoted in *41*, HBO documentary, aired June 14, 2012.

3. David J. Garrow, *Liberty and Sexuality: The Right to Privacy and the Making of Roe v. Wade* (New York: Macmillan, 1973), 120.

4. Timothy Naftali, *George H. W. Bush* (New York: Times Books, 2007), 8–9.

5. Quoted in *41*.

6. Lewis L. Gould, *Grand Old Party: A History of the Republicans* (New York: Random House, 2003), 28–29. See also John Robert Greene, *The Crusade: The Presidential Election of 1952* (Lanham, Md.: University Press of America, 1952), 91–94.

7. George Bush, *All the Best, George Bush: My Life in Letters and Other Writings* (New York: Scribner, 1999), 74.

8. Ibid., 85.

9. Quoted in Godfrey Hodgson, *The World Turned Right Side Up: A History of the Conservative Ascendancy in America* (Boston: Houghton Mifflin, 1996), 61.

10. Donald H. Critchlow, *The Conservative Ascendancy: How the Republican Right Rose to Power in Modern America*, 2nd ed. (Lawrence: University Press of Kansas, 2011), 57.

11. Herbert S. Parmet, *George Bush: Lone Star Yankee* (New York: Scribner, 1987), 93; and Hodgson, *The World Turned Right Side Up*, 60.

12. Quoted in *41*.

13. George Bush with Victor Gold, *Looking Forward: An Autobiography* (New York: Doubleday, 1987), 85.

14. Barbara Bush, *Barbara Bush: A Memoir* (New York: Scribner, 1994), 57.

15. Parmet, *George Bush*, 96.

16. Gladwin Hill, "Yarborough Pins Hope on Johnson," *New York Times*, November 1, 1964. The hatred between Johnson and Yarborough is treated in Robert A. Caro, *The Passage of Power: The Years of Lynn Johnson* (New York: Alfred A. Knopf, 2012), chapter 10.

17. Alexander P. Lamis, *The Two-Party South*, expanded ed. (New York: Oxford University Press, 1988), 196, 199.

18. "Feud Still Splits Texas Democrats," *New York Times*, August 16, 1964.

19. Hill, "Yarborough Pins Hope on Johnson."

20. Quoted in Parmet, *George Bush*, 96–97.

21. Marquis Childs, "The Wild Rodeo of Texas Politics," *Washington Post*, October 14, 1964.

22. Bush, *All the Best*, 87.

23. Quoted in John C. Topping Jr., John R. Lazarek, and William H. Linder, *Southern Republicanism and the New South* (Cambridge, Mass.: Ripon Society, 1966), 111.

24. Bush, *All the Best*, 88. Walter Reuther, an ardent liberal, headed the United Auto Workers.

25. Quoted in Numan V. Bartley and Hugh D. Graham, *Southern Politics and the Second Reconstruction* (Baltimore, Md.: Johns Hopkins University Press, 1975), 104.

26. Quoted in *41*.

27. Topping, Lazarek, and Linder, *Southern Republicanism and the New South*, 111.

28. Quoted in Jacob Weisberg, *The Bush Tragedy* (New York: Random House, 2008), 45.

29. Rowland Evans and Robert Novak, "Tangled Thicket in Texas," *Washington Post*, October 23, 1964.

30. "Democratic Party Split Is Making the Texas Senatorial Race a Toss-Up," *New York Times*, October 28, 1964; and Hill, "Yarborough Pins Hope on Johnson."

31. Quoted in Fitzhugh Green, *George Bush: An Intimate Portrait* (New York: Hippocrene Press, 1991), 91.

32. Quoted in Naftali, *George H. W. Bush*, 15.

33. Bush, *All the Best*, 90.

34. Ibid., 92.

35. George Bush, "The Republican Party and the Conservative Movement," *National Review*, December 1, 1965.

36. "Extremists Lose Texas G.O.P. Test," *New York Times*, July 4, 1965.

37. The alternative, as Governor Connally and the Democratic legislature knew, would have been court-ordered redistricting. Bill Porterfield, "Gov. Connally Faces Redistricting Test," *Washington Post*, January 21, 1965.

38. Quoted in Bush, *Barbara Bush: A Memoir*, 61–62.

39. Rowland Evans and Robert Novak, "The Birchite Republicans," *Washington Post*, July 28, 1966.

40. Treleaven's private account of the Bush campaign, "Upset: The Story of a Modern Political Campaign," is excerpted in Joe McGinniss, *The Selling of the President 1968* (New York: Simon and Schuster, 1969), 43–45.

41. Bush, *All the Best*, 95; and Richard Ben Cramer, *What It Takes: The Way to the White House* (New York: Random House, 1992), 13.

42. E. W. Kenworthy, "Turnout Is Key to Race in Texas," *New York Times*, November 6, 1966.

43. Rowland Evans and Robert Novak, "Battle for the Right," *Washington Post*, October 13, 1966.

44. M. S. Handler, "Negro Vote Rises as a Key in South," *New York Times*, November 9, 1964.

45. Topping, Lazarek, and Linder, *Southern Republicanism and the New South*, 120.

46. Bush, *Looking Forward*, 91. In the 1964 Senate election, Bush won an estimated 2 percent of the black vote against Yarborough in Houston. Topping, Lazarek, and Linder, *Southern Republicanism and the New South*, 119.

47. Bush, *Barbara Bush*, 59.

48. The Americans for Democratic Action's Annual Voting Records since 1947, along with the annual Liberal Quotient of each member of Congress, are available at http://www.adaction.org/pages/publications/viting-records.php.

49. The idea that Bush was a Republican moderate during his years in the House of Representatives prevails in every book about him. See for example Naftali, *George H. W. Bush*, 16–20; Tom Wicker, *George Herbert Walker Bush* (New York: Viking, 2004), 20–21; Parmet, *George Bush*, chapter 7; and John Robert Greene, *The Presidency of George Bush* (Lawrence: University Press of Kansas, 2000), 18.

50. Quoted in Parmet, *George Bush*, 134.

51. The extent of Goldwater's support for Planned Parenthood, and especially that of his wife Peggy Goldwater, is discussed in Robert Alan Goldberg, *Barry Goldwater* (New Haven, Conn.: Yale University Press, 1995), chapter 3.

52. David M. Kennedy, *Birth Control in America: The Career of Margaret Sanger* (New Haven, Conn.: Yale University Press, 1970). For example, Sanger came to believe that "working-class misery was attributable not to economic and political dislocation, but to the fecundity of the working class itself. In that view ... the artificial restriction of fertility was seen as an instrument with which the dominant classes could check threatened social disruption" (Ibid., 112–113). See also Garrow, *Liberty and Sexuality*.

53. Jean M. White, "Panel Urged to Earmark Family Planning Funds," *Washington Post*, March 23, 1967; and Webster Griffin Tarpley and Anton Chaitkin, *George Bush: The Unauthorized Biography* (Progressive Press, 1992).

54. Paul R. Ehrlich, *The Population Bomb* (New York: Ballantine Books, 1968), xi, 131.

55. U Thant is quoted in James H. Scheuer, "To Curb Population," *New York Times*, May 27, 1969.

56. Naftali, *George H. W. Bush*, 18; and Parmet, *George Bush*, 134.

57. Bush, *All the Best*, 124.

58. Quoted in Randall Balmer, *Thy Kingdom Come: How the Religious Right Distorts Faith and Threatens America* (New York: Basic Books, 2006), 12.

59. Bush, *All the Best*, 116.

60. Ibid., 111.

61. Ibid., 109.

62. Bush, *Looking Forward*, 93.

63. See, for example, Eileen Shanahan, "Mills and Panel Back Rise in Tex, Cut in Spending," *New York Times*, May 7, 1968; and Edwin L. Dale, Jr., "House Unit Backs Cut in Allowance for Oil Depletion," *New York Times*, July 22, 1969.

64. See, for example, Rowland Evans and Robert Novak, "Young Texas Congressman Bush Gets Nixon Look as Running Mate," *Washington Post*, June 5, 1968; Robert B. Semple, "Nixon Considering a Moderate on Ticket," *New York Times*, June 30, 1968; and "Reagan Avows Candidacy Agnew for Nixon," *New York Times*, August 6, 1968.

65. Bush, *All the Best*, 117–118.

66. Evans and Novak, "Young Texas Congressman Bush Gets Nixon Look as Running Mate."

67. A. D. Horne, "Eyes of Texas Are on Yarborough," *Washington Post*, January 1, 1968.

68. Warren Weaver Jr., "Nixon Recruiting G.O.P. Candidates for Senate Bid," *New York Times*, September 28, 1969.

69. Bush, *All the Best*, 128.

70. "Texas Rep. Bush Seeks Yarborough's Senate Seat Again," *Washington Post*, January 14, 1970.

71. Tom Wicker, "Mr. Nixon on the Stump," *New York Times*, October 29, 1970.

72. Jack Bass and Walter DeVries, *The Transformation of Southern Politics: Social Change and Political Consequences since 1945* (Athens: University of Georgia Press, 1995), 313. See also Martin Waldron, "Conservative Beats Yarborough in Democratic Primary in Texas," *New York Times*, May 3, 1970.

73. Waldron, "Conservative Beats Yarborough in Democratic Primary in Texas."

74. James Baker III with Steve Fiffer, "*Work Hard, Study . . . and Keep Out of Politics!*": *Adventures and Lessons from an Unexpected Public Life* (New York: G. P. Putnam's Sons, 2006), 20.

75. Quoted in Wicker, *George Herbert Walker Bush*, 23.

76. Michael Barone, Grant Ujifusa, and Douglas Matthews, *The Almanac of American Politics: The Senators, Representatives—Their Records, States and Districts 1972* (Boston: Gambit, 1972), 778.

77. Martin Waldron, "Johnson Stumping in Texas to Bolster Democrats," *New York Times*, September 20, 1970; and Martin Waldron, "2 Texas Amendments Drew Enough Voters for Bentsen to Win," *New York Times*, November 5, 1970.

78. Tom Wicker, "What Price Party Loyalty?" *New York Times*, June 2, 1970; and R. W. Apple Jr., "Similarities Mark Texas Rivals," *New York Times*, October 30, 1970.

79. Ken W. Clawson, "Chotiner Sees '70 Gains in GOP Senate Races," *Washington Post*, June 18, 1970.

80. Joseph Kraft, "GOP Chances in Texas," *Washington Post*, October 13, 1970.

81. Richard Halloran, "Large G.O.P Fund Is Given to Texas," *New York Times*, October 2, 1970; and "Tower Committee Spreading Funds among G.O.P. Candidates," *New York Times*, October 28, 1970.

82. David S. Broder, "Nixon May Find '72 Mate," *Washington Post*, October 27, 1970. See also James M. Naughton, "Agnew Rumor May Have Been a Trick," *New York Times*, November 11, 1970.

83. James E. Anderson, Richard W. Murray, and Edward F. Farley, *Texas Politics: An Introduction*, 2nd ed. (New York: Harper and Row, 1975), 74.

84. Waldron, "2 Texas Amendments Drew Enough Voters for Bentsen to Win."

85. See the data in Numan V. Bartley and Hugh D. Graham, *Southern Elections: County and Precinct Data, 1950–1972* (Baton Rouge: Louisiana State University, 1978).

86. Waldron, "2 Texas Amendments Drew Enough Voters for Bentsen to Win."

87. Robert B. Semple Jr., "President Claims a Working Margin," *New York Times*, November 5, 1970.

88. Bush, *All the Best*, 284.

89. Bush, *Looking Forward*, 207.

90. Jack W. Germond and Jules Witcover, *Blue Smoke and Mirrors: How Reagan Won and Why Carter Lost the Election of 1980* (New York: Viking, 1981), 117.

91. Theodore H. White, *America in Search of Itself: The Making of the President 1956– 1980* (New York: Harper and Row, 1982, 238.

92. Bush, *All the Best*, 303.

93. Critchlow, *The Conservative Ascendancy*, 222.

94. Bush, "The Republican Party and the Conservative Movement."

95. Barry Goldwater, *The Conscience of a Conservative* (Shepherdsville, Ky.: Victor, 1960).

CHAPTER 2

1. Unless otherwise noted, all quotations relating to the Bush presidency are from the George H. W. Bush Oral Histories, available on the Miller Center Web site, at http:// millercenter.org/president/bush/oralhistory. These quotations and references are identified in this chapter's endnotes by the interviewee's name and relevant page numbers in the Miller Center transcripts.

2. I have brazenly lifted this term from Irving Kristol, "America's Exceptional Conservatism," *Wall Street Journal*, April 18, 1995. While I follow Kristol's lead in seeing the new conservatism as a populist movement, my account gives greater emphasis to anti-communism as an early force in grassroots mobilization of the movement. See his 1996 essay, "The Right Stuff," reprinted in *The Neoconservative Persuasion: Selected Essays, 1942–2009*, ed. Gertrude Himmelfarb (New York: Basic Books, 2011).

3. Louis Hartz, *The Liberal Tradition in America: An Interpretation of American Political Thought since the Revolution* (New York: Harcourt, Brace, 1955).

4. For the sake of brevity, I am indulging in an anachronistic blending of Toryism and conservatism. Strictly speaking, one should draw this contrast between English Tories and Whigs, with Whiggery subsequently dividing into liberal and conservative ideological wings.

5. Elizabeth Fox-Genovese and Eugene D. Genovese, *The Mind of the Master Class: History and Faith in the Southern Slaveholders' Worldview* (New York: Cambridge University Press, 2005).

6. Pre–World War II conservatism in America had a great deal in common with Michael Oakeshott's account of conservatism. See Oakeshott's 1956 essay, "On Being Conservative," reprinted in his *Rationalism in Politics* (New York: Basic Books, 1962); and Michael Oakeshott, *The Politics of Faith and the Politics of Skepticism*, ed. Timothy Fuller (New Haven, Conn.: Yale University Press, 1996).

7. Ian Ker, *G. K. Chesterton: A Biography* (New York: Oxford University Press, 2011), 200.

8. Taft's run for the Republican presidential nomination in 1940—opposing New Deal policies and American support for England in World War II—was a bold but forlorn crusade after he had served only two years as a U.S. senator. (This also serves as a reminder that lusting for the White House after only two year's Senate (in)experience did not begin with Senator Barack Obama). In 1948, Taft lost to the moderate/liberal Dewey forces that dominated the Republican Party. After a close and bitter convention fight in 1952, Senator Taft lost the nomination to Dwight Eisenhower; he was outmaneuvered by the same East Coast moderate and internationalist establishment that occupied the center of the Republican Party. On these issues, see James T. Patterson's two books, *Congressional Conservatism and the New Deal: The Growth of the Conservative Coalition in Congress 1933–1939* (Lexington: University Press of Kentucky, 1967), and *Mr. Republican: A Biography of Robert A. Taft* (New York: Houghton Mifflin, 1972). The struggle within the Republican Party is analyzed in Michael Bowen, *The Roots of Modern Conservatism: Dewey, Taft, and the Battle for the Soul of the Republican Party* (Chapel Hill: University of North Carolina Press, 2011).

9. George Nash, *The Conservative Intellectual Movement in America since 1945* (New York: Basic Books, 1976). See also Lee Edwards, *The Conservative Revolution: The Movement That Remade America* (New York: Free Press, 1999); Jonathan Schoenwald, *A Time For Choosing: The Rise of Modern American Conservatism* (New York: Oxford University Press, 2001); and Geoffrey Kabaservice, *Rule and Ruin: The Downfall of Moderation and the Destruction of the Republican Party from Eisenhower to the Tea Party* (New York: Oxford University Press, 2011).

10. Marion Clawson, *New Deal Planning: The National Resources Planning Board* (Washington, D.C.: Resources for the Future Press, 2012).

11. Jennifer Burns, *Goddess of the Market: Ayn Rand and the American Right* (New York: Oxford University Press, 2009).

12. American Catholics in this period had every opportunity to pay attention to the pope's warnings about the communist threat. See, for example, "St. Peter's Crowd Hears Pope Speak," *Life*, September 22, 1947.

13. Rick Perlstein, *Before the Storm: Barry Goldwater and the Unmaking of the American Consensus* (New York: Hill and Wang, 2001).

14. Lisa McGirr, *Suburban Warriors: The Origins of the New American Right* (Princeton, N.J.: Princeton University Press, 2001); Bruce Schulman and Julian Zelizer, eds., *Rightward Bound: Making America Conservative in the 1970s* (Cambridge, Mass: Harvard University Press, 2008).

15. By 1962, the John Birch Society, which had been founded in 1958, may have had upward of 100,000 members in grassroots chapters spreading the conspiracy theories of its founder, Robert Welch. Wherever he looked, including at President Eisenhower himself, Welch found communist forces manipulating men and events to bring about totalitarianism in America.

16. The conservative figures involved in this meeting were William Baroody, head of the American Enterprise Institute; political philosopher Russell Kirk; William F. Buckley Jr., editor of the *National Review*; publicist Jay Hall; and (in disguise) Goldwater himself. At this time, January 1962, the John Birch Society was the only group publicly urging Goldwater to run for the GOP presidential nomination. William F. Buckley Jr., "Goldwater, the John Birch Society and Me," *Commentary*, March 2008. Buckley's brother-in-law and the *National Review's* Washington editor, Brent Bozell, had ghostwritten Goldwater's book, *The Conscience of a Conservative*, which brought the senator to national attention in 1960.

17. Barry Goldwater, *With No Apologies* (New York: Morrow, 1979).

18. George Marsden, *Fundamentalism and American Culture: The Shaping of Twentieth-Century Evangelicalism, 1870–1925* (New York: Oxford University Press, 1982).

19. Hugh Heclo, *Christianity and American Democracy* (Cambridge, Mass.: Harvard University Press, 2007), 113. These developments are described in detail in William Martin, *With God on Our Side: The Rise of the Religious Right in America* (New York: Broadway Books, 1996).

20. Kiron K. Skinner, Annelise Anderson, and Martin Anderson, eds., *Reagan: A Life in Letters* (New York: Free Press, 2003), 256, 257, 259.

21. Thus, in his 1965 autobiography, Ronald Reagan contended that classical liberalism was "now the conservative position." Ronald Reagan and Richard G. Hubler, *Where's the Rest of Me?* (New York: Duell, Cloan, and Pearce, 1965), 297.

22. George Nash, "Ronald Reagan's Legacy and American Conservatism," in *The Enduring Reagan*, ed. Charles W. Dunn (Lexington: University Press of Kentucky, 2009), 70n12.

23. "Conservatism is not an ideology, but rather a group of general principles concerning human nature and society." Barry Goldwater, "America's Best Hope for the Future Lies in Political Conservatism," in *The Great Ideas Today, 1962*, ed. Robert M. Hutchins and Mortimer J. Adler (Chicago: Encyclopedia Britannica, 1962), 21.

24. George Bush with Victor Gold, *Looking Forward* (New York: Doubleday, 1987), 26. Bush dedicated this memoir to his mother and father, "whose values lit the way."

25. In comparing the political careers of these two men, I am drawing on a number of the arguments and sources cited in my chapter "Ronald Reagan: The Making of a Politician," in a forthcoming collection edited by Charles Dunn.

26. William F. Buckley Jr., *God and Man at Yale* (Chicago: Henry Regnery, 1951).

27. Henry Catto interview, 2, 5.

28. Ronald Reagan and George Bush "The Republican Party and the Conservative Movement," *National Review*, December 1, 1964, 1053–1055.

29. James C. Humes, *Confessions of a White House Ghostwriter* (Washington, D.C.: Regnery, 1997), 176.

30. Edward Derwinski interview, 6, 9.

31. A week before the election, President Nixon made one brief stop at Longview, Texas, to endorse the Republican ticket of Paul Eggers for governor and Bush for senator. Richard Nixon: Remarks at Longview, Texas, October 28, 1970, The American Presidency Project, http://www.presidency.ucsb.edu/ws/index.php?pid=2776#ixzz1YnFmrOP7, accessed September 15, 2011.

32. Charles Ashman, *Connally: The Adventures of Big Bad John* (New York: William Morrow, 1974), 62.

33. Ben Barnes with Lisa Dickey, *Barn Burner, Barn Builder: Tales of a Political Life from LBJ to George W. Bush and Beyond* (Albany, Tex.: Bright Sky Press, 2006), 189. Connally stepped down as treasury secretary to head Democrats for Nixon in the 1972 campaign against McGovern. Finally, in May 1973, Connally fulfilled Nixon's hopes by switching parties and falling into place as another piece of the southern strategy.

34. On August 6, 1974, Nixon called a cabinet meeting to announce that he had decided not to resign because it would weaken the presidency and he did not believe he had committed an impeachable offense. According to the account by White House chief of staff Alexander Haig, as Nixon tried to steer the discussion on to economic issues there was a stir from the group sitting away from the cabinet table. George Bush, who sat in one of the chairs along the wall, seemed to be asking for the floor. When Nixon failed to recognize him, Bush spoke anyway. Watergate was the vital question, he said. It was sapping public confidence. Until it was settled, the economy and the country as whole would suffer. Nixon should resign. As Haig observed, it was unprecedented for the chair of the Republican National Committee to advise a Republican president to resign from office at a cabinet meeting. The cabinet sat in shocked silence, even though most realized that Nixon's resignation was inevitable. Bush, who thought that Nixon looked "detached from reality," felt that the issue had to be squarely addressed. In a public letter the next day, RNC chair Bush repeated the call for resignation, adding that his view was "held by most Republican leaders across the country." Nixon resigned on August 9th. Alexander M. Haig Jr. with Charles McCarry, *Inner Circles: How America Changed the World: A Memoir* (New York: Warner Books, 1992), 492–493.

35. Richard B. Cheney interview, 24, 26–28.

36. Robert M. Gates interview, 16. See also Bob Woodward, *Bush at War* (New York: Simon and Schuster, 2002), 21–22.

37. George Bush with Victor Gold, *Looking Forward*, 153–159; Gerald Ford, *A Time to Heal: The Autobiography of Gerald R. Ford* (New York: Harper & Row, 1979), 325–326, 337–338; Loch K. Johnson, *A Season of Inquiry: The Senate Intelligence Investigation* (Lexington, Ky.: University Press of Kentucky, 1985), 158–159. See also Richard B. Cheney interview, 29–30.

38. Bush, *Looking Forward*, 164–179.

39. James A. Baker III, January 29, 2000, 21.

40. "Bush and Reagan to Debate," *Washington Post*, February 13, 1980, A3.

41. The complexities of the conservative coalition are well described in Nash, *The Conservative Intellectual Movement in America Since 1945*; and Ted V. McAllister, "Reagan and the Transformation of American Conservatism," in *The Reagan Presidency: Pragmatic Conservatism and Its Legacies*, ed. W. Elliot Brownlee and Hugh Davis Graham (Lawrence: University Press of Kansas, 2003).

42. Edwards, *The Conservative Revolution*, 225–241; William Rusher, *The Rise of the Right* (New York: William Morrow, 1984), 313–314.

43. Whittaker Chambers, *Witness* (New York: Random House, 1952). Chambers's personal account as a well-meaning liberal duped by Communists matched Reagan's own earlier experience in dealing with Communist-infiltrated organizations in Hollywood immediately after World War II. *Witness* remained one of the most physically worn books in Reagan's home, wherever he resided after the early 1950s.

44. James A. Baker interview, March 17, 2011, 20.

45. Before directing Rockefeller's campaign against Goldwater in the California presidential primary, the political management firm that young Stuart Spencer and Bill Roberts formed had worked successfully for local and congressional Republicans of all types and thus was deeply distrusted by southern California's die-hard conservatives. Reagan brushed those concerns aside in favor of employing the most competent political management team he could find. Lou Cannon, *Governor Reagan: His Rise to Power* (New York: PublicAffairs, 2003), 134–136.

46. James P. Pinkerton interview, February 6, 2001, 3, 7, 36.

47. James A. Baker interview, March 17, 2011, 5–6.

48. Henry Catto interview, 14.

49. Craig Fuller interview, 13–14, 22–23.

50. Michael Boskin interview, 6.

51. During Reagan's 1984 reelection campaign, Bush's relations with reporters were notoriously poor. At one point during that summer, Bush carelessly admitted to a reporter that future tax increases might be necessary and then was forced to issue a hasty retraction. Pinkerton interview, 4, 10.

52. Baker interview, 19–20.

53. Phillip P. Brady interview, 15ff.; Baker interview, January 29, 2000, 3.

54. Despite Reagan's landslide victory, Bush was quite dejected by his performance against Walter Mondale's running mate Geraldine Ferraro and by his disastrous relations with the press during the 1984 campaign. It appears that Bush seriously questioned whether he had a future in politics. His friends Jim Baker and Nicholas Brady soon helped revive his spirits, and by Christmas of 1984, Bush and his closest advisors in Texas were already planning for a run at the 1988 Republican presidential nomination. Barbara Bush, *Barbara Bush: A Memoir* (New York: Scribner's Sons, 1994), 194–197; Bob Schieffer and Gary Paul Gates, *The Acting President* (New York: Dutton, 1989), 318; Pinkerton interview, 4.

55. For his 1966 congressional race (in a newly created district that cut a swath through Houston's new middle- and upper-middle-class suburbs) Bush hired the top-tier New York ad agency J. Walter Thompson to help design and implement a comprehensive campaign strategy that would "sell" the candidate like any other product. Media buys and professionally produced commercials appealed to voters to make a "purchase" in terms of the persona rather than in terms of party or policy issues. The results were so impressive that Bush's political consultants wrote a history of his 1966 campaign as a model for the new way of doing politics. See Elizabeth Mitchell, *W: The Revenge of the Bush Dynasty* (New York: Hyperion, 2000), 91–95.

56. Fuller interview, 60; John Sununu interview, 8, 38–39, 42–43; Pinkerton interview, 37–41.

57. John Brady, *Bad Boy: The Life and Politics of Lee Atwater* (Reading, Mass.: Addison-Wesley, 1996).

58. Fuller interview, 54; Pinkerton interview, 41.

59. Pinkerton interview, 5, 14.

60. For the origin and subsequent transformation of Reagan's tax policies, see W. Elliot Brownlee and C. Eugene Steurle, "Taxation," in *The Reagan Presidency*, ed. W. Elliot Brownlee and Hugh Davis Graham (Lawrence: University Press of Kansas, 2003).

61. Nash, "Ronald Reagan's Legacy and American Conservatism," 60.

62. Pinkerton interview, 18, 22.

63. Fuller interview, 63; Pinkerton interview, 12, 16.

64. Richard Darman, *Who's in Control? Polar Politics and the Sensible Center* (New York: Simon and Schuster, 1996), 191–192. See also Boskin interview, 52; Pinkerton interview, 25; J. Danforth Quayle interview, March 12, 2002, 35.

65. Bush could have avoided making his presidency a hostage to the tax pledge by simply adding language such as—"Read my lips: no new taxes! And let me be clear. That does not mean we should shy away from closing tax loopholes that erode the revenue base and treat Americans unfairly. On the contrary, we should carry forward the work so bravely begun by President Reagan with the Tax Reform Act of 1986." Why was such an obvious path not taken? The most likely reason is that by this time the two camps of campaign-focused and governing-focused Bush advisors were caught up in a zero-sum fight over a speech phrase.

66. The full statement of Bush's promise was as follows: "And I'm the one who will not raise taxes. My opponent now says he'll raise them as a last resort, or a third resort. But when a politician talks like that, you know that's one resort he'll be checking into. My opponent, my opponent won't rule out raising taxes. But I will. And the Congress will push me to raise taxes and I'll say no. And they'll push, and I'll say no, and they'll push again, and I'll say to them, 'Read my lips: no new taxes,'" http://www.americanrhetoric.com/speeches/georgehbush1988rnc.htm.

67. Boskin interview, 56.

68. However, Baker also privately warned Quayle during these transition months that Darman and Brady were going to try to get the president to break his tax pledge. Baker interview, 26.

69. Quayle interview, 37.

70. Pinkerton interview, 57.

71. To deal with the growing deficit, Bush had made his economic advisor's "flexible freeze" plan a prominent part of his 1988 presidential campaign. This plan, devised by Michael Boskin, would have held spending growth to a rate at or a little below the rate of inflation. But it would also be flexible about what would be cut or increased within that ceiling. Under such a control regime, a modestly growing economy would slowly but surely lead to a balanced budget over the long term. Instead of this approach, the president-elect accepted the recommendations of Budget Director Darman and Senate minority leader Dole to pass an interim budget in his first year in office. The next year, the Bush administration would charge forward to secure a more far-reaching budget that contained enforceable caps on future federal spending. The result of this strategy was the 1990 budget deal that broke Bush's no-new-taxes pledge. Boskin interview, 6–8, 50, 78.

72. While Quayle could not be said to have built his Indiana political career in the conservative movement, he became an important liaison with conservative columnists and politicians. He gained added credibility with neoconservatives when Irving Kristol's politically astute son William was appointed Quayle's chief of staff.

73. Quayle interview, 34–39.

74. Baker interview, March 17, 2011, 21.

75. Boskin interview, 57; Quayle interview, 36.

76. Boskin interview, 7, 52–54; Quayle interview, 41.

77. Sununu interview, 73–74; Baker interview, January 29, 2000, 27.

78. Quoted in Steven Mufson, ""Read Their Lips," *Washington Post*, July 31, 2011, B4.

79. Boskin interview, 52; Quayle interview, 36, 38; Fuller interview, 76.

80. William P. Barr interview, 71.

81. Quoted in Roman Popadiuk, *The Leadership of George Bush: An Insider's View of the 41st President* (College Station: Texas A&M University Press, 2009), 180.

82. Baker interview, January 29, 2000, 12. The exception, which turned out to help the Bush campaign, was the Reagan administration's attempt to negotiate with Panamanian dictator Manuel Noriega. Fuller interview, 56–57.

83. Paul Taylor, *See How They Run* (New York: Knopf, 1990), 6. See also Jack W. Germond and Jules Witcover, *Whose Broad Stripes and Bright Stars: The Trivial Pursuit of the Presidency, 1988* (New York: Warner, 1989); and Pinkerton interview, 32–33.

84. Of his own volition Craig Fuller, who had been Vice President Bush's chief of staff but was viewed by long-term Bush loyalists as too much a Reagan Republican, left government. Phillip P. Brady interview, 22–23; Fuller interview, 71–72.

85. For example, after finishing second to the liberal Warren Rudman in the 1980 Republican Senate primary, Sununu agreed to serve as Rudman's campaign chairman in order to hold conservative Republicans in line. Sununu interview, 3.

86. Danforth interview, 25; Sununu interview, 107–108.

87. Fuller interview, 74; Sununu interview, 30, 33, 45–46, 49, 59.

88. Boskin interview, 79.

89. Pinkerton interview, 97, 105–106.

90. Phillip P. Brady interview, 51; Sununu interview, 42–43.

91. Jim Lehrer, *Tension City: Inside the Presidential Debates, from Kennedy-Nixon to Obama-McCain* (New York: Random House), 2011.

92. Sununu interview, 151.

93. Quayle interview, 41–42; Baker interview, March 17, 2011, 37; Sununu interview, 140; Boskin interview, 46.

94. Pinkerton interview, 64.

95. Morton Kondracke, *Jack Kemp: An American Idealist* (forthcoming).

96. Quayle interview, 42.

97. Baker interview, January 29, 2000, 25–26, Baker interview, March 17, 2011, 37.

98. Phillip P. Brady interview, 51–52; Baker interview, January 29, 2000, 35.

99. Boskin interview, 53; Derwinski interview, 91; Baker interview, January 29, 2000, 32–33, 35.

100. Phillip P. Brady interview, 55; Baker interview, January 29, 2000, 38.

101. Barr interview, 71. See also Baker interview, March 17, 2011, 8; Sununu interview, 57–58.

102. Matthew Scully, "A Bush League of Their Own," *Washington Post*, January 17, 1993, C1–C2. See also John interview, 150; Pinkerton interview, 99.

103. Quayle interview, 37.

104. Having described this general pattern of abuse that Bush suffered during his earlier political career, it is fitting to conclude with a last example from the end of his public life. In the close-knit world of Texas politics and entrepreneurship, George Bush and businessman Ross Perot had come to know and like each other long before the 1980s, and Perot had financially supported a number of Bush's early ventures in Texas politics. When the Vietnam War ended, Perot became intensely interested in the issue of American soldiers missing in action who might be prisoners of war. Investing his considerable resources to investigate, Perot became convinced that there were Americans still alive in hidden Vietnamese prisons.

In 1986, Perot asked the Reagan administration to review the evidence and to send him personally to Vietnam in order to ascertain the facts on the ground. Perot's proposal was thoroughly reviewed by the relevant executive agencies, and the unanimous view they presented to President Reagan was that there were no Americans involuntarily living in Vietnam and that a Perot mission would negatively affect America's developing relations with Vietnam. President Reagan made the decision to reject Perot's offer and asked Perot's fellow Texans, Secretary of State James Baker and Vice President Bush, to convey the message. Not knowing Perot, Baker demurred. Bush happily offered to deliver Reagan's decision to his friend Ross Perot. It appears that from that moment onward, Perot held a bitter personal grudge against George Bush. Baker interview, January 29, 2000, 25, 38–39.

Given Perot's long record of harboring and acting on personal grudges, it would have been extremely odd if this instance of Bush's loyal service to President Reagan in 1986 was not an important factor in Perot's third-party challenge to Bush's reelection in 1992. Polling subsequently indicated that of the 19 percent of voters for Perot in the 1992 presidential vote, two-thirds were Republicans. Given these facts, the arithmetical conclusion seems clear. Since Bush received 38 percent of the 1992 vote with Perot in the race, adding two-thirds of the Perot voters to the Republican total would have given 51 percent of the popular vote to Bush (38 percent + 13 percent [2/3 of 19 percent] = 51 percent). Thus, one could say that Vice President Bush's well-meaning effort in 1986 to give President Reagan's frank assessment to Perot cost the future President Bush a second term six years later. Here, of course, we are also entering into the misty and delightful realm of speculative history.

105. Hugh Heclo, "The Corruption of Democratic Leadership," in *America at Risk: Threats to Liberal Self-Government in an Age of Uncertainty*, ed. Robert Faulkner and Susan M. Shell (Ann Arbor: University of Michigan Press, 2009), 249–266.

106. Norman J. Ornstein and Thomas E. Mann, eds., *The Permanent Campaign and Its Future* (Washington, D.C.: AEI Press, 2000). On this theme, see also Sununu interview, 19, 29, 58; Baker interview, March 17, 2011, 36–37.

107. Cardinal Joseph Ratzinger, 1981 address to the German Bundestag, published in his book *The Church, Ecumenism and Politics: New Endeavors in Ecclesiology* (San Francisco, Calif.: Ignatius Press, 2008), 151.

CHAPTER 3

1. All quotations in this chapter are from the George H. W. Bush Oral Histories unless otherwise noted. The interviews are available on the Miller Center Web site, at http://www.millercenter.org.

2. See Ivo Daalder and I. M. Destler, *In the Shadow of the Oval Office: Profiles of the National Security Advisers and the Presidents They Served: From JFK to George W. Bush* (New York: Simon & Schuster, 2009); David J. Rothkopf, *Running the World* (New York: PublicAffairs Books, 2005); John P. Burke, *Honest Broker? The National Security Advisor and Presidential Decision Making* (College Station: Texas A&M University Press, 2009).

3. See, for instance, Dennis Ross interview.

4. James A. Baker, III, *The Politics of Diplomacy: Revolution, War, and Peace, 1989–1992* (New York: G. P. Putnam's, 1995), 18–20. Baker reveals that Bush offered the job to him two days before the election. Once they were together in the White House, Bush would occasionally tease Baker by asking him, "If you're so smart, why aren't you president?" The same day Bush announced Baker's appointment, the day after the election, Bush announced that Boyden Gray would serve as his counsel and Chase Untermeyer would be director of presidential personnel.

5. Senators John Tower and Edmund Muskie were the other two members of the Tower Board, formerly known as the President's Special Review Board. The Tower Board, or Tower Commission, as it was often called, was established on December 1, 1986, with a mandate to investigate the national security process in the wake of the Iran-Contra affair. Scowcroft was also a member of the two Townes Committees, the immediate predecessors to the President's Commission on Strategic Forces, which was established on January 3, 1983, for the purpose of resolving how to base the MX ICBM and how to update the U.S. strategic force structure in light of the stalemate in the early 1980s between the Republican Reagan administration

and the Democrat-controlled House of Representatives. Scowcroft later served on the Packard Commission, which, among other things, looked at ways to reorganize defense procurement. He did not work closely with Bush during the 1988 presidential campaign, although in June 1988 the two talked about foreign policy at length and Scowcroft appeared at some campaign rallies. But he said he was "quite comfortable" doing what he'd been doing and had not planned on a job in the White House were Bush to be elected.

6. Herbert S. Parmet, *George Bush: Life of a Lone Star Yankee* (New York: Scribner, 1997), 387. Both men were former fighter pilots, Bush with the navy and Scowcroft with the army air corps. They were also of similar temperament—modest, gentlemanly, and cordial.

7. Brent Scowcroft interview; see also Dennis Ross interview. There were two components of the Iran-Contra affair. One was a secret arms-for-hostages deal carried out by Lt. Col. Robert (Bud) McFarlane, the national security advisor, who was assisted by several U.S. and Israeli middlemen. The other was a secret transfer of funds from the sale of U.S. weapons in the Middle East to the contras in Nicaragua, led by Col. Oliver North of the marine corps and Vice Admiral John Poindexter, helped by several middlemen. The first secret deal went against President Reagan's explicit policy of not negotiating with terrorists, and the second contravened the two Boland amendments passed by Congress that denied aid to the Nicaraguan contras.

8. Scowcroft interview; Richard Haass interview.

9. Robert Gates interview; Arnold Kanter, interview with the author, March 24, 2009. Although Gates had to withdraw as a nominee for director of central intelligence in 1987, he had served in the Carter and Reagan administrations and thus provided continuity. He was also widely respected. In his oral history, Scowcroft said that the fact that Gates withdrew was to his credit: his action had protected President Reagan and the White House from further embarrassment and political attacks.

10. Marcus Mabry, *Twice as Good: Condoleezza Rice and Her Path to Power* (Emmaus, Pa.: Rodale, 2007), 111.

11. Antonia Felix, *Condi: The Condoleezza Rice Story* (New York: Newmarket Press, 2002), 12, 198.

12. Mabry, *Twice as Good*, 112.

13. Scowcroft interview; Frank Carlucci interview, Miller Center, University of Virginia, Ronald E. Reagan Oral History Project, Miller Center.

14. Baker, *The Politics of Diplomacy*, 34–35.

15. See Roman Popadiuk, *The Leadership of George Bush* (College Station: Texas A&M University Press, 2009), 62; and Haass interview.

16. Baker, *The Politics of Diplomacy*, 26.

17. In an interview with the author, Carlucci said that Shultz had been "burned" by the NSC; Frank Carlucci, interview with the author, September 29, 2011.

18. See Popadiuk, *The Leadership of George Bush*, 58–61.

19. John G. Tower, Edmund S. Muskie, and Brent Scowcroft, *The Tower Commission Report: The Full Text of the President's Special Review Board* (New York: Times Books, 1987), 90–91. Scowcroft's prescriptions resembled many of Alexander L. George's recommendations and much of his analysis in "The Case for Multiple Advocacy in Making Foreign Policy," *American Political Science Review* 66, no. 3 (1972): 751–785.

20. Scowcroft would also get his "geographic principals reading the cables going out from State and Defense, because policy is really made by the outgoing cables from State and Defense." Otherwise, Scowcroft said, it would be "like that game of telephone with kids in a room."

21. This is consistent with the national security advisor's custodian role, in which he or she ensures that multiple advocates have a voice in the national security policymaking system. See George, "The Case for Multiple Advocacy in Making Foreign Policy."

22. See Daalder and Destler, *In the Shadow of the Oval Office*, 184–186.

23. Robert L. Hutchings, *American Diplomacy and the End of the Cold War: An Insider's Account of U.S. Policy in Europe, 1989–1992* (Washington, D.C.: The Woodrow Wilson Center Press; Baltimore, Md.: Johns Hopkins University Press, 1997), 22–24.

24. Scowcroft, interview with the author, October 6, 2010.

25. See George, "The Case for Multiple Advocacy in Making Foreign Policy," 763–765. The "Group of Eight," or "Big Eight," of the Desert Shield period and Desert Storm was but a slightly expanded Core Group. (Actually, it was a group of nine, since press secretary Marlin Fitzwater routinely sat in. But Fitzwater's name was purposefully not included on the circulation lists.)

26. Hutchings, *American Diplomacy and the End of the Cold War*, 23.

27. Daalder and Destler, *In the Shadow of the Oval Office*, 186–187.

28. Susan Koch, interview with author, January 2009; Daalder and Destler, *In the Shadow of the Oval Office*, 188–189.

29. Daalder and Destler, *In the Shadow of the Oval Office*, 188–189.

30. "Welcome Back Professor: Interview with Condoleezza Rice," *CREES Newsletter* (Stanford University), Spring 1991, 8.

31. See Barton Gelman, *Angler: The Cheney Vice Presidency* (New York: Penguin Press, 2009), 328–342; Daalder and Destler, *In the Shadow of the Oval Office*, 257–258; Donald Rumsfeld, *Known and Unknown: A Memoir* (New York: Sentinel, 2011), 321–330; David J. Rothkopf, *Running the World*, 407, 414–415; Alexander Cockburn, *Rumsfeld: His Rise, Fall, and Catastrophic Legacy* (New York: Scribner, 2007), 134–138; Jane Mayer, *The Dark Side* (New York: Doubleday, 2008), 187–188.

32. Rothkopf, *Running the World*, 404–405.

33. Richard Clarke, *Against All Enemies: Inside America's War on Terror* (New York: Free Press, 2004), 229–238; Daalder and Destler, *In the Shadow of the Oval Office*, 262–267; Mayer, *The Dark Side*, 20–24.

34. See Burke, *Honest Broker?* 259–260.

35. See Elisabeth Bumiller, *Condoleezza Rice: An American Life: A Biography* (New York: Random House, 2007), 134–229; Dick Cheney, *In My Time* (New York: Threshold Editions, 2011), 448–449; Mayer, *The Dark Side*, 143–144; Rothkopf, *Running the World*, 404–441. For possible pitfalls in the national security policy process, many of which characterized the George W. Bush White House, see George, "The Case for Multiple Advocacy in Making Foreign Policy," 769–781.

36. See Bumiller, *Condoleezza Rice*; Mabry, *Twice as Good*; Rothkopf, *Running the World*.

37. Peter Rodman, *Presidential Command* (New York: Knopf, 2009), 259.

38. Burke, *Honest Broker?* 267–273; Rodman, *Presidential Command*, 260–266. See also Richard Haass, *Wars of Necessity, Wars of Choice: A Memoir of Two Iraq Wars* (New York: Simon & Schuster 2009), 254–263.

39. Gelman, *Angler*, 339–342.

40. Rothkopf, *Running the World*, 414.

41. Gelman, *Angler*, 50; Rothkopf, *Running the World*, 407–408.

42. See Gelman, *Angler*, 50–60; Rothkopf, 413–414.

43. Cheney also had the much stronger views about the legitimacy of executive power and privilege in the face of a highly dangerous new international environment.

44. Gelman, *Angler*, 54. See also Stephen F. Hayes, *Cheney: The Untold Story of America's Most Powerful and Controversial Vice President* (New York: HarperCollins, 2007), 326–356.

45. Rothkopf, *Running the World*, 406.

CHAPTER 4

1. Unless otherwise noted, quotations in this chapter relating to the Bush presidency are from the George H. W. Bush Oral Histories. The interviews are available on the Miller Center Web site, at http://millercenter.org/president/bush/oralhistory.

2. On Hull and Cold War exceptionalism, see Thomas J. McCormick, *America's Half-Century* (Baltimore, Md.: Johns Hopkins University Press, 1995), 28–33.

3. Francis Fukuyama, *The End of History and the Last Man* (New York: The Free Press, 1992).

4. Bruce Cummings, "Time of Illusion: Post-Cold War Visions of the World," in *Cold War Triumphalism: The Misuse of History after the Fall of Communism*, ed. Ellen Schrecker (New York: The New Press, 2004), 75. Echoing the point, journalist Peter Beinart accurately noted that it did not matter to political conservatives—whose political powers were in the ascendancy—if the conclusions about history and causality embedded in their triumphant narrative of the end of the Cold War were correct. "Conservatives had come to *believe*" they were right. Quoted in Julian Zelizer, *Arsenal of Democracy: The Politics of National Security from World War II to the War on Terrorism* (New York: Basic Books, 2010), 354. Even British pop bands agreed with the confirming zeal of the times. As Jesus Jones sang, "Right here, right now: there is no other place that I'd want to be; Right here, right now, watching the world wake up from history." Significantly, the song never proved as popular in Britain or throughout Europe as it did in the United States, where it nearly topped the charts.

5. Jeffrey A. Engel and George H. W. Bush, *The China Diary of George H. W. Bush: The Making of a Global President* (Princeton, N.J.: Princeton University Press, 2008), 257.

6. "I didn't quote Shelley or Kant," Bush admitted after his presidency. "I didn't remember exactly what Thucydides had mean[t] to me when I was only twelve." Martin J. Medhurst, "Why Rhetoric Matters: George H. W. Bush in the White House," in *The Rhetorical Presidency of George H. W. Bush*, ed. Martin J. Medhurst (College Station: Texas A&M University Press, 2006). See also Catherine L. Langford, "George Bush's Struggle with the 'Vision Thing,'" in Medhurst, *The Rhetorical Presidency of George H. W. Bush*, 35.

7. Bush, "Inaugural Address," January 20, 1989, in *Public Papers of the President: George H. W. Bush*, vol. 1 (Washington, D.C.: US Government Printing Office, 1990), 1–4.

8. James Mann, *The Rebellion of Ronald Reagan: A History of the End of the Cold War* (New York: Viking Press, 2009), 320.

9. Scowcroft quoted in Jeffrey A. Engel, "'A Better World . . . but Don't Get Carried Away': The Foreign Policy of George H. W. Bush Twenty Years On," *Diplomatic History* 34, no. 1 (2010): 34.

10. David Hoffman, "Gorbachev Seen as Trying to Buy Time for Reform; Scowcroft Offers Guarded Assessment of Recent Soviet Peace Initiatives," *Washington Post*, January 23, 1989, A1.

11. Michael Kakutani, "The Deciders and How They Decided," *New York Times*, May 8, 2009, C27.

12. Gates made this point so often while at the Bush School of Government & Public Service that it became part of the institution's core identity and mission, told and retold by faculty members who were employed there during his tenure.

13. Ronald Steel, "Moscow: End the Cold War," *New York Times*, December 11, 1988, D25.

14. "The NATO Summit," March 20, 1989, Arnold Kanter Files, File: NATO Summit—May 1989, From Scowcroft to Bush, George Bush Presidential Library and Museum.

15. Ronald Reagan, "Remarks at the Annual Convention of the National Association of Evangelicals in Orlando, Florida," March 8, 1983, Public Papers of the President, The American Presidency Project, http://www.presidency.ucsb.edu/ws/index.php?pid=41023&st=&st1=, accessed June 4, 2013. The ideal starting place for Reagan's strategic transformation is Mann, *The Rebellion of Ronald Reagan*.

16. The literature on Gorbachev is rich and growing. See his own *Memoires* (New York: Doubleday, 1995); Archie Brown, *The Gorbachev Factor* (New York: Oxford University Press, 1996); Robert G. Kaiser, *Why Gorbachev Happened: His Triumphs and His Failure* (New York: Simon and Schuster, 1991); David Remnick, *Lenin's Tomb: The Last Days of the Soviet Empire* (New York: Vintage Books, 1994); Stephen White, *After Gorbachev* (Cambridge: Cambridge University Press, 1993); and William Taubman and Svetlana Savranskaya, "If a Wall Fell in Berlin and Moscow Hardly Noticed, Would It Still Make a Noise?" in *The Fall of the Berlin Wall: The Revolutionary Legacy of 1989*, ed. Jeffrey A. Engel (New York: Oxford University Press, 2009), 69–95.

17. Gorbachev quoted in Melvyn Leffler, *For the Soul of Mankind: The United States, the Soviet Union, and the Cold War* (New York: Hill and Wang, 2008), 374.

18. John Lewis Gaddis, *The Cold War: A New History* (New York: Penguin, 2006), 234.

19. Jeffrey A. Engel, "1989: An Introduction to an International History, in *The Fall of the Berlin Wall: The Revolutionary Legacy of 1989*, ed. Jeffrey A. Engel (New York: Oxford University Press, 2009), 21–22.

20. Ibid.

21. Ibid.

22. Mann, *The Rebellion of Ronald Reagan*, 304.

23. Don Oberdorfer, "Thatcher Says Cold War Has Come to an End; Briton Calls for Support of Gorbachev," *Washington Post*, November 18, 1988, A1.

24. Gorbachev quoted in William Hitchcock, *The Struggle for Europe: The Turbulent History of a Divided Continent, 1945 to the Present* (New York: Anchor Books, 2004).

25. Svetlana Savranskaya and Thomas Blanton, eds., "Reagan, Gorbachev and Bush at Governor's Island," National Security Archive Electronic Briefing Book # 261, posted December 8, 2008, http://www.gwu.edu/~nsarchiv/NSAEBB/NSAEBB261/index.htm, accessed September 24, 2011.

26. Quoted in Ibid.

27. Quoted in Ibid.

28. Thatcher quoted in Oberdorfer, "Thatcher Says Cold War Has Come to an End."

29. Mann, *The Rebellion of Ronald Reagan*, 304–306.

30. "The Presidential Debate; Transcript of the First TV Debate Between Bush and Dukakis," *New York Times*, September 26, 1988.

31. Jack F. Matlock, *Reagan and Gorbachev: How the Cold War Ended* (New York: Random House, 2004), 306.

32. Mann, *The Rebellion of Ronald Reagan*, 308.

33. For a discussion of the Bush administration's "strategic pause" and its subsequent policy of "beyond containment," see Christopher Maynard, *Out of the Shadow: George H. W. Bush and the End of the Cold War* (College Station: Texas A&M University Press, 2008), 1–26.

34. David Hoffman, "Gorbachev Seen as Trying to Buy Time for Reform," *Washington Post*, January 23, 1989, A1.

35. Robert M. Gates, *From the Shadows: The Ultimate Insider's Story of Five Presidents and How They Won the Cold War* (New York: Simon & Shuster, 1996), 445. Gates quoted in Michael R. Gordon, "CIA Aide Sees Soviet Economy Failing to Gain," *New York Times*, October 15, 1988, A1.

36. For "see no slackening," see Gordon, "CIA Aide Sees Soviet Economy Failing to Gain"; for "most dangerous time," see Gates, *From the Shadows*.

37. "Remarks at the Swearing-In Ceremony for Richard B. Cheney as Secretary of Defense," March 21, 1989, George Bush Presidential Library and Museum, http://bushlibrary.tamu.edu/research/public_papers.php?id=208&year=1989&month=3, accessed May 23, 2013.

38. Gorbachev, *Memoires*, 496–497; Anatoly S. Chernyaev, *My Six Years with Gorbachev* (University Park: University of Pennsylvania Press, 2000), 215.

39. Engel, "1989: An Introduction to an International History," 28.

40. Richard Haass Memorandum for Scowcroft, Subject: Secretary Cheney's Speech for Tomorrow Evening, May 10, 1989, File: USSR Collapse: US-Soviet Relations Thru 1991 (January–April 1989), Box 11, Series: USSR Collapse Files Subseries: US-Soviet Relations Chronological Files, Brent Scowcroft Papers, George Bush Presidential Library and Museum.

41. Ibid.

42. For "save us," see Tony Judt, *Postwar: A History of Europe since 1945* (New York: Penguin, 2006), 603.

43. Engel, "The Transformation of Europe and the End of the Cold War," 14.

44. Baker quoted in Randy Kluver, "Rhetorical Trajectories of Tiananmen Square," *Diplomatic History* 34, no. 1 (2010): 87.

45. For Bush, see Martin Walker, "NATO Is a Winner, Says Upbeat Bush," *Guardian*, May 24, 1989.

46. Scowcroft to Bush, March 20, 1989, Subject Files, Folder: NATO Summit—May 1989, Arnold Kanter Files, National Security Council Series, George Bush Presidential Library and Museum.

47. Michael Dobbs, "The Great Global Shake-Up," *Washington Post*, June 11, 1989, C1.

48. James Lilley, *China Hands: Nine Decades of Adventure, Espionage, and Diplomacy in Asia* (New York: PublicAffairs, 2004), 300.

49. Engel, "The Transformation of Europe and the End of the Cold War," 33.

50. George H. W. Bush, *All the Best, George Bush: My Life in Letters and Other Writings* (New York: Scribner, 1999), 433.

51. George H. W. Bush and Brent Scowcroft, *A World Transformed* (New York: Vintage Books, 1999), 149.

52. Public Papers of the President, "The President's News Conference in Brussels, December 4, 1989," The American Presidency Project, http://www.presidency.ucsb.edu/ws/index.php?pid=17907&st=&st1=, accessed June 4, 2013.

53. Zelizer, *Arsenal of Democracy*, 357.

54. For "Americans have always believed," see Public Papers of the President, "Remarks and a Question-and-Answer Session at a Luncheon Hosted by the Commonwealth Club in San Francisco, California," February 7, 1990, The American Presidency Project, http://www.presidency.ucsb.edu/ws/index.php?pid=18128&st=&st1=, accessed June 4, 2013. For Zoellick and Bush, see Jim Ciconni notes, "Briefing of Press on NATO Summit Walker's Point," July 2, 1990, Box 109, Folder 3, 7/3/1990, James A. Baker III Papers, Princeton University Library.

55. For "historic vision," see George H. W. Bush, "Address before a Joint Session of the Congress on the Persian Gulf Crisis and the Federal Budget Deficit," September 11, 1990.

56. Bush and Gorbachev Telcon, February 23, [1993], Box 46, File: Iraq—February 1991 [1993], Richard Haass Papers, George Bush Presidential Library and Museum.

57. For a discussion of the Bush administration's strategic pause and the president's prudence, see Maynard, *Out of the Shadow*, 1–26.

58. For Fitzwater, see Roy Joseph, "The New World Order: President Bush and the Post–Cold War Era," in Medhurst, *The Rhetorical Presidency of George H. W. Bush*, 97.

59. For Buchanan, see Joseph, "The New World Order," 97.

60. George McGovern, "'Come Home America': The New World Order and the 1992 Election, *SAIS Review* 12, no. 2 (1992): 141–147.

61. Telcon with President Mikhail Gorbachev of the USSR on February 23, 1991, and Telcon with President Mikhail Gorbachev of the USSR, August 21, 1991, Presidential Memcons and Telcons, George Bush Presidential Library and Museum.

CHAPTER 5

1. Pat Towell, "The Tower Nomination: Senate Spurns Bush's Choice in a Partisan Tug of War," *Congressional Quarterly Weekly Report*, March 11, 1989, 533.

2. John McCain, *Worth the Fighting For* (New York: Random House, 2002), 150.

3. Quoted in Larry Sabato, *Feeding Frenzy: How Attack Journalism Has Transformed American Politics* (New York: Free Press, 1991), 178.

4. Tower died in a plane crash in 1991 after writing a bitter memoir that focused on his defeat in the Senate confirmation battle.

5. See Sabato, *Feeding Frenzy*; McCain, *Worth Fighting For*; and Suzanne Garment, *Scandal: The Culture of Mistrust in American Politics* (New York: Random House, 1991).

6. John Robert Greene, *The Presidency of George Bush* (Lawrence: University Press of Kansas, 2000), 51.

7. Bob Woodward, *The Commanders* (New York: Simon & Schuster, 1991), 56–57.

8. William G. Phillips quoted in James D. King and James W. Riddlesperger, "The Rejection of a Cabinet Nomination: The Senate and John Tower," in *From Cold War to New World Order*, ed. Meena Bose and Rosanna Perotti (Greenwood, Conn.: Greenwood Press, 2002), 380.

9. The president admits that Scowcroft would have preferred to be secretary of defense, "but I needed him at my side in the White House." George H. W. Bush, *All the Best, George Bush: My Life in Letters and Other Writings* (New York: Scribner, 1998), 426. There was speculation in the press about other candidates for the post, including Sam Nunn, Don Rumsfeld, and corporate CEOs Paul O'Neil and Norman Augustine. See Fred Barnes, "Tottering Tower," *The New Republic*, December 19, 1988, 8.

10. Suggested Talking Points for Tower-Bush Meeting, NA 59-4, John C. Tower Collection, Southwestern University Library.

11. All quotations in this chapter relating to the Bush presidency are from the George H. W. Bush Oral Histories unless otherwise noted. The interviews are available on the Miller Center Web site, at http://millercenter.org/president/bush/oralhistory.

12. For a summary of the *New York Post* stories and others that appeared at the time, see Mark Hosenball and Michael Isikoff, "Psst: Inside Washington's Rumor Mill," *The New Republic*, January 2, 1989.

13. Maureen Dowd, "Conflict over Ethics Divides 2 of Bush's Closest Advisers," *New York Times*, February 15, 1089.

14. Greene, *The Presidency of George Bush*, 53; Bob Woodward, *Shadow: Five Presidents and the Legacy of Watergate* (New York: Touchstone, 1999), 176.

15. John Tower, *Consequences: A Personal and Political Memoir* (Boston: Little Brown, 1991), 46–47. Of course Tower may not be the best source for this conclusion.

16. Ibid., 50.

17. Quoted in Suzanne Garment, "The Tower Precedent," *Commentary*, May, 1989, 43.

18. Quoted in Tower, *Consequences*, 7.

19. "Towering Inferno," a reference to the title of a popular disaster movie of 1974, was the headline used for an article by Martin Schram in the May 1989 *Washingtonian* magazine. It was also the title for a William Safire column in the *New York Times*, February 13, 1989.

20. "Tower's Troubles," *Newsweek*, March 6, 1989, 20.

21. McCain, *Worth the Fighting For*, 139.

22. Alyson Pytte, "Questions of Conduct Delay Vote on Tower," *Congressional Quarterly Weekly Review*, February 4, 1989, 222.

23. U.S. Federal Bureau of Investigation, "Report on John Goodwin Tower," February 13, 1989, Vertical File, 28–32, John G. Tower Collection, Southwestern University Library.

24. Ibid., 28.

25. Ibid., 34.

26. Tower, *Consequences*, 182. A *New York Times* story on February 7, four days after Nunn spoke to Combest, quoted Senator Exon as saying that Nunn would vote no on the nomination.

27. Tower, *Consequences*, 196.

28. Tower reports that the story is not true; Tower, *Consequences*, 296. The same conclusion was reached by various media organizations after they finally saw the redacted FBI files on Tower. See John Elvin, "Investigators Couldn't Catch Tower with Pants Down," *Insight*, March 27, 1995.

29. McCain, *Worth the Fighting For*, 149.

30. Tower, *Consequences*, 90–91.

31. Pat Towell, "Senate Panel Deals Bush His First Big Defeat," *Congressional Quarterly Weekly Review*, February 25, 1989, 397.

32. Bob Woodward, "Incidents at Defense Base Cited; Drunkenness, Harassment of Women Alleged," *Washington Post*, March 2, 1989.

33. Dan Balz and Bob Woodward, "Senate's Debate over Tower Becomes Partisan Free-for-All; Allegations about Visit to Base Challenged," *Washington Post*, March 3, 1989.

34. McCain, *Worth the Fighting for*, 154.

35. Woodward, *Shadow*, 545.

36. George H. W. Bush, Statement on Death of John Tower, April 5, 1991, George Bush Presidential Library and Museum, http://bushlibrary.tamu.edu.

37. Herbert S. Parmet, *George Bush: The Life and Times of a Lone Star Yankee* (New York: Scribner, 1997), 371–375.

38. Bush, *All the Best*, 414.

39. Parmet, *George Bush*, 374.

40. George H. W. Bush's diary, quoted in Ibid., 375.

41. Woodward, *The Commanders*, 57–58.

42. Tower, *Consequences*, 317.

43. Greene, *The Presidency of George Bush*, 57.

44. Parmet, *George Bush*, 375. A similar view was expressed in Jack Germond and Jules Witcover, "Memories of Harsh '88 Race Haunt Bush," *National Journal*, March 11, 1989.

45. Joe Klein, "The Least and the Dullest," *New York Magazine*, March 27, 1989, 16.

46. Ibid.

47. Woodward, *The Commanders*, 57.

48. George H. W. Bush, Inaugural Address, January 20, 1989, George Bush Presidential Library and Museum, http://bushlibrary.tamu.edu.

49. Tower, *Consequences*, 335–336.

50. Paul Light, "Late for Their Appointments," *New York Times*, November 16, 2004.

51. Towell, "The Tower Nomination," 530–534.

52. Quoted in Greene, *The Presidency of George Bush*, 144.

53. Parmet, *George Bush*, 373. See also Barbara Bush, *Barbara Bush: A Memoir* (New York: Scribner, 2003), 268.

54. In his memoir, the president admits that Tower was not perfect. He "had shortcomings, but none so glaring that he did not deserve my loyalty, my standing by him when the going got downright tough." George Bush and Brent Scowcroft, *A World Transformed* (New York: Knopf, 1998), 22.

55. Robert Gates, *From the Shadows: The Ultimate Insider's Story of Five Presidents and How They Won the Cold War* (New York: Simon & Schuster, 1996), 454.

CHAPTER 6

1. In addition to the sources cited below, this essay is based on my interviews with members of Congress, congressional staff, and informed observers.

2. On the campaign see Gerald Pomper, ed., *The Election of 1988: Reports and Interpretations* (Chatham, N.J.: Chatham House Publishers, 1989); John Robert Greene, *The Presidency of George Bush* (Lawrence: University Press of Kansas, 2000), 27–44; Michel Duffy and Dan Goodgame, *Marching Place: The Status Quo Presidency of George Bush* (New York: Simon and Schuster, 1992), 15–35.

3. Barbara Sinclair, "Agenda Control and Policy Success: The Case of Ronald Reagan and the 97th House," *Legislative Studies Quarterly* 20 (August 1985): 291–314.

4. James Sundquist, *The Decline and Resurgence of Congress* (Washington, D.C.: Brookings Institution, 1981); Barbara Sinclair, *Majority Leadership in the U.S. House* (Baltimore, Md.: Johns Hopkins University Press, 1983); Barbara Sinclair, *Legislators, Leaders, and Lawmaking: The House of Representatives in the Post-Reform Era* (Baltimore, Md.: Johns Hopkins University Press, 1995).

5. For a discussion of the conditional party model of government that makes the same argument, see David Rohde, *Parties and Leaders in the Postreform House* (Chicago: University of Chicago Press, 1991).

6. Sinclair, *Legislators, Leaders, and Lawmaking*, 260–280.

7. Based on interviews conducted by the author.

8. Quotes taken from White House text of the president's address, printed in *Congressional Quarterly Weekly Report*, February 11, 1989, 276.

9. As a result of economic conditions, misguided regulatory changes, and bad business decisions, a large number of savings and loans were insolvent by the late 1980s and the deposit insurance system lacked the money to close them down and pay off covered deposits without a government bailout. See Lawrence J. White, *The S&L Debacle: Public Policy Lessons for Bank and Thrift Regulation* (New York: Oxford University Press, 1991).

10. *New York Times*, February 10, 1989, 1; *Washington Post*, February 10, 1989, 1.

11. All quotations in this chapter relating to the Bush presidency are from the George H. W. Bush Oral Histories unless otherwise noted. The interviews are available on the Miller Center Web site, at http://millercenter.org/president/bush/oralhistory.

12. *Congressional Quarterly Weekly Report*, January 7, 1989, 16.

13. *Congressional Quarterly Weekly Report*, January 14, 1989, 63.

14. Matthew N. Beckmann, "Up the Hill and Across the Aisle: Explaining Washington's Inter-Branch, Inter-Party Interactions," paper prepared for the conference New Directions in Congressional-Presidential Research, Miller Center, University of Virginia, May 2011, 24, Figure 1.

15. Duffy and Goodgame, *Marching Place*, 51.

16. In addition to the McClure oral history interview, see Kenneth E. Collier, *Between the Branches: The White House Office of Legislative Affairs* (Pittsburgh, Pa.: University of Pittsburgh Press, 1997), 233.

17. Interview by Kenneth Collier quoted in Collier, *Between the Branches*, 234–236.

18. Ibid., 238.

19. Ibid.

20. Shirley Anne Warshaw, *The Domestic Presidency: Policy Making in the White House* (Boston: Allyn and Bacon, 1997), 163.

21. Ibid., 168.

22. In addition to the McClure oral history interview, see also Duffy and Goodgame, *Marching Place*, 115–120. On Darman, see *Congressional Quarterly Weekly Report*, February 25, 1989, 373.

23. Greene, *The Presidency of George Bush*, 153.

24. Warshaw, *The Domestic Presidency*, 163. See also Paul J. Quirk, "Domestic Policy: Divided Government and Cooperative Presidential Leadership," in *The Bush Presidency*, ed. Collin Campbell and Bert Rockman (Chatham, N.J.: Chatham House Publishers, 1991), 211.

25. Regular vetoes are defined as those that are not pocket vetoes or vetoes that Bush labeled as pocket vetoes but nevertheless sent back to Congress, which then treated them as regular vetoes. This happened twice. See *CQ Almanac 1992* (Washington D.C.: Congressional Quarterly, 1993), 6–7.

26. Charles M. Cameron, *Veto Bargaining: Presidents and the Politics of Negative Power* (New York: Cambridge University Press, 2000), 47.

27. *CQ Almanac 1989* (Washington D.C.: Congressional Quarterly, 1990).

28. Samuel Kernell, "Introduction," in *Presidential Veto Threats in Statements of Administration Policy: 1985–2004*, ed. Samuel Kernell (Washington, D.C.: CQ Press, 2005), CD ROM. The CD includes PDF files of all the SAPs containing veto threats that were issued during the years 1985–2004. The introduction explains how Kernell obtained the SAPs for years before posting on the Internet became standard.

29. Executive Office of the President, Statement of Administration Policy, April 25, 1990, in "101st Congress (1989–1990)," 107, in Kernell, *Presidential Veto Threats in Statements of Administration Policy: 1985–2004*.

30. *Congressional Quarterly Weekly Report*, September 22, 1990, 2992.

31. Executive Office of the President, Statement of Administration Policy, April 25, 1990, 108.

32. Kernell, "Introduction," 4.

33. The first figure is my calculation based on the list of SAPs in "101st Congress (1989–1990)," 1–6; the second is from Kernell, "Introduction," 5.

34. Executive Office of the President, Statement of Administration Policy, June 18, 1990, in "101st Congress (1989–1990)," 225.

35. Executive Office of the President, Statement of Administration Policy, August 2, 1990, in "101st Congress (1989–1990)," 216.

36. For more on the data set, see Barbara Sinclair, *Unorthodox Lawmaking: New Legislative Processes in the U.S. Congress*, 4th ed. (Washington, D.C.: Congressional Quarterly Press, 2012), 8–9. Regular appropriations bill appear in the data set only through *CQ* key votes, not through *CQ*'s list of major legislation.

37. *Congressional Quarterly Weekly Report*, September 22, 1990, 2991.

38. Ibid., 2990.

39. Ibid., 2991.

40. *Congressional Quarterly Weekly Report*, December 2, 1989, 3287.

41. *Congressional Quarterly Weekly Report*, August 5, 1989, 2044.

42. See *Congressional Quarterly Weekly Report*, March 17, 1990, 837.

43. *Congressional Quarterly Weekly Report*, May 26, 1990, 1657. "A March 12 letter from Attorney General Dick Thornburgh to Rep. Steny Hoyer, D-Md., who is coordinating the bill's movement through the House, reiterated administration concerns first aired at a Feb. 22 hearing of the House Small Business Committee. . . . At issue are the proposed remedies for employment discrimination against the disabled. The compromise language negotiated last year specifies that remedies under ADA are to be the same as those provided to women and minorities under Title VII of the 1964 Civil Rights Act. Under existing law, those remedies are primarily injunctive relief and back pay. But in response to a series of controversial 1989 Supreme Court rulings, separate legislation (HR4000, S2104) has been introduced that would amend Title VII to permit aggrieved parties to sue for monetary damages. Hearings have begun in both chambers. . . . The administration opposes expansion of Title VII remedies and wants to make sure that no monetary damages are possible under ADA, either." Quote from *Congressional Quarterly Weekly Report*, March 17, 1990, 837.

44. *Congressional Quarterly Weekly Report*, July 14, 1990, 2227.

45. *Congressional Quarterly Weekly Report*, September 22, 1990, 2991.

46. *Congressional Quarterly Weekly Report*, October 6, 1990, 3234.

47. *Congressional Quarterly Weekly Report*, October 20, 1990, 3511.

48. Richard E. Cohen, *Washington at Work: Back Rooms and Clean Air* (New York: Macmillan Publishing Co, 1992), 60–61.

49. Warshaw, *The Domestic Presidency*, 170–171.

50. Cohen, *Washington at Work*, 58–62.

51. See the Sununu oral history interview.

52. Cohen, *Washington at Work*, 84.

53. Ibid., 154.

54. *Congressional Quarterly Weekly Report*, November 4, 1989

55. *Congressional Quarterly Weekly Report*, May 21, 1990

56. *Congressional Quarterly Weekly Report*, November 3, 1990

57. Ibid.

58. See the Michael Boskin oral history interview; and *Congressional Quarterly Weekly Report*, October 27, 1990, 3587.

59. Cohen, *Washington at Work*, 152–154.

60. *Congressional Quarterly Weekly Report*, October 27, 1990, 3587.

61. Ibid.

62. *Congressional Quarterly Weekly Report*, November 4, 1989.

63. Cohen, *Washington at Work*, 168–169.

64. For a more detailed discussion see Barbara Sinclair, "Governing Unheroically (and Sometimes Unappetizingly): Bush and the 101st Congress," in *The Bush Presidency*, ed. Colin Campbell and Bert Rockman (Chatham, N.J.: Chatham House Publishers, 1991).

65. *Congressional Quarterly Weekly Report*, March 4, 1989, 467; see also Richard Darman, *Who's In Control?* (New York: Simon and Schuster, 1996), 208.

66. *Congressional Quarterly Weekly Report*, April 5, 1989, 804.

67. *Los Angeles Times*, November 8, 1989.

68. Darman, *Who's In Control?*, 248

69. On Bush's job approval numbers, see Gallup's historical statistics at http://www.gallup.com/poll/116677/presidential-approval-ratings-gallup-historical-statistics-trends.aspx?. The events of the summer of 1990, of course, occurred before the Gulf War, but Bush's numbers were high before the Gulf War.

70. *Congressional Quarterly Weekly Report*, June 30, 1990, 2094.

71. *Houston Post*, June 29, 1990.

72. See the oral history interviews with James Pinkerton and Dan Quayle; and Darman, *Who's in Control?* 265. Only Darman seems to have believed that the no-new-taxes pledge was a mistake from the beginning. A number of Bush administration officials blamed Darman for what happened.

73. *Congressional Quarterly Weekly Report*, September 22, 1990, 2991.

74. *Congressional Quarterly Weekly Report*, October 6, 1990, 3184–3191.

75. Ibid.

76. *USA Today*, October 11, 1990.

77. On the negotiations and how winners and losers were perceived at the time, see *Congressional Quarterly Weekly Report*, October 1990, 3574.

78. In late September, Bush's job approval in the Gallup Poll still stood at 67 percent. On the inability of presidents regularly to translate even high popularity into support for their policies and subsequently into congressional support, see George C. Edwards III, *The Strategic President: Persuasion and Opportunity in Presidential Leadership* (Princeton, N.J.: Princeton University Press, 2009). In the light of the findings of Edwards and other political scientists, the argument that Bush could have translated his impressive popularity in the wake of the first Gulf War into support for various domestic policy legislative victories is not persuasive.

79. Darman, *Who's In Control?* 273.

80. According to Bruce Bartlett, who served in both the Reagan and Bush administrations, Bush's loss to Bill Clinton in 1992 "proved for all time that even though tax increases may be justified economically, they are never justified politically if you're a Republican. . . . Since then it's been Republican dogma that deficits don't matter and the only thing that matters for the economy is cutting taxes." Quoted in Lori Montgomery, "Among GOP, Anti-Tax Orthodoxy Runs Deep," *Washington Post*, June 5, 2011.

CHAPTER 7

1. All quotations in this chapter relating to the Bush presidency are from the George H. W. Bush Oral History unless otherwise noted. The interviews are available on the Miller Center Web site, at http://millercenter.org/president/bush/oralhistory.

2. Republican Party Platform of 1988, American Presidency Project, http://www.presidency.ucsb.edu/ws/index.php?pid=25846#ixzz1bjlaXjAl/.

3. George H. W. Bush, Republican National Convention Acceptance Address, August 18, 1988, New Orleans, Louisiana, American Rhetoric Online Speech Bank, http://www.americanrhetoric.com/speeches/georgehbush1988rnc.htm (bullets added).

4. *West Virginia State Board of Education v. Barnette*, 319 U.S. 624 (1943).

5. The Bush campaign ad was filmed in black and white, a tactic often used to portray negativity about an opponent and/or his policies. Although no African Americans or Hispanics moved through the ad's revolving door, the film's black, white, and gray tones may have had racial connotations for viewers. It would have been easy for voters to link the Bush and Willie Horton ads.

6. Timothy Naftali, *George H. W. Bush* (New York: Times Books, 2007), 61–62.

7. Henry J. Abraham, *Justices, Presidents, and Senators: A History of the U.S. Supreme Court Appointments from Washington to Bush II*, 5th ed. (Lanham, Md.: Rowman & Littlefield, 2008), 39.

8. Barbara A. Perry, "*The Supremes*": *An Introduction to the U.S. Supreme Court Justices*, 2nd ed. (New York: Peter Lang, 2009), 78.

9. See Perry's book-length study of this topic, *A "Representative" Supreme Court? The Impact of Religion, Race, and Gender on Appointments* (New York: Greenwood Press, 1991). In addition to passive representatives who simply mirror societal characteristics or active ones who pursue their group's interests, representative justices may also bring differing perspectives or life experiences to the bench. Sandra Day O'Connor, who brought a new gender perspective to the Court as its first woman, observed that she was "profoundly influenced" by her judicial colleague Thurgood Marshall's compelling stories of racial discrimination that he had faced throughout his life. Sandra Day O'Connor, *The Majesty of the Law: Reflections of a Supreme Court Justice* (New York: Random House, 2003), 132.

10. Abraham, *Justices, Presidents, and Senators*, 2.

11. Perry, *A "Representative" Supreme Court?* 10.

12. Warren B. Rudman, *Combat: Twelve Years in the U.S. Senate* (New York: Random House, 1996), 162. Rudman's book contains an entire chapter on his friendship and professional association with David Souter.

13. Sununu did not explain why he thought Justice O'Connor might leave the Court. She had only been on it for nine years and was just sixty years old, a young age by Supreme Court justice standards. Perhaps he saw her 1988 breast cancer diagnosis as a career-ending illness. O'Connor was successfully treated for her cancer and did not retire from the high bench until 2006.

14. Ann Devroy, "In the End, Souter Fit Politically," *Washington Post*, July 25, 1990, A6; David J. Garrow, "Justice Souter Emerges," *New York Times Magazine*, September 25, 1994, 52; Abraham, *Justices, Presidents, and Senators*, 304.

15. Perry, "*The Supremes*," 79.

16. Ibid.

17. "President Bush's Announcement and Excerpts from News Conference," *Washington Post*, July 25, 1990, A12.

18. Ibid.

19. Perry, "*The Supremes*," 80.

20. Rudman, *Combat*, 162, 152.

21. Abraham, *Justices, Presidents, and Senators*, 291.

22. Ibid., 291–292.

23. Perry, "*The Supremes*," 87–92; "President Nominates Clarence Thomas to Court of Appeals for the District of Columbia," *Civil Rights Monitor* 4, no. 3 (1989), http://www.civilrights.org/monitor/fall1989/art5pl.html, accessed December 11, 2012.

24. Abraham, *Justices, Presidents, and Senators*, 296.

25. Barbara A. Perry and Henry J. Abraham, "A 'Representative' Supreme Court? The Thomas, Ginsburg, and Breyer Appointments," *Judicature* 81 (January–February 1998): 160.

26. Clarence Thomas, *My Grandfather's Son* (New York: Harper, 2007).

27. Perry, "*The Supremes*," 93.

28. Abraham, *Justices, Presidents, and Senators*, 298.

29. Perry, "*The Supremes*," 94.

30. Abraham, *Justices, Presidents, and Senators*, 298.

31. For a different interpretation of Hill's credibility, see Jane Mayer and Jill Abramson, *Strange Justice: The Selling of Clarence Thomas* (New York: Plume, 1995).

32. Abraham, *Justices, Presidents, and Senators*, 299.

33. Ibid.

34. Thomas, *My Grandfather's Son*, 280.

35. Perry, "*The Supremes*," 94.

36. Abraham, *Justices, Presidents, and Senators*, 299.

37. Perry, "*The Supremes*," 81.

38. Tinsley E. Yarbrough, *David Hackett Souter: Traditional Republican on the Rehnquist Court* (New York: Oxford University Press, 2005), 160.

39. Perry, "*The Supremes*," 81.

40. Scott P. Johnson and Christopher E. Smith, "David Souter's First Term on the Supreme Court: The Impact of a New Justice," *Judicature* 75 (February–March 1992): 240.

41. Perry, "*The Supremes*," 81.

42. Ibid.; Abraham, *Justices, Presidents, and Senators*, 293.

43. Abraham, *Justices, Presidents, and Senators*, 294–295.

44. David H. Souter, "In Memoriam: William J. Brennan, Jr.," 111 *Harvard Law Review* (November 1997): 1.

45. *Planned Parenthood of Pennsylvania v. Casey* 502 U.S. 833 (1992); Perry, "*The Supremes*," 82.

46. Perry, "*The Supremes*," 82.

47. See David J. Garrow's insightful analysis of how Souter's jurisprudence evolved in "Justice Souter: A Surprising Kind of Conservative," *New York Times Magazine*, September 6, 1994, 36.

48. Henry J. Abraham and Barbara A. Perry, *Freedom and the Court: Civil Rights and Liberties in the United States*, 8th ed. (Lawrence: University Press of Kansas, 2003), 344; Perry, "*The Supremes*," 82–83.

49. Yarbrough, *David Hackett Souter*, 231.

50. Perry, "*The Supremes*," 83.

51. Ibid., 84–85.

52. Lincoln Caplan, "Clarence Thomas's Brand of Judicial Logic," *New York Times*, October 22, 2011.

53. Abraham, *Justices, Presidents, and Senators*, 299; Perry, "*The Supremes*," 96; Perry, *The Michigan Affirmative Action Cases* (Lawrence: University Press of Kansas, 2007), 147.

54. Thomas, National Bar Association Speech, Memphis, Tennessee, July 29, 1998, http://voxygen.net/classes/contemporary-public-address/clarence-thomas-national-bar-association-address/ (accessed June 14, 2013).

55. "The Justice Nobody Knows," *60 Minutes*, CBS, September 30, 2007.

56. Perry, "*The Supremes*," 98.

57. Bruce Schreiner, "Justice Thomas Says Bench Questions During Health Care Oral Arguments Weren't Helpful to Him: Thomas Chides Colleagues for Too Many Questions," Associated Press, April 5, 2012.

58. Dana Milbank, "Let's Do the Time Warp Again," *Washington Post*, November 16, 2007, A2.

59. Abraham, *Justices, Presidents, and Senators*, 301.

60. Robert Carp, Donald Songer, C. K. Rowland, Ronald Stidham, and Lisa Richey-Tracy, "The Voting Behavior of Judges Appointed by President Bush," 76 *Judicature* 302 (1993).

61. Perry, "*The Supremes*," 15.

CONCLUSION

1. George Herbert Walker Bush, Acceptance Speech at the Republican National Convention, August 18, 1988, New Orleans, Louisiana, http://millercenter.org/president/speeches/detail/5526. Engel notes that Bush was more reluctant to let go of Reagan's "evil empire" view of the Soviet Union than was Reagan, who developed a strong diplomatic relationship with Gorbachev.

2. For a more detailed analysis of the "new" party system, see Sidney M. Milkis, Jesse H. Rhodes, and Emily J. Charnock, "What Happened to Post-Partisanship? Barack Obama and the New American Party System," *Perspectives on Politics* 10, no. 1 (March 2012): 57–76.

3. For a more complete discussion of the importance of the 1912 election, see Sidney M. Milkis, *Theodore Roosevelt, the Progressive Party and the Transformation of American Democracy* (Lawrence: Kansas University Press, 2009).

4. Arthur Schlesinger Jr., *The Vital Center: The Politics of Freedom* (Boston: Houghton Mifflin, 1949).

5. William Galston and Elaine Kamarck, "The Politics of Polarization—A Path Back to Power," Washington, D.C.: Third Way, 2005), http://content.thirdway.org/publications/16/Third_Way_Report_-_The_Politics_of_Polarization_-_A_Path_Back_To_Power.pdf.

6. Donald Critchlow, *Conservative Ascendency: How the GOP Right Rose to Power in Modern America* (Lawrence: University Press of Kansas, 2011), 222.

7. On the modern presidency and social movements, see Sidney M. Milkis, Daniel J. Tichenor, and Laura Blessing "'Rallying Force': The Modern Presidency, Social Movements, and the Transformation of American Politics," *Presidential Studies Quarterly* 43 (September 2013): 641–670.

8. William Greider, *The Education of David Stockman and Other Americans* (New York: Dutton, 1982), 23.

9. Roman Popadiuk, *The Leadership of George Bush: An Insider's View of the Forty-First President* (College Station: University of Texas A&M Press, 2009), 35–36.

10. Stephen Skowronek, *The Politics Presidents Make: Leadership from John Adams to Bill Clinton* (Cambridge, Mass.: Harvard University Press, 1997), 40–41, 429–441.

11. Kenneth Duberstein, interview with Sidney M. Milkis, August 3, 1989.

12. Newt Gingrich, interview with Sidney M. Milkis, July 26, 1988.

13. Benjamin Ginsberg and Martin Shefter, *Politics by Other Means: Politicians, Prosecutors, and the Press from Watergate to Whitewater*, revised and updated version (New York: Norton, 1999).

14. Eastwood's prime-time appearance at the 2012 Republican National Convention suggests that his iconic status among conservatives endures, but his awkward performance there, which involved a rambling dialogue with an empty chair (cast as President Obama), may suggest that his star power has faded, especially for a generation not familiar with his movies.

15. George H. W. Bush, Inaugural Address, January 20, 1989, http://millercenter.org/president/speeches/detail/3419.

16. Eisenach quoted in Burt Solomon, "Bush's Zeal for Partisan Duties Tempered by His Bipartisan Style," *National Journal*, October 28, 1989, 2651.

17. Mary Matalin, chief of staff for Lee Atwater, interview with Sidney M. Milkis, August 4, 1989; and Solomon, "Bush's Zeal for Partisan Duties," 2651.

18. Philip Kawior, head of the Research Division, Republican National Committee, "The State of the GOP: A Review of the Recent Polling Data, February 1990," in author's possession.

19. Woodrow Wilson, *Constitutional Government in the United States* (New York: Columbia University Press, 1908), 69.

20. For a fuller discussion of the no-win situation Bush faced in regulatory politics, see Richard A. Harris and Sidney M. Milkis, *The Politics of Regulatory Change: A Tale of Two Agencies*, 2nd ed. (New York: Oxford University Press, 1996), chapters 7–9.

21. *Willie S. Griggs v. Duke Power Company*, 401 U.S. 642 (1971); *Wards Cove Packing Company v. Frank Antonio*, 490 U.S. 642 (1989).

22. Congressional Record, Senate, October 25, 1991, S15277.

23. George Bush, "Statement on the Signing of the Civil Rights Act of 1991," November 21, 1991, 27, http://www.presidency.ucsb.edu/ws/?pid=20258.

24. Charles Tiefer, *The Semi-Sovereign Presidency: The Bush Administration's Strategy for Governing without Congress* (Boulder, Colo.: Westview Press, 1994), 3.

25. Skowronek, *The Politics Presidents Make*, 441.

26. OMB Watch, "President Bush's Regulatory Moratorium," *OMB Watch Alert*, January 24, 1992, 3.

27. Although he reiterated his own formal opposition to abortion, Bush pledged his active support to several Republican candidates in the 1990 elections who were supporters of abortion rights. Robin Toner, "GOP Blurs Abortion Focus, Dismaying Some in Party," *New York Times*, January 18, 1990, http://www.nytimes.com/1990/01/18/us/gop-blurs-focus-on-abortion-to-dismay-of-some-party-faithful.html.

28. *Rust v. Sullivan*, 500 U.S. 173, 111 S. Ct. 1759, 114 L. Ed. 2d 233, 1991 U.S.; Linda Greenhouse, "5 Justices Upheld U.S. Role Curbing Abortion Advice," *New York Times*, May 24, 1991, A1, A18–A19.

29. George H. W. Bush, speech before the Republican National Convention, August 20, 1992, Houston, Texas, http://millercenter.org/president/speeches/detail/3431.

Contributors

HENRY J. ABRAHAM, the James Hart Professor of Government, Emeritus, at the University of Virginia, was the recipient of the first Lifetime Achievement Award of the Organized Section on Law and Courts of the American Political Science Association. A leading authority on constitutional law, civil rights and liberties, and the judicial process, he is the author of thirteen books, including *The Judicial Process: An Introductory Analysis of the Courts of the United States, England, and France* (7th ed.), *Freedom and the Court: Civil Rights and Liberties in the United States* (8th ed., with Barbara A. Perry), and, most recently, *Justices, Presidents, and Senators: A History of U.S. Supreme Court Appointments from Washington to Bush II.*

JEFFREY A. ENGEL is founding director of the Center for Presidential History at Southern Methodist University. He has authored or edited seven books on American foreign policy, including *Cold War at 30,000 Feet: The Anglo-American Fight for Aviation Supremacy* (Harvard University Press, 2007), which received the Paul Birdsall Prize from the American Historical Association; *The China Diary of George H. W. Bush: The Making of a Global President* (Princeton University Press, 2008); *The Fall of the Berlin Wall: The Revolutionary Legacy of 1989* (Oxford University Press, 2009); and *Into the Desert: Reflections on the Gulf War* (Oxford University Press, 2012). He is currently writing *When the World Seemed New: George H. W. Bush and the End of the Cold War.*

HUGH HECLO is Robinson Professor of Public Affairs at George Mason University. Formerly a professor at Harvard University and a senior fellow at the Brookings Institution, his recent books include *Christianity and American Democracy* (2007) and *On Thinking Institutionally* (2008). He was honored by the American Political Science Association with the John Gaus Award for lifetime achievement in political science and public administration.

SIDNEY M. MILKIS is the White Burkett Miller Professor of Politics and a faculty associate at the Miller Center of Public Affairs at the University of Virginia. His books include *The President and the Parties: The Transformation of the American Party System Since the New Deal* (1993), *Political Parties and Constitutional Government: Remaking American Democracy* (1999), *Presidential Greatness* (2000, coauthored with Marc Landy), *The American Presidency: Origins and Development, 1776–2011* (2011, with Michael Nelson), *Theodore Roosevelt, the Progressive Party, and the Transformation of American Democracy* (2009), and *The Politics of Major Policy Reform Since the Second World War,* co-edited with Jeffery Jenkins (forthcoming). He is currently working on a major project on the relationship between the modern presidency and social movements.

MICHAEL NELSON is the Fulmer Professor of Political Science at Rhodes College and a senior fellow of the Miller Center at the University of Virginia. He has published several books on the American presidency, the most recent of which are *Governing at Home: The White House and Domestic Policymaking* (2011, with Russell L. Riley), *The Evolving Presidency: Landmark Documents, 1787–2010* (2011), and *The American Presidency: Origins and Development, 1776–2011* (2011, with Sidney M. Milkis). He has published numerous articles in scholarly journals such as the *Journal of Politics,* the *Journal of Policy History,* and *Political Science Quarterly* and in periodicals such as *Newsweek*, the *New York Times*, and *Virginia Quarterly Review*. He writes frequently for the *Claremont Review of Books*. He is editor of the American Presidential Elections book series for the University Press of Kansas and has just completed a book about the 1968 election.

BARBARA A. PERRY is co-chair of and a senior fellow in the Miller Center's Presidential Oral History Program at the University of the Virginia. She was formerly the Carter Glass Professor of Government at Sweet Briar College, a U.S. Supreme Court Fellow, and a senior fellow at the University of Louisville's McConnell Center. Her recent books include *Rose Kennedy: The Life and Times of a Political Matriarch*, *"The Supremes": An Introduction to the U.S. Supreme Court Justices*, *The Michigan Affirmative Action Cases*, and *Jacqueline Kennedy: First Lady of the New Frontier*.

RUSSELL L. RILEY is associate professor and co-chair of the Presidential Oral History Program at the University of Virginia's Miller Center, where he has spent over a thousand hours recording confidential interviews with senior officials from the administrations of Jimmy Carter, Ronald Reagan, George H. W. Bush, Bill Clinton, and George W. Bush. He is the author of *The Presidency and the Politics of Racial Inequality: Nation-Keeping from 1831 to 1965* (1999) and editor of *Bridging the Constitutional Divide: Inside the White House Office of Legislative Affairs*.

BARBARA SINCLAIR is professor emerita of political science at the University of California, Los Angeles. She is a former vice president of the American Political Science Association and an elected member of the American Academy of Arts and Sciences. She is the author of six books, including mostly recently *Unorthodox Lawmaking: New Legislative Processes in the U.S. Congress*, 4th ed. (2012), *Party Wars: Polarization and the Politics of National Policy Making* (2006), and *Legislators, Leaders, and Lawmaking: The U.S. House of Representatives in the Postreform Era* (1995).

BARTHOLOMEW SPARROW is professor of government at the University of Texas at Austin. He is the author of *The Insular Cases and the Emergence of American Empire* (2006), *Uncertain Guardians: The News Media as a Political Institution* (1999), and *From the Outside In: World War II and the American State* (1996) and numerous articles and book chapters. He is currently completing a biography of former U.S. national security advisor Brent Scowcroft.

ROBERT A. STRONG has taught international relations, the presidency, and American foreign policy at Tulane University and Washington and Lee University, where he recently served as interim provost. He is the author of books on Henry Kissinger and Jimmy Carter, and his collection of presidential foreign policy case studies, *Decisions and Dilemmas*, has been published in two editions. Strong has participated in all of the Miller Center's oral history projects from Ford to Clinton and served as assistant director of the center's project on the Carter presidency.

PHILIP ZELIKOW is the White Burkett Miller Professor of History at the University of Virginia, where he is also associate dean for the Graduate School of Arts and Sciences. As a career diplomat, he was posted overseas and in Washington, including service on the National Security Council staff for President George H. W. Bush. In 2003–4 he was the executive director of the 9/11 Commission. He served from 2005–7 as the counselor of the Department of State, a deputy to Secretary Condoleezza Rice. His books include *Germany Unified and Europe Transformed: A Study in Statecraft* (with Condoleezza Rice), *The Kennedy Tapes: Inside the White House during the Cuban Missile Crisis* (with Ernest May), and *Essence of Decision* (with Graham Allison).

Index

Note: Page numbers followed by *t* indicate tables.

abortion, 40, 45, 55–56 passim. *See also* population control; Roe v. Wade
    Gonzales v. Carhart, 180–181
    Planned Parenthood of Pennsylvania v. Casey, 180
    Stenberg v. Carhart, 180
Acheson, Dean, 116
Adelman, Kenneth, 138
African Americans, 37, 193. *See also* NAACP
Agnew, Spiro T., 42
Aid to Families with Dependent Children, 38
Alito, Samuel, 180–181, 184
Americans with Disabilities Act (1990), 5, 157, 201
Anderson, John, 62
Armed Services Committee, Senate, 122–139 passim
Arms Control and Disengagement Agency, 94
Atwater, Lee, xviii, 23, 65, 70, 73, 187, 202–206 passim, 210

Baker, Howard, 45
Baker, James A. III, viii, ix, 10, 19, 43, 67, 82–99 passim, 100–105 passim, 109, 125, 127, 138, 168, 186, 194, 200
Bartholomew, Reginald, 94
Bates, David, 14
Belarus, 94
Bennett, William, 204
Bentsen, Lloyd, 33, 125, 132
    presidential campaign of 1988, 46
    Senate campaign of 1970, 42–44, 60
Berger, Sandy, 97
Berlin Wall, fall of, viii, 7, 18, 21, 22, 100, 118, 121, 185
Biden, Joseph, 174
Blackmun, Harry, 179–180
Blakley, William, 124
Bork, Robert H., 34, 172, 174, 177, 183
Boskin, Michael, 22
Bosnia, 81
Bradley, Bill, 74

Brady, Nicholas, viii, 67–68, 125, 127
Bremer, L. Paul, 98
Brennan, William J. Jr., 169–174 passim, 179–180
Breyer, Stephen, 179
Briscoe, Frank, 37
Brzezinski, Zbigniew, 83, 89
Buchanan, Patrick, 69, 120, 211
    presidential campaign of 1992, 46, 58, 75
Buckley, William F., 58–59
Bush, Barbara (nee Pierce), xviii, 32, 38, 58, 62
Bush, Dorothy Walker, 28
Bush, George H.W.
    American exceptionalism and, 101–102
    approval ratings, 3*t*, 3–6, 164
    career, xvii–xix
    Central Intelligence Agency director, 44, 61, 83, 87, 186
    challenges to presidency, 7–24
    character, vii–ix, 27–29, 77, 133–139
    childhood, 28–29
    China, ambassador to, 44, 61, 83, 87, 186
    conservativism and, 27–77, 185–212
    early political career, 30–32, 47, 57–59, 190–192
    HBO documentary, vii
    historical reputation, 1–7, 46–47, 192–198
    House of Representatives career, 35–41
    leadership, 81–138
    Looking Forward (1987), 41
    presidency assessed, 186–212
    presidential cabinet, 82–99
    presidential campaign of 1980, 45, 55, 62
    presidential campaign of 1988, xviii–xix, 45–46, 65–67, 109, 187–188, 198–200
    presidential campaign of 1992, 2, 23, 46, 70, 72–75, 121
    Reagan legacy and, 7–10
    Republican National Committee chair, 44, 60, 83
    Republican Party and, 5, 10, 13, 30–31, 47, 160–166, 187–212